MW01519665

Professional Indian

EARLY AMERICAN STUDIES

Series editors:
Daniel K. Richter, Kathleen M. Brown,
Max Cavitch, and David Waldstreicher

Exploring neglected aspects of our colonial, revolutionary, and early national
history and culture, Early American Studies reinterprets familiar themes and
events in fresh ways. Interdisciplinary in character, and with a special emphasis
on the period from about 1600 to 1850, the series is published in partnership
with the McNeil Center for Early American Studies.

A complete list of books in the series
is available from the publisher.

PROFESSIONAL INDIAN

The American Odyssey of Eleazer Williams

Michael Leroy Oberg

PENN

UNIVERSITY OF PENNSYLVANIA PRESS

PHILADELPHIA

Published by
University of Pennsylvania Press
Philadelphia, Pennsylvania 19104-4112
www.upenn.edu/pennpress

Printed in the United States of America
on acid-free paper
1 3 5 7 9 10 8 6 4 2

Library of Congress Cataloging-in-Publication Data
Oberg, Michael Leroy.
  Professional Indian : the American odyssey of Eleazer Williams / Michael Leroy
Oberg. — 1st ed.
    p.   cm. — (Early American studies)
  Includes Bibliographical references and index.
  ISBN 978-0-8122-4676-6 (hardcover : alk. paper)
  1. Williams, Eleazer, 1787–1858. 2. Mohawk Indians—Biography 3. Missionaries—
Canada—Biography. 4. Missionaries—United States—Biography. 5. Indians of
North America—Kings and rulers—Québec—Kahnawake—Biography. 6. Indians of
North America—Missions—History—19th century. 7. Indians, Treatment of—North
America—History—19th century. 8. North America—Ethnic relations—History—19th
century. I. Title. II. Series: Early American Studies.
E99.M8O14   2015
974.7004'975542092—dc23   2014028285

Albie Burke

CONTENTS

This book is about Eleazer Williams, a descendant of an unredeemed Puritan captive carried away to the Catholic Mohawk town of Kahnawake early in the eighteenth century, a Mohawk missionary to the Oneida Indians in central New York and Wisconsin, and an active supporter of the effort beginning early in the nineteenth century to "remove" eastern Indians to new homes in the American West. It is also about the many worlds of the nineteenth-century Iroquois that Williams traversed during his long public career, from the pressed-upon Indian towns in New York and Wisconsin to the centers of Anglo-American power in Albany, New York City, and Washington. It tells the story of the Iroquois in an era of culture change, dispossession, and relocation. By following Eleazer Williams on his American odyssey, it also presents a story of identity, of self-fashioning, in Indian America in the decades between the American Revolution and the Civil War, and the varied roles Indians might play in the white man's republic. It is, finally, a story about getting by and making do, and the struggles one important, if underappreciated, native leader confronted as he attempted to do so.

There is a revealing anecdote about Williams. According to Albert Gallatin Ellis, who worked with him at the Oneida mission in New York beginning in 1820, and who continued to cross paths with him over the years that followed, Williams once looked into a mirror hanging on the wall at the mission station. Still early in his career, Williams studied closely his own reflection, and wondered aloud "is this the face of a savage" and if, "in time . . . the Indian or the white man prevails in this face."[1]

It's an image I like very much. Who might Williams be, and who would decide? If we accept the accuracy of Ellis's recollection, it seems that Williams himself was uncertain. Over the course of writing this book, I have often wondered what Williams was like when he was alone, with no audience watching him. It is easy to tell what he did with his time, where he went. He left a clearly marked paper trail. But Williams described more fully the events in which he participated than the sentiments he felt. There is much about

Williams that I wish I knew and, indeed, I wish I knew him better. I wonder what he thought of himself. When Williams looked in the mirror, what did he see?

This book is an attempt to answer these questions. Williams saw himself as a Christian. That is certain. He saw himself as a messenger of God's word who long toiled with little reward in the mission field. Did he see, too, a tireless advocate who helped the New York Indians establish themselves in new homes in Wisconsin beginning early in the 1820s, or a veteran of America's second war for independence, or, toward the end of his life, a claimant to the throne of France? He performed all these roles, as well. Williams thus might have seen many things as he examined his reflection. But did he see his imperfections? Did he reflect on his failings? I think so, but answering these sorts of questions is not an easy thing for a historian to do.

We all make choices about how we present ourselves to the world. To some extent, we all play roles. We might conform to or challenge at times the expectations that come with these roles. Eleazer Williams clearly made choices. He played roles. On occasion, he created characters for himself, with elaborate backstories and complex plots. He told tales as he sold his services. But as an Iroquois Christian living in white America, he found himself confronted by a variety of forces that starkly limited the options available to him. As an Indian, or a person of mixed race, or a European; as a preacher, a broker, or a king—all identities he claimed—Eleazer Williams found himself staring down the expectations held by the varied audiences before whom he appeared. Williams struggled not to disappoint. His livelihood depended on it. And if Eleazer Williams was almost never all that he claimed for himself, he always was more than he seemed.

On the Northern Line

The Reverend John Holloway Hanson boarded the Northern, or Ogdensburg, Railroad in the autumn of 1851. Leaving for good his home way up in
St. Lawrence County, Hanson planned on attending the Episcopal Diocesan
Convention in New York City before beginning his next assignment as a missionary chaplain at Calvary Chapel, spreading the word of God to Protestant
immigrants in the spiritual wilds of Lower Manhattan. Hanson did not look
forward to his new job, and he left northern New York with many regrets.[1]

Since 1846 Hanson had served as rector at St. Paul's Episcopal Church in
Waddington, a beautiful village along the banks of the St. Lawrence. Among
the founders of the church had been land speculator David A. Ogden, he who
had played so large a role in attempts to remove New York's native peoples to
new homes in the West. Many of the "persons of intelligence and refinement"
in the congregation loved Hanson, his sister later wrote, but love clearly had
its limits. By 1851 the church seemed to have entered a period of decline; several of the wealthiest and most influential congregants moved away or died.
David Ogden passed on well before Hanson arrived in Waddington, and the
widow Ogden, who had done more than anyone else to support St. Paul's and
its rector, sensed that she, too, was not long for this world. She "advised the
clergyman she had loved as a son," Hanson's sister recalled, "to seek another
field of labor."[2]

Hanson sought out other prospects, but with little success. Finally, Francis
Hawks, the rector at Calvary and a close family friend, obtained for Hanson
the position in New York City. It was an act of charity for Hanson who, his
friends recalled, had "endured years of discouragement and the acute suffering
of hoping against hope, to do the work of his Master."[3] These discouragements
had induced Hanson to move often during his career. Born in England in

November 1815, he decided to immigrate to the United States at age twenty-five. He joined his mother and sister, who had crossed the Atlantic before him, in Hoboken, New Jersey. There, he recalled, he aspired to the clergy, to "willingly bind myself . . . to the ministration of the Gospel," a sacred calling that offered benefits "far superior to anything which can be derived from the pleasures of society or the applause of the world."[4] Hanson served first for one year as a missionary in Belvedere, New Jersey, and then spent the two years following in Connecticut, where he met the woman who became his wife. In 1843 he traveled to Florida to serve as a missionary in Key West. The call to Waddington came in 1845. Hanson, it seems, would have remained along the St. Lawrence if the congregation could have paid him what he felt his efforts warranted. Now he was on the move once again, uprooting his wife and his small family.[5]

Among the items of unfinished business at Waddington, Hanson had hoped to meet the Reverend Eleazer Williams, the well-known missionary who ministered to the Mohawk Indians at the St. Regis Reservation in New York, a place the Mohawks called Akwesasne. Once the easternmost of the Six Nations of the Iroquois, whose "great league of peace and power" stretched across upstate New York (including, from east to west, the Oneidas, Onondagas, Cayugas, Tuscaroras, and Senecas as well), most of the Mohawks had left New York State after the American Revolution. Akwesasne was all that remained of a once-vast estate. Hanson would have heard much about Williams, arguably one of the best-known native Christians in the country. He certainly knew of Williams's long and well-publicized career as a missionary, most notably with the Oneidas in New York and Wisconsin. He likely would have known something of his role in the fighting in northern New York during the War of 1812, and in the relocation of many of the New York Indians to new homes in Wisconsin. But Hanson found most interesting a small piece he had stumbled across in a New York City newspaper. It contained "the strange and, at first sight, most improbable announcement, that" Williams was the son of Louis XVI, the French king who died on the guillotine during the Revolution. Williams, Hanson learned, "was said to bear a strong resemblance to the Bourbon family." St. Regis was less than forty miles from Waddington and on the Ogdensburg line, but Hanson never found the time to visit a fellow Episcopalian clergyman who just might have a claim to the throne of France.[6]

Hanson had a long journey ahead of him. It took more than four hours to travel by rail from Waddington to Rouses Point on Lake Champlain. Once there, he would board a steamboat to carry him down to Burlington, Vermont, where he would board another train bound for New York City.[7] Hanson settled into his seat. As the train moved eastward, he noticed "a

Figure 1. Quarter length studio portrait of Eleazer Williams,
ca. 1854, from an original daguerreotype.

Courtesy of the Wisconsin Historical Society, Madison.

somewhat stout old gentleman" speaking with "two Indians in their own
language." Hanson knew nothing of what they said but found the conversation fascinating. The older man spoke "in a very animated manner." He spoke
with grace and style, it seemed to Hanson, and "used much gesticulation," as
he "worked his hearers into a state of excitement more remarkable compared
with the usual stolid expression of the Indian face."[8]

Hanson was not the only passenger who took an interest in this conversation. "He must be a half-breed," said the man seated a row in front of him. Hanson shared his neighbor's surprise "at the freedom with which one of evidently European figure and face spoke the Indian tongue." Then it dawned on Hanson. Perhaps this elderly gentleman who seemed so unlike the Indians Hanson imagined was Eleazer Williams, the man he had for so long wanted to meet. Hanson's neighbor did not know, but he did him the favor of asking the conductor. The elderly man was indeed Eleazer Williams.[9]

Hanson walked to the front of the car and eagerly introduced himself. He apologized for not having visited him during the six years he had lived only a short distance away. Williams was gracious. He explained to Hanson that he had been trying to convince his two Mohawk friends of the errors of their Roman Catholic faith, and was making some progress before Hanson intruded into the conversation. Williams must have asked Hanson where he was going. Hanson told him. Williams said that he was heading toward Burlington, Vermont, and then on to Boston, and that he would be traveling with Hanson to Rouses Point and then together with him down Lake Champlain in the evening. They might have ample opportunity to speak at length. Hanson looked closely at Williams. He later claimed he "was perfectly familiar with the Indian lineaments and characteristics." He was not, but he compared Williams's appearance "with that of his reputed countrymen and, the closer my examination, the more my curiosity was raised, for though his dress was not such as to show him to advantage, he presented in every respect, the marks of different race and station from theirs." Hanson looked at Williams and saw a white man. He wondered how "any attentive observer should ever have imagined him to be an Indian."[10]

*   *   *

John Holloway Hanson had already seized on one story. It drew him in and dominated and displaced all the other stories that Williams might have told about himself, or that others might have told about him. Hanson never understood—how could he?—the challenges Williams faced as an Indian and a Christian living in the American republic. Williams derived his income from white men in church and state. A professional Indian, Williams played roles and assumed characters. He staked claims, and exposed those claims to challenge. The questions Hanson asked Williams as the train moved slowly eastward—in essence, Who are you? How did you get here? What is your story?—were nothing new to him. For his entire life Williams, like other native peoples who lived or worked close to the centers of Anglo-American power, confronted questions of identity, of self-fashioning. Like them, he gave answers that emerged from his experiences, his beliefs, his fears, and his needs. Williams always kept his audiences in mind. He had to in order to get by.

Williams wrote much and said much, but assessing the record he left behind is complicated by the readiness with which he told audiences what he sensed they wanted to hear. Excavating the documents necessary to tell the story of an individual's life can be difficult enough, as we sort the knowable from the unknowable, as we determine what is plausible, what is impossible, and what makes for a persuasive educated guess, but even more so when we write about a teller of tales, a performer, who appeared before audiences white and red. We can tell where Williams went, with whom he met. But this information takes us only so far. We are, after all, all of us, more than what we do, whom we know, and where we have been. We make choices about the stories we tell. These tales—stories of creation and stories of vindication, self-discovery, denial, deception, and defeat—are the matter historians shape and examine as they work not only to understand a life, but to fit that life in a meaningful way into some broader context. Detecting how Williams felt about the roles he played requires a historian to travel in unfamiliar territory. We move carefully when we travel, untethered, into the minds, the sentiments, and the feelings of those about whom we write. When they did not commit their feelings to writing, we speculate very uneasily. This caution is a valuable thing, but it can also serve as a limitation, a brake on what we might learn from the small pieces of the past that we study.[11]

Like all people, Eleazer Williams made choices about his identity, and about how he presented himself to others in church and state and Indian town. Yet as a Mohawk, an Iroquois, an Indian, a Christian, or a king, Williams confronted and contended with forces that constrained and limited those choices in ways that Hanson would never understand.

*   *   *

There were very good reasons indeed to imagine Williams to be an Indian, and ample cause to dismiss the notion that somehow he was the Dauphin, that most unfortunate child of Louis XVI and Marie Antoinette. But Williams knew what Hanson wanted to hear, and he told him the only story he could tell given the circumstances of their meeting.

Hanson wondered if Williams might oblige him, "if it was not intrusive," to tell him "if he believed the story of his royal origin and upon what evidence the extraordinary claim was based." Williams told Hanson, as he had told many others, that the subject was difficult for him, that discussing it stirred up deep emotions. "There seems to me," Hanson interrupted, "one simple and decisive test of the truth of your claim." If Williams were the Dauphin, Hanson continued, "it seems scarcely credible that . . . you could have passed through the fearful scenes of the Revolution, without a strong impression of the horrors attendant on your early years." Hanson wondered if Williams possessed "any memory of what happened in Paris, or of your voyage to this country?"[12]

Those memories, indeed, would have been chilling, if Eleazer Williams had the capacity to recall them. Louis-Charles, second son of Louis XVI and Marie Antoinette, had been born at Versailles in March 1785. Hanson learned that this "captivating child" possessed a great deal of "infantine beauty." His face was "noble and smiling, his head adorned with beautiful curls which hung down over his shoulders." He lived a charmed life until "for the first time he gazed upon the demoniac heavings of the wild tempest of democracy." That was how the utterly-Whig Hanson described the beginning of the French Revolution. In the same year that Parisians stormed the Bastille, Louis-Charles became the heir to the throne, the Dauphin, upon the death of his elder brother. He was only four.[13]

As the French Revolution generated its own momentum, the royal family faced the increasing hostility of the crowds and significant limits on their freedom. In the summer of 1791, Louis XVI and his family, traveling in disguise, attempted to flee to northeastern France where the king intended to rally anti-Revolutionary forces. They did not get far and found themselves imprisoned at the Temple in Paris. The king's flight generated intense hostility and by fall of 1791, the National Convention had abolished the monarchy and created the French Republic. Louis XVI died on the guillotine in January 1793, Marie Antoinette the following October. Beginning that summer the Dauphin found himself in the custody of his sadistic jailer, Antoine Simon, who, with his wife, "did all that lay in their power to destroy the child's bodily and mental faculties."[14]

Simon demonstrated a "demoniac devotion" to "breaking down the constitution, deforming the appearance, corrupting the morals, and weakening the mind of his pupil." He beat the child mercilessly, "compelled him to drink to intoxication, and, in this state, taught him to swear, to sing revolutionary songs, and repeat odious tales concerning his mother." Simon and his wife fed the boy only what sufficed to keep him barely alive. He lived in utter squalor. He became ill, and the barbaric treatment reduced the child, Hanson said, to a "vegetable condition of life."[15]

The French ultimately grew weary of the Reign of Terror, and in its aftermath some sympathy appeared for the Dauphin. Simon was executed and more compassionate keepers took his place. The child's "wasted frame and delirious mind, generous and affectionate even in its delirium, moved their compassion and their tears." They cared for the child, but "the little Louis" could do nothing more than gaze "with a vacant air, hardly knowing, after more than two years of hatred, execration, and abuse," what to think of those expressions of gentleness and mercy. It was too late, and the weakened child died in 1795. He was one of many tens of thousands whose death resulted from the violence of the French Revolution.[16]

Or so it seemed. On the announcement of the Dauphin's death, rumors began to circulate at once that the child had somehow survived, that he escaped from the Temple. Perhaps, some hopeful supporters of the monarchy whispered, devoted royalists had carried the child to North America. Eleazer Williams could shed no light on any of this. He had no memories, he claimed, of the early parts of his life, and did not know how he arrived in America. "Everything that occurred to me is blotted out, entirely erased, irrecoverably gone," he told Hanson. The young Williams was, in Hanson's words, an "idiot" with no memory, no past, until, sometime around his tenth birthday, "he clambered with the fearlessness of idiocy to the top of a high rock," from which he dived into the waters of Lake George. He hit his head on a stone hidden just beneath the surface. His friends rescued him, but he remained unconscious for a time. When Williams came to, he told Hanson, "there were the mountains, there were the waters. That was the first I knew of life."[17]

Stories started flowing back to Williams. Images became clear through the mists of time. Williams told the willing Hanson these stories, and others he had heard or manufactured out of whole cloth. What Williams claimed to have remembered and what he had heard blurred together in ways that might have awakened Hanson's concerns, but Hanson was not that sort of thinker. Williams told Hanson of the French family who called themselves de Jardin, who arrived in Albany from France in 1795. They had called the youngest of the two children with them "Monsieur Louis." The Madame de Jardin carried in her possession many objects that had belonged to the dead king and his queen, and she showed them to curious visitors. This, evidently, was difficult for her, and she had been through quite a lot. Hanson learned that the Madame de Jardin spent her time in New York "in a state of high mental excitement" and could not recount the events of the French Revolution without wildly breaking into a rendition of the "Marseillaise" and bursting into tears.[18]

A significant number of Frenchmen and women sojourned in northern New York, as they fled the violence and turmoil of the Revolution. But Williams could learn nothing more of the de Jardins. They disappeared as quickly as they had arrived. Other French exiles, however, arrived to illuminate Williams's story. He told Hanson about two Frenchmen who arrived at Fort Ticonderoga a short time after the de Jardins disappeared. They had with them, according to one account, "a French boy, weak and sickly, whose mind was wandering so much that he seemed to be almost imbecile." They left this child in the care of Thomas Williams, Eleazer's father.[19]

These stories convinced Hanson that Royalists fleeing the Revolution had carried the Dauphin, a damaged child who remembered little of his tortured past, to North America. That child became Eleazer Williams. For Hanson, all the evidence seemed to fit. Two French gentlemen, for example, came on occasion to visit young Williams. According to the story Williams told Hanson, one of them "had on a ruffled shirt, his hair was powdered, and [he] bore . . . a very splendid appearance." Whatever composure this well-coifed French gentleman possessed quickly disappeared one afternoon when the boy, at his father's urging, approached the visitor. Asking young Eleazer to stand before him, the Frenchman "shed abundance of tears, said Pauvre garçon, and continued to embrace him." The Frenchman took hold of Eleazer's bare feet and his dusty ankles. The child bore scars consistent with the torments inflicted by Simon on the Dauphin. The Frenchman, once again, shed many tears.[20]

Williams's stories enthralled Hanson. Williams may have told Hanson, as he told other people, "about wonderful visions of beautiful scenes and splendidly dressed people which haunted him, and which seemed to be fleeting reminiscences of what had really happened in his childhood." Hanson provided Williams with a perfect audience, a man as eager as he was credulous and utterly free from doubt.[21]

The train finished its journey. As they waited at the dock at Rouses Point, Hanson asked Williams about his mother. She lived at Akwesasne. Surely she could shed some light on the question of his royal descent. Williams anticipated the question. He found that "many of the Romish priests had been tampering with her, and that her mouth was hermetically sealed." These crafty Catholic priests threatened the elderly woman with excommunication should she reveal to Williams anything about his origins. Williams said that "my efforts to extract anything from her were unavailing," and "her immovable Indian obstinacy had hitherto been proof against every effort I could make." It was a masterful answer, or at least masterful enough to convince the entirely guileless Hanson, combining the vigorous anti-Catholicism popular in Protestant New York with stereotypes of the stolid and savage "squaw drudge."[22]

They boarded the steamboat. If theirs was the *Burlington*, or a ship similar to it in service at that time on Lake Champlain, Hanson and Williams would have found "a perfectly exquisite achievement of neatness, elegance and order." The cabins were well appointed, "choicely furnished with prints, pictures, and musical instruments," with "every nook and corner of the vessel ... a perfect curiosity of graceful comfort and beautiful contrivance." Fit for nobility, "the internal drawing rooms are so truly splendid that you might fancy yourself in the drawing room of a ducal palace."[23]

It was not Versailles, but it might have been close enough. Williams explained to Hanson how he had come to learn that he was the Dauphin. He described for Hanson the interest taken in him by French observers who wondered what Williams would do to prosecute his claim. Williams made his case: The Dauphin was supposed to have died from scrofula, which had manifested itself on the boy's knees. "My knees," Williams told Hanson, "are eaten up with scrofula, and there are no other scrofulous marks on my body." Just like the Dauphin.[24]

Williams explained to Hanson that he looked like members of the Bourbon family. He had been mistaken in the past for Louis XVIII, he said, an incredible claim that Hanson, somehow, managed to believe. And then began the show-and-tell. Hanson accompanied Williams from the deck where they had been sitting to the empty and quiet saloon. Williams felt the need for privacy, he said. He opened his valise. He showed Hanson some miniatures and a daguerreotype depicting Williams seated with "a broad band fastened by an ornamental cross passed over the shoulder as worn by European princes." The miniatures were of Marie Antoinette and of Williams's wife, whom, he told Hanson, he had left behind years before in Wisconsin, with one now-grown child and the grief and wreckage left after the death of another more than a decade before. He showed Hanson a dress that he claimed had once belonged to Marie Antoinette. He carried it with him on his frequent journeys, a surrogate perhaps for the wife he had all but abandoned. It was a beautiful dress of faded brocade silk. Hanson knew he could not say "whether the dress which he showed me is what it is asserted to be." It could have been any dress. But Hanson wanted to believe. "There is a pleasure in believing in the truth of memorials of the past"; he could not, he wrote revealingly, "envy the critical coldness of one who would ridicule me for surrendering myself, under the influence of the scene, to the belief, that the strange old gentleman before me, whose very aspect is a problem, was the son to the fair being whose queenly form that faded dress had once contained."[25]

Williams knew that there were those who doubted his story. He told Hanson that he had contentedly placed his fate in God's hands. "He has cast my lot among this poor Indian people, and I have ministered and will minister to them, if it pleases Him, until death." Williams did not need a crown. "I am convinced of my royal descent; so are my family."[26] Time was running short as the steamboat approached Burlington. "You have been talking," Williams told Hanson, "with a king to-night." This he said, Hanson thought, with a smile "between jest and earnest." Williams explained to Hanson that he lived alone at St. Regis, "in a little hut, almost destitute of the necessaries of life, without books, without companions, except the Indians, and that he occupied his time in teaching a few children." He could rest there content.[27]

Hanson took one last look at Williams's face. Like others who described him, Hanson saw a man in his sixties, a few inches short of six feet tall. His complexion, one observer wrote, "is rather dark, but not as much as so very many Americans, and especially Europeans from the Continent." He had dark eyes, though not black, and black hair interspersed with gray. "His eyebrows are full," his nose "aquiline." His mouth was "well-formed, and indicative of mingled firmness and benignity of character." The ship had arrived at Burlington. Hanson thought Williams's "manner of talking reminds you of a Frenchman, and he shrugs his shoulders and gesticulates like one." He seemed, to Hanson, "to possess the port and presence of an European gentleman of high rank; a nameless something which I never saw but in persons accustomed to command." Others, less oblique than Hanson, pointed out "the full protruberant Maximilian lip, the distinctive feature of the Austrian family," a feature "never found in the aboriginal, and very rarely among the Americans themselves." There was little doubt, in Hanson's eyes. He bought the act, and found the performance absolutely convincing. As he watched Williams depart Hanson thought, "I should never have taken him for an Indian."[28]

*   *   *

Hanson learned much that evening, but he wanted to learn more. He recognized "all the difficulties" with Williams's story. He understood that many Americans would find the notion that an Indian from the northern wilds possessed a claim to the throne of France completely ridiculous. False dauphins, after all, were in some places "as plenty as blackberries." It was a role that others had played. But Hanson found something compelling in the way Williams told his story. Williams did not engage in a hard sell, and he seemed to Hanson curiously content to accept his humble station in life. Hanson admired that. Williams convinced Hanson that he had told him merely what he believed to be true. He suggested that "there might be evidence fuller and more explicit" than that which he had offered thus far, but he freely left it up to Hanson to believe or disbelieve. Williams's story haunted Hanson. "I could not get rid of it," he wrote, "and when I tried to throw it off, it would recur again."[29]

It surprised Hanson to learn that nobody had bothered to write Williams's story. Hanson spoke with his friends in New York and New Jersey. They encouraged him to undertake the project. They provided him with bits of additional evidence—hearsay, to be sure—but these anecdotes further confirmed Hanson in his belief that the Dauphin had survived his brutal imprisonment, been rescued by his supporters, and carried into the wilds of America.[30]

His new job bored Hanson, even before he arrived there, and he always had fancied himself a writer. He wrote poetry in his spare time. "Primeval Bard! Young Fancy's first born son," he wrote in an unmemorable ode to Homer. And "Sleep, sleep, sweet babe—I envy thee thy rest / The angel silence of that throbless breast," he wrote in another, a poem entitled "On a Dead Infant." Little came of these efforts, thankfully, save for a slim volume published posthumously as a tribute by his sister.[31] But now, Hanson felt, he had a story worth telling.

So he wrote to Williams, seeking additional information, but also to ask if Williams minded if Hanson told his story. Williams did not object. He provided Hanson with a copy of what he claimed was his journal for the years 1841 and 1848, important points in his growing awareness that he was the Dauphin. He encouraged Hanson, while modestly making sure that the aspiring biographer understood that Williams sought "not an earthly crown, but heavenly, where we shall be made kings and priests unto God."[32]

In November 1852, Hanson left the city for the North Country to speak further with Williams and gather material for his biography. He found the reservation a "miserable, lonely" place, and he seems to have shared the views of New York antiquarian Franklin B. Hough who, in 1853, thought that St. Regis "exhibits nothing but an air of decay and listlessness, peculiar of the Indian character, when it assumes the habits of civilization."[33]

About three hundred Mohawks lived on the American side of the Akwesasne reservation. Twice that number lived on the Canadian side. The state of New York exerted its haphazard influence over the St. Regis Reservation. It appointed trustees to manage the affairs of the Akwasasne Mohawks living in the state. The state funded a small school. It half-heartedly acted to protect the Indians from alcohol vendors, loan sharks, squatters, and thieves, but these efforts seldom succeeded. Nor did the state adequately protect the Mohawks' lands. The atmosphere of decline that Hough identified might have been due at least in part to dispossession. A reservation originally established in 1796 had been reduced significantly as the result of a number of land sales to speculators and the state of New York. By 1845, only 14,000 acres of the reservation remained.[34]

While the Mohawks at Akwesasne lost much of their land, they also lost valuable timber on what remained to white encroachment and to accident. "Unhappily," one observer noted, "the timber which formerly abounded has been all but cut off or destroyed by fire, and not enough remains for a sufficient supply of fuel for the tribes." And against this backdrop of encroachment and dispossession, smallpox struck the reservation, and "swept off great numbers" of Indians in 1829. Three years later, cholera and typhus killed 120 more. The "filthy and negligent habits of these people," Hough wrote, "appear to have rendered them fit subjects for any pestilence that might chance to make its appearance."[35]

Hanson had little interest in life and death on the reservation, aside from the fact that these conditions might have made things difficult or uncomfortable for Williams. The Dauphin, he found, lived an impoverished existence in the town of Fort Covington on the east side of the reservation. "The rigors of the climate are excessive; the thermometer in winter being frequently thirty degrees below zero, and one can scarcely conceive a situation for an intelligent mind more lonely, more unfriended, more destitute." At the time of his visit, Hanson found that "dead evergreen swamps, decayed vegetation, rude fences, half prostrate" surrounded the "rickety shed" in which Williams lived. He did not, however, find Williams, who Hanson learned had left the reservation "on missionary service." Indeed, there must have been little for Williams to do at home. Hough, in describing the dispirited state of the Akwesasne reserve, noted that "the St. Regis Indians observe none of the festivals or ceremonies of their ancestors, and no public demonstrations are made, except those imposed by the canons of the Catholic Church." Ardently Catholic, in Hough's view, the Akwesasnes went all out to celebrate the feast of Corpus Christi, which took place in early June and for which preparations

began well in advance. One can hardly blame Williams, a lonely Episcopalian, for wanting to stay away.[36]

Undeterred, Hanson commenced his investigation. Williams's landlady,
responding to Hanson's leading questions, said that "I do not know whether
he is Indian or not." He did not look like one, she said, and "if I had not
heard that he was one, I should not suppose that he was." A Mr. Harrington,
who lived in the town of Moira near Williams, declared that he was certain
that Williams was a European. "The general impression among intelligent
people, in this neighborhood, who know Mr. Williams, is that he is not an
Indian." Harrington said confidently that "I know an Indian as well as I know
a cow or a horse." Eleazer Williams, Harrington continued, did not look like
his brothers and "his reputed mother does not acknowledge him to be her
son." Because Williams "bears an excellent character among us, and is highly
respected," Harrington implied, he could not possibly be an Indian.[37]

Having accomplished all that he felt he could at Akwesasne in Williams's
absence, Hanson traveled down river to Kahnawake, the town across the
St. Lawrence from Montreal where Williams spent his early years. There he
confirmed Williams's claim that his name did not appear in the parish baptismal records alongside his many brothers and sisters, suggesting that he
may indeed have been born outside the community. This was not proof that
Williams was the Dauphin, but it was valuable evidence nonetheless. Hanson returned to New York City, and set out to write his book. Hanson hated
"shams" and said that he would not participate in one. He claimed that in his
research, "there has been no attempt to impose on" the public's "credulity."
Williams, Hanson wrote, "stands in the position of one who asserts facts."
Hanson sought "only to establish a historical fact, and let that fact take care
of itself."[38]

*   *   *

If we return to the beginning of Williams's story, and if we follow the many
paths he traveled before he encountered Hanson on that Northern Line train,
we will see that there were of course many facts, and so other stories, that
Hanson might have told. His tunnel vision—each bit of information Hanson
uncovered he assessed only in regard to its value for establishing Williams's
identity as the Dauphin—led him to miss much of the significance in Williams's life, for this Mohawk missionary to the Oneidas, a man who interacted with low-level Indian policy-makers and presidents, Indians seeking

salvation and speculators seeking their lands, played important roles in the many stories of the Iroquois in the American republic. On his American odyssey, Williams was no mere oddity, and much more than an old man telling far-fetched tales to a guileless minister. He stood close to the center of the Iroquois experience during the first half of the nineteenth century. William's story, one reconstructed from words and deeds and tales untrue, involved native peoples in New York, Wisconsin, and Canada; political leaders in Albany, New York City, and Washington; and the hierarchies of the Episcopal Church in two states. It involved missionaries, land speculators, political operatives, and Indians Christian and Pagan. Hanson tried to tell this story, but in the end he never understood completely the challenges Williams confronted as a native Christian leader, and the many worlds of the Iroquois through which he traveled.

CHAPTER ONE

Pilgrim and Patriot

Eleazer Williams's family could trace its roots deep into the rocky soil of New England's past, and his story rested at the core of the region's long and violent history. Born in 1788 at or near Sault Ste. Louis in Lower Canada, a place known to the Mohawks as Kahnawake, Williams wrote in the draft of an early autobiography that his "father was the great grandson of the Rev. John Williams of Deerfield." Even Sunday school children in New England learned that the well-known Indian missionary Eleazer Williams descended "from Rev. John Williams . . . in the town of Deerfield, a place pleasantly situated on the Connecticut River, between Northampton and Brattleboro."[1]

When John Williams, Eleazer's great-great-grandfather, arrived in Deerfield in 1686, the struggling settlement, still recovering from the ravages of King Philip's War a decade before, could hardly be considered "pleasant." It remained an exposed and vulnerable frontier outpost, a target attractive to hostile Indians and French Catholics, who, the town's settlers feared, might descend upon them in fury in the night. Nonetheless, John Williams, twenty-two at the time, accepted the town's invitation "to dispense the blessed word of truth unto" the rugged Puritans settled there. It was a rough place to serve the Lord, which might explain why two candidates before Williams had turned down the town's call to serve as its minister. Indeed, not until 1694 did the townspeople bother to build Williams a meeting house thirty feet square.[2]

The Reverend Williams nonetheless worked his land and preached to his congregants. He toiled hard in the fields of the Lord. With his neighbors, Williams understood that the resumption of war between France and England threatened Deerfield and, late in February 1704, its horrors came once again to the community. Four dozen Frenchmen, accompanied by approximately two hundred Indian allies, marched nearly three hundred miles to attack the poorly guarded village. Aided by high snowdrifts and sleeping guards, the attackers easily breached the palisades and overpowered those few surprised and horrified defenders capable of getting to their weapons. Forty-nine of the town's residents died in the initial attack. The raiders took dozens more captive, including the Reverend John and his family. They killed his wife—a new mother for the seventh time—because she could not move quickly enough.[3]

The Indians who joined in the attack included Abenakis from Algonquian towns in northern New England such as Cowass, Pennacook, Pigwacket, and Winnipesaukee. Others came from mission settlements in the St. Lawrence Valley: Catholic Abenakis from St. Francis, Hurons from Lorette, and Mohawks from La Montaigne and Kahnawake. Many of them sought captives. A Mohawk woman from Kahnawake, who may have lost her daughter in the smallpox epidemic that struck the St. Lawrence settlements in 1701, accompanied the party, and adopted Williams's young daughter Eunice both to take her dead child's place in the community and to assuage her own considerable grief.[4]

The Reverend John remained a captive until 1706, when finally the French ransomed him from his captors and sent him home to New England. He had experienced the horrors of frontier warfare, pressure to accept Catholicism, and the death of his wife and two of his children. He returned to Deerfield. He published an account of his family's ordeal, *The Redeemed Captive*, in 1707. The book sold well, and Williams and his surviving children attempted to put their lives back together. Only Eunice remained unredeemed. She stayed at Kahnawake, the Catholic Mohawk settlement situated across the St. Lawrence from Montreal. She converted to Catholicism. After some time, she married a Mohawk. She went native, assimilating into the mission community. Despite returning on occasion to visit her brothers and sisters in Deerfield, she remained at Kahnawake, apparently content, for the rest of her life. Yet despite her obvious attachments to Kahnawake and her new community, she still gave her children her father's name. Her daughter Sarah was the mother of Thomas Williams, a "warrior of wide renown during the conflict of the American Revolution, fighting against the struggling colonies," and, ultimately, the grandmother of Eleazer, who was born sometime in spring 1788. Eleazer, one of thirteen children, was named after Thomas's great-uncle, the first minister in Mansfield, Connecticut. At Kahnawake, people called him Lazar.[5]

Williams grew up in one of the most ethnically diverse communities in North America, a settlement older than the established colonial centers at Charleston, Philadelphia, and Savannah. Founded in 1667, Kahnawake blended French, Catholic, and Iroquois influences into something new.

French Jesuits entered the territory of the Iroquois in the middle decades of the seventeenth century. Some of the converts, Oneidas at first, followed by significant numbers of Mohawks, migrated to the St. Lawrence Valley hoping to avoid tension between Christians and non-Christians, and the turmoil and disorder caused by French and Dutch traders who poured alcohol into the Mohawk Valley settlements.[6]

Within a decade of its founding, five hundred Indians called Kahnawake home. Mohawks made up a slight majority of the town's population, but all the Iroquois nations were represented as well as Abenakis, Catawbas, Chickasaws, Hurons, Mahicans, Susquehannocks, and a dozen or so more. Those who came to Kahnawake symbolically left behind the turmoil in their lives. They entered the settlement after ceremonially passing by two trees, planted at opposite ends of the town. At the base of one they ritually surrendered their lusts, the sexual depravity that the Jesuit fathers perceived and derided but mostly imagined in Iroquois communities. At the other, they left behind their alcohol, even this early the source of so many problems. They pledged to remain both chaste and sober. Catholicism blended with Iroquois traditions at Kahnawake.[7]

Yet as much as the immigrants sought to avoid the chaos colonization brought to their homelands, they did not turn their backs entirely on Iroquoia. The settlement of Kahnawake allowed Iroquois people to reoccupy with the blessings of the Jesuit fathers territories in which they had hunted, raided, and traded for centuries.[8] The Kahnawake Iroquois maintained ties to their Longhouse kin, and there is evidence of considerable movement and communication between Iroquois communities in the St. Lawrence and Mohawk valleys. Intended by the French as a mission settlement of Catholic Iroquois, Kahnawake became a frontier post on the margins of Iroquoia. The settled Indians interacted frequently with the French, traded with the *habitant* community across the river at Montreal, but maintained and preserved Kahnawake's character and identity as an Iroquoian town.[9]

Kahnawake was one of a number of settlements planted outside of the territorial boundaries of the traditional Iroquois Longhouse. Onondagas and Cayugas settled at a site called Oswegatchie in northern New York, near present-day Ogdensburg. Senecas moved westward in the eighteenth century to a number of sites in the Genesee Valley. And migrants from Kahnawake moved roughly sixty miles up the St. Lawrence in the 1750s to Akwesasne, a site chosen perhaps for the quality of its soil and superior access to water and timber.[10]

The St. Lawrence Iroquois participated actively in the imperial warfare between France and England in the late seventeenth and eighteenth centuries. They joined French forces in raids on New England and on New York's frontier settlements. While Iroquois warriors fought on both sides in these colonial wars, they avoided conflict with their Longhouse kin, shared intelligence with each other of impending attacks, and certainly never played the pawn in a European struggle for domination in eastern North America.[11]

The independence they sought to preserve always remained tenuous, and became especially difficult to maintain after the English defeated the French in 1761 and, later, after the Anglo-American colonists' protest movement flared into a revolutionary war in 1775. The American rebels lacked the resources to support an alliance with the Indians, and urged native communities to remain neutral in the coming conflict. The British used threats, at first, to attempt to persuade the St. Lawrence Iroquois to join them in attacks on the American frontier, but Daniel Claus, the Indian agent at Quebec, appealed to their interest instead. Should the rebels succeed, he told the Mohawks at Kahnawake and Akwesasne, the Indians stood in "danger of loosing their lands and hunting grounds" to land-hungry American settlers.[12]

Experience would prove Claus right, but most Iroquois preferred neutrality. They understood fully that they would have to live with the eventual winner and recognized the risks that came with choosing the wrong side. But because they feared that Indians not with them might be against them, the British in Canada kept up the pressure. Thomas Williams fought with the British in "various expeditions against the inhabitants of the northern frontiers of the American colonies." So said Eleazer, his son. Far from being one of the bloodthirsty savages described by Thomas Jefferson in the Declaration of Independence, however, Thomas Williams accompanied the war parties "with the view of preventing, if possible, the massacre of feeble and defenseless women and children; and on various occasions he exerted himself to excite feelings of humanity and kindness towards the Americans who fell into their hands." He fought with the Tories, but he behaved well as he did so.[13]

Yet the acts of compassion Eleazer attributed to his father, if indeed they occurred, counted for little to the victorious New Yorkers who claimed, at war's end, the right to acquire all the Indian lands within the state's asserted boundaries. The Mohawks fled. Some settled at the refugee haven established outside the British post at Fort Niagara before moving on to Grand River, eighty miles to the west in Ontario, under the leadership of Joseph Brant. Others moved to the Bay of Quinté under John Deserontyon. Those Indians who remained behind faced settlers who at best viewed the Iroquois as temporary occupants of land that would be put to better use if in their own hands.[14]

In the early 1790s, after concentrating for several years on the Onondagas, Oneidas, and Cayugas who held the valuable lands in central New York, land commissioners from the state of New York turned their attention toward the Mohawks at Akwesasne. After the Revolution, the Akwesasnes had joined the Seven Nations Confederacy based at Kahnawake, a coalition of native communities made up of mission settlements in the St. Lawrence Valley formerly allied with the French. Together, they claimed a vast tract of land in northern New York, much of which (3.84 million acres) the state had sold for a small sum to the land speculator and fur trader Alexander Macomb in 1791.[15]

State officials well understood the Seven Nations' interest in these lands. A year after the sale to Macomb, a Seven Nations delegation complained about what it considered unauthorized settlement along the shores of Lake Champlain and on the banks of the St. Lawrence. State officials purchased the Indian title to these lands from Joseph Brant and John Deserontyon, the leaders of the Mohawk communities at Grand River and on the Bay of Quinté, but they did not consult with the Seven Nations.[16]

They opposed this sale, and challenged the right of Brant and Deserontyon to sell lands in New York that the Seven Nations still claimed. Three men, with ties to the Mohawks of varying and debatable strength, represented the Seven Nations in its diplomacy with New York State. Colonel Louis, or Louis Cook, had fought with the Americans during the American Revolution and passionately hated Joseph Brant. Cook's aid to the rebels caused him to fall out of favor among his Mohawk neighbors. The son of a Black father and an Abenaki mother, he left Kahnawake for the duration of the war but settled at Akwesasne, with the support of the state of New York, afterwards. William Gray, a child of settlers on the New York frontier who "when he was a boy he was taken prisoner . . . by the Indians at the Seven Nations of Canady among whome he has ever since continued to reside" and, he recalled some years later, "by adoption and marriage he has become entitled to all the Rights and privileges of one of that Peaple," worked with Cook. Thomas Williams, Eleazer's father, rounded out the group.[17]

State officials told the Seven Nations "to possess your minds in peace," for the state intended to treat with them in a just and equitable manner "about land which is within our state and which you say belongs to you." Cook, Gray, and Williams met with the state's commissioners and one federal official who attended to provide some oversight from the national government in May 1796. Williams played little role in the negotiations, for he was "confined at his lodging by Sickness." There is no word as to whether Eleazer, who would have been nearly eight at the time, accompanied him.[18]

Louis Cook spoke for the Seven Nations, as he had on a number of previous visits to meet with state officials. They wanted justice with regard to lands the state claimed but that the Seven Nations felt still were theirs. They wished, as well, "to enjoy our own laws and you yours so far that is any of our People Indians should commit a crime to any of their brothers the white people of the United States, that he may be punished by his own Nation and his Chiefs to make good all damages." A white person committing crimes against Indians, on the other hand, would be pursued according "to the Laws of his Nation." The Mohawks wanted to be left alone. The Seven Nations were willing to sell land to the state, but they also understood the tricks the state might use to "deprive poor ignorant people of their property and bring them poverty and at last to become Beggars and Laughing Stocks." They had already seen it happen many times.[19]

Louis Cook described the boundaries of the lands the Seven Nations claimed, but the state's commissioners considered it "scarcely reasonable in you to expect we should admit your Claim." The state offered to make a payment to the Seven Nations because New York wanted to be good neighbors, but not because of "any supposed merit or justice in the claim itself." The Seven Nations simply asked for too much. With the purchase from Brant and Deserontyon, and the peace agreement that ended the Revolution, the New York commissioners could assert that the Seven Nations' claim lacked any legitimacy, and they played hard ball with the delegates. The state had power and its people had numbers. They were coming to settle these lands, whether or not Cook and Gray agreed to terms. They could sell now and receive something for their people, or run the risk of having their lands in New York overrun by settlers or seized by force. This, all too often, was how Native American peoples lost their lands. Certainly fraud and coercion took place, and to these the Iroquois were no strangers. But far more often, Indians faced a Hobson's choice—accept a paltry sum for lands colonial settlers showed they would overrun and exploit, or lose them outright to white men who would not respect the property rights of native individuals and communities. On the last day of May, the delegates signed a treaty in "the name of the Seven Nations or tribes of Indians," in which they ceded to the New Yorkers "all the claim, right, or title of them, the said Seven Nations . . . to lands within the said state" with the exception of a block six miles square at St. Regis and an annuity.[20]

Eleazer Williams long complained that his father and "his heirs have been denied a share in the lands and annuities enjoyed by the American portion of the tribe." The Akwesasne Mohawks, it seems, felt that the 1796 sale, even if it was the best the Mohawks could have achieved at that time, was unjust. They blamed the men who signed the agreement. All three men benefited from their willingness to work with the New Yorkers. Louis Cook, William Gray, and Loren Tarbell, another descendant of white captives, were appointed "trustees for the said tribe, for the purpose of leasing the ferry over St. Regis River, with one hundred acres of land adjoining, and also one mile square on Grass River." The revenues from these rents, the state legislature said, would be applied to support "a school for the instruction of the children of the said tribe." With state support, they would play an important role in governing Akwesasne for the next decade and a half.[21]

*   *   *

It is not surprising how little evidence exists for Eleazer Williams's early years. Like many people born at Kahnawake—if, in fact, he was born at Kahnawake—his would have been a life of little significance to the non-Indians who produce the documents on which historians rely. Huge gaps in the historical record existed, waiting to be filled by mythmakers, liars, and men on the make, by those who craved for whatever reason to claim that they knew royalty, and the mistaken, the confused, and the easily entertained. Eleazer Williams and John Holloway Hanson would fill those gaps, but not all that they said was correct or true.

Before Eleazer Williams could play the Dauphin, he was a boy, a Mohawk child living at Kahnawake. The Englishman John Long thought that the two hundred houses he saw there near the time of Williams's birth had "a mean and dirty appearance" but that Kahnawake still was "the most respectable of all the Indian villages." Its people lived lives "in a great degree civilized and industrious," yet they felt little fondness for "laborious work." They hunted still, exchanging the furs they took with traders from Montreal and New York, yet their appetite for luxury and extravagance "contributed to make them more idle; and in proportion as their vanity increases, ease and indolence are the more eagerly coveted and gratified, insomuch that hunting is in danger of being totally abandoned." It was a mix. They hunted and they farmed. They prayed at the Catholic Church and they drank. Some outsiders thought the Mohawks had changed too much and for the worse from their contact with settlers, while others believed little had changed at Kahnawake since its founding. Williams spent the first decade of his life here, descended from that unredeemed Puritan captive, Eunice Williams, but also from many Mohawks over many generations.[22] Eunice's many relations in New England could not set aside their ties to her. They always hoped to recover her from captivity, to bring her back to the banks of the Connecticut River. Though she visited her relations in Deerfield on a number of occasions, she always refused their entreaties that she return to the place she long since had ceased to consider home.

Thomas Williams continued this tradition of visiting and in so doing kept alive hopes for the redemption of at least some of the "captive" Williams family. He first visited his Massachusetts kin after the American Revolution. The "attention and hospitality" his New England relations showed him, Eleazer Williams remembered much, much later, made "a deep impression on his mind" and that day when he first arrived in southern New England "was one of the happiest days of his life." In 1797, these long-hopeful relations proposed to Thomas that he bring his children to Massachusetts to receive an education in proper Christianity and civility. At least some of Eunice's descendants might thus be redeemed from Catholicism and savagery, and a painful chapter in the region's history might at last be brought to a close.[23]

Thomas Williams did not respond immediately, but his kin along the Connecticut kept after him. Finally, in January 1800, deacon Nathaniel Ely recorded that "Mr. Thomas Williams with his two sons viz. Lazau aged 11 and John Sunawattis 7" arrived at his house in Longmeadow, Massachusetts, a short distance south of Springfield. Ely had married a granddaughter of the Rev. John Williams, and stood at the center of a group of clergymen and "past keepers" interested in the return home of "our Cousins from Cannawaga."[24]

Neither of the boys could speak a word of English, Ely claimed, and they arrived in Longmeadow wearing "Indian dress." Eleazer wore "blankets worked into the forms of a loose great coat" along with "beaded wampum . . . about the loins" and his hair "carelessly stuck with feathers." Perhaps Ely's description of the boys was on target. It is hard to imagine that they would not have dressed like their friends and neighbors at Kahnawake and that they would not have dressed well for this special occasion. At the same time, it is difficult to believe that the boys emerged from the Canadian wilderness completely untouched by European ways. Kahnawake was hardly isolated. We must remember, as well, that the boys' father spoke English well enough to serve as a translator in intercultural diplomacy, and he wrote the language well enough to carry on a correspondence with his New England relations.[25]

Thomas Williams placed his sons in Ely's care to obtain for them an English education. Many other Indian parents, over the preceding decades, had sent their children to New England for schooling. Williams must have hoped to equip his boys with the tools they needed to succeed in a world increasingly shaped by the rising power of the empire state. Native peoples actively sought out education, and recognized that knowledge meant power in Anglo-America. For some, a colonial education brought significant change: new norms for conduct and behavior, in addition to a new language, a new religion, and, at times, a new home. For others, however, the changes might not have been so drastic. Indians in many parts of Anglo-America had lived in close contact with non-Indians, and likely understood quite well the outlines of Anglo-American culture, even if they found that culture strange and anathematic to what they recognized as familiar and right. The Williams boys more likely fell into the latter category. Though uneducated by John Hanson's standards, Ely was a "worthy and intelligent" tutor, and "a man of sound, clear, understanding, and remarkably methodical habits." Even if he felt himself pressured by the burden of two additional mouths to feed, Ely, Eleazer Williams later noted, had "warmly at heart the project of converting the aborigines" from the twin perils of "Paganism and Romanism." Williams admired Ely immensely as "a worthy gentleman" in "whose piety & zeal for the cause of the Redeemer's Kingdom, it may be truly said, few excelled him."[26]

Ely, his friends, and his neighbors took on the responsibility of educating the two boys. One would have expected it to be a difficult task. According to one Longmeadow legend, the boys found adjustment to school difficult. Their classmates made fun of their efforts to learn English. The boys did not understand at first the behavior their tutors expected of them. But Thomas Williams's sons soon learned to play their parts, and they performed to the satisfaction of their teachers. "Indefatigable pains," Ely noted a short time after the boys arrived, "have bin taken to learn them to read and write and also to give them some knowledge of agriculture and the arts of civil life." The boys made progress, quite rapidly it seemed, "larning to speak, read, and write our language." All who observed the boys agreed: Eleazer, four years older than his brother and within a short time a more reliable and consistent speller than Ely, was the better student.[27]

*   *   *

John Hanson wondered about Eleazer Williams's arrival in southern New England. Hanson knew that Williams "repayed the affection of the Williams family with gratitude and love," but he suspected that there was much more to the story. That Williams's father brought Eleazer and his brother to live and learn with members of the extended Williams family in Massachusetts certainly provided evidence of the strength of their connections to the family's

Puritan forebears. Why, indeed, would Thomas Williams bring the dauphin to southern New England to receive an education among the Calvinist descendants of Anglo-American Puritans?[28]

Hanson expected that the clues he unearthed from these early years might shed light on Eleazer's origins. He gathered evidence. He filled in gaps in the record with his own wishful thinking. Every ambiguity he resolved in favor of his claim. Williams told Hanson that at first he took as "much pride and pleasure in considering himself a descendant of Eunice, as her relatives took in calling him so." But he never felt it wholeheartedly, he said. "Against the tangible and evident claims made on him by his reputed kinsmen, the every day realities of life, and all the endearing associations which spring from the reception of a thousand marks of kindness, social and pecuniary," Williams still felt out of place. He told Hanson that he sulked; he felt sad and distant, for reasons he did not understand. Eleazer, Hanson learned, "had nothing to oppose but thick clouds and darkness brooding over his early childhood, faintly lighted up by mysterious dreams of unknown things, to which he could assign neither date nor place." Hanson believed he knew why.[29]

Hanson corresponded with people who had known Eleazer and his brother during the period in which they lived in Longmeadow and in other small towns in the Connecticut Valley. Hanson's informants, recalling events a half-century old, remarked upon the differences between the two boys. Though these informants could offer relatively little about the younger brother, they suggested that Eleazer "carried a mystery with him" that "enshrouded him" and "could not be explained." Urania Smith, who as a child lived next door to Deacon Ely, told Hanson that the two boys "were entirely unlike each other in complexion, appearance, form, and disposition, John having the look of an Indian, and Eleazer that of an European." Julia Jenkins, also a neighbor, recalled that "the prevalent opinion" about Eleazer in Longmeadow "seemed to be that, he was a French boy, who was stolen from his family, and brought away at so early an age, as to render his recollections of other than Indian life, vague and unsatisfactory." Martha Temple, a daughter of Nathaniel Ely, wrote to Williams to "state in writing, as you desired, that there was an entire and striking dissimilarity between yourself and your brother John, in the features of your face, your general appearance, and also in your predilections and character." Williams dutifully passed this information along to Hanson, who in the meantime learned of a pencil sketch, done of Eleazer at the time, that "strongly resembles . . . the earlier pictures of the Dauphin in France and exhibits in the most marked manner the lineaments of the Bourbons."[30]

Figure 2. Image of Eleazer Williams as a child, from John Hollway
Hanson, *The Lost Prince* (New York: G. P. Putnam, 1854).

Other mysteries presented themselves to Hanson. How, he wondered,
could Thomas Williams afford to pay for the boys' education and upkeep in
Massachusetts? Even if he did come across the necessary funds, Thomas Williams "would have been the last man in the world to remit the money with
any punctuality." *That* was something, Hanson suggested, that Indians simply
could not do. Hanson dug around farther. He learned, or at least claimed to
have learned, that the boys' upkeep was paid "with great promptness, show-
ing a mercantile attention." Because, Hanson argued, this proved "that a man
of exact business habits must have been the agent through who the payments
were made," the funds could only have originated with Royalist supporters of
the Dauphin![31]

Indeed, Hanson believed that Nathaniel Ely knew Eleazer Williams's secret. According to Urania Smith, neighbors quizzed him about the differences in the boys' appearance. Ely told Smith that "there was something about it which he should possibly never reveal, but would say this much, that Eleazer Williams was born for a great man, and he intended to give him an education to prepare him for the station."[32]

Hanson believed every bit of evidence that corroborated his identification of Eleazer Williams as the dauphin. He believed Williams's story that his mother, prior to her sons' departure for Longmeadow, told Thomas Williams to carry away Eleazer, "the strange boy," for whom "means have been put into your hands for his education."[33] Hanson challenged nothing, and Williams must have thought him an easy mark. He told Hanson stories—these were not the only stories Williams might have told, but he knew what Hanson wanted to hear. And nearly every claim Hanson made about Eleazer Williams's time in Massachusetts turned out to be wrong.

*   *   *

Nathaniel Ely surely knew better than John Holloway Hanson. Nothing Ely wrote ever hinted that he saw the two boys as being in any way different. He never suggested Eleazer seemed more white, or more burdened by the weight of the past, or more tormented by dark secrets, than his younger brother. Ely viewed both boys as Indians and descendants of Eunice Williams. Ely saw it as his job to provide them both the education in Christianity and civility he and his neighbors believed they needed. To achieve this, Ely assembled a network of patrons for the two boys and a haphazard system for their support and upkeep. Thomas Williams played a role in maintaining this network, meeting with ministers and other Williams family members from Albany to Hartford, joining them on occasion to support and hold together what was, at heart, a little missionary enterprise. The work of educating Indians often took place on a very small scale.[34]

To share the expense of caring for the boys they moved around from minister's house to minister's house. Both stayed with Ely at the outset, but it is not at all clear that they remained together. Toward the end of April 1803, Eleazer recalled that "I was placed under the care or Instruction of the Rev. Mr. Brockway of Ellington, Connecticut."[35] In January 1804 the boys received a visit from their parents. They traveled together with Ely and others through Hartford and the smaller river towns. At the end of February, their parents decided to return home. They took his younger brother John back to Kahnawake with them. Later, Eleazer recalled that this decision originated with his mother. The Catholic parish priests at Kahnawake threatened her with excommunication if she did not return with the boys. She hoped that these malevolent and scheming priests—and in the tales Eleazer told nearly all Catholic priests were malevolent and scheming—would somehow rest satisfied if she managed to return with only one.[36]

This is the story Williams recorded long after the fact and that he related to John Holloway Hanson. It is difficult not to wonder how the departure of his mother, father, and brother made him feel. His mother, after all, returned home with the younger brother who, Williams recalled, "appeared to be his mother's favorite." A lonely child, he remained behind with feelings of "great regret and sorrow."[37] These words ring true. Over the course of his long career, Williams wrote frequently and fondly of his father, but he never wrote a single flattering word about his mother. When he returned to Kahnawake for a brief visit, he went to see his father, he said, and not his mother. He did not begin to broadcast his claim to be the Dauphin until after Thomas Williams had died. Of course his father might easily have discredited these claims, but perhaps Williams respected him enough to spare him the insult of a denied paternity. Toward his mother he showed no such courtesy. Feelings of abandonment might account for his obvious estrangement from her, as well as his later decision to adopt a new persona and thereby play a role in which he repudiated his own origins.

After his parents departed, Eleazer stayed with "Dr. Williams of Tolland, and Dr. Strong of Hartford," but he still managed to spend much time with Ely. He accompanied Ely to meetings of the Massachusetts General Court, on which Ely served. They attended sermons together, some at Congregationalist churches, some at Episcopal Churches, and once at a Baptist meeting. These journeys, Ely hoped and Eleazer remembered, would strengthen the boy's fragile health. Sixteen years old when his brother returned to Kahnawake, Eleazer suffered from periodic painful respiratory infections that, he recalled, provoked episodes of "bleeding of my breast" and that caused him to fear that "I might die in my younger days."[38]

In October 1804, Ely placed Williams in the care of Moses Welch in Mansfield, Connecticut, where he would remain for much of the next three years. Here, Williams wrote in his journal, "I hope, by the grace of God, so to conduct myself as to meet the approbation of my instructor, & my friends—and above all, so to live & walk before that God to whom I must one day render an account of my thoughts, words, & actions." He missed

Ely greatly, and though he gained from Welch "more knowledge on the doctrines of Christianity than all his reading before," his health remained fragile. Welch made the most of the time he had. Williams late in life recalled "more than one instance" when Welch "took me away to a retired spot and conversed with me in regard to my spiritual state, not only with great solemnity, but even with tears."[39]

Like other native peoples living and learning in New England, he was never completely isolated from his Mohawk family. Eleazer traveled to Akwesasne in fall 1805 to visit his father. He rejected, he wrote, an offer from the Catholic priest there "to accept authority from their Bishop as a teacher to the Indians of his tribe." Why the Catholics so desired the services of a teenager receiving his education among Calvinists in southern New England, Williams did not say. If he took the opportunity this incident offered, if in fact it actually happened, to reflect upon the theological and doctrinal differences between Catholics and Protestants, Williams did not share with anyone in writing his insights. He rejected the offer, he said, and returned to southern New England. He visited Ely at Longmeadow before returning to Mansfield in May 1806.[40]

Eleazer Williams went where he was told and did what his patrons asked him to do. He left one minister's house for another when the cost of maintaining him grew too great. Ely did what he could to raise money to cover Williams's costs. On a number of occasions, for instance, Ely delivered sums of money to Mr. Brockway to lighten the burden of caring for Eleazer and, perhaps, his younger brother. After five months, however, Williams "was impelled from necessity to leave him." Brockway, even with support, could not provide for the two boys.[41]

Ely, indeed, continually raised funds to care for Eleazer and provide for his education. In spring 1803, Ely received fifty dollars from a "Committee for Patronizing the Indian Lads in my Care." Ely and his sons frequently petitioned the Commonwealth of Massachusetts to provide funding for the maintenance and education of Williams. The boys were, he said, "very tractable, and have made considerable improvements, and are sober, discreet young men, piously inclined and bid fair to make good Indian missionaries, if their education can be completed." Congregationalists in Newport, after receiving an appeal for funds, sent Ely twenty-five dollars. A couple of dollars here, several more there: Ely managed to cobble together enough funding to pay for Williams's education. Eleazer, too, contributed to these fundraising efforts. In a letter most likely written in 1806, he asked one of Ely's wealthy friends for financial help, for he hoped "to become a member of some college by next fall," but he had no means with which to pay. Williams learned how to sell himself, to tell the white patrons of Indian missions that he could become what they hoped he might become—a missionary to Indians.[42]

A number of interested New Englanders eagerly watched Williams's progress. Arthur Burt, a family friend from Hartford, urged him to remember "that you have such advantages for improvement," and rejoiced "that you make so good progression: you cannot value your opportunities too high." Don't blow it, Burt suggested, for there was much at stake. He expected Williams to pursue to the end of his life "the path of humility, of wisdom, and the fear of God."[43]

*   *   *

Nathaniel Ely placed the education of the boys, at the outset, in the hands of his wife. Though later Longmeadow lore emphasized the boys' unfamiliarity with the classroom and its discipline, much of their education appears to have taken place not in schools but in the minister's house under the close supervision of Mrs. Ely. She taught the boys to memorize their prayers, the psalms, and the hymns. Mrs. Ely gave the boys presents when they successfully committed to memory one or another biblical passage, piece of verse, or line of hymnody.[44]

Eleazer learned much about religion, but he learned as well of patriotism, and love of country, even if his ties to his new country were ambiguous at best. He copied into his notebook an "Ode to Independence Composed by Dr. Willard" and published by his relative Nathan Williams in 1793. Copying a poem written just as the French Revolution descended into a reign of terror, young Eleazer seems not to have paused when Willard urged his readers to observe how

> Lo! Meek-ey'd peace, with lenient hand,
> Waves o'er the plains her olive wand,
> And mildly bids War's rude commotions cease:
> While Europe's guilt-stain'd barbarous realms
> A mighty sea of blood o'erwhelms,
> And death's vast Empire finds a swift increase.[45]

America was a special place, Williams learned, a refuge free from the tumults and the violence that had overwhelmed the Old World.

If Williams learned something of the history of America and Europe from his studies, he also learned about Indians. As a student in New England, he read George Caleb Bingham's popular *Catechism*, from which he might have learned that at the time Europeans discovered America, the continent "was peopled by various tribes of savages, who still occupy the largest part of the continent." He would have learned from Bingham nothing about the Iroquois, but he would have read that all Indians but the "Mexicans and Peruvians" were "ignorant of letters, and the arts of civilized nations."[46]

Not all of his learning about Indians came from books. In 1805, during one of his many journeys through southern New England with his patrons, Williams crossed the sound over to Long Island. Enamored with the surf and tides and the Long Island shore, Williams said little about the Indians living there. Perhaps he had internalized the beliefs of his patrons, the widely shared belief in the early republic that Indians would, ultimately, disappear unless they chose Christianity and civility. Chief among their virtues, in this sense, was their capacity to become something else. Williams visited a "remnant of an Indian tribe at Montag Point," where he enjoyed a wonderful meal. But he said nothing else of his encounter.[47]

Williams attended two sermons that day. He enjoyed listening to sermons. And he learned from them. Adolescent children in New England appear to have learned more from the sermons they listened to than from the books they read. According to a sampling of diaries written by adolescents, sermons conveyed lessons about the power of God, the importance of living one's life in compliance with the Bible, and the importance of feeling gratitude toward Jesus.[48]

Williams learned all these lessons, and like his contemporaries, he thought much about death and its meaning in his young life. Young people in New England thought about death frequently. A catechism that Williams acquired during his years there, like so much of the devotional literature directed toward young people, urged its readers to

> Let the sweet work of prayer and praise,
> Employ my youngest breath;
> Thus I'm prepared for longer days,
> Or fit for early death.

Work hard, children learned, and pay attention to the means of grace, for one could never know how short his or her time was. Death—in one's family, in one's community—always remained near, so young people must be ever vigilant.

I, in the burial place may see
Graves shorter far than I;
From Death's arrest no age is free,
Young children too may die . . .
My God, may such an awful sight
Awakening be to me!
O that by early grace I might
For death prepared be.[49]

In such an environment, some young people feared for their souls, and they thought much about heaven and hell.[50]

Eleazer Williams, as a sickly adolescent living in New England far from home, must have felt himself closer to death than many of his peers. It is not difficult to imagine why. In February 1803, Williams received a letter from his father. "Son I wrote to you last month that we lost your oldest sister and one younger by their deaths," he informed Eleazer. That earlier letter had miscarried, so this was all news. In the intervening month, his father continued, "we have lost one of your Brother six years old by Daths wich we must submit on to the will of God and I hope it will work for our Good." The boys learned of their family's suffering from afar. The feelings of isolation—of disconnect— must have been intense. The "distressing news" understandably threw the family into crisis. It was during the following winter when the boys' grieving mother traveled south to take Eleazer's younger brother home.[51]

While some sort of terrible illness lacerated his family at Kahnawake, Eleazer himself frequently experienced illness in southern New England. "A general debility," accompanied "by pain on my left side," struck Williams in the winter of 1803. The cause, he speculated late in life, Eleazer thought could be found in "the deep distresses I suffered in mind on the account of the Death of my two supposed sisters and a brother." Williams inserted the word "supposed" some time after he initially composed these lines. The illness returned in spring 1804, shortly after his brother's departure.[52]

The combined weight of these experiences led Williams to think much about religion, to reflect upon "the Supreme Author of all the Stupendous works that were before me, and the irresistible power which sustains them." Religion, one of his patrons reminded him early during his stay in New England, "is the Light of the New Jerusalem," and "the one thing needful without which we can neither be happy here nor hereafter."[53]

He lived in an environment that made easy thoughts of this kind. Early in 1802, when a "Great revival of religion" began in Longmeadow, Ely saw "the minds of the children affected," and he believed that "the Spirit of the Lord is at work." Ministers frequently visited the Ely household during the revival and thereafter, and Williams attended with him many lectures and sermons in and around Longmeadow.[54] He remembered that he resisted much of this religious teaching. In time the "fortress which I had erected, to defend myself against the batteries of the Christian faith, came crashing down." He saw clearly then "the vileness of my heart, my baseness & Ingratitude to that God, whose distinguishing goodness & kind providential care of me, which had been displayed in multiplied instances." He kept the resulting feelings: shame, confusion, and humility, to himself. He said little about religious topics. He let others do the talking, many of whom he thought were "too forward in expressing of their feelings and [who] appeared to be overly righteous."[55]

Williams was not an uncritical consumer of religious information. He wrestled with the correctness of the positions advocated by the Catholics with whom he was raised and the Congregationalists with whom he resided now. In this effort, Williams recalled later, "I was highly favored and assisted by several Rev. Gentlemen, whose attentions were excited to see a young Iroquois who being so inquisitive upon a subject which is considered belonging to a student of theology and one who had already made a considerable [progress] in that science." Williams began to question, at least inwardly, not only the truths he carried with him to the Connecticut Valley as a child, but what his patrons taught him as well. "A spirit of independence existed in my breast," he wrote, "which is characteristic of my nation, and a spark of honesty still inflamed my breast, sufficient to abhor and detest the idea of deceiving my best friends." So he wrote, years after he departed from New England.[56]

Williams could mouth all the familiar Puritan denunciations of Catholicism, but at the same time his journeys and his study led him to conclude that the Congregationalists had gone too far in the opposite direction. He worried that religiously minded men and women had "too little elevation of mind to be much affected with those forms and methods of worship, in which there is nothing striking to the outward senses." Episcopalianism, it seemed to Williams, offered a middle path between these extremes of ceremony and austerity. The Episcopal Church, he believed, was "apostolic, her doctrines pure—her government agreeable to scripture—her authority of ministry descended from the Apostles—her discipline and ceremonies not repugnant to the word of God."[57]

Williams claimed later that he came to these opinions in 1804 and 1805 as a teenager in New England but that he kept them concealed from his patrons. This seems unlikely. In fall 1804, Williams attended with Ely a lecture by the

Rev. Enoch Hale at the Hampshire Missionary Society in Boston. Hale took as his texts Matthew 28:19–20 and Mark 16:15–16. Hale's words moved Williams. He responded to the call to "go and make disciples of all nations, baptizing them in the name of the Father and of the Son and of the Holy Spirit and teaching them to obey everything I have commanded you." Williams found himself inspired by Hale to "Go into all the world and preach the good news to all creation."[58]

Williams admired his patrons. He felt "an attachment to the clergy and their sacred office." Their teaching and encouragement inspired in Williams "a missionary spirit." At the age of nineteen, Williams "began to have a desire to become a messenger of the Prince of Peace and manifested a great anxiety for the Salvation of the red men of the forest." He would help non-Christian Indians, people quite different from himself. This was good news to the men who had struggled to support Williams during his stay in New England. It brought them enormous joy to think that Williams, as President Timothy Dwight of Yale told him in 1807, "will be useful to your countrymen by preaching to them Jesus Christ and him crucified."[59]

They made plans to send him to Moor's Charity School, the Indian school that stood as a companion institution to Eleazer Wheelock's Dartmouth College. Williams traveled to New Hampshire, but remained at the school for less than one month. One historian speculated that the experience humiliated Williams. During his stay at Moor's Charity School, Geoffrey Buerger wrote, Williams learned what his New England patrons really thought of him: "that he would remain always a rehabilitated savage in their minds, no matter what level of education or repertoire of social graces he might acquire." Williams, in this view, admired the New England clergy and aspired to join their ranks as an equal, and not a mere missionary to Indians. Consignment to Moor's he viewed as a "demotion and repudiation" by his patrons, so he left the school.[60]

Williams clearly understood the purpose of Moor's Charity School. Williams never had expressed any objection to the numerous suggestions that he become a minster to the Indians. Though he certainly experienced "unpleasant feelings in regard to my late journey," the source of his frustration may have rested elsewhere. He may have suffered from one of his frequent bouts of illness while at the school. Or his patrons might have struggled to send the funds needed for his tuition. And the school's president, Eleazer Wheelock's son John, was according to Williams a difficult and ill-tempered man, who simply did not like his new student. Wheelock received Williams "with certain airs which I am told are peculiar to himself," but Williams could never discover why, precisely, Wheelock treated him so callously. "To me," Williams recalled, "it was an unfortunate affair but gained many friends by it, and no additional credit I believe as to the President."[61]

So he returned to Connecticut to live once again with Moses Welch. He continued to battle ill health. But he was an adult now. Nathaniel Ely died in spring 1808. Williams visited his ailing patron on 18 March but learned of Ely's death several weeks later from the newspapers. Williams wrote a heartfelt letter to Elizabeth Ely, sprinkled with biblical language. Writing from Mansfield, he told Mrs. Ely that God is sovereign, and we are his creation. We all die, return to dust. "We have forfeited all title to his favor and might justly experience the effects of his displeasure; and whatever good thing we enjoy is of grace." God was all-powerful. "The afflictions we suffer are greatly merited: the blessings we enjoy are God's free gift." God "afflicts men for their profit, that they may become partakers of his holiness."[62]

Williams wrote to Mrs. Ely toward the end of July, nearly two months after her husband had died. The news of Ely's death devastated him, he wrote. The moment he heard of Ely's death, he called out "in anguish and bitterness of my soul—*O let me die, the death of the righteous and let my sad end be like his.*" But Williams was preparing to move on, and he wanted to let Mrs. Ely know that. In the same letter in which he tried to console Mrs. Ely, he asked her for financial support. It was a jarring transition. He had come to the point of his letter. He needed a new coat, and his shoes were worn out. His board with Welch had been paid, but Williams still was in want.[63]

In May 1810, almost twenty-two, Williams left New England. Advised by his doctors to journey to the seaside, he hoped that there he might recover at long last from "a turn of bleeding in my lungs and it has made me very weak." He left for New Haven and moved on to New York City. It was not a beach town, strictly speaking, nor known for its healthfulness. Still, like many who go there, even if on a mere "jaunt," Williams found his time in Gotham entirely transforming.[64]

*   *   *

Eleazer Williams left for New York with the blessings of his patrons, who believed that the journey would benefit his health. One of these patrons, the Rev. Enoch Hale, described a young man who "has obtained a degree of information of men and historical facts relative to the country, beyond what is common, to gentlemen of his years." Williams, Hale noted, "has also a talent for writing, which I think may be cultivated to advantage." Yet Williams's "conversation," Hale wrote, "like that of all foreigners, evidences that it is not easy to gain the sounds of the English Alphabet, unless they be learned in early childhood." He struggled, as well, with Latin and Greek and, in Hale's view, he was not ready to go to college. "His present knowledge of languages," Hale wrote, "I do not think sufficient to enable him to be admitted without some further study."[65]

So with the limited financial support of Congregationalists who thought Williams not yet ready to begin his formal training for the ministry, Williams traveled to New York where he became an Episcopalian. He told the Rev. R. S. Storrs in Longmeadow that the Episcopalians invited the promising young man "to place himself under their care, for missionary service." This offer must have attracted Williams, for it came along, Storrs wrote, "at a time when we were difficulted to procure money for his support." Storrs still hoped to raise the money to train Williams properly in New England so that he might "administer the ordinances of the kingdom of God amongst the aboriginals of this Continent," but the Episcopalians viewed Williams as more ready to begin this work than his friends in the Connecticut Valley.[66]

At the center of this group of New York Episcopalians stood John Henry Hobart, soon to become the bishop of the Diocese of New York. Committed to revitalizing an Anglican establishment that had by the early nineteenth century "degenerated into the expression of ruling class propriety," he hoped to expand the range of the Church's missionary endeavors, and saw in Williams a means to that end.[67]

For some, ritual and ceremony constitute the marrow of their Christianity. Beliefs about ceremony and ritual and their meaning at least in part marked the boundaries between Christian denominations. And for many Christians, these differences mattered deeply. But not, it seems, for Eleazer Williams, who was on his way to his third religion. Williams seems to have had little time for doctrinal differences. Other than a vague statement that Episcopalianism seemed a happy medium between Calvinism and Catholicism, he said nothing at this stage of his career critical of the religious practices and beliefs of the denominations he left behind. Religious truth could be a difficult thing to find. Catholicism and the variety of Calvinism embraced by his New England relatives both claimed that they offered believers the way of the light and the truth. From an early age, Williams became a theological dabbler, one who recognized that one's standards might be flexible, that one might be a Christian but believe many things. This ecumenicalism was not rare among Indian Christians who often found themselves living in close proximity with ministers from multiple denominations. With Williams, however, this flexibility, this early recognition of the contingent nature of truth, would clearly serve him well in the future.

Episcopalians in New York immediately began raising funds to send Williams as a missionary to Kahnawake, his natal community. Congregationalists in New England, not to be left behind, chipped in as well. He had learned from very early in his career that religious profession, in both senses of the word, might provide a livelihood for a person of native descent. And Williams, like other Indian missionaries, took advantage of the opportunity offered by his patrons. Writing in *The Christian's Magazine* in summer 1811, Williams remarked on the kindness and confidence shown him in New York. It had long been, he wrote, "my earnest prayer, that God would fit and enable me, by his grace, to go among my *brethren according to the flesh*, and preach to them the unsearchable riches of Christ." Now he saw "hopeful symptoms" that he believed "presage the approaching conversion of some of the savages of the wilderness, to Christ." Williams, with enormous enthusiasm, looked forward at last to joining "the fervent ministers of Jesus traversing the wilds of America, and sounding the Gospel trumpet among the remotest of savage tribes."[68]

His supporters instructed Williams to get along with the non-Indians he encountered near the mission. From them he might learn much about how to approach his prospective converts. "Let your journey be a journey of improvement to gain that knowledge which may be helpful to you," and in the greater program of "sending the Gospel to the Native Indians." Williams should take it easy, for his patrons knew about his frail health. He should not be boastful or impolite, and must always be "very prudent and grave in your deportment among the Indians of your tribe." He should "do everything suitable to gain their confidence and interest in their affections—you will strive to preserve the knowledge of your native language in its purity; you will learn the state of your brethren and connect yourself with those who are most respectable and who may be of future service to you, should you be employed among them in the service of Christ." It was a trial run, of sorts, with his backers looking forward to seeing what their new missionary might achieve.[69]

On the surface, Williams had many of the attributes that made him a perfect candidate for missionary service. He spoke Mohawk and he was a Christian, of course, and he knew a lot about "Indians." This point Williams himself raised in his letters to clerical supporters. The American Board of Commissioners for Foreign Missions published in *The Panoplist* some of Williams's correspondence from the mission field. Williams asserted that "there is much room for improvement in the system of missionary instruction among the Indians, especially in the choice of teachers." A missionary, he continued, "should be well-acquainted with the Indian temper and character" if he is to succeed in "Christianizing the American ancients."[70] He spoke here with the voice of authority, even though he had little firsthand experience. He played the role his supporters provided for him. Indians could become Christians. They should be led to the word of God. This profound transformation might occur if churches could persuade native peoples to minister to their own. Williams understood what his audience wanted to hear, and he played his part to perfection. He convinced many of them that their hopes could be fulfilled if they placed their trust in him.

But little came of his first attempt, and despite these high hopes, Williams remained for only a short time at Kahnawake, a wayfarer who never really put down any roots. The Catholic priest, Williams recalled much later, "not only inculcated the peculiarities of his Church, but prejudiced the minds of his people against the Protestants." Perhaps the priests at Kahnawake had conspired against Williams's mission. But there were other possibilities. The Kahnawake Mohawks, for instance, had assembled a way of living in which they sustained themselves and their community, contentedly Catholic and Mohawk, as they met their physical and spiritual needs. They had little reason to listen to Williams who, by 1812, they may have viewed as an outsider connected to the men who had surrendered Mohawk land to the state of New York in 1796. He brought them nothing that they needed, and what he sold, however attractive and full of promise that product seemed to his clerical sponsors, they had no interest in buying.[71]

*   *   *

In 1812 new opportunities presented themselves to Eleazer Williams. The aspiring missionary became a soldier. The young man who wanted to save the souls of the Indians helped save the American nation instead. Williams told Hanson, and many others, about his experiences during the war with England. His story fascinated Hanson who, once again, believed every incredible claim Williams made about his heroism and his ability to lead men under the most difficult circumstances.

The War of 1812 emerged from issues left unresolved after the American Revolution. Great Britain respected neither American independence nor American sovereignty. As Britain's war against France intensified in the last decade of the eighteenth century, British captains began stopping American ships on the high seas, violating America's rights as a neutral nation and raising troubling questions about the viability of a republican form of government.[72] Those Americans who supported the declaration of war believed that well-led forces might easily overwhelm the British troops in Canada. They underestimated how difficult finding that leadership could be, as well as the competence of the battle-tempered British army and navy. They also failed to foresee how quickly the conflict devolved into a civil war, with both the American republic and the British Empire competing for the allegiance of English-speaking settlers and native communities from the St. Lawrence Valley in northern New York to the western Great Lakes. Many of these Indian communities saw in the war an opportunity to protect their remaining lands from the surging population of the new nation.[73]

Much of the war would be fought in New York state and its strategically critical waters. Control of the Niagara portage determined the ability to move men and materiel into the West. The traditional invasion route for armies advancing against the Americans cut through the St. Lawrence, Lake Champlain, Hudson River corridor. Control of both of these borderlands, long claimed and used and occupied by Iroquois peoples, meant that the Senecas and Mohawks, especially, would find themselves positioned once again to choose sides. The sparse population, moreover, made northern New York a smuggler's paradise. American Federalists, who largely opposed the war, were loath to encourage or cooperate in the prosecution of smugglers, and thousands of head of American cattle as a result passed through St. Regis into Canada.[74]

Because the Mohawk reserve at Akwesasne stood on both sides of the St. Lawrence, white settlers in northern New York feared that their Indian neighbors might ally with the British. Governor Daniel D. Tompkins refused to follow the state assembly's advice to extract a land cession from the Mohawks in 1812 "in consequence of the delicate situation of affairs between the United States and Great Britain" and how that act might effect "an Indian tribe divided in their attachments and affections between Great Britain and the United States," but he still received numerous complaints from "the St. Regis Indians of trespasses of white people upon their lands." Tompkins and many other New Yorkers feared that settler aggression might force more of the 750 Mohawk warriors in three different communities into the arms of the British.[75]

Tompkins hoped to confine the St. Regis Mohawks to their reservation. They could not leave without a pass stating that "the bearer was a quiet and peaceable Indian." This made hunting and trading difficult on a reserve already reduced in size by sales of land to the state. To try to preserve the

loyalty of the Akwesasnes, the New York State Legislature approved a measure delivering five hundred rations per day to St. Regis, and cash payments
to Iroquois military leaders to encourage them to keep their men at home.
The entire annuity the United States had divided among the Mohawks at St.
Regis and Kahnawake it now paid solely to those on the American side. The
policy may have had its effect, however heavy-handed. In spring 1812, these
Mohawks pledged to the American agent at Buffalo, Erastus Granger, their
neutrality in the coming conflict.[76]

British agents, of course, sought to unravel this neutrality. They asked
Thomas Williams to rally the northern Iroquois to the British cause. According to Eleazer, the elder Williams refused. With his family he left Kahnawake
and settled on the American side at St. Regis. Along with his pro-American
associates Colonel Louis Cook and William Gray, he believed that alliance
with the Americans served their own and their community's best interests.[77]
Eleazer Williams joined his father in service to the American cause, and he
provided John Holloway Hanson with a copy of the wartime journal that
he claimed proved it. This was the story that he told. He wanted those who
listened to him to understand that he did not serve as a mere scout or go-
between. He did not do the sort of work white Americans expected allied
Indians at war to perform. His was not a savage warfare of massacre and
reprisal. Indeed, the military leaders of the young republic sought out Williams and actively enlisted his support, he claimed. "I am sent for," Williams
wrote in an entry dated 27 July 1812, "to prevent the Indians from taking the
hatchet against the Americans."[78]

That call to serve came from General Henry Dearborn, a colonel during
the American Revolution, former secretary of war under Thomas Jefferson,
and commander of American forces in northern New York. If he was the
most experienced officer the Americans had available, he was also a clumsy
and slow-moving sixty-one-year-old with little initiative. Williams arrived at
Dearborn's camp near Plattsburgh in early August. The general and his senior
staff, Williams wrote, received him "with a courtesy that was not only gratify-
ing but highly flattering."[79]

Williams recalled that he shared the officers' beliefs about the threat
posed by British allied Indians. He understood, he wrote, "their mode of warfare . . . which is known to spare neither age nor sex, and to be distinguished
by features peculiarly shocking to humanity." Unless he helped Dearborn, he
claimed, "many hundreds, yea it may be thousands of innocent and defenceless women and children would fall a sacrifice under the tomahawk of these
merciless warriors." Perhaps Williams thought of his own family's experience

in frontier warfare when he wrote these words. Perhaps he decided merely to trade in stereotypes about savage warfare that resonated with his military patrons. Perhaps he never said these words at all—Williams is the only source for this meeting. Dearborn claimed later that he recruited Williams, "a half-blooded Indian of the Cachnawaga tribe" to "carry on such a correspondence with certain chiefs of that, and other tribes, as I considered necessary." Williams, Dearborn told militia officer Major-General Benjamin P. Mooers, belonged to a family that had "considerable influence with the Indians" in northern New York. He might help keep them "on neutral ground." Dearborn gave Williams a salary of four hundred dollars per year, a travel allowance, and the "means in the winter seasons for improving your education." Williams claimed that in addition Dearborn appointed him "Superintendent-General of the Northern Indian Department and Commander of the Corps of Observation," a title similar to that of Warraghiyagey, Sir William Johnson, the king's man in charge of Iroquois diplomacy during and after the Great War for Empire. It was not the only or the last time Williams made use of Johnson's name.[80]

Hanson never asked, nor did Williams offer, an explanation as to why the commanding officer in the American war effort would have placed such great responsibility in Williams's hands. He had no military experience, and he had only occasionally visited the Mohawk communities in New York and Canada over the twelve years he was away. Thomas Williams might have put in a good word for his twenty-four-year-old son.[81] Mooers, under whom Eleazer Williams seems to have served in 1813 and 1814, and who agreed with Dearborn that "he may be of essential service," noted simply that "he talks good English and writes a good hand & is pretty well informed" and, despite his long absence, "believes he has the confidence of the Indians generally." He would make a good messenger and might gather some useful intelligence along the way, and he convinced Dearborn that he might provide some important assistance.[82]

Williams told Hanson that the men Dearborn placed under his command were among "the most reckless, daring, and unscrupulous in the Army." Williams described them to Hanson as his "terrible corps." They spread out on foot and on horseback, and reported to Williams "every movement of the British forces." This was, for Hanson, important stuff. The army's marches and movements in the North Country, Hanson believed, were governed by information the senior officers received from Williams. Williams, Hanson claimed, was to a great extent "thus the instrument of defeating the English, both by land and water, in the north and west."[83]

Williams tried to create the impression in his war stories that he had been born to lead. He wrote that in September 1812, Dearborn sent him north to Rouses Point where he met with Sir William Johnson's son, Sir John Johnson, the crown's superintendent of Indian affairs in Canada during the War of 1812. There they discussed the importance of Indian neutrality but could not overcome their differences. But Williams, according to his own account, did very much impress Johnson. Williams told Johnson that the British king "styles himself the Defender of the Christian Faith." Would the king, then, "league himself with the ruthless savages of the wilderness, whose tender mercies are to be manifested by the Tomahawk and the scalping knife—and that not only upon the wounded and captive of the American soldiery, but upon defenceless women and children?" It was a familiar theme for Williams, playing upon images of Indian savagery. "I have too exalted an opinion of British humanity," he claimed to have told Johnson, "and of the principles of religion by which the English nation is governed, to admit this unholy alliance." Johnson thought Williams "moved like a young lion upon the subject," and "that he not only pleaded upon principles of humanity and civilization, but of religion, which would not add savage barbarity to the other evils of the war."[84]

Williams traveled frequently between Albany, St. Regis, and Plattsburgh. He carried messages for Dearborn and Mooers and New York's Governor Tompkins. He carried messages from the chiefs at St. Regis, and served as an interpreter and translator. All of this can be documented.[85] He also may have fought, at least on occasion. In 1855, Williams told Benson Lossing, a chronicler and historian of the war, that he had participated in the fighting around St. Regis that resulted in the capture of a small British force in fall 1812. But fighting was sporadic on the northern frontier, and like many couriers, Williams spent much of his time in camp. He thought much of matters religious. "O, how sweet it is when I am with Him by prayer and in reading His holy word." He asked the Holy Spirit to "sanctify my heart by thy divine influence, and make me a true child of God." He pledged, "O my God, I once more give myself up to thee, and wilt thou accept of me, unworthy as I am."[86]

Given the conduct of the war, as well as the quality of life in camp, Williams likely found ample cause to contemplate his relationship with God and the state of his immortal soul. Nearly a third of the men in camp at any one time suffered from illness that rendered them unfit for service. Williams continued to struggle from bouts of poor health. In December 1813, the cold weather of the northern New York winter reminded Williams "of the uncertainty of my existence here." By the end of March, four months later, he was a mess. "My nervous system is in a feeble state," he wrote, "and my eyes are so weak that I am unable to read." He hoped that "this sickness may have the effect of weaning me from the world."[87]

Meanwhile, American military operations in the North Country accomplished little. The unwillingness or inability of American leaders to challenge the British for control of the St. Lawrence, their most critical line of supply, amazed British officers. American officials seemed more interested in socializing while their soldiers suffered from cold and disease.[88] The only significant attempt at an invasion in late 1813 ended disastrously, and the American troops withdrew once again from the valley. Smuggling resumed, and Major General George Izard, who replaced the disgraced General Wilkinson and who, Williams claimed, recognized the importance of his "Corps of Observation," complained that, "From the St. Lawrence to the ocean, an open disregard prevails for the laws prohibiting intercourse with the enemy. The road to St. Regis is covered with droves of cattle and the river with rafts destined for the enemy. The revenue officers see these things and acknowledge their inability to put a stop to such outrageous proceedings." These smugglers returned home with British manufactured goods, in great demand in the United States.[89]

The Americans seemed uncommitted and their forces poorly led, and the British obtained further cause for optimism early in 1814. The defeat of Napoleon on the continent allowed the British to send veteran reinforcements to America. As these forces arrived in Montreal, American commanders decided to shift many of their troops from the north to the Niagara frontier. Williams noted in his journal in August 1814 his fears that "if our army is withdrawn from this part, the enemy may invade this section of the country and attack Plattsburgh." He told Major General Izard, who had been ordered to march his troops to Buffalo, that he thought the plan unwise. "I am a soldier, and must obey my superiors," Izard told him. Recognizing, it seemed, Williams's natural ability to lead men and assess grand strategy, Izard added, "Friend Williams, you ought to be at the head of the War Department instead of those who now control the army."[90]

Two days after Izard departed with his 3,500 soldiers, a British invasion force of 10,000 men crossed into the United States, a force larger than the armies commanded by Burgoyne and Cornwallis during the American Revolution. Commanded in person by the British Governor General Sir George Prevost, the British army intended to advance on Albany. Before he could get there, however, Prevost had to deal with the American forces at Plattsburgh, on Lake Champlain. American major general Alexander Macomb had 1,500 regulars at his disposal, most of them untested in battle, and militia troops from New York. The overly cautious Prevost would not attack them until the Royal Navy first defeated an American squadron on Lake Champlain under the command of Thomas McDonough.[91]

Macomb sent Williams to collect information, to watch the British troops as they advanced. His brother John joined him on some of these missions. "The anxiety of the General is now so great, at the movements of the enemy," Williams wrote, "as to require a report from me once in ten hours." Major General Mooers, meanwhile, led his militiamen out to skirmish with the advancing British soldiers. By 4 September, Prevost's advance guard was eighteen miles from Plattsburgh. "All fell solemn," Williams recalled, "knowing as we do our weakness, and the strength of the enemy, but brave resistance will be made, whether to effect or not."[92]

Williams may have engaged in some of these skirmishes, though there is no solid evidence that he did so. If he was involved, he would have joined with Mooers's militia forces in felling trees and tearing up bridges to slow the advancing enemy. Prevost drove back defenders who had set up an ambush just north of Plattsburgh on 6 September, and he might have taken the town had he not decided, foolishly, to await the outcome of the naval battle. It had been, Williams thought, "a day of anxiety and gloominess in the little American army."[93]

The next night a council of war took place in Plattsburgh. Williams delivered the intelligence he had gathered to Macomb and Mooers. Upon their recommendation, he claimed, Williams, who had no training or experience in firing such weapons, "decided to place myself at the head of the artillery, with such volunteers as might be collected."[94] Prevost's forces at last attacked on 11 September. Williams's battery stood above the Saranac River, located there to challenge any British effort to cross and advance on the town. Williams "saluted" the British troops "with such a storm of shot and grape from our battery as to compel them to fall back." The British tried several more times, and Williams's men "either answered the enemy's fire, or poured shot into every body of their troops, that presented a tolerable mark."[95]

While Prevost's men tried to ford the Saranac, the naval battle raged out on the lake. When he heard the cheers of Vermonters who had watched the fight, and saw his flagship defeated by the Americans, Prevost decided to withdraw. He snatched defeat from the jaws of victory. He called off the attack and proved "how useless the best troops in the world may be in the hands of an incompetent general."[96]

And it was, Williams claimed, because of his own cleverness that the British withdrawal became a complete rout. Williams's plan for a "coup de main" won the approval of Macomb and Mooers. He sent out runners to carry rumors to the British camp. From these stories, Prevost gathered that thousands of Vermont militiamen were on the march to occupy a village to Prevost's north. Unless he moved quickly, his entire army would be cut off. Fearing such a colossal defeat, his men began a rapid return march to Canada, leaving behind their wounded, and much of their equipment and materiel. In the biography of his father Williams wrote very late in life, he claimed that "this *coup de main* . . . saved the defenses at Plattsburgh, the honor of the American troops, and the flag of the United States." Through this heroic act, Williams claimed later, American "honor was sustained, her troops, with immense quantities of property, were saved, and the whole northern frontier was relieved from a troublesome enemy."[97]

In the battle's final hours, Williams received a wound in his side, the result of one of Prevost's last artillery barrages. It was not so serious that it forced Williams to leave the field. Indeed, he joined in the pursuit. Rain fell, and the British carts moving northward tore up the roads. The going was difficult, and after a day Williams began to feel the effects of his wound. He washed it with brandy, but had done nothing more, until the wound had become "extremely painful and somewhat alarming in its features." Williams spent the next five weeks confined to his room, his father attending him as his physician. Hanson assumed that Thomas Williams used "Indian herbs" to treat him, but that was pure supposition.[98]

During his confinement, Williams had plenty of time to think and reflect. Restricted largely to reservations defined geographically by the State of New York and the United States, and surrounded by a surging white population, Iroquois peoples had to consider their choices carefully. Though they would have preferred neutrality, many came over to the American side as the war advanced, hoping to maintain positive relations with outsiders in order to preserve their remaining autonomy and lands. But never again would the United States rely upon the sort of assistance that Williams and his neighbors offered them. Armed resistance to American expansion, in the Ohio Country, the Great Lakes, and in the southern states, largely came to a close. Pressure on native land increased immensely after the war. The conflict thus marked an important turning point. Williams seems not to have thought about the effect of the war on the peoples of the Longhouse. He could not claim to belong to any of the communities in Canada and New York that together comprised a broader Iroquoia. An Indian alone in white America, he focused on his career, his options, and the things he hoped to accomplish once he recovered. During these long hours, he wrote, "I resolved again and again, if God willing, to carry to the Indians that 'faithful saying, and worthy of all acceptation, that Christ Jesus came into the world to save sinners' [1Tim. 1:15]."[99] He committed himself anew to "the glory of God, and the advancement of the Redeemer's kingdom."[100]

*   *   *

Eleazer Williams told his war stories to John Holloway Hanson, and Hanson, as far as we can tell, believed everything that Williams told him. Williams told these stories to many people, over many years. Williams appears on occasion in the war's rich documentary record, but he is the only source for descriptions and accounts of his military service. There is no doubt that Williams simply made up much of what he related to Hanson and others as his wartime experience. An "Eleazer Williams, Jr.," served in Captain Braddum Yale's New York militia company based in Rensselaer County, but this clearly was not our Eleazer Williams. Another "Eleazer Williams" served in Vosburgh's Ninth New York Militia from Kinderhook. This, too, does not appear to be our man. No other military service records exist for individuals from New York named Eleazer Williams.[101]

If Williams served in some secret capacity, as he claimed, perhaps this explains why no evidence exists to describe his military career. But Williams never succeeded in persuading anyone in the military establishment that this was the case. At the end of the war, for example, Williams sought back pay he claimed the army owed him for his service. General Henry Dearborn had no memory of Williams's service after the war's first year and referred the matter to Benjamin Mooers. In 1814, Mooers had told the army's inspector general "that Thomas Williams and his sons had done much good by their timely and repeated interference with the hostile Indians," but by 1816 he had done nothing to help advance Eleazer Williams's claim.[102]

Williams told tales of his military service on a number of occasions. Sometimes he sought money for his own injuries, and at other times for property losses allegedly suffered by his father during the war. Always he did so with the hope that it might bring some financial reward. It was, in a sense, the American way. Once a certain identity brought with it access to resources, whether a grant of land or a pension, it was not long before a certain segment of the population began scheming to claim that identity and their share of those resources. Williams wanted a pension for himself and compensation for his father, and he sought out allies in that cause. He offered his assistance in 1817 to the Ogden Land Company in removing the New York Indians to new homes in the West, for instance, at least in part in expectation that David Ogden, a congressman, "will attend to my Father's case for his losses during the war."[103] He told Michigan's territorial governor Lewis Cass, probably in 1827, of the wounds he suffered leading an infantry charge at Plattsburgh, evidence, he hoped, of both the strength of his commitment to the United States and his fitness for a government job in managing Indian affairs.[104] The U.S. Senate in 1829 considered a petition from Williams seeking relief for property losses he and his father allegedly had suffered during the war. He asked specifically for a grant of lands. Two committees considered the petition, but neither took action in his behalf.[105] Two decades after that, Williams told the author of an article that appeared in the *Democratic Review* that he had "shed his own blood at the siege of Plattsburgh" in the "defence of American rights, and the honor of its flag."[106] Later that year, on Christmas Eve 1849, Williams submitted to the U.S. Senate a memorial "praying a pension for services rendered during the last war with Great Britain." Dearborn had approached Williams, he claimed, "to perform certain duties in behalf of the Government, which were then and now too private and confidential in their nature to be mentioned." This service was "frequently hazardous in the extreme," but Williams still had not received the pay to which he was entitled.[107]

Williams explained to the Senate that his service "was planned in secret, and executed in secret, and it is believed that it proved in the end to be one of the most important auxiliaries in the discomfiture of the enemy at Plattsburgh in 1814." During that battle, in which he displayed such great heroism, Williams "received a serious wound, from which he still extremely suffers, and at times disables him even from walking." Williams badly needed help.[108]

He included in his memorial affidavits from men who remembered seeing him at Plattsburgh three and a half decades before, and who knew that he was "very active during the war in these frontiers, in passing and repassing from Plattsburgh to St. Regis, with dispatches." He included a copy of a letter from Dearborn, in Williams's own hand, that spelled out the terms of his secret service. But he failed to persuade the Senate's Committee on Pensions that he deserved their assistance. They did not doubt that Williams had served during the war in some capacity, nor did they doubt that he had received a wound. But Williams did not provide the committee "with any proof as to the degree of the disability occasioned by the wound," and they could "not ascertain, by any papers in their possession, in what capacity he was engaged when he received said wound, and the amount paid him for the services which he rendered." The committee dismissed Williams's memorial largely because he did not have the evidence to substantiate his claims.[109]

Williams must have composed his war journal sometime after the Senate rejected his memorial. If he had the journal, surely he would have submitted a copy as supporting documentation, for it addressed every one of the concerns raised by the committee members. But like so much about Williams, the journal was a fabrication, an elaborately detailed fiction designed to convince whoever read it that Williams had played an essential role in preserving the new nation's independence. He constructed a story, and cast himself as the lead character in an effort to save the republic. He told the story late in the 1840s, when few still lived who might challenge his claim. It was, in the end, a con.

It would be nice to think that Williams had no reason to be ashamed of his service during the War of 1812. If he served as a courier and as an interpreter—and the evidence allows us at least to go that far—he did important work that at times must have been both physically arduous and extremely dangerous. If his health was as frail as his journal indicates, his ability to carry out his orders is indeed commendable. Desertion was common on both sides during the war, but Williams continued to serve, it seems, even at times when the outcome of the war remained in doubt. It is entirely possible, as well, that he found himself on occasion under fire. Would anybody have dismissed his service as inconsequential?

Williams needed a better story. The ordinary was never adequate. Always keenly aware that he lived in a country with a short historical memory, he attempted to invent for himself a greater role in the nation's story. He was, in his version of the past, no mere courier carrying messages for the high command, but the Superintendent of Indian Affairs, a man holding a lofty title with an ample salary. Perhaps Williams understood something of the disdain, the condescension, and the fear, the hatred, and the nostalgia, that colored non-Indian perceptions of native people. So many non-natives saw Indians as part of the past, ready to exit the stage of history through extinction or "civilization." Williams's war stories, perhaps, challenged these narratives. But he mostly told his stories to impress, to magnify his importance in the eyes of others, and to supplement his meager and episodic stipend as a missionary. It never seems to have dawned on Hanson that Williams wrote the journal late in his life to bolster his claim for a pension, and Hanson sought in this record only for material that confirmed his supposition that Eleazer Williams was the Dauphin. Hanson, who read but did not analyze, and who missed entirely the reasons why Williams might have felt compelled to tell these stories and to act this part, believed that Williams conversed easily with generals and demonstrated his toughness, his heroism, and his ability to lead men, all fitting qualities for a gentleman—or, for that matter, a king. But Williams was as much the "Superintendent of Indian Affairs" during the war as he was the ill-fated son of Louis XVI and Marie Antoinette.

CHAPTER TWO

Soldier of Christ

In the weeks and months following their first meeting on the Northern Line, Eleazer Williams and John Holloway Hanson remained in touch. Their correspondence, which must have been extensive, has not survived. Nevertheless, they met on a number of occasions—in Albany, in New York City, and in Hoboken, New Jersey, where, Hanson's sister recalled, Williams regularly visited the family home. Williams must have provided Hanson with drafts of the autobiography he never published, copies of his correspondence, and a range of newspaper clippings documenting his career. They spoke for hours. Hanson took notes. He gathered his evidence, looking for material to confirm the identity of Williams as the dauphin. Williams objected to none of this, of course. He could play the dauphin, but whatever biographical work Hanson might produce would lend his assertions additional weight, scholarly heft, and the authority provided by an independent observer, seemingly wary of fraud, committed to excavating nothing but the facts. Hanson might approach the subject with an air of disinterestedness that Williams could not provide. Williams was the claimant, Hanson the impartial investigator. Williams valued the publicity and attention Hanson's story, when published, might generate.[1]

After Plattsburgh, Williams wrote, he "retired from the seat of war & like a monk entered into a cell for meditation & reflections." He prayed and read the Bible and prayed some more. He employed the language of performance: "It seemed to me as if I was entering into a new scene of the theatre of the human life—a scene to me most solemn in its consequences both in this life & that which is to come." Williams selflessly turned his back on this grasping world, he said, and committed himself "to do something for the benefit of the St. Regis Indians, who were at this period in a most deplorable condition in regard to their morals and whose children were growing up without education."[2]

Perhaps this is how it went. But Williams's patrons had groomed him for missionary work, and after the war it is not surprising that he returned to the career path they had marked for him. Williams might have understood, even this early in his career, that for an acculturated and educated Indian male who hoped to succeed in American life, religion and reform offered perhaps the only visible, viable, and socially acceptable avenues for doing so. The examples offered by other Indian ministers, like the Mohegans Joseph Johnson and Samson Occom, and scores of lesser known New England Algonquians who ministered at times to small flocks, offered a template. Williams followed a familiar path, one that involved a difficult balancing act, maintaining ties both to native Christians and to white patrons who looked toward the "civilization" of the Indians. He ministered to them, while answering to white men who hoped to transform native Christians culturally and spiritually.

Williams traveled from Plattsburgh, where he had last been stationed, to Albany. He began to sell his wares, and play his part. He visited with New York's lieutenant governor John Tayler, who oversaw much of the empire state's Indian policy, including its aggressive program to acquire Iroquois land. He met with Episcopal clergymen in Albany and in nearby Troy, generating support for his missionary enterprise. And then he headed for New York City, to reacquaint himself with John Henry Hobart, now bishop of the Episcopal Diocese of New York.[3]

Williams reminded Hobart of his determination "to proclaim the unsearchable riches of Christ to my poor brethren." They met together in the city several times. They discussed missions, but they also discussed theology. Williams claimed to have little interest in the issues that divided Arminians, Calvinists, and Lutherans. He told Hobart that "I am somewhat free & independent in my views in regard to the great doctrine of the Gospel." But not too independent. He would never, he assured Hobart, "receive any article as an article of faith, which I may view it as repugnant to the word of God." Hanson admired this independence of spirit and thought it consistent with Williams's royal origins, even if it more accurately reflected a sort of ecumenicalism not uncommon among Indian preachers.[4]

Hobart envisioned an important role for Williams. He wanted his church to enter the mission field with Indians and to do so energetically. Hobart learned from the land baron Thomas Ludlow Ogden that Indians living in the vicinity of white people had "lost all the virtues of the Savage State and have adopted all the low vices of the lowest class of society." One of the founders of the Ogden Land Company, a business syndicate possessed of nothing more than the right to purchase the Seneca Indians' remaining lands in western New York, Ogden told Hobart that the Indians suffered as whites pressed on their lands. "Their men are drunkards and their women prostitutes," he stated, matter-of-factly. If Hobart accepted Ogden's claim that "the hunter must yield to the Civilized State, and that the presence of the Indian tribes in their collective and national character in the midst of the White population is inconsistent with the interests of both," he did not yet let on.[5]

But he did back Williams. Williams made his First Communion and received Confirmation at St. John's Church in New York City in May 1815.[6] Two days later, Hobart addressed a letter to *The Churchman's Magazine*. "An opportunity offers of extending, under the most favorable circumstances, the blessing of civilization and religion among the Indian tribes, through the instrumentality of Mr. Eleazer Williams, a young man of Indian extraction." Hobart asked his readers for donations. Williams—talented, educated, and committed—could produce a translation of the Book of Common Prayer in the Mohawk language with the support of dedicated Christians. Hobart sent Williams on the road to raise money. Williams met with "some of our worthy church people" over the course of three days in June. He visited Washington, as well, and met, he claimed later, with President James Madison and his secretary of state, James Monroe. He met with several senators and congressmen, and the men who immediately oversaw the conduct of federal Indian policy on the New York frontier, the federal agent Erastus Granger and the interpreters Jasper Parrish and Horatio Jones. Here is the irony. Jones and Parrish provided Williams, he claimed, with valuable information about the state of the Six Nations. Williams knew the language, but he learned much about conditions in Iroquoia not from the Indians themselves, but from the powerful white men who oversaw their relations with the federal government and the state of New York. These men supported efforts to save the Indians' souls, but they also hoped to acquire their lands.[7]

Hobart directed Williams to head for Akwesasne, to act as a lay reader, catechist, and school teacher for the Indians. All the signs seemed favorable. If Williams raised less than his sponsors had hoped, the project still generated considerable interest. Bishop Hobart placed his hopes on the twenty-seven-year-old missionary, and expected him to perform well. The mission had the blessings of both church and state. Yet seven months after his arrival at St. Regis in August 1815, Williams declared the mission a complete failure.

Williams explained that he faced two insurmountable problems. Much bad blood remained at St. Regis after the War of 1812. Those who had aided the British during the conflict had returned to the community, Williams said, and the resulting tensions defeated "those objects I had in view." But Williams said little specifically about how these dynamics worked against him, or of the nature of postwar relations between the pro-British minority and those who had opposed them during a divisive conflict. Nor did Williams say anything of his family's ties to St. Regis. His parents left Kahnawake in 1813, feeling themselves unsafe there during the war. They settled at Akwesasne. That Mohawks there might have associated Williams with those who in the past (and would again in the future) sell lands the Akwesasne Mohawks claimed might have reduced his effectiveness as a missionary. But Williams wrote of his failures only in generalities, and he was quick to find excuses. There always was something, or someone else, to blame.[8]

Such as the "young Romish missionary" at St. Regis, Williams wrote, "whose object is, from his conduct, to foment those jealousies and stimulate the opposition party to continue in their present feelings." The priest had advantages unavailable to Williams. He possessed, on the one hand, "the powerful support of the British government," which supplied him with gifts to distribute to a people "already tinctured with the Catholic tenets." Williams had only "persuasion & influence" on his side to counter Catholic largesse. On the other hand, Williams watched as his Catholic opponent employed "the terrors of the Romish Church" against those reluctant to follow him. The priest "thunders forth the anathemas of his Church to terrify them." Against these forces, Williams could not prevail, and he began to make plans to try again as a missionary at another location, even though some in the American party at St. Regis reportedly wished him to continue his efforts.[9]

These were excuses as much as explanations, but what Williams told his superiors after the Akwesasne failure had the desired effect. They kept their faith in him. Just two months after the Battle of Plattsburgh, Williams received a letter from the Oneidas inviting him to come minister to them "in our own language." Dissatisfied with their present missionary, they hoped that Williams might teach them "to learn the way to heaven and we wish also that our children may learn to read and write." When Williams told John Holloway Hanson this story many years later, the aspiring biographer was truly impressed. "Other persons," Hanson believed, "with his endowments, would have despised the wigwam of the Indian, and sought for popularity and status in cities, and in the applause of the wealthy and intellectual." Not Williams. He took little interest in such earthly vanities, and committed himself only to advancing the Redeemer's kingdom. Hanson listened eagerly as Williams opened for him the next chapter in his life story.[10]

*   *   *

Eleazer Williams convinced John Holloway Hanson that he could have had so much more, but as a humble man he trusted in God and accepted his will. The riches of Versailles and the power of a prince interested him less than the spiritual rewards he might acquire toiling in the mission field. He accepted the Oneidas' invitation. He arrived on 23 March 1816. Seldom did Indian preachers arrive on native ground without the support of a larger missionary organization, or state and federal officials, who encouraged their efforts. Mission service meant balancing sometimes antagonistic interests. The challenges Williams faced, in this sense, were not unique. He wanted to preach to the Indians, but Williams journeyed to the Oneida country because powerful white men in the state, some of whom saw it as their primary responsibility and interest to acquire Oneida land, thought he might be an effective missionary. At the time the Oneidas wrote to him, Williams had as yet no credible experience or success as a missionary. There is no reason the Oneidas would have known of him unless they had been told about him. Perhaps the same officers in church and state with whom Williams had met promoted his talents. Lieutenant Governor Tayler, for instance, provided Williams with a letter to the Oneida chiefs encouraging them to accept Williams, and strings of wampum "which when delivered . . . was received with peculiar marks of respect."[11]

And Williams, to the Oneidas, might have seemed a promising prospect. Oneidas over a span of several decades sought men out to help broker their relations with their white neighbors. All these men, all of them white, had let the Oneidas down. Perhaps Williams, if he possessed the talents men like Hobart and Tayler claimed he did, and connections to powerful men in the East, could perform this function and play this role more effectively than his predecessors. Indeed, Williams learned from the non-Christian chiefs, several days after his arrival, when "they congratulated me on my safe arrival once more among them, and thanked the Great Spirit for his protection and for moving my heart to come to them in the character of a religious instructor," that it was the very same "Pagan" party that extended the Oneida invitation to Williams.[12]

He received warm greetings everywhere he went, but what he saw left him deeply disturbed. The problem at Oneida was not bad blood left over from a divisive war as at Akwesasne, or the powerful influence of a Catholic priest, but "the morals of the nation," which Williams thought "most deplorable." A decades-old factionalism divided the Oneidas into Christian and

Pagan parties. The Christians, Williams wrote, "were still ignorant of the way of salvation by Jesus Christ—they scarcely understood the meaning of having faith—had no idea of evangelical repentance," and "they needed further instruction in the character of Jesus Christ and the end and design of his coming into the world and the great moral duties which our Creator has required of us, as rational and accountable beings, to perform." Drunkenness occurred too frequently, Christians attended church too infrequently, and their morals stood in a tattered state.[13]

The divisions Williams described stemmed from the Oneidas' long history of interaction with their non-Indian neighbors. While native peoples farther to their west found inspiration in the teachings of a number of nativist leaders, the Oneidas faced growing numbers of European colonists living in close proximity to them. Some of these white people they considered friends and neighbors. But others pressed on their lands, cut their timber, and allowed their livestock to roam free and damage Oneida fields. Some outsiders they welcomed as teachers, others as buffers to insulate their community from the frontier population. Some Oneidas at the polyglot town of Onoquaga in the southern edge of their still-vast territory, for instance, attended mission schools in New England and welcomed into their midst a small number of Protestant missionaries. The Oneidas invited Christian Brothertown and Stockbridge Indians from southern New England to settle on the eastern periphery of their territory, closest to the surging white frontier settlements. These Indians brought with them literacy, fluency in English, political connections to Protestant leaders in New England, and a knowledge of English-style agriculture. They seemed to bring the prospect of peace with their white neighbors. Those Oneidas who supported this experiment viewed it not as a capitulation to their colonial overlords but as a way to strengthen and protect their community from the outside forces that threatened its very existence.[14]

In 1766 Presbyterian minister Samuel Kirkland arrived in Oneida country. Kirkland called upon the Oneidas to give up drinking. He told them to begin to farm their land like their white neighbors. Some Oneidas followed Kirkland's advice, and his followers ultimately became the Oneida "Christian Party" whose lack of religious knowledge Williams later decried. Others, including many traditional chiefs, rejected key parts of Kirkland's message. These "Pagans" opposed Kirkland's challenge to traditional beliefs, and to the religious and cultural system that upheld their authority. They understood the basic tenets of Christianity but they rejected those beliefs. The Pagans, whose views had been tempered by the aggressions of frontier whites, asserted that

Indians and non-Indians were not alike, and that Indians should not follow religious practices intended for grasping and land-hungry settlers. The
experience of living with Kirkland, and the Presbyterian missionary's dogged
determination to transform them, led some Oneidas to view white people as
hypocrites, aggressive and exploitative, committed to dispossessing the weak.
Some of the Christian Oneidas came to share these beliefs. Oneidas and their
native neighbors, both Christian and Pagan, in short, confronted the complicated question of how best to deal with this significant threat.[15]

Kirkland maintained close ties to his fellow churchmen in New England,
and as a result imperial officials like Sir William Johnson, the king's superintendent of Indian Affairs in the Northern Department, grew to distrust him.
Johnson overstated Kirkland's influence, but many Oneidas did indeed side
with the United States during the American Revolution. They never committed unanimously—some Oneidas joined with the British; others cleared
out, hoping to lay low while the war raged. After the disastrous battle of
Oriskany in 1777, in which Oneidas took part in a bloody losing battle with
American forces against a British force that included Iroquois from the
other League nations, they avoided conflict with their Longhouse kin. They
seem to have shared intelligence on American intentions with their British-
allied Iroquois brethren. Oneidas agreed that league members should not
spill each other's blood. They agreed that they had more to fear from the
neighboring whites than from the distant British tyrants. Warren Johnson,
the brother of Sir William, pointed out that some of these white settlers wore
"an Indian's skin for a Tobacco Pouch," a menacing and terrifying symbol of
past violence. Most recognized that they would have to find a way to live in
the company of these white people, though they could not agree on how to
best achieve that end. Iroquois communities, whether they sided with the
British or not, based their decisions on a consideration of which side they
believed offered them the best chance of preserving their lands and their
way of life after the war.[16]

And despite their alliance with the victorious American patriots, Oneida
country lay devastated at the war's end. Much of the livestock the Oneidas
had accumulated over the previous decades had disappeared: over 100 pigs,
120 horses, and five dozen head of cattle. Oneidas claimed that British raiders and allied Indians took from them steel traps, rifles, and metal hand tools
obtained through trade with their non-native neighbors as well. The Oneidas treated this property as private and personal, another significant change
in how they lived and how they saw the world. The Oneidas kept trunks
and chests to store their possessions. Many Oneidas lived in single-family

dwellings, not longhouses, many of which they erected in the 1740s during a period of relative peace in Iroquoia.[17]

Houses can be rebuilt. Livestock and other property, with difficulty, can be replaced. The war's other wounds proved harder to heal. Alcohol and domestic violence occurred with more frequency, according to non-Indian observers. Oneida Christians who had accepted Kirkland's Calvinist message began to believe that the God to whom they prayed despised Indians as much as did the Oneidas' war-weary neighbors. Factionalism reemerged between traditional chiefs and warriors, between "Christians" and "Pagans." Christianity, and the cultural change that in varying degrees accompanied its acceptance, exacerbated divisions in communities, at Oneida as elsewhere. Two thought worlds, two ways of comprehending the historical experience of a people, and two sets of lenses for perceiving a difficult reality: Oneidas, like other native peoples at other times and in other places, hurled blame at one another as they debated how best to move forward. It is not difficult to understand the anguish they might have felt. Christianity, or the rejection of Christianity, could not provide immediate answers for problems that had brewed for many years. As a result, many Oneidas seemed to lose hope for the future, a trite line perhaps, but one that suggests something of the wreckage with which the community lived.[18]

And in this atmosphere of crisis, the Oneidas faced growing assaults upon their lands, a determined drive to dispossess them and push them out of their New York homelands that would dominate their history for the entire span of Eleazer Williams's association with them and beyond. The state of New York needed Iroquois land. Control of the Oneida "Carrying Place," that small strip of territory that connected the Mohawk River to Oneida Lake and from it the waterway to the Great Lakes and the interior of the continent, was essential to the state's economic development. Men like Elkanah Watson, who traversed Iroquoia shortly after the Revolution, envisioned a canal cutting across the state, one that channeled the trade of the Northwest eastward through New York rather than south down the Ohio. To make this dream a reality required carving up the Iroquois estate. Moreover, a state like New York, cash-poor and deeply in debt, saw in the sale of Iroquois lands a way to pay for its government without resorting to a politically inexpedient program of taxation.[19]

The Articles of Confederation, the first American constitution, possessed an ambiguity in its language related to Indian affairs that allowed both state and federal officials to view the conduct of diplomacy with the Six Nations as a matter within their exclusive jurisdiction. The Confederation government, late in 1783, appointed commissioners to negotiate a treaty of peace with the Six Nations. New York state officials questioned the right of the federal commissioners to meet with Indians in the state, and the legislature appointed its own commissioners, who raced to Fort Stanwix (present-day Rome, New York) and arrived ahead of those sent by Congress.[20]

In 1784, the Oneidas chose to negotiate with the officials appointed by Congress, and from the United States they obtained a pledge to secure them "in the possession of the lands on which they are settled." But within a year, the Oneidas reluctantly sold 200,000 acres to the state of New York, whose governor George Clinton would not take no for an answer. And this was only the beginning. Through a fraudulent agreement negotiated in September 1788, Governor Clinton and the state's appointed Indian Commissioners acquired another massive swath of Oneida land. The state completed this transaction just before the new federal Constitution went into effect and clarified and significantly strengthened, at least on paper, the powers of the national government over Indian affairs.[21]

In 1790 the new Congress under this Constitution enacted the first of several Trade and Intercourse acts, an attempt to control contact between Indians and whites, and give force to the language in the federal constitution. The legislation required, among other things, that purchases of Indian land take place with federal oversight, and that the Senate ratify the resulting agreements. But the state ignored these laws and purchased the Oneidas' lands anyway, and the federal government was at times a willing partner. Dispossession may have exacerbated other tensions already existing in the community. According to Paolo Andreani, an Italian visitor who passed through Oneida country in 1790, the Indians suffered from "inflammatory fevers caused by the immoderate use of strong liquors and various kinds of venereal diseases." Alcohol abuse, according to some observers, continued to devastate the community. Andreani saw progress, but he described the Oneidas as "half-civilized." They had adopted many of the customs of their neighbors, a product of "the frequent intercourse that this nation had with European colonists." Though the Oneidas did not "separate their fields from their pastures in the English mode," as Jeremy Belknap observed six years after Andreani passed through, and they did not fence their fields like their Stockbridge and Brothertown neighbors, they were adjusting to the new economic realities around them. They bought and sold corn from their neighbors. They attempted to rebuild and increase their herds of livestock. Some practiced trades like their non-Indian neighbors. Still, they encountered a relentlessly aggressive state government ever desirous to acquire their lands.[22]

In 1794, when U.S. commissioner Timothy Pickering met with the Six Nations at Canandaigua, New York, to secure their alliance with the republic and ensure that Iroquois warriors did not join with a massive native uprising in the Ohio country, the Oneidas aired their grievances about the state's conduct. They told Pickering that they felt troubled. "Our minds," the Oneida speaker Captain John told Pickering, "are divided on account of our lands." These difficulties could not be blamed upon the Oneidas. "'Tis you, Brothers of a white skin," Captain John said, "who cause our uneasiness. You keep coming to our seats, one after another. You advise us to sell our lands. You say it will be to our advantage." Captain John said that his people were willing to accommodate the outsiders. They always had been, he said. The Oneidas sold their lands when asked, he delicately stated, "because we wish to live in friendship with our brothers the white people," and they feared that their white neighbors "would not be pleased if I did not comply with their requests." Captain John described for Pickering the Oneidas' poverty after the war. Pickering understood that the state would offer the Oneidas and their Indian neighbors no protection from the surging white population without land cessions. Factionalism, meanwhile, offered a wedge for whites interested in acquiring additional Indian land. Alcohol, sold illegally to the Oneidas, also offered opportunities for those willing to defraud intoxicated Indians. Captain John aired his grievances carefully, but Pickering understood well that for the Oneidas to refuse to sell their lands to the New Yorkers meant risking the wrath of a land-hungry state with a frontier peopled by unprincipled men willing to use any means fair or foul to dispossess them.[23]

In his response, Pickering told the Oneidas that they should become civilized like white men, even though they already had made many changes to their modes of subsistence. They should learn as well to read and write, for it would then be less likely that "bad whites" could dispossess them through agreements the Indians did not understand. But Pickering did more than lecture the Oneidas about their shortcomings. He sympathized and understood their plight. He reminded them that they did not need to part with their lands. He reminded them that the Trade and Intercourse law declared "that no sale of Indian land should be valid, unless made at a public treaty, held under the authority of the United States."[24]

In Article II of the completed Treaty of Canandaigua, the United States acknowledged "the lands reserved to the Oneida, Onondaga, and Cayuga nations, in their respective treaties with the state of New York, and called their reservations, to be their property." The United States would never claim these lands, on which the Six Nations possessed the right to "free use and enjoyment," and it agreed that "the said reservations shall remain theirs until they choose to sell the same to the people of the United States who have the right to purchase." But the state once again ignored a federal treaty, and the United States simply lacked the power to prevent the state's relentless efforts.[25]

The state acquired Oneida land in 1795, 1798, and again in 1802, the first purchase in direct defiance of federal authority and the latter two with its cooperation. And the state did not rest. In March 1805, state officials oversaw the negotiation of an "indenture" between the "Christian" and "Pagan" parties, in which they agreed to divide their remaining lands into two parts, one controlled by each faction. As a result, state negotiators would thereafter meet separately with the Christian and Pagan parties. The Christian Party in March 1807 negotiated the cession of two parcels of its land in return for the payment of an annuity. Two years later, in February 1809, Governor Clinton acquired from the Christian and Pagan parties additional cessions. The state acquired even more Oneida land later that year and again in 1810. Clinton's successor, Daniel D. Tompkins, a man who Eleazer Williams came to know during the war, acquired even more lands from the Christian Party at a treaty held in February 1811. The following July, "the Tribe or Nation of Indians called the Oneidas" ceded lands lying east and south of its reservation to the state.[26]

The federal agents tasked with protecting the Indians and enforcing the Trade and Intercourse acts found doing so a difficult job. The New Yorkers did what they wanted. They ignored the provisions of federal law. Federal officials, aware that power claimed but not exercised was power lost, did little about it. The federal agents in the state, moreover, lived distant from the Oneidas, and only visited them on occasion. But the biggest challenge, Agent Erastus Granger said, was that "there exists in the minds of many white people a strong prejudice against Indians." The New Yorkers, Granger said, "want to root them out of the Country, as they own the best of the land. Those people," he continued, "are often on juries." Exasperated, Granger believed that the two federal agents could not curb the desire of local whites for Indian land, and that the Six Nations would continue to suffer if they remained where they were. Granger called the attention of his superiors to the Louisiana Purchase, that vast expanse of land west of the Mississippi River acquired by the United States from France in 1803. If the United States, Granger suggested, "would dispose of a sufficient tract of land in that purchase to the Six Nations, so as to make it an object for them to remove, I think I could persuade them to go." Even their guardians wanted them to leave.[27]

*   *   *

Eleazer Williams arrived in this community, at once divided over matters religious, under siege from those non-Indians who coveted their lands, and wracked by self-doubt and insecurity, in spring 1816. He was, according to the memories of one man who knew him at the time, "a man of elegant figure straight and portly, with broad shoulders, and limbs tapering with very small hands and feet." So said Sewell Newhouse, a New Yorker prone to the same sort of fantasy which tugged at John Holloway Hanson. Williams, Newhouse recalled, seemed more "like a Caucasian than an Indian."[28]

The dauphin craze that Hanson and Williams fueled beginning in the 1850s influenced that recollection. At the time Williams arrived at Oneida Castle, nobody doubted that he was an Indian and a missionary, one of a number of men who had attempted to bring Christianity to the Oneidas. Williams certainly knew something of these earlier efforts. He knew of Samuel Kirkland, whose arrival preceded his own by half a century. He knew as well about Samson Occom, the Mohegan missionary who played a leading role in the settlement of the Brothertown community in New York. The Oneidas welcomed Occom, who assumed "such an air of importance" that he offended them. His zeal, Williams believed, "was not sufficiently tempered with the mild and gentle spirit of the religion he taught." He treated his congregants "with great severity." Williams drew the obvious conclusion. Only when Occom relaxed and began to accept the Oneidas as they were did his audiences view him as "agreeable and exemplary, easy and unassuming in conversation." A decade after Occom died, Quaker missionaries arrived. They tried between 1798 and 1800 to bring civility, private property, and Christianity to the Oneidas before they left to devote their attention to the Senecas farther west. By this point some Oneidas had begun, as they told the New York State legislature, "to abandon our Savage life—to adopt your mode of life in cultivating the land, to raise grain, to be sober, and many other good things."[29]

Occom died three decades before Williams arrived. The Quakers had given up and left the same year Williams arrived as a child in southern New England. The Seneca prophet Handsome Lake had some followers in Oneida Country, but Williams faced little competition from them. Kirkland died in 1809. William Jenkins, a Presbyterian and Kirkland's successor, and a man described as "weak, inefficient, and without influence," could not follow in his predecessor's footsteps. For one thing, unlike Kirkland, he could not communicate with his audiences in their own language. He attracted few adherents, and the Christian Party dwindled in numbers.[30]

Visitors to the Oneida country reported signs of an "incipient civilization" among them. Oneida farmers cultivated fields in which they grew the traditional "Three Sisters"—maize, beans, and squash—while tending apple orchards and the sheep and cows they kept in nearby pastures. They gathered ginseng in the forests and sold it to passing traders. They fished on Wood Creek or on Oneida Lake for eels, salmon, and catfish. They preserved important parts of their traditional way of life, but also selectively adopted elements of white culture that they believed might allow them to weather the crisis caused by the growing numbers of white settlers. Christianity, for those Oneidas who converted, was only one of these creative adjustments. It is important to point this out. The Oneidas could have lived well enough on their remaining lands, but those who coveted them would not leave the Oneidas alone, regardless of the changes they had made. New Yorkers across the board ignored the provisions of the federal Trade and Intercourse Act. Many New Yorkers ignored, as well, their state's own laws designed to protect Indians from sharps, cheats, and alcohol vendors.[31]

By 1816, the year of his death, the great Oneida leader Skenandoah, a Christian who had tried to cooperate with the New Yorkers, concluded that his hope for intercultural peace and accommodation had failed. He attributed what he saw as the Oneidas' downfall to the anger of a Christian God, who refused to protect the Oneidas from their relentlessly advancing white neighbors. "No Indian sleeps," he said shortly before Williams arrived in Oneida Country, "but those that sleep in their graves." He expected that soon white men would occupy his house, and that they would drive the rest of the Oneidas from their homes.[32]

The Oneidas gave to Williams, according to one source, the name "Sky Had Been Crossed," perhaps a reference to the dark clouds that hung over the Oneida Country, both figuratively and literally, at the time of his arrival.[33] Commissioned by Bishop Hobart once again as a lay reader, catechist, and schoolmaster, Williams saw reasons for optimism. The state government supported him. He enjoyed the patronage of the Episcopal bishop of New York. Powerful supporters in Christian circles, both New England Congregationalists and New York Episcopalians, provided support as he commenced both his mission and his translation of the Book of Common Prayer into the Mohawk language. And in addition to this, and in addition to his being "tolerably versed in the Christian system and theology," Williams, his supporters noted at the outset, had mastered "the Indian language, his mother tongue, besides being a natural orator and powerful speaker, the *sine qua non* of persuasion and success with the Indians." It was

Williams, and not a grasping white man, who moved into Skenandoah's recently emptied house.[34]

Williams approached the Christian Oneidas first. He thought they possessed a shallow understanding of the doctrines of Christianity, and believed that they "scarcely understood the meaning of *saving faith.*" But Williams succeeded in winning some of these Christians over, and they told the Northern Missionary Society, the Rev. Jenkins's sponsor, that they vastly preferred Williams to Jenkins. The directors of the society conceded that the new missionary "is capable of benefiting his brethren beyond almost any other man." They already had paid Williams to complete some translation work for them by the time they decided to recall Jenkins and turn their organization's attention toward Indians in the Michigan Territory.[35] Williams, like other missionaries, may have exaggerated how far these Indians had fallen in order to boost his own achievements. His writings reveal the critical and discerning quality of their Christianity, their active, rather than passive engagement, with their missionary. They told him, shortly after he arrived, that they did not care for the prayers of the Episcopal Church. Williams opted for flexibility. He suggested to the Oneidas that if they learned the church's principles they would find that "its doctrines were pure, its ceremonies few, proper & primitive, its method exact, and phrases were taken out of scripture with the purest antiquity." But the choice remained theirs, he said. He would condemn no one who appeared truly pious, and "with this answer, they appeared to be satisfied."[36]

Williams continued to meet with small groups of Christians. He tried to explain why different Christian denominations disagreed over ritual, ceremony, and belief. He explained to them the disputes that led to the Reformation. He addressed the fears of Presbyterian Oneidas, Kirkland's former followers, who worried that Episcopalianism bore too many similarities to Catholicism. He might have explained to them that he had been born into a Catholic community, that like Kirkland he had been educated by New England Calvinists, but now had embraced the doctrines of the Episcopal Church. These believers returned to their homes, and discussed among themselves the best path to follow.[37]

Williams succeeded in strengthening and revitalizing the Christian Party. But his greatest success as a missionary—he would refer to this achievement for the rest of his life, and certainly told Hanson about it in detail—came with the Pagan Party. From the time of his arrival Williams made the conversion of the Pagan Party the particular focus of his mission, he wrote. He held councils with them. He explained to them "the *nature & design of Christianity,*" but they raised "many objections and arguments, some of which were against the religion of the white man." He succeeded in overcoming this opposition by integrating himself into the community. A "Collection of Occasional Prayers" cobbled together from the Book of Common Prayer and other sources reveals this; Williams copied into his papers a prayer to be delivered "On the Birth of a Child," another when that child grew ill, and yet one more when that child died. He shared in the pain of a community where diseases still took a toll in Indian lives.[38]

As he taught the Pagans that "God, the *Great Creator* of all things, doth uphold, direct, dispose, and govern all Creatures, actions & things, from the greatest even to the least, by his most wise and holy providence," Williams proved himself a patient catechist, willing to instruct the Oneidas, in a native tongue, on the rudiments of Christian faith.[39] He also captivated his audiences as a preacher. According to an account published in the *Boston Recorder* in 1818, Williams held his audiences in rapt attention. Men and boys seated themselves to his left; the women sat to his right. He read the service "in the Indian language," with a large part of the congregation, and especially the women, "repeating the responses and prayers in a very devout, distinct, and harmonious manner." Williams "displayed the gestures of eloquence and Christian zeal." The congregation, the Boston correspondent wrote, "listened with as much attention and solemnity, as any I ever witnessed."[40]

Williams claimed that he drew his inspiration from Luke 14:23, and in his own view, at least, he spared no effort to "go out into the highways and hedges, and compel them to come in, that my house may be filled." He used spectacle to draw the Oneidas to services. He decorated the altar of the chapel with evergreens for the Christmas service in 1816, and, in "white robe, chanted at the altar of that Angelic hymn, *Gloria in Excelsis* and *Te Deum Laudamus.*"[41] Williams translated English hymns and employed singing instruction to communicate his message, even if this meant that he spent less time teaching the Oneidas to read and write in English than his sponsors may have wished. He encouraged his audiences, as well. If the Pagan Oneidas tried "to denounce the sins of the devil, the world, and the flesh; if they sincerely believe all the articles of the Christian Faith, even though their faith be weak; and if it is the desire and purpose of their hearts to keep God's holy will and Commandments, and to walk in the same all the days of their lives, even though their obedience is marked with much imperfection," they could find eternal happiness. He assured them of this. They had to make the effort, but the effort required was not great. It could be done. They could avoid alcohol, if they chose, and find happiness. Their past sins could be forgiven.

"Light is sown for the righteous," his audience would have heard when Williams preached on Psalm 97:11, "and gladness for the upright at heart." Converts, he said in a sermon on the 107th psalm, undertake "a change of their course, from the broadway that leads to Hell, to the narrow way that leads to Heaven," beginning "that great work, and Journey, their whole lives should be devoted to, and spent in."[42]

If they chose to stray from that path, Williams readily changed his tone. He demanded that his audiences listen closely to him, one observer recalled, and he "challenged them either to obey or refute the Gospel." Those who "deserted the standard under which they had enlisted to war," and "had drawn back from the engagements into which they had entered," stood in "the most debased condition of man." In his most fiery sermons, Williams expressed little patience for those who chose to ignore God's law. He did not describe eternal suffering, or torment forever in a fiery Hell. But he did make clear to them the loneliness, and the pain, that came with forsaking God. The suffering he described was one of isolation, of being left alone to confront the many dangers of a sinful world, a vision of torment that might have resonated with Oneidas.[43]

It is difficult to overestimate the importance of preaching, and Williams was indeed an extraordinarily talented preacher. All accounts agree on this. But it was only part of Williams's job, and he spent much more of his time with small groups of Oneida seekers and individual Indians who lived in fear. In these small encounters—these intimate performances—Williams made his greatest impact. He labored "day and night," he wrote, "to strengthen the faith" of the Oneidas and to "lead them in the path of virtue & piety."[44] He answered their questions. He told them stories. Early in April 1816, for instance, he met with four "Pagan Chiefs." They asked Williams why Christians suffered. Some Oneidas and their New England Indian neighbors had chosen Christianity, but still they lost their lands, still they faced racism, and still they experienced poverty and the ravages of alcohol. New Yorkers injured Indians, whether Christian or not. Some Christian Indians had concluded that God cursed them, that they suffered God's wrath because of who and what they were. Why did Christians, they asked, the followers of a God that Williams said was both almighty and merciful, not live lives of constant comfort? It is unclear if Williams's answer helped them, for he responded to these probing questions with the same sort of indirection that Christians long have used when confronted by the problem of evil and suffering. "If we want to be partakers of Christ's holiness," Williams told them, "we must also be partakers of his sufferings, and if we suffer with him patiently, we shall reign with him eternally."[45]

Williams challenged drunkards. The abuse of alcohol led to the violation, he told four Pagans in May 1816, of each of the Ten Commandments. "What sin is it that a drunken man stands not ready to commit," he asked. "Fornication, murder, adultery, incest, what not?" Alcohol transformed "a man into a beast," and made "him the shame & reproach of human nature." He had seen it happen too many times. Other observers, in other Indian communities, documented amply the devastation wreaked by alcohol. It imperiled souls and communities. "The intemperate man is his own tormentor, yea, his own destroyer, as appears by the many diseased & untimely deaths which surfeiting & drunkenness daily bring upon them."[46]

Conversations like these continued throughout the year. In July, Williams challenged the small number of Oneida Pagans who followed the Seneca prophet Handsome Lake, an "idolator," an "imposter," and a "false prophet" in Williams's view. They asked Williams "*Why the Great Spirit had made known his mind & will to the white people and not to the Indians?*" He told them that "it is enough for us . . . to know for certain that he is good & just in every thing he does, or permits to be done," and that "we may be assured sooner or later, every tongue shall confess and every soul acknowledge, the justice and equity of God's proceedings with mankind." Williams explained that God worked in mysterious ways, but that Christians believed "the God we serve to be the most perfect of all beings." One of Williams's listeners asked about this perfection. Williams answered, with some circularity, that God was great and omnipotent, and his "perfections" included "his eternity & providence, his holiness & justice, his wisdom & truth, his goodness & mercy," and "the unspeakable riches of his exceeding abundant grace & love."[47]

Faith. Williams thought believers needed some basic knowledge "in the Doctrines of our Divine Redeemer" for salvation and he did not believe that "persons will be taught the things which essentially belong to their peace" by dreams and rituals. He could not excuse the sins of the unconverted, and told the Pagans "that mens unbelief" could not "take off & extinguish the guilt of all their other sins." But all he asked was that they do their best to follow God's laws and believe in him. The choice as to whether to do so was theirs.[48]

In October 1816 a young Indian, "very melancholy," approached Williams. He was, he said, "sick with my sins, my soul is sick, I am seeking for its remedy—I want to be healed." Jesus could heal him, Williams said. He was the "great physician of souls, who is ever ready to heal all who apply to him with penitent hearts." Jesus will not refuse you, Williams told the young sinner. "Look at his cross & all those streams of blood flowing from his visage, side, hands, and feet—they will wash away our sins with true repentance."

A month later another sinner, an Oneida Williams did not know, asked the missionary to help him. "Such a miserable creature as I am," the Oneida said, worthless, frightened, and in his own words "evil," and "polluted with sin and yes, a great sinner": How could he hope to repay "that love & that precious blood spilt on my account?" God's love was great, Williams told him, and it knew no limits. This comforted the stranger, who said that "I will now throw away my great pack of sins & search after this loving father and when I find him, I will follow him all the days of my life."[49]

We cannot know for sure whether these conversations actually took place. Williams wrote them down long after the fact. He may well have made up these conversations out of whole cloth. But much of the material Williams included in the autobiographical drafts that appear in his papers is devoted to the few short years he spent at Oneida Castle, clearly an important period in his life. In 1818, he told a group of Pagans "from the west" that "as I love you, I tell you the truth." He wished for nothing more, he told them, than "your soul's eternal happiness in the world to come." And in ministering to the Pagan Party at Oneida Castle, Williams achieved what he viewed as his greatest success, and the achievement of which he remained most proud.[50]

In January 1817, the chiefs of the Pagan Party wrote to Governor De Witt Clinton. "We have abandoned our Idols and our sacrifices and have fixed our hopes on our blessed Redeemer." They informed the governor that they now believed in "God the Father, the creator and preserver of all things— as omniscient and omnipresent—most gracious and most merciful." They believed in Jesus, too, and that "all must believe in him and embrace him in order to obtain salvation." To provide evidence that they had accepted Christianity, the chiefs offered to Clinton unequivocally "our abjuration of paganism and its rites."[51]

It was quite a letter. Williams wrote it—not only does its language not ring true for Oneidas who spoke little or no English, but Williams used similar language in a letter he wrote to Bishop Hobart some years later. The Christian newspapers in New York and elsewhere in the Northeast reprinted the letter widely nonetheless, and Williams became something of a celebrity in mission circles for transforming the Pagan Party into the Oneida "Second Christian Party."[52]

Williams worked with forty to fifty children each day, he told his superiors and sponsors. He catechized them twice a day, and they did very well, he wrote. Williams knew that he could take credit for "turning some of them from darkness to light, and from Satan to true God." He received from fellow missionaries and his superiors in the Episcopal establishment "congratulatory letters of my success among the Oneidas, expressed in a language most encouraging and flattering to my feelings." Hobart himself left New York City to travel to the Oneida Country. A hundred Oneidas rode out to greet him, their horses lining the road as he passed by them. Hobart acknowledged the gesture, this greeting at the edge of the woods, as the gathered Oneidas asked him for his help. Despite their recent profession of faith, they announced to the bishop that "we are ignorant, we are poor, and need your assistance. Come, venerable father," they asked, "and visit your children and warm their hearts by your presence in the things which belong to their everlasting peace."[53]

The bishop replied with a message that offered to transcend the racial lines that separated Indians and whites on the New York frontier. God, he said, "hath made of one blood all the nations of the earth, and hath sent his son Jesus Christ to teach all and to die for them all that they might be redeemed from the power of sin." Hobart suggested, unlike his protégé, that the Oneidas learn not only Christian doctrine but the "arts of civilization," and that they start working the land like their white neighbors. Hobart, it seems, knew little of how the Oneidas actually lived. Still, he held the congregation's attention. Williams thought it "an affecting sight to see the aged and venerable chiefs, councilors, matrons and warriors, with uplifted hands, and with countenances indicating their minds were deeply affected," renounce their paganism. Hobart concluded his visit by consecrating the Oneida chapel and confirming ninety-four new Christians.[54]

Hobart energetically supported missionary enterprise. He wanted devoted young Episcopalians to become missionaries and he wanted other Episcopalians to support these efforts financially. In a summary of diocesan missionary activity, Hobart mentioned at the end of a long list of missionaries "Mr. Eleazer Williams, [who] acts as a Catechist, Schoolmaster, and Lay Reader among the Oneida Indians." Writing as "An Episcopalian" in the *Onondaga Gazette* in summer 1817, either Hobart or one of his supporters trumpeted Williams's accomplishments. "Hundreds of those once-bewildered beings, who joined in the war song of murder on their foes, are now uniting in the anthems and responses of our church, singing praises to the Savior who had brought them out of heathenish darkness into marvelous light." With additional funding, Williams might expand his mission to the nearby Onondagas.[55]

Hobart returned to visit the Oneidas in fall 1818. The Indians thanked the bishop for sending Williams to them. Hobart baptized twenty-four children, and confirmed eighty-nine more, all of whom Williams had "previously prepared." It was, according to the small number of non-Indians able to witness the visit, a powerfully emotional ceremony. "The reverence and devotion with which the Indians joined in the confessions; the supplications and praises of the Liturgy; the solemn attention with which they listened to the instructions and exhortations of the Bishop; the humility and thankfulness, evidenced by their prostration on their knees, and by their tears which flowed down the cheeks of several of them, with which they devoted themselves, in the apostolic 'laying on of hands,' to the God who made them, and the Savior who shed his blood for them, powerfully interested the feelings of all present." Hobart was impressed. "I have admitted Mr. Williams as a Candidate for Orders," he told the annual convention of the diocese, "and look forward to his increased influence and usefulness, should he be invested with the office of the ministry."[56]

Williams, one correspondent who visited him later that year reported, still lived in Skenandoah's old house. Two women, one of them his cousin, and two young men made up his household. We know nothing about these people, but "the deportment" of Williams's family, the correspondent wrote, "was such as the most refined in manners would have been pleased with." Williams, who the correspondent noted "is too well known to need my encomiums," "appears to be a lover of science, and his parlor was ornamented with a very handsome library." The congregation of nearly 150 sang hymns beautifully, listened to sermons with "much attention and solemnity," and seemed to be making extraordinary progress.[57]

It is a revealing profile. To earn respect, to gain credibility among potential patrons and backers for his mission, Williams not only had to put in his time on the ground, come to where his congregants were, and share in the experiences of a pressed-upon native community. He had to keep up an appearance of refinement and something very much approaching gentility. He headed a household. He understood white expectations of mannerly behavior, and he could act the part. Not merely literate, Williams was immersed in the world of print culture, his ample library standing in the parlor as evidence. The correspondent who wrote so enthusiastically about Williams's success and good work never hinted that this catechist and lay reader faced burdens white clergymen seldom worried about. He never appreciated that service as an Indian missionary compelled Williams to perform for audiences often far removed from the mission field.

Some Oneidas supported Williams, but others criticized him. After Hobart returned to Oneida again in fall 1819 to formally consecrate an Oneida Church "that was most tastefully illuminated by the matrons of the nation,"

Williams addressed the misrepresentations of those "who were inimical to the mission, to the church, and to myself." He stood accused of maintaining his ties to Catholicism. Williams could have addressed what he viewed as a slander at any point, but he believed that the bishop needed to hear what he had to say. "As I was educated in the Roman Catholic Church, and an impression may be entertained that I am yet, in heart, attached to that communion," he told Hobart "I here . . . sincerely & solemnly declare, that I am in principle & practice firmly opposed to the doctrines, discipline, and worship of the Romish Church, as far as they are contrary to the word of God." Charges of doctrinal laxness, of a willingness to lean toward an excess in ceremony, would continue to dog Williams.[58]

But they were not enough to keep him from broadening his horizons, and expanding the reach of his missionary enterprise. In May 1819, Williams visited the Senecas, then engaged in a struggle with the persistent Ogden Land Company to hang on to their remaining lands and in an internal dispute over the presence of Christian missionaries on their reservations. He worked in the Company's behalf. Williams met with Red Jacket, a leader "most violently opposed to the introduction of Christianity among his people," but he could not win him over. He did send the Seneca Jacob Jemison to Hartwick College, where a missionary organization had sprung up interested in education and Christianizing the Indians. Williams also interpreted for Baptist missionaries who visited the Oneidas, as well as the Stockbridge and Brothertown communities. He spoke at the Baptists' annual convention in Buffalo in early 1820. He traveled and he spoke, and accounts of his success and his words were carried in the pages of a vibrant and growing Christian press. An Indian who had converted other Indians to Christianity, his story spread and his influence grew.[59]

So why, John Holloway Hanson asked him, did Williams not ask for more? Williams received a salary of $125 per year but received nothing else from the church. He expended his own meager funds until he had exhausted them. Too small an amount of money existed in the Missionary Fund to provide adequate salaries, much less to establish and support missions in all the places Episcopalians believed were ripe for conversion. Williams met many important people, and he showed that he had the capacity "to have attached himself everywhere to the highest and most gifted minds." He could have had anything, Hanson believed. But Williams was a humble and a selfless man, Hanson concluded, and to preach to the Indians "the glad tidings of salvation was the one absorbing desire of his heart."[60]

*   *   *

A distinctly different picture of Eleazer Williams emerges from the writings of Albert Gallatin Ellis, who published three essays in the *Collections of the State Historical Society of Wisconsin* that documented his time with Williams at Oneida Castle and, later, in Wisconsin. His "Advent of the New York Indians into Wisconsin" appeared in 1856, two years before Williams died far to his east at Hogansburg, New York. The other essays, "Fifty-Four Years' Recollection of Men and Events in Wisconsin" and his "Recollections of Rev. Eleazer Williams," appeared in 1876 and 1879 respectively, two decades later, and after Williams and many of those who had known him as the Dauphin had passed.[61] Ellis, who wrote his accounts "in a remote part of the State" of Wisconsin, far "out of the reach of libraries, without a scrap of the records of the transactions, and only from a recollection of events transpiring more than thirty years ago," believed Williams to have been a con man and "the most perfect adept at fraud, deceit, and intrigue that the world ever produced." Indeed, Ellis saw himself as Williams's first victim.[62]

Born in Oneida County in 1800, Ellis served a brief apprenticeship in the printing office of the Herkimer *American* until, in fall 1820, he "yielded to the solicitations from Rev. Eleazer Williams . . . to join him at the Oneida Castle as a teacher to the Oneida Indians." Ellis believed at the time that an association with Williams, who had been at Oneida for more than three years and who was already celebrated in the broader Protestant community, offered him an opportunity to leave behind his own humble origins. There was some irony in a young white man attaching himself to an Indian missionary in order to advance his career. Ellis felt, he told Williams in a letter written sometime at the beginning of their acquaintance, a "duty and a desire to be the humble instrument in the hands of my Lord & Master, of promoting the furtherance of his Kingdom among them who have long been sitting in paganism and heathenish darkness, and thereby be useful to some part of this fallen race of man."[63]

Ellis's accounts have exerted an enormous influence over how historians have interpreted Williams's life and career, and that is unfortunate. During his time with Williams, Ellis certainly saw much, but his accounts nonetheless possess significant flaws. Ellis at times misunderstood or misrepresented Williams's actions, remembered inaccurately stories about Williams's past and, quite possibly, fabricated stories about Williams. In so doing, Ellis devalued and dismissed the missionary work that was so important to Williams's own understanding of himself, and viewed actions

Williams sincerely undertook and beliefs he deeply held as shams not worthy of trust.[64]

Ellis depicted Williams as a pompous and incompetent windbag who deceived him about the terms of his employment at the mission. Instead of working with children at the mission school, Williams brought the humble and hard-working Ellis to Oneida to teach the missionary himself "to read, to pronounce, and to write the English language." It turned out to be an enormous and frustrating job. Ellis claimed that Williams "not only failed in the pronunciation" of the English language, but that "he could not write the simplest sentence correctly." Williams forced Ellis "to spend hours every day in helping him to utter words, to get correct sounds, and to pronounce as to be understood." Williams was a poor student to boot, Ellis claimed, for "in all the time I was with him, he made almost no progress perceptible in the construction of the language," and "the cases of nouns, the moods and tenses of verbs were unintelligible to him; and to the last of my acquaintance with him, he could not write five lines of English decently."[65]

Ellis resented that Williams expected him to act as a secretary during his time at the mission. Ellis claimed that "it was my business to render his attempts into intelligible English which, when I had done, he carefully copied out." Williams never sent off a letter until Ellis had corrected the grammar and language. Ellis complained that he spent much of his time deciphering and copying old manuscript sermons Williams had acquired from his New England ancestors.[66]

Ellis had hoped to learn from Williams Latin and Greek, languages, he learned later, that Williams did not know. He had hoped to immerse the Oneida children in Scripture, and he resented Williams's instructions that he teach them instead "to sing the songs and chants of the church." Ellis could not accept that music might work better than the written word in ministering to a largely nonliterate audience. Williams built an addition to the Skenandoah house that he intended to use as a schoolroom but, Ellis complained, Williams used the room every Thursday afternoon for "levees of the Indians." No prayers, no sermons, and no lessons, Ellis complained, but rather Williams speaking in Mohawk, for an hour and a half or two hours at a time, with "his discourse without exception . . . concerning himself, and how it happened that he was the 'Great Man he was.'" Williams, Ellis recalled, was methodical. "From week to week," Ellis wrote, "he had marvelous stories to tell of his ancestors, the Williams family, and how he was descended from the Whites; of his accompanying his father in his hunting, trading and fishing excursions," and of his time in Massachusetts and Connecticut.[67]

Yet Ellis, who at best at this early stage of his career understood only the rudiments of Mohawk, and who suggested that during his time at Oneida he did all the work while Williams took all the credit, pointed out that Williams possessed an impressive library. Williams was fond of his books even if, Ellis sniffed, his reading interests lay in areas other than theology. Ellis knew well about Williams's revised translation of the Book of Common Prayer, a task that certainly required facility with language. Williams, Ellis noted, employed eleven characters to write the Mohawk language, rather than the twenty characters used by the Anglican Mohawk Joseph Brant, a reflection of his ties to the community at Kahnawake and his familiarity with the Jesuit tradition in the translation of Iroquoian languages. This change, Ellis claimed, "simplified the orthography so much that an Indian child could be taught to read in a few lessons." Ellis noted, as well, that Williams composed "and got printed a small spelling and rudimental book, which greatly facilitated the learning of the young people to read Oneida or Mohawk." Ellis's depiction of Williams as unlettered and uncouth simply does not stand up.[68]

Ellis did not stop there. In addition to describing Williams as a functional illiterate who had ascended to a social position he did not deserve, Ellis charged Williams with dishonesty, fraud, and theft in his dealings with his white neighbors. "The white denizens of Oneida Castle, of which there were quite a number," Ellis wrote, "were coming to him almost daily with claims, large and small, for labor and other supplies." Nearly every day, Ellis continued, these neighboring whites complained that Williams refused "them justice in every way." At times, Williams argued with these men. To their accusations of dishonesty and "all manner of injustice," Ellis noted, Williams "seemed perfectly indifferent."[69]

There is little doubt that Williams was a poor and careless bookkeeper, and he struggled to pay debts. But Ellis's wounded complaints once again go too far. On a New York frontier where native peoples, however refined and however civilized, faced the hatred and derision of thugs and thieves, witnessed firsthand the racist injustice of New York's court system, and knew the impotence of federal agents who could not and would not protect the Oneidas and their Indian neighbors from alcohol vendors, land speculators, timber strippers, and horse thieves, Ellis identified Williams as the greatest crook in the region.[70] Other native peoples living in the vicinity of the Oneidas learned to hate their white neighbors for these aggressions. It is, then, perhaps as likely that Williams defrauded his white neighbors and failed to pay the mission's debts in a timely manner as it was that his "indifference" to the New Yorkers' charges was the reasoned response of a community leader who understood well the sort of justice that his white neighbors demanded from Indians and preferred to dispense.

Ellis's most well-known claim was that Williams dreamed of "the establishment of an Indian empire west of Lake Michigan," a "grand confederacy of the Iroquois cantons" "all under one federal head; the government to be a mixture of civil, military and ecclesiastical, the latter to be pre-eminent." Williams "had no mind or thought for anything but Indian empire." It was "the dream of his life," Ellis wrote.[71] Many historians have repeated Ellis's claim that Williams aspired to some lofty position of political leadership in the West, but Ellis made these claims after the publication of Hanson's book identifying Williams as the dauphin, and the belief that Williams acted the part of a claimant to the throne of France clearly colored Ellis's depiction of earlier periods in Williams's life.[72]

Certainly some Americans active in the formulation of American Indian policy suggested that an Indian state might be carved from the unsettled lands in the old Northwest, where native peoples might be isolated from aggressive and land-hungry whites. While Williams did tell Hanson in the early 1850s that he hoped "that all the remains of the Indian race in the United States, should be there gathered into one vast community, where the savage tribes might be won over to civilization and Christianity, by intercourse with their already civilized brethren," there is little evidence that he or anyone else thought he might lead the movement, and he certainly was not alone in expressing sentiments such as these.[73]

The Baptist missionary Isaac McCoy, for instance, began to call on the government in 1823 to establish an asylum in the West for "improved natives," Christian and educated, who he believed found little acceptance in their own communities and among neighboring whites. Indian leaders required training in medicine, religion, and government for his colonization scheme to work. With the support of Congress, McCoy hoped, the relocated Indians could develop "a country of their own" where they might at long last "feel their importance, whereby they can hope to enjoy, unmolested, the fruits of their labors, and their national recovery need not be doubted."[74]

Williams does not seem to have ever met McCoy, but he certainly knew and admired the Rev. Jedidiah Morse, who supported Williams's first mission effort at Kahnawake before the war. Long interested in Indian affairs and active in missionary enterprise, Morse responded in 1819 to secretary of war John C. Calhoun's call for advice from missionary societies on how best to spend moneys appropriated by Congress for the "civilization" of the Indians.[75] Morse had "conceived a plan for the rescue of these outcasts from civilized society, dwelling yet in the midst of a Christian people." Indians in the East would sell their lands, raising funds to support their relocation to a tract in the West "sufficiently large to accommodate these scattered . . . tribes." There, with the help of missionaries and educators, the Indians would learn "to hold their lands by the same tenure as their white neighbors, become freemen and citizens, and ultimately be represented in the Government."[76]

Calhoun offered Morse his support. After visiting the West, Morse told Calhoun that he had concluded that "it would be wise in the government and good for the Indians to set apart the whole of the NW Territory for the Indians exclusively, to grow up into a new State, in due time, & admitted, as are other new States into the Union." Morse believed that Williams could help him carry his plan into effect. In November 1819, Williams recalled, he was "unexpectedly" visited by Morse, who was traveling through New York on his way "to make a visit of observation and inspection . . . to acquire a more accurate knowledge of the actual condition, & to devise the most suitable plan to advance their civilization and happiness." Williams called a council, and Morse made his pitch to the gathered Oneidas. He told them that "the best and most successful means which could be employed by Government & religious societies to civilize the Indians, was to learn them to cultivate the soil, as the whites do."[77]

Morse approached Williams undoubtedly because he viewed him as a man of influence in his community. But if McCoy and Morse dreamed of an Indian state in the west, and federal authorities to at least some degree listened to their proposals and entertained the idea, nobody at the time viewed Williams as the prospective leader of that Indian state. If Williams dreamed of placing himself at the head of an Indian confederacy or empire or state in the West, as Ellis claimed, he said absolutely nothing about it in his papers. For missionaries who sought regeneration and revival for Indians in the West, and for aggressive land companies that sought to effect their relocation for pecuniary reasons, Williams offered merely a means to an end. Ellis's oft-repeated claims about Williams's imperial design simply cannot be confirmed.[78]

*   *   *

How do you save a soul? It is a question Eleazer Williams and John Holloway Hanson, the would-be king and his chronicler, might have discussed as they met together in 1852 and 1853. It was one thing that bound the two men, that they held in common, despite their very different backgrounds and the very different paths they followed to the mission field. Both men, it is easy to imagine, felt unappreciated and that their efforts as missionaries had not received the recognition they deserved.

Williams took pride in nothing in his life so much as his conversion of the Pagan Party in 1817. He saw it as his greatest achievement. In the draft autobiographical writings that fill Williams's papers, the story of his work at the Oneida mission fills many pages, and much of what he wrote here rings true and heartfelt. Hanson surely understood the importance of this work to Williams, even if, as he wrote, he did not feel it was his purpose "to enter into the endless details of his labors among the Indians, which are ample enough to form a work of absorbing interest, to those who can sympathize with the struggles of the humble missionary." Hanson thought it sufficient "simply to state results and leading events."[79] Williams, if his autobiographical writings are any indication, surely would have described these labors and the struggles he faced, the efforts he made to build relationships, to establish trust, and to bridge the narrow linguistic divide between his native Mohawk and the Oneida language, to translate his Christianity into something meaningful and of value to the Oneida pagans, and to integrate himself into that divided community.

In this, for a time, he succeeded. He became a leader in the community among its Christians, and certainly in the eyes of those white people who supported his efforts. This presented him with additional challenges. He was not the only leader at Oneida, but nobody else there wrote English as fluently or spoke the language with his facility. When white people needed to speak to Oneidas they came to him. And most of those white people wanted the Oneidas' lands. He knew these men. He worked for some of them. Williams had resided in the Oneida country long enough to understand that there were other white men with whom the Oneidas might have to deal if they chose to ignore these men—the rustlers and the grog-sellers, the land sharps and the thieves. So the man who came to Oneida to save Indian souls became a man who facilitated the sale of Indian lands. Williams explained to Hanson that though he initially opposed the idea of any "removal" or relocation of the New York Indians to new homes in the West, he came to believe that leaving the Oneida country ultimately was in the Indians' best interest. Williams understood well, he explained to Hanson, that the Oneidas' growing number of white neighbors would continue to make their lives difficult. Despite the existence of laws intended to protect the Indians, Williams knew firsthand how the conduct of the neighboring New Yorkers could make Indian lives intolerable.

Williams might have believed this. Certainly he convinced Hanson that unless they sold their lands and removed "they would be entirely swallowed by the swelling tide which hemmed them in on all sides."[80] The white men who wanted the Indians' land came to respect Williams, at least in the sense that he seemed willing to make himself useful to the agents of Indian dispossession. But his willingness to aid these men, and to accept their money, witness the execution of their papers, and to sign their treaties, deeds, and receipts, ultimately cost him the support of those to whom he came to preach. To many Oneidas, Williams could not advocate land sales and removal while claiming to care about the community. Hanson never understood this part of the story. Listening closely to Williams, he could only conclude that the Oneidas had grown alienated "from the man to whom they were indebted for the faith of Christ, and who had been laboring to the best of his ability, and the neglect of his own interests, to promote their welfare and that of the whole body of the Indians."[81]

CHAPTER THREE

The Prospect of Great and Good Things

Eleazer Williams may have led in the effort to relocate the New York Indians, but he was not alone, and a surging white population, aggressive land speculators, and the economic and commercial development of the Empire State conspired at the same time to push the Indians out. Native peoples did not need Eleazer Williams to explain to them that they might improve their lives by leaving New York State. Indeed, Indian land sales in New York predated Williams's arrival in the Oneida country. They continued for more than two decades after he left. Still, no single figure has been more closely associated with the dispossession and relocation of the New York Indians than Williams. If, as a missionary, he brought a brief moment of unity to a divided Oneida homeland, his participation in the Oneidas' "Indian Removal" helped tear the nation apart.

From an early period Williams involved himself in the mechanics of Iroquois dispossession. In March 1816, he witnessed a real estate transaction signed by his father and two others in Albany that ceded one mile square of territory at St. Regis to the state in return for payment of an annuity of $1,300. He received from North Country land baron Michael Hogan "fifty dollars for services rendered by me in his negotiations with the Indians of St. Regis." Williams witnessed Hogan's payments to several other Mohawks from Akwesasne for the expenses they had incurred in traveling to Albany to cede to him their community's land. One day later, on 19 March 1816, Williams signed his name as one of seven "deputies of the Seven Nations of Canada Indians," to acknowledge an annuity payment for the 1796 cession. According to one report, Williams collected a state annuity amounting to $266 due to the Mohawks at Kahnawake from 1812 until 1820. He kept the money and apparently paid none of it over to the tribe.[1]

John Holloway Hanson paid relatively little attention to this part of Williams's career, even though Williams thought these the most consequential years of his life. Shortly after he succeeded in transforming the Pagan Party of Oneidas into the Second Christian Party, Williams accompanied their leaders on a journey to Albany to celebrate this accomplishment. There they met the governor and negotiated with him the sale of a share of their lands to raise the funds necessary to construct a church. A number of the group's leaders received grants in the ceded tract. Williams, who witnessed the transaction and served as an interpreter, benefited both personally and professionally. He received out of the ceded lands a parcel of 150 acres for his own use. Another 600 acres of the cession the state sold, with "the monies arising from such sale . . . appropriated in such manner as the said Governor shall judge most expedient for the building of a Church for the Second Christian Party in such place on their lands as they shall select for its site." Williams sold a third of the lands set aside for his personal use to the Lenox Iron Company, a business venture recently launched on lands the state acquired from the Oneidas. He received $750 for fifty acres, more than five times his ministerial salary for the year. Williams also leased an additional twenty-five acres to the Lenox Company for timber cutting and charcoal making. Within five years, he had sold the entire tract, netting $1,450 in all. He also witnessed, while in the state capital, along with his father and his brother John, the payment of that year's St. Regis annuity by the state.[2]

During his time at Oneida, Williams traveled frequently to Albany. He witnessed an 1818 cession of St. Regis lands, negotiated by his father and other Akwesasnes in February. That fall, and once again in January 1819, he put his pen to paper, acknowledging the state's past agreements with the New York Indians and his collection of the annuities the state paid for Mohawk land. In signing for the St. Regis, and for the Seven Nations of Canada, Williams claimed to represent communities with which he had little connection. Eleazer Williams had become a willing agent in the dispossession of the Oneidas and Mohawks, and he worked with those well-connected white New Yorkers who looked forward to a day when the state's Indian population lived someplace else.[3]

*   *   *

Williams told Hanson that as late as 1817 he had opposed the very idea of removal, and that he involved himself after that reluctantly, and only because others—officials with the national government, he said—actively sought out his assistance. Williams told Hanson that he considered removal west only after he concluded that a better life awaited the Indians there. He did not engage in these sales for money or fame or respect, and removal was in the end the only decision he felt he could make. So he told Hanson, who seems not to have understood the depth of his friend's involvement with the state of New York and the wealthy men who hoped to acquire the lands belonging to the Iroquois and their neighbors.[4]

A number of factors influenced Williams's behavior. Like many other native leaders, he may have agreed to sign deeds, receipts, and treaties in order to collect something for lands that the Oneidas would otherwise lose outright to aggressive and land-hungry settlers, a process that repeated itself on a continental scale. The state bought these lands low and sold them high, and native peoples received only a small fragment of what their lands were worth. But at least they got something. These sales, of course, made things more difficult for those who chose to remain behind. Opening land to settlement brought increased pressure on the community's remaining lands as more and more Anglo-American newcomers moved in. Once the cycle began, it proved difficult to stop.[5]

In many ways, the Oneidas, along with their Stockbridge and Brothertown neighbors, had done all that the white residents of the young republic had asked of them. They aided the patriots during the Revolution. They helped the Americans throw off the yoke of British tyranny. They professed and practiced Christianity. According to agent Jasper Parrish, writing in 1819, they had "within the last season, raised more corn, wheat, oats, potatoes &c than any have before in any one season, for thirty-five years." The Oneidas of the Second Christian Party sold their lands in 1817 to raise the funds necessary to build a church. Many of them thus clearly expected to remain on their lands in New York, members of a Christian and Indian community on the frontiers of the Empire State. Many of them must have believed that they deserved this right after all that they had done. They sold their lands not because they wanted to leave, but because they hoped they might relieve the pressure on what they retained. They wanted to stay.[6]

But none of this seemed to matter to those white people who coveted the Oneidas' land. The settlers took what they wanted. They rustled the Indians' livestock, and went unpunished by juries of their peers.[7] While state leaders and federal agents at times acted to protect the Indians—from the wreckage left after a bad harvest, or from alcohol vendors who sold their wares in violation of the laws of the United States, or from the loan sharks or the squatters who had usurped their lands—they often did so half-heartedly. Why pursue villains, after all, when juries refused to convict? Why enforce laws designed to protect native peoples who, the friendliest of their white neighbors believed, soon would disappear? In their public statements, these white leaders tended to ignore the changes the Oneidas and their neighbors had made to more securely tie themselves to their homelands and emphasized instead their degradation and their suffering, a product of white encroachments on their land in the first place. They saw what they wanted to see. De Witt Clinton, that governor who fancied himself a scholar, expected that the Iroquois would die off within half a century. Attitudes like these mattered. Of the Indians, one sympathetic Christian observer reported, "too frequently they are treated by individual white men as being possessed of no *unalienable rights.*" It is not surprising, perhaps, that some native peoples in New York state contemplated relocation to move out of the path of the surging white population whose aggressions white policy-makers viewed as the inevitable consequence of the meeting between savagery and civilization. Some of the Oneidas and their New England Indian neighbors thought they might outrun their problems by moving west.[8]

American officials with responsibility for Indian affairs believed that removal, a policy they had discussed for years, would benefit both Indians and non-Indians. Thomas Jefferson discussed the possibility of removal as early as 1803, as he sought to quiet his own constitutional scruples and justify the expansion of federal power necessary to purchase Louisiana from France. The United States could relocate eastern Indians to the newly acquired territory west of the Mississippi. Jefferson acted on this belief several years later in negotiations with the Cherokees.[9] Removal, indeed, had many supporters, long before the election of Andrew Jackson, with whom the policy is most often associated, and many of those most in favor came from New York State. Shortly after the War of 1812, for instance, Governor Daniel D. Tompkins suggested to President James Madison the possibility of relocating New York's Indians to the northwestern frontier. The acting secretary of war, Alexander Dallas, informed Tompkins that the president wanted "to accommodate your wishes." A movement of friendly Indians to the Northwest, Dallas believed, might do much to bring security to the region. Madison suggested to the Senecas that they abandon all their remaining reservations save one, and concentrate themselves at Allegany, the most remote by far.[10]

Removal resulted from the refusal of white Americans to respect the property rights of native peoples living on their own lands. White frontier settlers pressed relentlessly on Indian lands. The settlers' livestock destroyed

Indian cornfields. The frontier population cut timber on Indian lands, cheated them in trade, and provided the alcohol that tore gaping holes in the fabric of native communities. All this despite federal laws and treaties that guaranteed Indians the undisturbed possession of their remaining lands. State officials abetted these trespasses through their inaction. Among the Creeks and Cherokees in the South, and the powerful Indian confederacies of the Ohio River Valley and Great Lakes Region, native prophets emerged to preach a message of resistance against these rending changes. At times, and in places, warfare erupted. The followers of the Shawnee prophet Tenskwatawa and his brother Tecumseh challenged the security of American frontiers in the north and those in their communities who chose to accommodate themselves to the growing power of the United States. Among the Creeks, "Red Stick" militants fought a civil war with those of their kin willing to work with the American "Long Knives," until Andrew Jackson and his Cherokee allies wiped them out at the Battle of Horseshoe Bend in 1814. Many Senecas, meanwhile, followed the nonviolent but transforming and cathartic message of Handsome Lake. All Indians, sympathetic whites noted, whether they accepted or rejected the new religions or stood somewhere in between, seemed to suffer from their contact with American settlers. The national government seemed powerless and much of the time uninterested in halting the onslaught.[11]

Proponents of the removal policy believed that as the Indians faced the rising tide of white settlement, and as they picked up the vices but not the virtues of neighboring settlers, those in government had a responsibility to act. Indians faced certain extinction unless the "Great White Father" preserved his "Red Children." Removal to the far side of the Mississippi would free Indians from the problems caused by non-Indians pressing on their lands. Removal would buy them time to become civilized before once again they contended with a surging white population. Removal promised to "save" the Indians, bring order to the frontier, and open the Indians' lands in the east to white settlement. Taking, as the historian Gregory Evans Dowd pointed out, became giving.[12]

The federal government wanted removal at an early date and so did the state of New York. But no organization played as important a role in the efforts to remove the New York Indians as the Ogden Land Company. David A. Ogden, that founding member of the church where Hanson later preached, had purchased from the Holland Land Company in 1810 the right of preemption, or the right to first purchase, of the eleven Seneca reservations that remained after the Treaty of Big Tree of 1797. He acquired the title thereby to lands still possessed and occupied by the Senecas, nearly 200,000 acres, for fifty cents an acre, leaving the Indians with nothing more than what Chief Justice John Marshall would describe as a mere right of occupancy. To pay his debt, Ogden created an association of well-connected and wealthy investors. Once they cleared the land of its Indian occupants, they could sell it to settlers.[13]

The Ogden Company received the assistance of state and federal officials. Indeed, the company's small circle of investors held numerous positions in government. The Ogden Company hoped to remove the Senecas to some location in the West. Robert Troup, one of the company's most active members, thought Arkansas best, but failing that, a spot in the Michigan Territory, "in the neighborhood of Green Bay," would do. The company called upon its allies for support. Jasper Parrish, at company expense, traveled to Washington in 1817 to convince secretary of war John C. Calhoun, of the benefits removal would bring to the Indians. The company focused on the Senecas, but its leaders believed that if other Iroquois tribes could be persuaded to remove, pressure on the Senecas would increase.[14]

Ogden claimed that removal served the national interest, even as he knew it served his own. Surveying all that he saw across the state of New York, and ignoring the evidence that untidily contradicted his claims, Ogden said that "the extensive forests" possessed by the Indians posed "a barrier to the progress of improvement." The Indians, who did not pay taxes, contributed "neither towards the expenses of roads or any other object of public utility." Their removal, he said, could only "add to the general prosperity and resources of the state." They were useless, and they ought to go away.[15]

An appeal to benevolence followed. "The history of every Indian tribe on the Atlantic Coast," Ogden wrote, "proves that they cannot long exist in their savage character in the Neighborhood of civilized Society, that becoming partly Christian, partly Pagan, partly civilized and partly savage, they are rendered more and more debased and degenerate and finally become extinct, without having rendered themselves capable of any national enjoyment, or having contributed in any degree to the stock of the public good." To Ogden, this was historical fact, and mawkish sentimentality served no purpose. The government must act, for the company could not act alone. "The Savage," Ogden wrote, "must and ought to yield to the civilized state, and . . . this change cannot be effected otherwise than by the Agency of Government."[16]

That was, across the United States, the premise that underlay most of the support for removal, an early expression of a sentiment that would, by the 1830s, come to be known as Manifest Destiny. Ogden found the assistance he sought. The New York State Legislature, in a report published in March 1819, agreed that alcohol had ravaged the Indians as squatters overran their lands, both problems "highly injurious to the interests of the state." The Assembly declared that the state's Indian population "ought to yield to the public interest, and by a proper application of power they ought to be brought within the pale of civilization and law and that if left to themselves, will never reach that condition." The State Senate, shortly afterward, called on the governor to "cooperate with the Government of the United States in such measures . . . to induce the several Indian tribes within this state to concentrate themselves in some suitable situation" and, if necessary, to act "either with or without the cooperation of the government of the United States."[17]

Rhetoric such as this from the New York State Legislature mirrored arguments occurring at the same time in the southern states. As the federal government and its agents among the Creeks and Cherokees sought to protect the Indians there from the aggression of their white neighbors, and as missionaries and philanthropists sought their "civilization" and "improvement," southern state legislatures and state courts argued that all who resided within a state, including Indians, must conform to its laws. The Marshall Court, later, would reject this limited federalism, but southerners claimed and asserted the power largely to ignore officials of the national government. The resolution of 1819, which reveals the strength of the forces arrayed against the Oneidas and their neighbors, shows that New York's political leaders possessed a similar states' rights ideology, at least where Indians were involved.[18]

After laying all the groundwork, Ogden requested of Secretary of War Calhoun "that a commissioner may be appointed to hold a treaty with all or any of the Tribes composing the Six Nations of Indians residing in this State."[19] Calhoun appointed Morris Miller to serve as federal agent "in a treaty which the Proprietors of the Seneca Reservation in the State of New York wish to hold with that nation." Calhoun believed whole-heartedly in the philanthropic justifications for removal, but at the same time he believed that the practice of treating with Indians was flawed and dated. The national government protected the Indians, Calhoun believed, and "is their best friend."[20] The Indians depended on the United States like a child relied upon its parents. Calhoun believed that the Indians had not flourished in their homelands. In this sense, removal seemed to Calhoun a logical solution to the new nation's "Indian Problem." If Indians relocated to the western side of the Mississippi River they would distance themselves from frontier whites, and gain time to become "civilized."[21] He believed that the United States, rather than the tribes themselves, should determine what was in the Indians' best interest. "They neither are, nor ought to be, considered as independent nations," he wrote, and "our views of their interest, and not their own ought to govern them."[22]

Aware that they had the support of the federal government, the Ogden associates played their cards carefully. The object was limited: concentrate the Senecas at their Allegheny reservation, and open their other lands to white settlement. The best thing the Company could do, Ogden investor William Troup told Jasper Parrish, is "to be perfectly still, and to make no appearance whatever" at the Council, and "to leave everything entirely in the hands of the Commissioners of the General Government, in full confidence that the Agents will do everything in their power, according to their instructions from the government, to induce the Indians to accept of a grant of land to the West."[23]

The Senecas, aided by Quaker missionaries and led by Red Jacket and others, refused to sell their lands to the Ogden Company in 1819. But the Oneidas lacked the resources and allies Senecas drew on to resist dispossession. No Quakers opposed to the efforts of the Ogden Company petitioned Congress on the Oneidas' behalf. The Oneidas faced the state's agents alone, divided among themselves and without friends in high places. The best friend they had—and the most well connected—was Eleazer Williams, and he, unlike the Quakers, favored removal. Williams, who had tried to convince the Senecas to accept concentration at the Allegany Reservation, was thus no bystander in these events. From an early point he visited with Jasper Parrish and discussed removal. He expressed to the agent his disappointment that negotiations at Fort Meigs in Ohio in fall 1817 had failed to result in the acquisition of a new homeland there for the New York Indians. Late that year, Williams offered his assistance to David Ogden and assured him "that if my influence is wanted in this business, it shall be exerted to the utmost."[24]

Williams earned his fame as a missionary. He achieved a significant success, and solved a problem that had eluded his predecessors in the Oneida country. He learned to make use of his fame and exploit the high regard in which he was held by his white patrons. But at the same time that he quite literally capitalized on his missionary success, other men, all of whom wanted the Oneidas' lands, made use of him. They needed his assistance. We should not be surprised that Williams supported Indian removal. It is what his patrons wanted. He likely understood, as well, that the white people he then encountered in the Oneida country were very different from these patrons, and from the friends and family he spent time with along the Connecticut. He said nothing about it directly, but he did suggest that native peoples lived lives of poverty and injustice. He knew that injustice himself. Perhaps things might be better in the west. He may have wanted to get away from the Indian-haters. In this he certainly was not alone.

That year, according to Ellis, Williams began "to broach cautiously among his Indian people a proposition of removing all the Indians" to new homes in "the neighborhood of Green Bay." Stockbridges, that year, looked to move to the White River in Indiana to save their people from New Yorkers who never ceased their encroachments on Indian land. Williams claimed that many Iroquois had "become sensible that there must be a change not only in regard to their present residence, but their civil polity and the manner of obtaining their livelihood." Their lands overrun, their timber cut, many recognized "that it cannot be long before they must leave in want."[25] John Metoxen, Solomon U. Hendrick, and Hendrick Aupaumut, leaders in the New England Indian communities settled in the Oneida country, understood all this. When Williams told Jabez Hyde, a catechist associated with the New York Missionary Society, that he feared that "if the Oneidas were not removed away from white people, all attempts would prove fruitless in preventing their degeneracy and annihilation," at least some New York Indians would have agreed.[26]

But Williams took his support a large step farther than other native advocates of removal. Through David Ogden, Williams met representatives and senators, secretaries and presidents. These facts complicate Williams's claim that he came to removal reluctantly, that he would have preferred to stay in New York if the Oneidas and their native neighbors could find some meaningful protection of their rights to person and property. Williams found that many Oneidas opposed his efforts, and began to question his motives. Some Oneidas complained to President Monroe late in 1818 that "much pains have been taken by sundry individuals to poison the minds of your children, and to make them disenchanted with their present residence and desirous of removing to the lands of their brethren in the west." They did not want to leave New York, even if they recognized fully that the assaults on their lands and their lives would continue. The question of whether or not to leave New York, which Williams answered earlier than many of the Oneidas to whom he preached, generated deep divisions within the community. His connections to that community, and their homeland, were much weaker than his connection to his patrons. He did their work now, and many Oneidas knew it.[27]

Opportunities. Williams had been given plenty of them, but they all came from these white patrons. He was Iroquois, he was literate, and he was a Christian, but unlike cultural brokers and mediators more deeply committed to their communities, Williams could never claim much of a following. His patrons believed that he could help them, and Williams told them tales to maintain the appearance that he had more influence than he actually possessed. And as his involvement in removal grew, Williams found himself confronted by Oneidas willing to challenge his claims, to call out his lies, and resist his efforts to help those who wanted to dispossess them. Many Oneidas did not trust him.

*   *   *

When Jedidiah Morse visited the New York Indians in November 1819, he explained to them what he saw as the benefits that would follow from their relocation to new homes in the West. With the financial assistance of Morse, the Ogden Company, and John Henry Hobart, Williams traveled to Washington "to ascertain the views of the general government." Though he later claimed he made the journey at Calhoun's invitation, the evidence shows clearly that powerful men in New York State orchestrated his visit to the capital. They saw Williams as their man.[28]

Bishop Hobart wrote Williams a letter of introduction to Secretary of War Calhoun. Williams's opinions "with regard to the best means of improving the condition of his countrymen," Hobart pointed out, "correspond in substance . . . with the judicious & benevolent views which you have exhibited in your reports to Congress." All involved knew what that meant. Thomas L. Ogden, David's brother, wrote Williams a letter of introduction to Peter Buell Porter, an Ogden Company investor well connected in Washington. Williams, he wrote, recognized "that a removal to the west under proper protection & Assistance from the Government" was the best measure "calculated for the welfare of these Tribes."[29]

Williams traveled east from Oneida. He might have taken the recently opened Erie Canal, the first fifteen miles of which covered the distance from Rome to Utica. He looked for financial support there. Then he traveled from Utica to Albany, where he met with the governor and other interested parties, and then traveled down the Hudson to New York City. From there, he proceeded to Washington. In the capital, Williams reunited with Morse, who served as his guide and host. On the same day early in February when Morse made his pitch for a commission to travel westward to learn about the condition of the Indian tribes, Williams presented Calhoun with a "statement of pecuniary assistance, which the six nations of Indians would require, in order to enable them to explore certain parts of the North West Territory, and to make arrangements with the Indians there residing, for a portion of their Country, to be hereafter inhabited by such of the six Nations, as may choose to emigrate thither." It was to this point the fullest explication of Williams's plan for the relocation of the New York Indians, and Morse's fingerprints can be seen all over the request for funding. For a proposed delegation of ten Indians, Williams suggested, Calhoun ought to provide three hundred dollars, a blanket for each traveler, twenty pounds of gunpowder and "a proportionate quantity of lead, two tents, a copy of Morse's geography and his Gazetteer, two compasses, one or two mappes, a telescope, and an order for rations to be received at the different posts for seven or eight months."[30]

Calhoun told Morse that the president approved an allocation of five hundred dollars to "make a visit of observation and inspection to the various Indian tribes in our immediate neighborhood." Williams's request for assistance so closely dovetailed with Calhoun's own policy that the secretary gladly agreed to lend his support. Williams and his patrons knew what Calhoun wanted to hear. The secretary of war threw in an additional one hundred fifty dollars to defray any additional costs Williams might personally face.[31] Calhoun told Michigan territorial governor Lewis Cass that the expedition "has the approbation of the President, and I have to request that you will afford them every facility in traveling thro the Indian country and promote, as far as in your power, by your influence with the Indians, the object intended to be accomplished by their journey." Calhoun sent out orders to military officers along the way to support the New York Indians and Williams in any manner they could with provisions, ammunition, and supplies.[32]

The visit to the capital showed the extent to which the Oneidas, and other Iroquois in New York State, faced a powerful combination of interests directed toward acquisition of their lands. The executive, legislative, and judicial branches of the federal government all agreed that Indian communities had a lesser claim to the land than did the states in which their lands stood. All agreed in their public statements that Indians would benefit from removal. State political leaders, in New York as elsewhere, would have disagreed with none of this, and questioned only the extent to which they could act on their own without the federal government. Removal was a powerful force with a widespread white consensus behind it, and Williams, despite his protests, helped that machine move forward, well before the rise of Andrew Jackson.[33]

Williams returned home. He stopped in New York City once again to meet with Thomas Ogden, who kicked in some additional funds for Williams, while Episcopal clergymen provided him opportunities to preach and raise money in their churches. At Oneida, Williams called a council and explained the views of the federal authorities with whom he had met. That the Oneidas might part with their lands and accept new homes to the west, he recalled, generated an acrimonious debate. Williams worked the problem. He played his part. In the middle of May he reported to Hobart that he had "obtained the consent of the *Oneidas, Onondagas, St. Regis, & Seneca Indians*" to undertake an expedition to scout out the location for a new home. "The most sensible of these Nations are convinced, if they continue in their present situation much longer, it will prove to their destruction."[34] He told his sponsors what they wanted to hear. Neither Williams nor the idea of removal was as popular as he led Hobart to believe. But telling tales of this sort would become increasingly necessary for Williams, whose livelihood depended to the greatest extent on the influence his white patrons believed he wielded over the New York Indians.

Only the ignorant and intoxicated opposed Williams's planned trip west, he told Hobart. Those white people "who had been in habit of defrauding and cheating those poor Indians" cheered on and encouraged this benighted few. Afraid of losing their marks, these designing white men told the Oneidas that Williams was "deceiving them—my object was to ruin them—I had in view to get all their reservation to myself." The opposition of these "wicked men" did not discourage Williams.[35]

Williams may sincerely have believed in the benefits relocation might bring. He may have believed deeply that the future of the community where he preached might be brighter in the West. He claimed that he had gained the support of the Six Nations, yet it is impossible to believe him. Numerous petitions and appeals announcing the Oneidas' opposition to removal exist in the archives. Perhaps Williams was so convinced that removal advanced the best interests of the Indians that he went ahead with his venture despite all opposition. Perhaps he exaggerated the appeal of the relocation plan in order to impress his patrons, or to inflate his own sense of importance. It is difficult to tell. What can be known is this: although Williams obtained federal support for an exploring party of up to ten men, he managed to recruit only half that number. Most of the party consisted of members of the First Christian Party: John Skenendoah, son of the great Oneida leader; Daniel Bread, who later would play so important a role in establishing the Oneidas at Green Bay; John Brandt; and Cornelius Baird. Williams consistently overstated the support for removal. If those who supported Williams had doubts about their man, they said nothing because he still seemed to offer the prospect of relocating the New York Indians out of the path of future development.[36]

Before Williams and his party departed, he read to the Oneidas a letter prepared by Bishop Hobart. Williams's mentor wanted the Oneidas to know that it was "the benevolent wish of the Government of the United States, in all their plans, to promote your good." Williams, too, Hobart wrote, "has you constantly in his heart," and wanted "to make you good, and respectable, and happy." The Oneidas, Hobart wrote to his "Children," should "let Mr. Williams go, and aid him all you can in the important objects of his journey." Very few of them did.[37]

The land near Green Bay which Williams hoped to explore had come under control of the United States only recently. French traders established a fort at "La Baye" at the mouth of the Fox River way back in 1717. Perhaps 1,500 Indians gathered there each summer to trade. Many French traders married into the neighboring Menominee and Winnebago communities, establishing ties of kinship that further facilitated trade. Out of these "country marriages" emerged a métis culture at Green Bay, multilingual and Catholic even after the British takeover in the 1760s. The settlement at Green Bay maintained the quality of a base camp for fur traders. In 1785, only 56 people lived there year round, but the small town grew. On the eve of the War of 1812, 250 people lived at La Baye, and by 1820 that figure had doubled. The inhabitants, according to the explorer and geographer Henry Schoolcraft, were "with few exceptions, French, who have intermarried with Indian women."[38]

At the top of the settlement's social pyramid stood a small number of families. Charles de Langlade, one of the founders of the settlement, raised a large métis family that acquired a huge fortune through the fur trade. Pierre Grignon, who married one of Langlade's daughters, raised a large family as well. Four of Grignon's sons became prominent traders. Jacques Porlier, a descendant of French nobility who later would impress Albert Gallatin Ellis with his "culture and fine tastes," operated a mercantile business that supplied traders and settlers. The leading English trader, John Lawe, also raised a métis family. Through his trade fortune, he acquired vast tracts of land, on which he kept sizable herds of horses and cattle.[39]

When Americans arrived at Green Bay in 1816, victorious in their war against Great Britain, they found what they believed to be a "mongrel French settlement" inhabited by families "allied with the Indians whose language, habits and character most prevails with them." Americans viewed the métis population, which had allied itself with the British during the war, as a threat to the security of the entire Northwest Territory. Government officials put in place policies designed to control the region's population, Indian and non-Indian, that brought dramatic change to Green Bay.[40]

In the summer of 1816, American soldiers began constructing Fort Howard on the west bank of the Fox River where it emptied into Green Bay. In
1820, the small garrison moved four miles up the river, occupying the high
ground at a site they called Camp Smith. Settlers soon occupied the lands
in between the fort and Camp Smith, creating a "Shanty Town" where most
trading occurred. A bit more than two hundred men served as the garrison.[41]

Fort Howard, territorial governor Lewis Cass pointed out, along with
forts constructed at Michilimackinac, Chicago, and Prairie du Chien, was
"highly important" because it guarded "the principal avenues of Communication to the interior of our Western world." The forces stationed at Green
Bay in effect compelled the métis community to respect American authority. But Cass worried much more about the Menominees and Winnebagos,
both of which had allied with the British during the war. Cass understood
that "a display of the power of the United States in that remote quarter of the
world would be productive of salutary effects upon the minds of the Indians," and that "this weakest and most exposed frontier of the whole Union,
unless protected by troops and garrisons, could not for one hour resist" their
attacks.[42] The United States wanted to avoid war, so Secretary of War Calhoun appointed Colonel John Bowyer to serve as federal Indian agent at the
newly established Green Bay agency. He would enforce the Trade and Intercourse Act, establish and maintain peace with Indians who felt themselves
abandoned by the British, and attempt to bind them to an allegiance with the
United States.[43]

The Menominees indeed stood in a tattered state at war's end. Bowyer
reported that they feared starvation owing to "the frost having destroyed their
corn, and the wild rice failing." Meanwhile, women and children around the
Bay, Bowyer reported, had lost husbands and fathers during the war years. A
number of important leaders died as well, and the Menominees faced a significant crisis in leadership. A small number of Menominees signed a treaty
with the United States in March 1817 at St. Louis, establishing a "perpetual
peace and friendship between all the citizens of the United States and all
individuals composing the said Menominee tribe or nation," but Bowyer told
Cass that the Indians who signed "have no influence or character" and that
"this treaty has been made without the knowledge of the principal chiefs, and
of nine tenths of the nation knowing or even hearing of the transaction." The
Menominees wanted to work out some sort of peace with the United States,
but Bowyer seemed to recognize that much work remained to be done.[44]

Army garrison and federal agents constituted the emblems of American
power in the Michigan Territory. But the war opened Green Bay to John

Jacob Astor's American Fur Company as well. Though the trade in furs mattered little to the larger economy of the United States, and the Green Bay area already had begun a transition toward more extensive agriculture than had existed previously, the American Fur Company's efforts to monopolize the trade marginalized the Porliers, Grignons, and Lawes, who now found themselves cut out.[45] This old elite received rough treatment from American soldiers and settlers. The garrison soldiers bullied and abused the original settlers, John Lawe believed. Soldiers took livestock and vandalized property. Lawe believed that "oppression is the cry here" since the American takeover. Porlier found himself "loaded incessantly with most atrocious calumnies."[46] As more non-Indians moved into the region, the old connections that bound the Menominees and Winnebagos to their non-native neighbors eroded. The newcomers wanted farmland more than furs. They wanted to cut timber and dig mines, activities for which they did not need Indian partners. These settlers, along with American soldiers, brought great change to the region. They were not the only newcomers.[47]

*   *   *

Williams and his party left Oneida in spring 1820. They traveled westward along the Ridge Road, following that path toward the growing city of Buffalo. They boarded a steamboat there, the *Walk-in-the-Water*, for passage along Lake Erie, into Lake Michigan, heading toward Detroit. According to the *Detroit Gazette*, the Oneida party arrived in June, intent on finding a "suitable tract of country within the Territory, to which the Oneida Indians, or part of them, will remove." Jedidiah Morse caught up with Williams and the Oneidas in Detroit.[48]

Shortly after they arrived, the New York Indians learned that Bowyer had purchased from the Menominees the same lands upon which they intended to settle, an unwelcome surprise that threatened to scuttle their plans to move West. Williams told Morse that the Indians "conceived that the government had anticipated them, & got possession of the best tract of land, in the country, which they were encouraged by the governor to explore, & to select a spot for settlement with assurance, that a good title should be given them to the tract they should thus select." Distressed by Bowyer's action, and unclear what to do next, the Oneidas informed Governor Cass that "we think it altogether improper to proceed at this time, lest we should excite jealousies and troubles among our brethren to the west."[49]

Morse ultimately proceeded on to Green Bay, where he learned that the Menominees would willingly extend to the New York Indians "the hand of friendship," but Williams and the delegates returned home. Morse noticed some "very serious uneasiness among the Indians on account of this purchase." Morse insisted on learning from the government whether Bowyer acted under orders and what the government intended to do with his treaty.[50]

Bowyer died late in the summer of 1820, so he could shed no light on his actions. Cass believed that either "Col. Bowyer misunderstood his own authority or that he acted under instructions which had been issued long previously, and which were not at that time intended to be carried into effect." The treaty must be defeated. Cass told Williams that he opposed its ratification and that the treaty would not move forward. In the face of protests from territorial officials, from Indians in Wisconsin, and from those who joined in this expedition westward, President Monroe made the easy decision against submitting the treaty for ratification. He urged the Oneidas to try again the next year.[51]

And that is what Eleazer Williams intended to do. The forces that desired the removal of the New York Indians once again began to move. David Ogden in February 1821 urged Calhoun to undo the damage done the previous year by "providing a future seat for the New York Indians." Williams recalled that the desires of the younger Oneidas to relocate to the West "had been excited, [and] were not easily abated." Those Oneidas who favored removal—Cornelius Baird, John Brandt, and others—announced their firm support for Williams. "He is our minister as well as our brother," they wrote, and "he is an Indian, as well as ourselves, and we choose him before any of our White Brethren."[52]

Accompanied by Ellis, Williams took to the road once again to line up support for the expedition and to ensure that the previous year's debacle was not repeated. He might have stopped at Onondaga to meet with the Council of the Six Nations. He met with the Indians of Stockbridge and Brothertown, to shore up their spirits. He surely met with Thomas Ogden in New York City, who agreed to provide Williams with "the sum of four hundred and fifty dollars for defraying the expenses of a delegation of Indians to the west in the pursuit of a permanent seat in the state." From there, Williams and Ellis continued on to Philadelphia. He appealed to the members of the Episcopal Domestic and Foreign Missionary Society for support for his mission to Green Bay. And the secretary of war once again, offered his support. Calhoun ordered military officers at Detroit, Mackinac, and Green Bay to provision Williams's party as they passed through.[53]

Williams thus received the support of a number of New York Indians, government officials interested in the conduct of Indian policy, and private interests who hoped to acquire Indian land. Missionary organizations also watched this promising development, and considered lending Williams assistance. Each of these sponsors expected much from Williams. Each had invested, to some degree, in his ultimate success. Williams claimed that the Oneidas supported his plan as well. Many Oneidas attended the evening religious meetings he held after his return from Green Bay. Those in the crowded church, he remembered, "were aroused from their lethargy when they reflected on the greatness of their religious privileges and the love of God displayed towards them in this—and the miserable condition of their western brethren who were still sitting in darkness and in the shadow of death."[54]

Williams had fewer followers than he claimed, and there were many others at Oneida who thoroughly distrusted him. Their numbers grew with Williams's commitment to removal. He wanted Oneida lands, they said, but not what was best for the community. Some Oneidas, moreover, accused their religious teacher of misappropriating the funds for the construction of the church. The money received for lands sold by the state for the purpose of building the church, part of the 1817 agreement into which members of the Second Christian Party had entered at Albany, brought $4000. A. G. Ellis recalled, however, that Williams had erected "a small building of cheap construction," and that Williams had "no vouchers that would bear inspection." Ellis thought that the church cost between twelve and fourteen hundred dollars to build and that Williams could not account for the rest of the money.[55]

These charges bothered some of Williams's white critics. The Oneidas, however, thought much more dangerous the tales Williams told about removal and their supposed willingness to relocate. When, for instance, Jedidiah Morse once again visited them in the summer of 1821, he reminded the members of the Second Christian Party of their earlier interest in removing to Green Bay. The Second Christian Party leaders—Peter Summer, Moses Schuyler, and Martin Denny—told Morse that they did not know what he was talking about. Morse then read to them their speech from the year before, which Williams had translated into English. They could not conceal their anger. Williams, they said, had mistranslated the speech to make it seem like they supported removal when in reality, they told Morse, they asked Williams to state that "they would not remove to Green Bay, and that they would furthermore advise their people, young and old, to have nothing to do with the scheme, and that they would oppose it in every way possible." They caught Williams in the act, and his mistranslation, they told Morse, "was a lie, a wicked lie." They begged Morse to burn it.[56]

The Oneidas did not want to move to the Michigan Territory, but Williams made it seem like they did. Williams made it seem that Oneidas who stood steadfastly opposed to removal would willingly abandon their homelands and leave. The powerful white men who favored removal could achieve their goals if they relied on him. He had influence at Oneida, and the Indians there would follow him to a new homeland. Some did, but not all. Williams wanted the Ogden Company men, and their allies in the state and national governments, to recognize his indispensability, that they could achieve their goals most easily with his assistance. He attempted to convey to them the importance of the role he might play. He made his choice, and because he still offered the prospect of removing the Indians, Morse and others still supported him. But for some Oneidas he could not be forgiven.[57]

Summer and a number of other Second Christian Party delegates traveled to Washington a month after Morse's visit. The petition they submitted to the president offered a damning critique of Williams. "There is business," they wrote, "going on without our consent or authority." Williams, they believed, "is continuing a plan to get us from our land, and to have us settle among the wild Indians of the West, we don't know where." These Oneidas had no interest in leaving. "Our reservation is already diminished to a very small space; but we calculate to keep what we have got, and we think much of it, and intend it shall go down to generations after us." Williams did not represent them, they wrote. "We have not sent him to obtain land for us, and we shall not send any one to do so; and we now send our delegates to inform our Father the President accordingly."[58]

Williams clearly spoke with authority for very few, but neither did he let these criticisms, nor the obvious opposition he faced, bother him. He questioned his critics' motives: vendors and cheats, he asserted, who drew their livelihoods from the mouths of Indians; aspiring and ambitious missionaries like Solomon Davis or the Baptist Robert Powell who hoped to supplant him at Oneida. Respected by those in Washington or Albany who hoped to effect the removal of the Oneidas, and certainly better known than his opponents, Williams and his occasional supporters were able to cast their critics as petty and designing men who could not understand what Indians needed. Even if his neighbors began to question "seriously the character of the Rev. Eleazer Williams for truth and veracity," far from Oneida, Williams still possessed considerable influence.[59]

He and his party set out for the West at the end of June 1821. Ellis and Williams stopped in Geneva, in Ontario County, to collect the money Ogden had pledged for Williams's support. It took them four days, traveling by stagecoach, to reach Buffalo, little more than "a straggling village of a hundred houses much dispersed," in Ellis's eyes, that still bore scars from the War of 1812. At Black Rock, two miles up the Niagara River, they boarded once again the *Walk-in-the-Water*. After nine yoke of oxen towed the steamboat out onto Lake Erie, they began their journey to Detroit, where they arrived three days later.[60]

Ellis, a sour and miserable man, once again found little to his liking there. The population of Detroit, he recalled many years later, "was mixed, the French Canadian prevailing." There were, he said, "many half-breeds, and it being the season of the year when the Indians usually came in from their wintering grounds, the wild Chippewas seemed to be in undisputed possession." The party lingered here for several weeks awaiting the arrival of delegates from the Stockbridges, Senecas, Akwesasnes, and Tuscaroras. Ellis fell ill and could go no farther, but on the last day of July, the rest reboarded the *Walk-in-the-Water*, a party consisting of "Mr. Williams, five Stockbridge Indians, among whom are Kaunkapit and Hendrick two principal chiefs, five Oneidas, two Senecas, and one Onondaga." Five companies of American troops, bound for the "Upper Posts," traveled with them, as did C. C. Trowbridge, Governor Cass's personal secretary.[61]

It took them slightly more than a week to pass Mackinac and sail south along the western shore of Lake Michigan to Green Bay and Fort Howard, which stood on "an exposed point of sand, formed by the junction of the waters of the Fox River with the Bay, and a marsh of considerable extent lies to its rear, approaching within a few yards of it, rendering it bleak, dreary, and uncomfortable."[62]

On 8 August, sixty Menominee and Winnebago chiefs arrived at Fort Howard. The Stockbridge leader Solomon U. Hendrick opened the council. He told the gathered Indians that "we had a very important message to communicate to them." The Menominees and Winnebagos wanted to wait until more of their leaders arrived. The council resumed on the 16th. Cornelius Baird, an Oneida, spoke first. Hendrick, who followed him, then addressed the gathered Indians. According to Trowbridge, "he disclosed our object in a gradual and handsome manner, setting forth at the same time all the advantages" that would result from a cession to the New York Indians.[63]

The Menominees did not want to sell land to the newcomers. They did not have enough land to spare. A Winnebago speaker, Dog's Head, argued that "the lands are not ours." They belonged to "the Great Spirit who sits above and now sees and hears all that is done and said in this Council." But even though "the Great Spirit would be angry at the idea of receiving payment for lands," the Winnebagos were willing, "although we have a very small tract of country, to give you a part of that country the same right which we have; we are willing that you should come & live among us as we live with each other, and if you contemplate giving us anything we repeat to you that we shall not receive it as payment for these lands, but as a token of your love for us & your desire to assist us."[64]

The New York Indians, Williams recalled, could not live with this offer. They appreciated the generosity, but worried about what would happen if a later chief denied the gift. Williams noted that this would leave the Indian immigrants "in an unhappy situation." The French inhabitants of the Bay, as well, opposed any deal and, in Trowbridge's view, "opposed with zeal the progress of settlement and improvement in their country."[65] Nobody at the time commented upon the irony of New York Indians leaning heavily on the Wisconsin Indians for a cession of their lands. These problems threatened to unravel the negotiations, but a day later, on 18 August, the Menominees and Winnebagos ceded to the New York Indians "a small territory for themselves & other Indians in the state of New York, who may choose hereafter to emigrate thither."[66]

Williams played little direct role in the negotiations. He addressed the Menominees after the speech of Dog's Head, but did not speak again in council. He attempted to discuss with them matters religious, but, he wrote, "their minds were too much occupied with the treaty concerns and my own health was in such a feeble state as it did not permit me to be with them but little." Williams found in the Fort Howard garrison some Christians "in whose bosoms there is still a feeling of attachment which is not quite obliterated," but he did little at this time, noting only that the commanding officer "hoped that in due time the church may be planted here under the good Providence of God and become a Godly Tree." Williams may have acted as a cheerleader, trying to keep up the spirits of the New York Indians. Certainly Trowbridge, who traveled with Williams after the treaty had been completed to explore the bounds of the ceded lands, told Cass that "the correct moral deportment and statesman like conduct of the deputies from the Six Nations, under the direction of Mr. Williams, whose personal exertions in this business have been very great," impressed him immensely.[67]

As soon as the parties signed the treaty, problems emerged. The Menominees and Winnebagos charged that those who signed the agreement did not have the authority to do so, and that they did not represent their communities. The New York Indians who signed the agreement, for their part, also expressed reservations about the size and the location of the tract they believed they had just purchased. The lands lay farther from the bay than they had anticipated. Cornelius Baird told Calhoun that he wanted permission for another expedition to Green Bay to purchase additional Menominee land. Williams wanted federal officials to confirm the agreement, but he shared the New Yorkers' concerns about the size and location of the cession.[68]

But many Oneidas, and other Iroquois across New York State, rejected completely the notion that they ought to leave their homeland for any lands under any condition. Williams left the delegates as they returned home after the council. He fell ill on the journey, and stayed behind to recover at Mackinac. When he reached Buffalo late in September, Williams wrote that he "was informed by the public prints, that someone had been busy among the Oneidas to prejudice their minds against the policy of the general and state governments and the wishes of the first Christian party of the Oneidas and other branches of the Six Nations, and my own motives in aiding them, in regard to the Green Bay Country."[69] The Senecas, for their part, firmly believed that Williams had joined with their enemies to drive them from their lands; they did not know, but suspected correctly, that he worked for the Ogden Land Company. Members of the Second Christian Party informed the secretary of war that they intended to dismiss Williams as their religious instructor. Indeed, they wrote to William Lacey, an Episcopal minister in Albany, and asked him to tell Bishop Hobart that they did not support his protégé, that they did not need the sort of help Williams offered them. They no longer loved Williams, they told Lacey, for "he has tried every means in his power to draw us away from *our own lands.*" Williams, they continued, wished for the Oneidas "to leave the possessions we inherit from our fathers to our white brethren, but we cannot sacrifice our houses & our Church & go to the land of Strangers." They loved the Church, but not Williams. Would Lacey ask Hobart to send to them a new minister, "a young man of piety and disinterested benevolence, one who," like Solomon Davis, was "willing to conform to our mores & customs"?[70] They hoped so. It must have been a somewhat surprising request: the Second Christian Party Oneidas thought that the non-Indian Davis could conform more closely to their "mores & customs" than Williams. The Oneidas wanted an effective broker, and Williams clearly had let them down. Meanwhile, a council of the Six Nations informed their federal agent Jasper Parrish that they thoroughly opposed any relocation plan and that none of their annuity funds should be used to support Williams's program.[71]

Williams told John Holloway Hanson about the criticism he faced. The Indians, so easily manipulated by those who did not have their interests at heart, could not see how finding a new home at Green Bay offered solutions to the problems they faced. Hanson learned from Williams of the machinations of Powell and Davis, of their attempts to stir up discontent among the Oneidas, discredit the catechist, and usurp his position at Oneida Castle. Even if, as Williams told Hobart, only a missionary not previously identified with any faction could enjoy any success, Hanson could find no fault in any of this with Williams. "Political prejudices, fostered by certain religious teachers, for their own ends," Hanson wrote later, alienated the Second Christian Party from a clergyman who had their best interests at heart.[72]

Williams returned to Oneida at the end of September. The disagreements between those who supported and those who opposed removal must have been expressed openly. The vast majority opposed removal, but they also recognized that complaining about this would not have any effect on Williams. Criticisms of his religious conduct did draw a reaction, however, for Williams understood that these charges, more than complaints about removal, threatened his position as a leader and teacher. Bishop Hobart, Williams's patron and a man he greatly admired, fully supported removal to Green Bay. Williams had nothing to apologize for there. But the charge that he had misused the funds set aside for the construction of the church risked damaging Williams's reputation in Hobart's eyes, as did other charges leveled against him by Powell and Davis.

Williams obtained in February 1822 a "Declaration of Oneida Chiefs in General Council Assembled" that responded directly to charges that Williams had engaged in misconduct in his capacity as a catechist and lay reader. Williams's Second Christian Party critics charged that he had obtained the signatures on this "Declaration" by threatening that if the bishop removed him, the "Prayer Book and the Bishop's support would be withdrawn." Perhaps Williams did make this threat. Lacey could not tell. He could only conclude that "owing to a concurrence of circumstances," some of which were clearly unfounded, Williams "has lost his influence over the Oneidas, and that a removal as speedy as is consistent with his reputation, will contribute to the interest of the Church."[73] Williams's supporters argued in response to the Second Christian Party's charges that there was no evidence that their teacher maintained "a strong attachment to the Roman Catholic Church, and betrayed a want of decided preference for the Protestant Faith." Williams may have been a theological sampler, serving a dish flavored by each of the three faiths he had practiced, but he was no Catholic. Neither was he a crook, he told Hanson. After the construction of the Episcopal chapel, the Oneidas told Williams to take the surplus funds left over to defray the cost of translating and printing the Book of Common Prayer in Mohawk. Any money left over they gave to Williams as a gift, a claim that Hanson, but few others, appears to have believed.[74]

And despite the mounting criticism and growing opposition, Williams participated in another expedition west late in the summer of 1822. Though this party was larger than that of the year before, it cannot be considered at all representative of the Oneidas or the Iroquois generally. As in 1820 and 1821, the secretary of war provided support. The Indians' mission he considered an important one, and Calhoun recommended them "to the attention and kindness of all offices of government."[75]

They arrived at Green Bay on the first day of September. The first matter of business, Ellis recalled, "was to find shelter—some building to camp down in." When the council opened two weeks later, Solomon Hendrick, the Stockbridge leader, held out a string of wampum and addressed the gathered Winnebagos and Menominees. He felt thankful, he said, "that the Great Spirit has allowed so many of us to assemble around this council fire, to shake hands together, and smoke a pipe of peace and friendship." Hendrick hoped that the Menominees and Winnebagos could keep clean the chain of friendship that bound them to the New York Indians, as the newcomers came "to take possession of the land they had acquired the year before, an action that has the President's approval."[76]

A Menominee speaker responded. The arrival of the New York Indians, he said, "will enlarge our council fire and strengthen our nation." It was a theme a number of Menominee and Winnebago speakers picked up on. The Menominees, under the guidance of the Great Spirit, hoped to "become soon like yourselves." He hoped that the Menominees will soon "become like you, civilized, for we see no difference betwixt you and the white people." According to Williams, who once again took little direct role in the negotiations, the Menominees recognized that the New York Indians "know more of the ways of the white men than we do, and you know also by sad experience that he has long nails when he once puts his nails upon the land, then it is very uncertain whether you can take them off." Williams's memory may have been more than a bit self-serving, for it is highly unlikely that the Menominees wished "to put all the land belonging to us into your care and guardianship that the white man shall not get it from us." They would do this, Williams recalled, because the New York Indians "knew how to keep these long nails off from our lands."[77]

But not all Wisconsin Indians felt this way. Dog's Head, the Winnebago leader, told the New York Indians in council that "you are civilized, you have the fashion, knowledge, and understanding of the white people." The Winnebagos drank and occasionally acted like fools, he said, but the New York Indians did not. These were not compliments. The New York Indians, he said, were too much like the white people, and "therefore do I fear, should you be too much among us that we might be unhappy."[78]

The Winnebagos walked out rather than agree to the request of the New York Indians for more land. Hendrick and Williams continued to negotiate with the Menominees. According to Oneida accounts, Williams "was very persuasive with the Menominee and made all kinds of promises." The Menominees agreed to an additional cession of lands, approximately 6.7 million acres in exchange for four thousand dollars in goods. But it was pretty clear that the two parties understood the resulting agreement in very different terms. The Menominees granted the New York Indians a "right in common" to their lands. Williams told the Menominees that the New Yorkers intended only to "come and sit down with them." But what, precisely, did that mean? Had the Menominees, as they argued, granted to the New York Indians nothing more than the right to settle on their lands? Or, as Williams asserted, had the New York Indians become co-owners of a massive tract stretching inland from Green Bay? The resulting debate would last for another decade.[79]

*   *   *

"The Green Bay country became my adopted country," Williams wrote, after negotiation of the 1822 agreement. He took up residence in the house Bowyer had occupied. He preached on occasion to an audience of settlers and soldiers who drank too much and ignored the Sabbath. They were "in communion with the Church of Rome," he wrote, and clung to "many childish traditions." The young men who dominated life in Green Bay came to make their fortunes but lived "beyond the restraints of godly advice of parents & friends." They were nearly savage, Williams suggested, and their moral condition, he said, "was truly lamentable and perilous."[80]

One might argue that the New York Indians brought civilization to Wisconsin. One of the tragic ironies of the policy was that its supporters, some cynically, claimed that removal would save untutored savages from the perils of civilization. But these same Indians, occupying valuable land, had learned to farm it, and many of their leaders read and wrote English and practiced

Christianity. Removal quite often ensnared native peoples whose ways of living resembled closely that of their white neighbors. The New York Indians, for instance, built the first grist mill in the territory. They practiced the sort of settled agriculture that policy-makers hoped Indians might emulate, even if those same authorities gave the Oneidas little credit for doing so. They entered the territory at a point of transition. The land may have looked like a wilderness to the New York Indians, but that had clearly begun to change. Territorial government matured and administration improved. A territorial court system began to operate in an effort to bring order to relations between the garrison, the settlers, and the Indians.[81] Just as much a part of the westward movement of pioneers as the many thousands of white Americans and European immigrants who moved into the interior of the continent, the Oneidas and other New York Indians began to settle in. Williams, according to his own accounts, helped them make this transition. During a harsh winter he used his influence with the American officers at Fort Howard to provide the immigrants with extra supplies of "cloathing, flour, pork, and beans." When the roads permitted him to travel, Williams visited the Stockbridge community, ministered to them there, "baptized their children, and buried their dead," a spiritual leader with good connections to white men of influence. But this is all we can know for sure. Additional information on his activities is difficult to find.[82]

The Oneidas were an "ambitious people" when they arrived in Wisconsin, one member of the community reported in a WPA interview recorded in 1939. The Oneidas "did all kinds of work to make a living, such as cutting wood and selling it," along with trading the corn they planted and the hides and meat from the animals they hunted. They practiced the mixed economy of hunting, subsistence farming, and limited exchange with white outsiders that long had characterized their life near Oneida Lake. They began to farm as quickly as they could and their Green Bay neighbors frequently commented on their similarities to white people. But moving west did not mean a complete abandonment of Iroquois culture. They held land communally, and they organized large winter hunts.[83]

And they remained poor. The small number of newcomers struggled to obtain all that they needed. Relocation to Green Bay cost money. Those willing to go—and at the outset, far more Stockbridges and Brothertowns journeyed west than Oneidas—needed to pay for their travel by water from Buffalo to Green Bay, as well as the tools, the livestock, and the clothing they needed to get by. Some of them contracted debts with traders around the bay to meet their needs. Williams, himself, struggled to find the cash necessary to pay his own debts. They raised the funds they needed by selling their lands in New York. That the New York Indians quickly constructed the "settlements, houses, barns and cultivated fields" that "attest to the industry of the occupants, & exhibit most encouraging evidence of increasing order and sobriety," was no mean feat.[84]

Williams helped where he could, and spent a considerable amount of his time generating support for his missionary activity. He told John Holloway Hanson about his labors during these years. Williams possessed great influence in the fledgling community, he told Hanson. Indeed, Hanson concluded that Williams "might easily have gained wealth, had money been his object," and he "might have acquired political importance, had ambition been his ruling passion." But Williams "was simply an enthusiast for the welfare of others." Hanson really seems to have believed that.[85]

He began preaching, at least on occasion, an activity which he felt the need to justify to Bishop Hobart. The Oneidas constructed a log building to house Hobart Church. To make the mission work, Williams felt it necessary to improvise, and to claim more responsibility than he had originally been given, and to expand upon the role Hobart had assigned him. "I have deviated from the proper functions belonging to the rank which I hold in the Church," he informed Hobart, "in as much as I have been compelled to deliver sermons, part of the time of my own composition, and the other part, selected." He wished that Hobart had ordained him, for Williams felt "the want of proper authority to administer the ordinances." He needed authority, but he also needed funds. He paid for Ellis's room and board but he no longer had the money necessary to acquire prayer books in English and in French. He asked Hobart for additional support.[86]

Williams claimed that he had begun preparing Albert Ellis for the ministry. Certainly he asked Hobart to "empower him to baptize," and to appoint him "catechist and lay-reader, and the former if possible." Ellis named his firstborn son after Williams, but later neglected entirely to describe Williams's patronage. Late in 1822, Williams wrote to *Churchman's Magazine*, asking its readers to consider that the Wisconsin Indians, "totally destitute of religious instruction," might provide a "greater opportunity for the useful offerings of Charity" than Indian tribes elsewhere. He asked for donations of old clothing, for before he could begin educating the Indians, "their nakedness must be covered." Williams informed John Calhoun that December that a school had commenced, "tho, without a great pecuniary support." Thirty children attended regularly and they "are very fond of school." Williams wrote that "nothing now is wanting . . . but efficient means."[87] Ellis felt optimistic about the school's prospects because it "was immediately filled to the capacity of the room," and "the parents were interested, the scholars kindly disposed, and well-behaved, and the school on the whole all that could reasonably be expected." It stood on the west bank of the Fox River, opposite Shantytown in Bowyer's old agency complex.[88]

But the school serviced, Williams wrote, "the citizens' children and the half-breeds." It did little for the Menominees, Winnebagos, or immigrant New York Indians. The students and their parents liked Ellis, Williams wrote, and he was successful as a teacher. "Mr. Ellis," Williams told Hobart, had "discharged his duty to the satisfaction of the parents as well as myself."[89] Williams visited Ellis's school on occasion but, according to Ellis, he "bestowed more than common attention" on one of his pupils, Madelaine Jourdain, one of the two attractive daughters of a métis trader. According to one early historian of the Wisconsin Oneidas, Madelaine Jourdain was "very beautiful and of great personal attraction." She also brought with her a claim to 4,800 acres of land. Williams married the seventeen-year-old Madelaine early in 1823. Marriages of young women to older men were not uncommon in the western Great Lakes, and this convenient union connected Williams to the métis community at the Bay. Williams told Hanson and others much later that his wife "was a distant relative of the king of France from whom she had been honored with several splendid gifts and honors, among the rest a golden cross and star." Obviously this was not true, but marrying her still brought Williams significant short-term benefits.[90]

For Ellis, not so much. He surrendered the room in Bowyer's old agency building that he had used for a schoolhouse to the newlyweds, and the next day dismissed the "school indefinitely." Williams needed room for his new bride more than the children of the métis leaders and the garrison officers needed a school.[91] Ellis cast a critical eye on Williams's actions during these years. He viewed the marriage to Madelaine Jourdain as opportunistic. Ellis always depicted Williams as a schemer. Williams, Ellis recalled, frequently visited Pierre Grignon during his final illness, read him prayers, "and offered the comforts of religion." Grateful for this spiritual care, Grignon asked Williams how he might repay the kindness. Williams, Ellis wrote, had his eyes on an old sawmill built years before by Grignon. If Williams might have use of the mill for a year, he could cut "a little lumber with which to build him a house." Grignon obliged gladly but, Ellis suggested, his family saw through Williams's game. Grignon's heirs "took charge of the estate, and the ensuing fall they relieved Williams of any charge of the saw mill, he having cut at it" by early 1823 "about twelve million feet of boards."[92]

That's a lot of lumber, and it is difficult to reconcile Ellis's depiction of Williams's acquisitiveness and social climbing with Hanson's depiction of regal disinterestedness. Both authors wrote their accounts decades after the events they described. Williams often complained of poverty. He often sought additional support for his religious work. And relocation, from New York to Wisconsin, was not cheap. Williams may indeed have found it difficult to make ends meet.

In 1824 Williams sent Ellis to New York to visit Bishop Hobart and solicit funds to aid in "establishing a mission school." Williams asked Ellis to seek Hobart's permission to call upon "the church people of the city in that behalf." Ellis tried but raised little money, and thought his efforts "nearly a failure." Williams thought that Ellis "unfortunately obtained but a small sum for the object in consequence of his disposition." When Ellis returned in the summer, however, he recalled that Williams had done nothing to establish the mission for which he had been sent to obtain funding.[93]

Perhaps Williams was as lazy as Ellis remembered. Perhaps he shut down Ellis's school solely to make room for his wife in the agency building. But the fact is that the school project received only minimal support. Hobart did not feel that he could send funds from his diocese to support mission work in another diocese, Williams said. That Ellis was a man with a sour temperament seems clear from his bitter recollections of Williams. That he was an ineffective fund-raiser is beyond dispute.[94]

Williams did find some support. The secretary of war sent $250 to ease "the embarrassed state of Mr. Williams's establishment for the want of funds." The New York Episcopal Tract Society provided some religious literature "for distribution at Green Bay." All the evidence suggests that Williams had to make do with very little. The Oneidas, one chronicler recalled, "were very poor" in their new homes and "mourned for the old gardens and orchards, and fruit trees they had left behind them." They paid a high price, leaving New York for a home where, one métis community leader lamented, all was "wretched," with "dirty grog shops where every crime is committed" and where "Indians, squaws, soldiers all met together." There were, of course, missionaries who continued their efforts without significant support. Williams preached sermons, and likely continued to provide spiritual counsel for those who needed it. But he never did enough to convince Ellis, the man Williams had sent to raise the funds the mission needed, that he had done all that he could.[95]

When Ellis returned to Green Bay, the garrison commander at Fort Howard asked him to establish a school once again for his soldiers' children. Ellis asked Williams if he should accept the offer. Because, Ellis wrote, "the church committee had provided no funds for his school," Williams advised Ellis to "accept overtures of the officers." He did not stand in Ellis's way.[96]

Williams worked with the garrison as well. He preached there on occasion. The immigrant New York Indians, it is not difficult to imagine, may have attended these sermons, to listen, and to learn, as Williams himself had done as a young man. Williams stated repeatedly that relocation to Green Bay served the best interests of the Indians who migrated there. But removal brought with it "great difficulties," and Williams understood if some of the first immigrants felt like they had leapt from the frying pan into the fire. He understood the difficulties, and he wanted the financial support he felt was necessary to make relocation work.

On the Fourth of July in 1823, Williams preached a patriotic sermon at Fort Howard that might have left any immigrant Indians who heard it feeling confused, for the patriotism he performed so wholeheartedly was that of the nationalistic young republic. "While other nations," he said, "who are involved in the sable shades of despotism, meet to celebrate the births of monarchs and princes," his audience gathered on this edge of the western world to celebrate the "founding of our empire—the birth of freedom, and the rights of man." He asked his audience to "trace for a moment the rise and progress of our Independence—the beauty and excellency of our happy constitution & government, and anticipate with grateful joy the pleasing prospect which lies before us."[97]

American heroes and patriots fought for their freedom, and "our villages," Williams said, "poured forth the hardy sons of courage, who with unequaled animation met the insulting foe." Williams did not mean the Oneida villages, or those where the Stockbridge and Brothertowns had settled. These all fought with the Patriots. He did not describe how the Revolution had unleashed a scourge of land-hungry New Yorkers on Iroquoia. It seems not to have entered his mind.

Instead, he spoke of how God favored the Revolution, and how he "advocated our cause." He spoke of the brilliance of American institutions. "That excellent and invaluable, Constitution, that most illustrious work of human invention, abounding with strength, replete with wisdom, shining like a star of the first magnitude among those of the most enlightened nations, conveying a light dangerous to tyrants, dreaded by oppressors, and laying a permanent foundation for the enjoyment of our bought liberties," followed the Revolution and secured its blessings. "This Palladium of our country's rights, has laid a foundation for the most happy government on earth."[98] *Our country*, he said. For this great society to continue, Williams said, the republic's virtuous citizens must turn to God, for "government cannot exist without religion." Christianity might provide the unity necessary to hold together the Republic. Sin had no place in Williams's view of America. He told his listeners that "nothing will prove more effectual to destroy our Union, than falsehood, slander, and calumny, by which the nature of our government will be misrepresented, the measures adopted, stigmatized, and our rulers calumniated, to render them odious in the eyes of the world."

Williams's subsequent career shows that he knew much, indeed, about falsehood, and he continued to feel the slings and arrows of his growing numbers of critics. He continued to fend off charges that he "inclined to the doctrines of the Romish church," and that he had misappropriated mission funds in New York. Some of his religious supporters in the East, influenced by the objections of the mass of the Oneidas to removal, denounced him as a man who "at first promised fair, but like other hirelings, his own pecuniary interests got the ascendancy, and by management and intrigue, he got $1500 worth of their lands."[99]

It is difficult to know how heavily these charges weighed on Williams. He only occasionally responded to them. He said nothing in his sermon of the criticism he had received, nothing about Indians at all. He performed. He played the role of a patriotic minister. "What people, in any age or country," he asked, "ever had greater reasons for gratitude & joy, either from the real enjoyment, or the prospect, of great & good things, than the inhabitants of the United American States, at the present moment?" Williams seems to have understood that the small number of immigrant Indians who may have joined his audience did not enjoy fully the blessings of liberty, and he may have chosen the word "inhabitants" over "citizens" quite deliberately. They had little now, but there existed at Green Bay the "prospect" for a better future.

We can imagine the scene. Soldiers and officers from the garrison, listening to Williams's address along with the residents of Green Bay and the Christian Indians. Williams spoke to the officers and the soldiers, and he told them what they wanted to hear, on this day when the nation celebrated its independence. Perhaps this required dishonesty. But there seems little reason to doubt that in this instance Williams meant every word that he said, and that he drank deeply the notion that he had performed well enough to earn a prominent place for himself in an American nation that had showed it had no place for Indians.

CHAPTER FOUR

A Failed Performance

Close to five thousand Iroquois remained in New York State when Williams delivered his Fourth of July speech in 1823. Neddy Archiquette, a chief of the First Christian Party, led close to one hundred Oneida Christians to Wisconsin that year, but some of these returned home shortly thereafter. Oneida leaders like Daniel Bread attempted to persuade others in New York that removal offered an alternative to watching white settlers steadily overrun their lands. The Indians heard as well from federal officials like Thomas McKenney who wanted them to sell their lands and then find new homes away from the ravages of alcohol, the lawlessness of frontier whites, and the constant disorder that seemed to characterize their lives. State officials regularly leaned on them to sell their lands. The pressure never ceased. But many Oneidas found these arguments unconvincing, the pressure a force they must resist. Most Iroquois simply did not wish to go.[1]

Williams saw things differently. He believed he had done important work, and that he was a man of consequence. He claimed to have set the process of relocating the New York Indians in motion by leading the first delegation of emigrants to Wisconsin. He helped negotiate the treaties that secured for the New York Indians a homeland in the West, and this was a good thing. He argued that relocated New York Indians would extend the reach of Christianity into the western Great Lakes and become a missionary arm of the United States. At Green Bay, he believed, they might "ameliorate the unhappy condition of the neglected Indian tribes of the west, by imparting to them the blessings of the knowledge of Christianity and the arts of civilized life." Their civility and Christianity would shine like a beacon to native people living still in darkness. Williams told John Holloway Hanson, and other Episcopal clergymen with whom he corresponded, that owing to his efforts, the long-suffering Oneidas and their neighbors enjoyed "the bless-ings of liberty which has ever been prized by their ancestors." Throughout his career, Williams told one clerical correspondent, he consistently pursued plans and policies "calculated according to the best of my judgment, to ame-liorate the temporal and spiritual condition of my unfortunate countrymen." That's what some white Americans hoped might follow from removal, and Williams seems to have sincerely felt that he pursued the best interest of the New York Indians.[2]

He was hopeful. The Oneidas suffered at home, but to him the problems they faced seemed beyond any government's control. Williams believed that the Oneidas faced a truly lawless white population in the center of the Empire State, and that in the West things might be better, that there, less pressure might be placed on their lands. Unlike many Indians who lived their entire lives in these hard-pressed communities, he believed that he could help all parties, that each of his audiences would appreciate his performance.

But Williams talked a good game, and for some the act had worn thin. Albert Gallatin Ellis was right about this. Most Oneidas had had enough. The patience of all his patrons had begun to wear out. For his efforts—for the choices he made—the Oneidas grew to distrust him. This is not surprising. Over time, after his performances failed to produce results, his white patrons in church and state decided that they, too, no longer needed the assistance Eleazer Williams might offer them.[3]

In October 1823, Williams announced his intention to return to New York. He felt that he could be of more service to the Indians still there, fully aware that where he had led, thus far few had followed. He told John Hol-loway Hanson of his many relationships with the powerful men engaged in making Indian policy, and Hanson was impressed. But once again, Williams told tales and Hanson believed claims that a more critical thinker might have questioned. For when Williams left Green Bay that fall, only a handful of Oneidas remained behind, and it is not likely that many of them cared that he had gone away.[4]

*   *   *

Eleazer Williams spent much of the next three years in New York. He learned on his return to the Oneida country that Daniel Bread once again had con-spired against him with the assistance of Solomon Davis. Or so he wrote years later. Williams claimed to have learned from John Denny, an Oneida aligned with the First Christian Party, of Bread's boast that "if Mr. Williams has no sins which will remove him, he . . . would make sins for him, & which will, he was sure, draw the attention of the Bishop to him."[5]

In the story Williams related to Hanson, he struggled tirelessly to promote missions, with enemies on every side, defaming him, attempting to drag him down, and nipping constantly at his heels. They never relented. Meanwhile, he asked his patrons for funding. Indian missionaries could not perform their work without white allies, and in his quest for funding and support he had to remain attentive to his patrons' concerns. He needed Bibles and prayer books at Green Bay, after all. He needed money to build a schoolhouse. But he lavished attention on the Indians who already lived in Wisconsin and paid relatively less attention to the New York tribes. Williams told Bishop Hobart, and whoever else would listen, that he intended to educate the Menominee and Winnebago youth according to a "Lancastrian" plan, with a schoolhouse erected with a work house, a garden, and a large field nearby, "where they may occasionally be instructed in the most useful mechanical arts, and in agriculture." Young Indian students, Williams said, "cannot at first be made to spend their whole time in confinement." They needed the "profitable amuse-ment during the hours of relaxation from study" that the fields, the garden plots, and the work house provided.[6]

Williams's enthusiasm for the project, and his conviction that by fol-lowing it he could "raise" his Indian students gradually from "one stage of improvement to another, without subjecting them to a discipline, which would be at once irksome and unprofitable," convinced Hobart. The bishop endorsed and called on Episcopalians to support Williams's plan to teach the Wisconsin Indians "in the English language; in the various branches of com-mon school learning; in husbandry and the arts of civilized life," and give to them, "and through them to their parents and friends, a knowledge of the true God, and his Son, Jesus Christ; of virtue and true happiness, of glory, honor, and immortality."[7]

So many assumptions appeared in Hobart's broadside and in Williams's plans that inspired it: Indian children could be brought through education from one level of civilization to another, becoming more civilized as they approached the ideal personified by the American yeoman farmer, at once hardy, self-sufficient, and Christian.[8] Missionaries must target the children in order to succeed. They could achieve little by preaching to and teaching Menominee and Winnebago parents. Williams endorsed one of the cruelest beliefs undergirding the historical conduct of American Indian education, and in what he wanted to achieve in terms of his Indian policy, he advocated nothing that white policy-makers would have disavowed. All the children attending the school, he wrote, "must be maintained wholly independent of the parents." Hobart and Williams assumed, as well, that Christians "who love the prosperity of Zion" would contribute money for the school, and that Williams's "knowledge of the Indian character . . . and disposition will enable him to gain the confidence of the Christian public."[9]

All these assumptions appear to have been wrong. Williams, who often pleaded poverty, claimed he barely raised enough to defray his expenses. Perhaps this was so. But he did receive an appointment as an agent of the Domestic and Foreign Missionary Society of the Protestant Episcopal Church, with responsibility for procuring from "the Menominee and other Indians interested, such title to the lands that may be necessary for a missionary establishment." The position carried a small salary. Indeed, his entire livelihood came from those who wanted to remove the Indians, dispossess them, or Christianize them, and he said they barely paid him enough to get by. The school, could he have acquired the necessary funding, might have provided him a better livelihood in the West.[10]

Williams attempted to generate support for his missionary program, but he also remained involved at the margins in the dispossession of the New York Indians. The Akwesasne Mohawks on the New York side of the line resolved in the spring of 1824 to empower Thomas Williams and four other men as trustees to carry out "all necessary grants, conveyances, releases or receipts which may be required in consequence of any Bargain or Treaty" it struck with the state. While in New York, Williams accompanied his father to collect annuity payments, and he and his brother John signed statements witnessing these transactions: a family engaged in the transfer and sale of Akwesasne lands.[11]

It is difficult to tell what benefit the St. Regis community received from these annuities. Elsewhere in New York, Iroquois peoples complained to state and federal officials when annuity payments arrived late, suggesting that their communities relied at least to some extent on this small source of cash revenue. On highly disadvantageous terms, Iroquois people transformed their lands into annual cash payments from the state that helped them to obtain some of the material goods they needed to survive.[12] This is perhaps the best that can be said, and the payment could never have been enough. The Akwesasnes continued to sell lands. In March 1824, the St. Regis trustees met with Governor Joseph C. Yates. They agreed to cede to the state a mile square of territory in St. Lawrence County in return for a one-time payment of $1,920. Williams signed the deed as a witness. Three months later, Williams swore an oath and signed a statement acknowledging that he witnessed his father and other Akwesasne representatives cede an additional one thousand acres to the state.[13]

Family connections explain Williams's presence at the St. Regis transactions. The work brought him no direct financial rewards. But Williams's willingness to help state officials may have paid off in other ways, for he remained a useful Indian, and the state recognized this usefulness. In August 1824, for instance, a delegation of First Christian Party Oneidas traveled to Albany to meet with Governor Yates. They hoped to sell land to raise the money necessary to defray the costs associated with the 1821 and 1822 Menominee treaties. Williams was not there: he had returned for a short visit to Green Bay, but he benefited from the transaction nonetheless. The Oneidas agreed to grant Williams one hundred acres "in consideration of his pastoral services." In return for the cession, the First Christian Party received a small cash payment and annuities totaling three hundred dollars. Williams clearly possessed some small amount of support among the First Party Oneidas, and state officials valued his past efforts in helping to relocate the New York Indians and acquire their lands.[14]

During Williams's absence from Wisconsin, his wife had given birth to their first child, a son who was ten months old by the time Williams returned to Green Bay. Though the arrival of a child might have had the effect of tying him to the place, Williams still felt the need to be with the New York Indians. He claimed, much later, that he no longer wanted to minister to the garrison and to the white inhabitants of Green Bay, because he wanted to help another group of Oneidas make the trip West. They would settle at Duck Creek, a bit west of Green Bay, where Williams wanted to open a church. He hoped, he wrote later, that the Missionary Society might send another man to take his place in Green Bay, freeing him to undertake this important work. Williams told John Holloway Hanson that he came to this decision with some difficulty. He suffered from exhaustion, he said. With his pay he could not feed his family. His health broke down yet again.[15]

Help was on the way. In August 1825 Albert Gallatin Ellis returned to Green Bay from his own trip to New York, along with his new wife and the Reverend Norman Nash. Williams had long since moved out of the agency buildings at Green Bay. He took up residence on his wife's land at Little Kakalin, a bit upriver. Nash moved into the agency buildings but did little more. Nash, Ellis recalled, occupied himself "in his studies and sundry amusements, portrait painting, and boat building." Ellis always believed he was the hardest-working man in any vicinity, and he watched Nash "with much discouragement and impatience." Through the fall Nash did nothing. As winter approached, still no steps had been taken toward opening a school. Recognizing that "the views of myself and Mr. Nash as to matters in general, and the organization and conducting a school in particular, were at such variance as to preclude harmony of action between us," Ellis decided to leave Nash's service and open his own school. Ellis, who received an appointment as catechist and schoolmaster from the Missionary Society, made some progress. His school, according to his own account, "was very prosperous." Nash, meanwhile, with no forewarning and no subsequent explanation, left Wisconsin in June 1826, leaving all behind.[16]

It is not at all clear what Williams was doing during this period. Shortly after Nash's arrival Williams left Wisconsin for a return journey to New York. His wife and child journeyed with him. He fell ill once again. At Oneida Castle, where he stopped to recover, those Oneida who opposed him held a "defamatory council" that began late in November 1825. Williams saw in this the work of Solomon Davis, who once again accused Williams of misconduct. He did so "first by hints, then insinuations, and finally they were perfected into regular charges." Williams grew to hate Solomon Davis, a coward and schemer in his view, who betrayed the friendship and support Williams had provided him just four years before. Davis, Williams said later, "had an evil design against me," and recognized that he could ingratiate himself with the Second Christian Party by encouraging their opposition "to the movements of the first Christian Party in relation to Green Bay." Among the witnesses, Williams recalled, Davis brought before the Oneidas the merchant J. L. Williams, who made more trouble and "demoralized the Oneidas more than any other of his class in that neighborhood." An unrepentant liquor dealer, the merchant Williams sold so much alcohol to the Indians that "two or three of those poor people actually died near his door." These were the sorts of people who stood opposed to removal, Williams suggested, concealing the depth of Oneida opposition.[17]

Eleazer Williams was determined "to vindicate by every means in my power, and do away the aspersions which had been circulated by those who were inimical to me." As he convalesced at Oneida, he received support from Hobart. The bishop, and Thomas Ludlow Ogden, urged Williams to travel to New York City as soon as he felt strong enough. Of Hobart, Williams wrote, "I had great hopes that by his interference in some way the persecution which had been carried on against me may be arrested."[18]

While support and a sympathetic ear awaited Williams in New York, the Rev. George Boyd of the Episcopal Missionary Society in Philadelphia received a letter from "Magdalene W," Williams's wife, early in February 1826. Her husband had been laid up at Oneida now for four months. He was sick, and she feared that they soon would run out of money. "Misfortune and necessity have compelled me" to ask for financial support. The Oneidas, even those opposed to Williams, had been "kind and attentive to us," but still she and her husband stood in a "destitute condition and among strangers." Boyd failed to notice that the letter was not what it seemed to be. Eleazer Williams wrote the letter; it unquestionably appears in his hand. It was, in a sense, an act of ventriloquism in which Williams used his wife as a character to gain funding from the Episcopal establishment.[19]

Williams slowly recovered. By spring 1826, he felt well enough to travel. He, his wife, and his child arrived in New York City in May. While Williams rested and attempted to recover more of his strength, he recalled, Bishop Hobart baptized his wife at Trinity Church. Hobart gave to Madelaine the Christian name "Mary Hobart." The ceremony made clear that Williams still possessed the confidence of the bishop and his supporters, and he appreciated the effort.[20] Mary Hobart Williams wrote to Bishop Hobart's wife some months later. The letter, once again, appears in Williams's hand. Its language, once again, sounds like Williams and does not ring true for a twenty-year-old Franco-Menominee woman. "Whenever I am called by my Christian name," Mary Hobart wrote, "it always reminds me from whom I received it & of whom by whose office & ministry I was initiated into the visible church of Christ." She looked forward to helping her husband carry the gospel to the Indians, if only they could obtain some "means to aid them in this desirable object."[21]

Williams himself must have explained to Hobart the challenges he faced. He must have confided in him, and told him about the machinations of Solomon Davis and Daniel Bread. He told Hobart tales. He had to, in order to preserve his influence. Hobart had some familiarity with the dispute between Williams and his opponents. He had investigated it several years before. Hobart decided to support Williams publicly, and to do so at Oneida; that is, his actions make sense only if we conclude that he made such a decision. Williams, much later, told Hanson that he had not previously sought ordination because he had "little desire for self-aggrandizement" and "personal display was not in his nature."[22]

Williams returned to Oneida in June, with instructions to expect a visit from Hobart the next month. On 14 July, he received word that Hobart had arrived at Vernon, New York. Williams traveled the short distance to visit his patron, but after a short time, Davis and the First Christian Party leader

Martinus Denny arrived. They wished to speak to Hobart, and they did not want to do so with Williams in the room. Hobart excused Williams, but after Davis and Denny left, Hobart called him back in. He was, Williams recalled, "highly gratified with the object of their visit, which was that Mr. Davis and the chiefs had withdrawn all their complaints and they had nothing now against Mr. Williams and that they wished the Bishops would proceed to his ordination the same as if nothing had been said." Hobart evidently told Davis to drop the matter, and to halt his opposition to Williams. It was, Hobart told Williams, "a wise retreat" on the part of Davis and Denny, who learned that Hobart intended to support the missionary in whom the Oneidas had lost faith.[23]

Williams and Davis clearly distrusted each other, but Hobart could have seen that they agreed on nearly everything else. Both men felt missionaries needed more support than they received and both men agreed on what they felt was the best course for educating Indians and Christianizing them. Hobart valued Davis's work among the Oneidas, just as he appreciated Williams's. He did not want discord and rancor in his enormous diocese.[24] The next day Hobart, along with "eight prominent clergymen from the city of New York and elsewhere," arrived at Oneida Castle. Solomon Davis led the Morning Prayer, and then Hobart delivered a sermon that the numerous observers described as "appropriate" and "affecting." Davis served as Hobart's interpreter. Hobart assisted Williams, but did not do anything that would have discredited Davis, who he must have recognized was a skilled catechist, whatever his other faults. The bishop told the Oneidas to obey God's laws. Work hard. Do not drink. Bring your children to school and present them for baptism. Only then, Hobart continued, might they become "members of his holy church, children of their heavenly father, and heirs of the kingdom of Heaven." And, last, he told them to "be at peace among yourselves; for if you are divided and contentious, you will become weak and despised." He may have cast a silent glance at Davis as he spoke these words.[25]

Hobart then turned to Williams. "I have known you long," he said, and "have thought and do still think, that you desire to do your duty in the fear of God, and above all, to promote the temporal and spiritual welfare of your countrymen." Hobart, looking out at a congregation he knew was divided, said that "I now intend to carry into effect a design long contemplated, and to admit you into the holy ministry, that you may become the spiritual guide and instructor of these your people who are or will be settled in the west." With the blessings of the diocese of New York, Hobart authorized the new deacon to baptize converts, instruct his followers, and "to preach the gospel, not only by reading the Holy Scriptures and homilies, but by delivering your own exhortations and admonitions in the form of sermons."[26]

Hobart expected that the Oneidas would leave New York. They would travel to Wisconsin and become an "independent body of enlightened free-men" who would "participate in all the inestimable blessings of those civil and religious institutions which are the just prize of our happy country." Hobart made clear to all who heard his ordination sermon, and all who subsequently read it, that Eleazer Williams had his full support. "You go forth to aid in this great, and glorious, this most benevolent design," Hobart told Williams. "You go forth, the first Indian vested by our church with that commission, without which no man can minister in sacred things." After Hobart finished his sermon, he confirmed twenty-five Oneidas. Then several chiefs, members of the First Christian Party all, advanced toward the pulpit, "each one placing his right hand on the right shoulder of the chief before him, and the foremost placing his right hand on the right shoulder of Mr. Williams, as a token of concord." Eleazer Williams had been ordained deacon of the Episcopal Church, and the influential bishop of the diocese of New York had demonstrated his support for him in the most powerful form he had at his disposal.

Hobart lent this support fully aware of the breadth of Williams's activities, which might have given other mission patrons pause. For Williams's opportunism was clear to see. Shortly after the ceremony, for instance, Williams left Oneida. He traveled two hundred miles through the Adirondacks to Clintonville, New York. There, Williams reported in early August, he had engagements "too pressing" to permit him to visit Hobart, who was then staying in nearby Plattsburgh. Williams found there, he wrote to Hobart, "among the heterogeneous population which surround the establishment of the Peru Iron Company," and "particularly among the foreigners of whom there are a vast number employed there," an audience hungry for organized religion and "generally destitute of the Prayer Book."[27]

Williams told Hobart that he had preached in the vicinity of the Iron Works for the past two years, to an audience of "forty or fifty persons." This would have put Williams at Clintonville as early as 1824, when the entrepreneur Joshua Aiken founded the Peru Iron Company. Though Williams clearly exaggerated the amount of time he spent at Clintonville, Aiken and Williams indeed maintained some sort of business relationship. On the same day that Williams learned that Hobart was on his way to Oneida to ordain him deacon, the directors of the Peru Iron Company authorized Williams to build a house of brick or stone on company land, so long as its cost did not exceed eight hundred dollars. They also allocated three hundred dollars for the purchase of church pews, as well as a hundred dollars "per annum toward supporting a minister of the gospel" and another hundred to go toward the construction of a school house. Williams told Hobart that he had considered relocating to Clintonville permanently.[28]

It is not clear how Hobart responded to Williams's letter, and nothing came of the project at Clintonville, for Aiken sold out in 1828. But Hobart certainly knew what Williams was up to, and he found nothing to which he felt the need to object. Hobart saw ordination as a means to lend Williams support in his struggles against his rivals, and to quiet the increasingly acrimonious tensions in the community at Oneida. He wanted peace in his diocese. In so doing, Hobart helped a missionary who helped him, putting his influence behind Williams, a native Christian leader who unquestionably supported Indian removal, the sale of Iroquois land in New York State, and missionization.

Williams, his wife, and his child returned to Green Bay in the fall of 1826. He ministered to the small Oneida community at Duck Creek with the blessings of the church hierarchy. He had weathered the storm, and survived, it seemed, the challenges he faced in the first half of the 1820s. Williams looked forward, according to one account, "to spend his life among the people he loved, and who were now in larger numbers coming to their new homes in the west." All seemed to be going well. This is what Williams tells us in the autobiographical writings that appear in his papers. In the spring of 1827, however, Williams "heard like a distant thunder, that a treaty was to be held by the Government with the Menominees, in the ensuing season" that would threaten to undo all the work that the New York Indians had done to secure a new home in the West.[29]

*   *   *

There were other New York Indians who believed that relocation to someplace beyond the reach of grasping and land hungry whites—if, indeed, such a place existed—could help their people not only survive but prosper. Williams was not alone in this, even if nobody else worked so closely with those who sought their lands. Jacob Jamieson, a Seneca, told Secretary of War James Barbour that those New York Indians who had removed to the Fox River in Wisconsin "have vastly improved their condition," even if Jamieson himself did not join in the movement, and had little firsthand knowledge. Stockbridge and Brothertown spokesmen told Commissioner of Indian

Affairs Thomas L. McKenney that in the West they "might be enabled to put their rising generation in a way to get their living the same way as the white people," even if they already worked their lands in that manner in central New York and had done so even earlier in New England. Late in 1826, Daniel Bread led a party of Oneidas to the Michigan Territory, armed with the same hopes. He helped them to obtain supplies, and assisted them in making it through their first winter.[30]

Those Indians who hoped to remain in New York faced much more than a conspiracy of interests among politicians and speculators to seize their homeland. With the completion of the Erie Canal in 1825, thousands of migrants moved westward across and through Iroquoia. They came in search of land. This pressure drove up demand, and by the end of the decade, *Niles Weekly Register* reported that the growth of commerce and population along the canal increased the value of lands in the state by more than one hundred million dollars. Iroquois people made changes in an effort to hang on to their land and to secure "the free use and enjoyment thereof." But they were outnumbered, and each year their numbers relative to the settler population declined. The Iroquois were not alone in facing problems like these. The "Civilized Tribes" in the American southeast could have sympathized as the growth of cotton culture and expansion in the "Black Belt" took place on lands that once had belonged to Choctaws and Chickasaws, Cherokees and Creeks.[31]

Eleazer Williams hoped that more Indians would join the migration westward, but significant problems remained unresolved after the 1821 and 1822 treaties. The Menominees understood these agreements in terms dramatically different from the New York Indians. The Menominees believed they had agreed only to permit the immigrant Indians to settle on their lands. But the immigrant Indians, as the Brothertown chiefs told John Quincy Adams early in 1827, did not want to share the land, and they asked Adams to recognize their title as if they had purchased it outright.[32]

Federal officials recognized that the Wisconsin tribes' growing discontent and their sense that they had been cheated threatened frontier order. The Menominees and Winnebagos viewed the New York tribes as interlopers, much like other native peoples, in other places, viewed encroaching white frontiersmen. When Iroquois immigrants sold a chunk of land they acquired in 1821 and 1822 to the Brothertowns, the Menominees charged the Iroquois with acting less like Indians and more like white land speculators. While the New York Indians, wiser from their own experience in the East, sought a title to land that the United States would recognize and that they hoped would thwart the efforts of those non-Indians who already sought their lands in the West, some Wisconsin Indians threatened violence.[33]

But these same federal officials blamed the descendants of the original French settlers, the métis community, for provoking the Indians and fomenting discord. McKenney reported that "the French settlers in the neighborhood of Green Bay have very improperly interfered to prevent the carrying into effect" of the 1821 and 1822 agreements. Their conduct, he continued, "is highly reprehensible, and cannot be suffered by the Government with impunity." Peace between the Wisconsin and New York Indians could only be preserved if the government could protect the newcomers "against the arts of designing and intermeddling white men."[34]

Williams agreed entirely with McKenney's assessment. "Harmony and confidence," he recalled, "had prevailed among the western tribes & those of New York" until the French settlers at Green Bay undertook concerted "efforts to prevent the establishment of the New York Indians in that country." Self-serving, to be sure. The treaties of 1821 and 1822, Williams suggested, demonstrated his statecraft, his influence, and his competence. As Williams saw things, there could be no reasonable and legitimate opposition to the initial agreements into which the New York Indians, the Menominees, and the Winnebagos entered. So he believed. Thus, outside agitators must be responsible for the resulting discord. It was a familiar argument for Williams.[35]

Familiar, but also simplistic and incorrect. Territorial governor Lewis Cass recognized the Menominees' grave concern that "they will not ere long have a foot of land to stand upon" if the claims of the New York Indians went unchecked. The Menominees expressed deeply felt fears of dispossession, and they were nobody's fools. At Prairie du Chien in 1825 the United States attempted to create a general peace among Indians in the Upper Mississippi Valley, but nothing in that agreement addressed the Menominees' concerns about the immigrant Indians.[36] Meanwhile, thousands of white immigrants moved into the Michigan Territory, settling in the vicinity of Green Bay, a port which offered to the dreamers among them the prospect of linking the Mississippi through the Great Lakes and the recently completed Erie Canal to the Atlantic Coast. These settlers often came with greater resources than did the relatively small number of New York Indians, some of whom were so poor prior to their departure from New York that they reportedly scraped up the flour that spilled on the ground at loading stations along the Erie Canal. The Menominees saw the newcomers, both Indian and white, as a threat to their lands and their way of life.[37]

Cass and McKenney, who represented the United States when they met with the Wisconsin Indians at Butte des Morts in the summer of 1827, hoped to acquire Menominee lands that they could open to the growing numbers of land-hungry white settlers. John Metoxen, the Stockbridge leader, called upon Williams to attend the council "to act for the Seven Nations." Metoxen may have relayed this request from McKenney or Cass, who in turn might have believed that Williams could be of some service in the coming negotiations. Or perhaps Metoxen made this decision independently. He told Williams that "all the [New] York Indians are requested to come." Whatever the case, Williams journeyed to Butte des Morts as part of a New York Indian delegation, representing a Canadian Indian community that had not sent him, in response to a request that he attend delivered by men who had no apparent authority to appoint him. To prepare for his role, Williams studied closely the history of American Indian policy, and he copied lengthy extracts from congressional speeches, presidential addresses, and treaty proceedings into his notebooks. He understood the work required to perform well as an Indian diplomat.[38]

McKenney found the Christian hymn-singing of the New York Indians beautifully moving. They sang in three-part harmony, McKenney recalled, "with a time so true, and with voices so sweet, as to add harmony even to nature itself." Williams, known for using song in his ministry, may have led them. McKenney felt himself humbled, he claimed later, and "ashamed of my country, in view of the wrongs it had inflicted, *and yet continues to inflict*, upon these desolate and destitute children of the forest." Their singing, McKenney remarked, stood in sharp contrast to the "yelling and whooping of the wild Indians by whom they were surrounded." From these wild Indians McKenney hoped to extract a cession. If an agreement could be worked out with regard to the New York Indians, all the better.[39]

Thomas Dean, the Brothertowns' agent, argued on 7 August that the agreements of 1821 and 1822 had been negotiated with the encouragement and support at that time of the president of the United States and the secretary of war, and as such, that they should stand. The Oneida Cornelius Baird, as well, asserted the legitimacy of the 1821 and 1822 accords. The Menominees would have none of this, of course. Their spokesmen described how the Menominees took pity on the impoverished New Yorkers, who asked to live on their lands as guests. Their grant was a loan and not a gift, and the New York Indians misconstrued the agreements in ways that supported their unwarranted claim to an enormous swath of Menominee land.[40]

In the resulting treaty with the "Chippewa, Menominie, and Winnebago tribes of Indians," the commissioners obtained a strip of land along the Fox

River from Green Bay to Winnebago Lake, 200,000 acres in all. Well aware that this cession involved lands on which the New York Indians intended to settle, the commissioners and the Menominees agreed that the boundaries of the cession might be altered by the president if he thought it interfered "with any just claims of the New York Indians." The final treaty authorized the president "to establish such boundaries" between the Menominees and the New York Indians "as he may consider equitable and just."[41] Thus nobody viewed the Butte des Morts treaty as a definitive solution to the conflict between the New York Indians and their new neighbors. The Ogden Company directors, for instance, told Secretary of War Barbour in October 1827 that the New York Indians wanted permission to lay their complaint before the president and "to send a delegation of some of their leading chiefs to the seat of government." The Ogden Company saw the Butte des Morts treaty as a threat to their efforts to remove the Indians from New York. Of course Cass and McKenney approved of the removal of the New York Indians to Wisconsin, but they feared that the enormous size of the tract claimed in 1821 and 1822 would lead the immigrant tribes to return to the hunt and abandon settled agriculture. They hoped for a compromise, one that ended the threat of violence and that provided the foundation for a future solution to the problem. Cass and McKenney hoped that somehow, Menominees, New York Indians, and white settlers could share the lands around Green Bay. But the steps they took served instead to suggest only that the New Yorkers would be forced, at some point, to relinquish lands that they believed they had obtained legally and legitimately a half decade before with the support of federal officials, a forced cession that might rob those inclined to go West of a secure new home to which they might remove.[42]

*   *   *

A quarter century later, Eleazer Williams told John Holloway Hanson about the Butte des Morts treaty. The passage of time and geographic distance only hardened his criticism of the commissioners' conduct. They pursued "their unjustifiable course by encouraging the idea that the New York Indians had committed a fraud upon the Menominees." The New York Indians viewed Butte des Morts "as a violation of their just rights," and Williams saw it as a grave personal insult. He rejected any claim that he had misled the Menominees and Winnebagos. Hanson listened closely. He looked over the papers Williams provided him, including copies of the speeches given at the council.

"Of all the transactions in the history of the United States," Hanson concluded with more sentiment than knowledge, "the treaty of Butte des Morts is the most dishonorable."[43]

Williams described his efforts to defeat the treaty. He told Hanson how he headed east to protest. Steamboats and canal boats became instruments of Indian opposition, allowing native peoples, with difficulty, to work against unjust treaties, accords, and policies. "The hopes of the Six Nations," Hanson wrote, "depended on the efforts of Mr. Williams." He told Hanson that he fell ill once again as he subjected himself to the rigors of travel, and that he undertook this work at considerable expense. Those who supported ratification of the treaty worked to prevent Williams from carrying out his duties. But, Hanson wrote, Williams would not be deterred.[44]

Williams did not tell Hanson how the Ogden Company, once again, underwrote his journey east. When Williams fell ill in New York City, he convalesced in the home of Thomas Ludlow Ogden. He shared with Ogden information he had received and rumors he had heard, and Ogden used this information in his pursuit of a general removal of the New York Indians. If Williams succeeded and found the "good fortune to interest" many senators and representatives "in behalf of the New York Indians," it seems impossible that the well-connected investors of the Ogden Company did not help open a few doors for him.[45]

Williams led Hanson to believe that he had single-handedly presented the petition of the New York Indians against the Butte des Morts treaty. But Williams already had returned to Wisconsin when Congress received the "Memorial of the New York Indians" in January 1829. The memorialists recited the history of their relocation to Green Bay. There, they said, they had "hoped to enjoy a safe retreat for ourselves and our children; and that, to remote generations, we and they should remain undisturbed in the possession of this distant country." They hoped to avoid a repeat of their history in New York, and they explained to the members of Congress that "if this treaty, to purchase our land from us without our consent, and against our wishes, should be" confirmed, "it will serve wholly to discourage the emigration of our people from the East."[46]

The Senate ratified the treaty a month later, and President Adams proclaimed it in the final days of his presidency with the proviso that it "shall not impair or effect any rights or claims which the New York Indians . . . have to the lands . . . mentioned in the same treaty." Butte des Morts accomplished little, in this sense, and the dispute between the Menominees and the immigrant tribes remained for the incoming administration of Andrew

Jackson to resolve. Despite the cloud that remained over the New York Indians' claim, however, small groups of New York Indians—Brothertowns, Stockbridges, and Oneidas, too—continued slowly their relocation to Wisconsin. However uncertain the situation at Green Bay, for them New York had grown intolerable.[47]

Even before the Butte des Morts treaty, the federal agent in New York, Jasper Parrish, reported a drop in population on the reservations in the state caused by removal west. When Andrew Jackson took office in March 1829, Parrish believed, only 84 Munsees and 50 Stockbridge Indians remained in the state. They wished to leave in the spring, "as soon as the navigation opens" on the lakes.[48] First Christian Party Oneidas, too, looked forward to leaving. In February 1829, a month before Jackson took the oath of office, Daniel Bread and five others signed a treaty ceding lands to the state in exchange for fifteen hundred dollars and a small annuity. He departed with 110 Oneidas that summer for Green Bay.[49]

Federal officials recognized that the dispute between the Menominees and the New York Indians slowed the pace of this migration. But the poverty of the prospective emigrants posed a barrier as well. Parrish believed that the Stockbridges would depart if the government provided them with funds to finance their removal. Daniel Bread and the men of the First Christian Party presented a memorial to the New York State legislature expressing their desire to move west as soon as possible. But as a "once flourishing but now poor tribe," they believed that "without the receipt of a fair price for the lands," they "would never be able to locate themselves in their chosen vicinity" at Green Bay. Playing music to the ears of state legislators, Bread said that the First Christian Party would willingly sell all of its lands if doing so financed their removal to Wisconsin. They wanted out of New York.[50]

And in the meantime, former members of the Second Christian Party who converted to Methodism and became known as the Orchard Party began selling their share of Oneida lands as well. By October 1830, federal agent Justus Ingersoll reported that 5,267 Indians lived in all of New York State, of whom 1,766 were Oneidas; three and a half years later, agent James Stryker informed Cass that 4,716 Indians remained in the state, 1,146 of them Oneidas or Brothertowns.[51]

In his discussions with Hanson, Williams said little about the process through which these New York Indians became pioneers. Or, if he did, Hanson did not find the stories sufficiently interesting to include in his account of the life of the Dauphin. After the initial round of negotiations, Williams played little role in the actual removal, and he found his connections to the immigrant community becoming few and his welcome wearing thin. And as Williams's influence declined, Daniel Bread rose in prominence among the Oneidas. Like Williams, Bread considered removal inevitable, and like Williams, he accommodated himself to the outsiders who clamored for Oneida land. No Oneida signed more removal and land cession treaties than did Daniel Bread between 1817 and 1830. But unlike Williams, Bread's membership in the community stood beyond question and, in Solomon Davis's view, Bread's "assiduity" and "his kindness to his people, and his unbending integrity" earned him the respect of his fellow Oneidas. Unlike Williams, an outsider in so many ways, Bread displayed the qualities Iroquois people valued in their leaders. He was one with them, and he showed it.[52]

Bread represented the Oneidas in their interactions with state, territorial, and federal officials. He protested against the damage done by alcohol vendors who ignored laws regulating Indian trade. And he worked to heal the long-standing divisions that removal, and Williams's brief tenure in his community, had widened. According to Bread's biographers, he was "a quick learner who operated in the hard-boiled, real world of nineteenth-century America with its harsh racial attitudes about Indians and their future." Bread understood that Oneida culture had changed, and that they had lost much through removal. But despite these significant changes, "the Oneidas rebuilt their nation under Chief Bread's aegis by taking cultural elements of the past and by modifying them to serve the Indians' needs."[53]

There can be no denying the significance of Bread's leadership to the Oneidas over the course of the five decades prior to the American Civil War. Describing him as "a founding father of his Iroquois nation" is not without merit. But it is important as well to note that many Iroquois, who also "operated in the hard-boiled, real world of nineteenth century America," objected to any suggestion that they leave their homes in New York. The Onondagas clung to their dwindling homeland south of Syracuse, for instance, and clearly intended to remain there. The Senecas sold lands in 1823 and 1826, but they resolved thereafter to hang on to what remained.[54] And not all the Oneidas left their homelands for Green Bay. In this context, one historian's pragmatist becomes another historian's opportunist or failure, betraying those who hoped to resist the enormous pressure that they remove; and the sales of parcels of Oneida land to finance Oneida removal that Bread signed unquestionably tilted the odds sharply against those Indians who wished to remain behind.[55]

Bread represented the Oneidas, and because he so commonly interacted with outsiders, like Williams he appears frequently in the documentary record.

But caution is merited. Focus on leaders, at the expense of the communities which they led, is a trap that can ensnare any historian. The immigrant Oneidas quickly cleared and placed under cultivation "two hundred and thirty seven acres of land," and erected on those lands "thirty-three small log dwelling houses." Ordinary Oneidas worked these lands, built their houses, constructed a saw and grist mill, and successfully reordered their lives to enable them to survive in their new homeland. Focusing on leaders too closely can cause one to miss the small triumphs and the tenacity of the New York Indian pioneers.[56]

Williams played little direct role in this process. He continued to engage himself in at least some religious work. In the fall of 1828, he helped Bishop Hobart consecrate the newly constructed St. Paul's Church in Detroit. Upon returning to Green Bay several weeks later, Williams claimed that he officiated "(altho in imperfect health) every Sunday excepting one . . . to devout and orderly congregations." Though the Christian Indians, he wrote, "appear to be more animated, strengthened, & encouraged in the things of God and religion," a lack of resources and illness that left him "unable to perform the Divine Service either to the white congregation or Indians" meant that much of the heavy lifting was done by others. He probably preached at Holy Apostles, the Hobart church where the Oneidas worshipped. He may have preached at Christ Church, established in Green Bay. But Williams had nothing to do with the mission school established for the Menominees and Winnebagos by the Reverend Richard Fish Cadle. He moved upriver to Little Kakalin to be closer to the Oneidas, he wrote much later, but his connections to the community remained remote. According to one observer, Williams had "been in the habit of occasionally appearing on the scene and gathering a small congregation," though most of the time, "the community was destitute of regular spiritual instruction." Another noted that when Williams "happens to be in the country, which is very seldom," he spent most of his time at Green Bay and rented out the house at Little Kakalin.[57]

But Williams still possessed influence with those non-Indians who pushed for removal, and these men found an ally in Andrew Jackson, who won the election of 1828 with broad popular support. Jackson came into office determined to revolutionize the conduct of the republic's Indian policy, and his administration would resolve the crisis over the New York claims. Much of the national debate Jackson's plan provoked focused on the troubled relationship between the state of Georgia and the Cherokees, a testament both to the fierceness with which Georgians wanted to expel their Indian neighbors and the sophistication of the Cherokee political campaign of resistance, but his policies applied broadly to native people throughout the United States.[58]

In his first Annual Message to Congress in December 1829, Jackson said that the Indians should leave their homes in the East. This immigration should be voluntary, he wrote, "for it would be as cruel as unjust to compel the aborigines to abandon the graves of their fathers, and seek a home in a distant land." Nonetheless, Jackson said that the Indians "should be distinctly informed that if they remain within the limits of the States, they must be subject to their laws." It is in this sense that Jackson's Indian policy differed from that of his predecessors. Historians long have debated the nature of the limited "Democracy" that accompanied Jackson's rise to power. Historians have described the Jacksonian movement as one drawn from urban workingmen, Western interests, or Southern slaveholders. It was, in a sense, all of these things, but it was also a movement that native peoples had feared from the beginning. With Jackson's ascendancy, frontier federalism came to the fore, a variant of states' rights ideology opposed to the constitutional logic that had supported earlier laws like the federal Trade and Intercourse acts and that rested on the notion that Indians must yield in all things to the people of the states in which they lived.[59]

In February 1830, Jackson's supporters introduced the Indian Removal Bill in Congress. Opponents of the legislation, concentrated in the northeast but not in New York, quickly seized the moral high ground. Driving the Indians across the Mississippi, they argued, violated treaties. Jackson's critics knew that the policy rested at its heart upon coercion: in Georgia, for instance, that state's imposition of its own criminal and civil jurisdiction over the Cherokees deprived them of access to the courts. Providing native peoples with no protection for their rights to person and property, the state thus compelled its Indian population to remove. The policy of removal, in the eyes of Jackson's opponents, was unjust, immoral, and a violation of the nation's principles.[60]

Congress passed the Indian Removal bill that summer by a narrow margin. The president's policies elated those interested in removing New York's Indians. Thomas L. Ogden, with great satisfaction, told McKenney that he had found an enthusiastic and informed ally in the president, even if McKenney himself was about to break with Jackson over the coercive elements of his removal policy. Jackson's critics, Ogden believed, "with more zeal than knowledge, seem to imagine that nothing more is necessary to reclaim Savages from a state of Ignorance and barbarism than to preach to them the doctrines of Christianity." Comments like these must have stung Williams. One wonders what Ogden thought of the catechist and lay reader who had assisted his efforts. Ogden piously proclaimed that only removal could save the Indians from extinction. Like Jackson, Ogden ignored the abundant and inconvenient evidence demonstrating the cultural changes eastern Indians already had made, and the capacity they had shown to adapt themselves to changing conditions. None of that really mattered. Any land in Indian hands, to Ogden and men like him, was too much land in Indian hands.[61]

Some thought that Williams could help settle affairs in Wisconsin and encourage the remaining New York Indians to remove. The pro-removal Oneida leader Cornelius Baird and the Seneca Jacob Jamieson both thought Williams might serve the government well as the federal agent or sub-agent at Green Bay. Lewis Cass, in 1828, agreed and told the leaders of the New York Indians that he would seek Williams's appointment.[62] A year and a half later, Cass recommended Williams to Jackson's secretary of war, John Eaton, for the post of interpreter or sub-agent at the Green Bay Agency. Williams, Cass told Eaton, "was an Episcopal Clergyman of very respectable standing, and partly descended from the Iroquois Indians." He fought bravely during the War of 1812, Cass continued, having "led a heavy column at the battle of Plattsburgh," and received wounds "the effects of which will probably continue during his life." Because Williams knew the immigrant Indians so well, Cass suggested, he could "render important services, to the government and the Indians."[63]

No opening existed at Green Bay, but Williams still engaged himself in the government's efforts to remove the Indians. The state of New York continued to purchase Indian lands, but relatively few Iroquois left the state. The situation in Wisconsin remained unsettled. All of those interested in the removal of the New York Indians recognized that something must be done. Commissioner of Indian Affairs McKenney told the Ogden Company that he believed that if the government could see to "the judicious fixing of the limits at Green Bay for the New York Indians," then "a few years only need transpire to rid New York of its Indian population." Secretary of War Eaton appointed commissioners to travel to Green Bay and try to reach an agreement, at last, on boundaries with the Menominees and the Winnebagos.

The New York Indians did not trust the commissioners, and worried that they might face dispossession once again. Eaton, indeed, told the commissioners to settle the question in a manner that produced harmony, pointing out that "tribes in a hunter state" like the Menominees and Winnebagos require large tracts of land, while "tribes whose condition is essentially agricultural" like the New York Indians require less land. He warned that "to transfer them from fixed and reasonable agricultural limits, to boundless forests," risked encouraging them to peel off what he thought must be a thin veneer of civility, and return again to the roaming and hunter state.[64]

The commissioners arrived in early August, 1830. They spent the next two weeks exploring the region, familiarizing themselves with the lay of the land. They hired A. G. Ellis to accompany them as a surveyor and a guide. Ellis made clear the purpose of these explorations in the report he wrote for the commissioners. The white population in and around Green Bay had grown rapidly, he observed. Some of the same pressures they faced in New York now confronted the emigrant Indians in Wisconsin. Noting the quality of the region's waterways, the richness of its fisheries, and the quality of its soil, Ellis looked forward to seeing a day when, "under the fostering hand of this enlightened government," he might see "a second Genesee Country," and "a Rochester springing up west of Lake Michigan."[65]

Eleazer Williams attended the council. He claimed to represent the St. Regis Mohawks, even though no Akwesasnes sent him and none of them as yet had relocated to Green Bay. Once again, Williams attended a treaty council with no obvious mandate to represent anyone. Yet the Oneida delegates, John Anthony, Henry Powlis, Cornelius Stevens, Neddy Archiquette, and Daniel Bread, tolerated his presence. The commissioners, too, who must have understood something of the increasingly tenuous links connecting Williams to the immigrant Indians, saw value in his presence. Williams, the Oneidas knew, opposed any settlement that threatened to damage significantly the New York Indians' prospects in the West: he had staked too much of his reputation on his ability to obtain a homeland for the Indians there. In defending the Oneidas' claims, he defended his own efforts. Federal officials recognized that Williams still might help them effect the complete removal of Indians from New York State. Though they worked at cross-purposes, then, both the Oneidas and the commissioners believed that Williams might help them achieve their objectives.[66]

Several days before the council formally opened, Williams hosted a meeting between the commissioners and the Oneida leaders. At Williams's house, Daniel Bread once again rehearsed the New York Indians' arguments. They asked that the commissioners hold the council outside of Green Bay, and prevent "none but the parties concerned . . . to witness the deliberations of the Council." Bread wanted to prevent intermeddling by interested whites. This the commissioners refused to do. But Bread laid out the New Yorkers' arguments, and told them that they would accept a reasonable resolution. They were willing to compromise. They were unwilling, they said, after eight years of uncertainty "to remain longer under such a cloud, to see our families and our people dejected under the doubtfulness of their prospects, their courage subdued, and their former confidence in the repeated and solemn

assurances, of protection, and patronage, from the government, almost anni-
hilated." But the commissioners could not help them. The War Department
sent them without the power to negotiate a new treaty.[67]

The new federal agent at Green Bay, Samuel Stambaugh, invited the
Indians to travel with him to Washington. All of them recognized his sympathy for the Menominees and Winnebagos. Williams believed, he wrote
later, that "the New York Indians found they were at issue with the government instead of the Menominees." As a result, they remained "very jealous
to all the movements of the government and its agents toward them," and
only after a lengthy debate did they agree to send a delegation to the nation's
capital. Fourteen Menominees, along with Charles Grignon, Albert Gallatin
Ellis, and Stambaugh, left Green Bay in November. Williams and his wife
accompanied them. They must have done so with heavy hearts. They had
buried their second child, Margaret Anne, not yet eighteen months old, on
6 November on Oneida land at Holy Apostles. Hers was the first baptism
and the first burial entered in the church's records. The Oneida delegation
departed shortly thereafter.[68]

Indeed, the Oneidas caught up with Stambaugh and the others in Detroit,
and they arrived together in Buffalo two weeks before Christmas. Williams and
Bread, along with the Stockbridge John W. Quinney, presented themselves as
civilized, and Calvin Colton, for one, could "see nothing in their persons, dress,
or manners, to distinguish them from the white citizens of the State, except
their complexion, and those particular features and expressions of countenance
which belong to the Indian character."[69] Williams, however, made no friends
among his fellow travelers on the journey eastward. A. G. Ellis, who already
thought little of him, complained that Williams too often played to the sympa-
thies of those whom they met on the journey. In Detroit, for instance, Williams
and Ellis dined with an Episcopalian woman. Williams told her that he was too
sick to eat; he had only warm water and dry toast for dinner. Upon returning to
the hotel, however, Ellis reported that Williams ate nearly two pounds of ham.
Another observer noted that Williams was "built very much like a hogshead,
largest in the middle and tapering a little bit both ways, and if you could have
seen him eat . . . you would have thought him about as hollow." Ellis concluded
that it was Williams's "chief effort never to *speak* or *act* a truth, but always a
falsehood." And once a liar, Ellis suggested, always a liar. If Williams could not
lie, Ellis continued, "he would scarcely talk at all: with him words were not used
to exhibit, but always to conceal the truth." Ellis hated Williams's act.[70]

Stambaugh complained about the exorbitant hotel and travel bills Williams, his wife, and the other New York delegates rang up. He did not want

the New York Indians around and viewed them as a nuisance. Stambaugh believed that the government should pay these bills, but he believed as well that Williams had lived extravagantly on federal dollars. Within four months, Williams in fact wrote to the Episcopal leadership asking them to "contribute something to his present relief." He was broke again. For some, Williams's claims that he had been laid low "by a lingering disease and so much enfeebled from a recent severe bilious attack as to be incapable of mental and physical exertion" could not have rung true.[71]

A liar, indeed, his critics believed, and certainly a man that the New York Indian delegates did not trust. But Williams was well known in policy circles, even if the peevish Stambaugh thought him a nuisance. Government officials knew Williams, or knew of him, and they possessed a greater familiarity with him than they did with Bread. There were few good guys in the story of Indian removal, but some of the bad were worse than others. Williams presented the New York Indians with liabilities but also benefits. Williams offered the New York Indians access that they may otherwise not have gained with the alacrity they did. So Williams signed the petition sent by the New York Indians to President Jackson, to secure title to at least a portion of the lands they felt entitled to in Wisconsin. Williams did so, once again, as a representative from St. Regis. They reminded the president that since 1820, the government, with Williams's assistance, had attempted to "relieve the State of New York of its entire Indian population, and to provide for the Six Nations and their confederates a home in the vicinity of Green Bay, which should belong to them and their posterity forever." The Menominees' complaints threatened these plans.[72]

Despite the petition, the Menominees, in February, entered into two agreements with the United States. Stambaugh and Secretary of War Eaton acted as the principal negotiators. The Menominees asserted in the first agreement that "they are under no obligation to recognize any claim of the New York Indians to any portion of their country," and that "they never sold nor received any value, for the land claimed by these tribes." Nonetheless, they agreed that a tract "may be set apart as a home to the several tribes of New York Indians, who may remove to, and settle upon the same, within three years of the date of this agreement." In an amendment signed a few days later, the Menominees and the United States agreed that, "if, within such reasonable time, as the President of the United States shall prescribe for that purpose, the New York Indians, shall refuse to accept the provisions made for their benefit, or having agreed, shall neglect or refuse to remove from New York, and settle on said lands, within the time prescribed for that purpose, that then, and in either of these events, the lands aforesaid shall be, and remain, the property of the United States." The United States had taken steps to encourage the Oneidas to move west. If they did not go under the superintendence of the United States, they could remain on their ancestral lands, but they would lose any claim to lands set aside for them in Wisconsin.[73]

The delegates continued to fight. Josiah Quinney, a Stockbridge, wrote a "Brief Exposition of the Claims of the New York Indians to Certain Lands at Green Bay, in the Michigan Territory" with Williams's assistance. Including copies of much of Williams's correspondence with War Department officials, Quinney wrote that "the gradual extension of white settlements throughout every part of the State of New York long since admonished the Indians remaining within the limits of that state of the necessity of providing for themselves a new place of abode, in which, under the protection of the General Government, the scattered remnants of their different tribes should be collected together, and secured from further encroachment and disturbance." They wanted freedom from the constant pressure, the aggressions of white settlers. They thought they had found it near Green Bay. Thus Quinney, Williams, and others saw the recently negotiated Menominee treaty as "subversive to the rights of the New York Indians, and inconsistent with the public faith."[74]

Williams recalled later that he had been visited while in Washington by members of Congress and that "there were strong feelings with many in our favor." If it was true, it did not matter. The president and Stambaugh had combined against their interests. The Menominee delegates and Stambaugh, it seemed, got what they wanted. "No people," Williams wrote, "can be placed in a more humiliating situation than the Deputies of the New York Indians, to be thus viewed, as having intruded themselves upon the Menominees and their pretended bargain or treaties with them were no better than fraud!!" With the approval of the 1831 Menominee treaties, the hopes of the Ogden Company to relocate the Indians seemed forlorn.[75]

At least until the Menominees returned home. Stambaugh and the delegates presented the terms of the 1831 agreements to the rest of the tribe. The size of the grant to the New York Indians remained too large. Much dissatisfaction remained. To the immigrant Indians, the 1831 treaties left them with a tract of land that was too small and of too little quality. Thomas Ogden and his fellow investors worried that the continued impasse in Wisconsin might prevent the Iroquois from leaving New York. They emphasized to Lewis Cass, now Jackson's secretary of war, the importance to the state and the United States that the Indians "should have a tract of Country at the west suitable to all their purposes," and "to which they may remove after disposing of their lands."[76]

Williams remained in the East. His wife spent the winter in Canandaigua, staying with Jasper Parrish. Their son boarded with a family in Nassau, a bit east of Albany. Williams visited the boy enough to learn that he missed his mother terribly. But Williams spent little of his time with his small family. He visited Oneida for a while, and lived in a hotel in Vernon, not far from the Oneidas' remaining lands, while he recovered from yet another bout of illness. He visited Episcopalians in New York City and elsewhere. He visited with Thomas L. Ogden, who encouraged him to continue his missionary work and his efforts to persuade the remaining Oneidas to leave the state. The church granted him a salary of $250 per year to continue his work. At the end of 1831 he reunited with Bread and other New York Indian delegates in Washington. George Porter, Cass's successor as territorial governor in Michigan, accompanied the delegation. And whatever misgivings Bread retained about Williams, he appears to have found his presence useful as they met with Cass, with members of the Senate, and with President Jackson.[77]

Federal officials would not increase the amount of land set aside for the New York Indians, but they did send Porter back to Wisconsin to try to persuade the Menominees to allow the Oneidas, Brothertowns, and Stockbridges more say over the location of the tracts they retained. Porter assembled the Indians in the fall of 1832 and Williams played a large role in the proceedings. He claimed to represent both the Tuscaroras and the St. Regis.

Porter opened the council by explaining to the Menominees, once again, the terms of the 1831 treaties, which the Senate had ratified, conditionally, several months before. The senators hoped to secure an adequate supply of land for the New York Indians which if they did not settle in three years would be thrown open to white settlers. If Porter could not persuade the Menominees to accept the terms of the 1831 agreement as conditionally ratified, Cass instructed him, he was to strike the best deal he could.[78]

The Menominees showed little interest in compromise. Grizzly Bear, the Menominee speaker, pointed out that they had allowed the New York Indians 500,000 acres in the treaties of 1831. But still, the New York Indians hunted on Menominee lands, cut down their timber, and acted in a fashion similar to the white frontiersmen who earlier had encroached on Oneida lands. The New York Indians, Grizzly Bear told Porter, "are hard to be satisfied," for they acted just like white people. They "are like Dogs," he continued, and "when we give them a piece they want more. They have no hearts and souls," and "they behave so badly that we hate them."[79]

Porter told Grizzly Bear that he would ask the New Yorkers not to hunt on Menominee land, or intrude onto their sugar lands, or cut down their trees. Clearly no resolution could be reached without the participation of the immigrant Indians. Porter approached them after his contentious meeting with Grizzly Bear. They would accept nothing less than what had been spelled out in the treaty. Porter found the sailing rough, until Williams involved himself closely in the discussions. On 27 October, he told Porter "that we are willing to make a sacrifice, for the sake of having the dispute settled." Williams must have felt the need to resist the loss of lands in Wisconsin. He believed in removal. He thought it in the Indians' best interest, and had staked his reputation to make it happen. He worked against all that jeopardized the program. He needed to compromise. The New York Indians understood this, too. Williams told Porter that he had been instructed by the New York Indians to accept 200,000 acres of better soil on the southern side of the Menominees' land in exchange for the 500,000 acres reserved for them in 1831. Both sides, exhausted, accepted the agreement. The contending parties, after "much labor and pains," signed the treaty on a Sunday afternoon late in October. Williams, however, was not there. He left the council, he told Porter, to work on his Sunday sermon. He never signed the treaty that secured the New York Indians at last a home in the West.[80]

*   *   *

In the aftermath of the 1832 treaty, Eleazer Williams remained in Wisconsin. He had been away for much of the preceding two years. He tried to resume his clerical career. He preached where he could. Williams recalled much later that change had come to the Indians in the vicinity of Green Bay. "The younger part of the tribe," he wrote, "were much contaminated with the vices of their white neighbors." He called for a revival. He exhorted "the people to refrain from their evil ways." His private counsel, and his public preaching, he confessed, bore little fruit. He blamed the younger generation for its spiritual malaise, and he accused his critics of undermining his good work.[81]

Daniel Bread and Solomon Davis, who had joined the relocation to Wisconsin in 1830, resumed their long campaign to destroy Williams's ministry. This is what Williams told anyone who would listen. He claimed he had attempted to discipline Bread for his conduct. Williams was indirect about what Bread had done, but he hinted that it involved behavior "too delicate in its nature to be mentioned here." Williams attempted to keep Bread and a number of others "from the communion table, as . . . open and notorious evil livers," a decision quite likely that explains the animus that developed toward him.[82]

Williams still had some credibility left. He was not entirely without friends. In May 1832, the Episcopal diocese of New York authorized him as an agent "to solicit funds, with the concurrence and approbation of the Respective Rectors or Ministers of the Parishes through which he may pass, to aid in sustaining a mission among the Oneida Indians at Green Bay." A handful of Indians from the "Oneida, Mohecownnuck, or Stockbridge & Munsee, St. Regis, and Tuscarora tribes," at nearly the same time, deeded to him and his wife the lands they lived upon at Little Kakalin. Williams well understood that under American law this cession meant nothing—owing to the 1823 Supreme Court decision in *Johnson v. McIntosh*, native people could not transfer title of land to individuals because they possessed a mere right of occupancy, subordinate and inferior to the rights of preemption held, in this instance, by the United States—and he continued to seek federal recognition of his ownership of the lands he claimed his wife brought into the marriage.[83]

But more and more, people in Green Bay, Indian and white, thought of Williams as "a fat, lazy, good for nothing Indian" whose words counted for little. Bread signed as many deeds as any other Oneida, but this was not a cardinal sin among the emigrant Indians, and Bread had done much of the heavy work in organizing Oneida removal and helping the community reestablish itself in the West. He had been there during a tough period, and he maintained ties to the community that Williams never possessed. Solomon Davis was hardly a paragon of virtue. In New York, he encouraged impoverished Oneidas to beg passengers aboard passing stagecoaches for whatever they could spare. A tenacious backbiter and frontier Fagan always ready to accuse Williams of misconduct but never willing to confront Williams directly, Davis was nonetheless present in the community and willing to stick around. Bread helped lead the community and conduct its relations with outsiders. Davis tended to its spiritual concerns, in New York and, now, in Wisconsin. The Rev. Richard Fish Cadle opened a school in 1829, and even if he later stood accused of beating the children in his care, he was part of a trio of men who could speak of affairs in the West now with more authority than Williams.[84]

The story Williams told Hanson about attempting to discipline Bread was a lie. Williams, quite simply, no longer had support in the community adequate to bring a complaint of this sort even if he wanted to. The fact is that most Oneidas had grown tired of Williams. Those who supported him—if, indeed, any did—chose not to speak in his behalf.[85] Bread accused Williams of pursuing his own financial interests more than the spiritual good of the Oneidas. He never preached more than six times in a given year at Holy Apostles or Christ Church, Bread charged, and was "more agreeable to receive his salary than to render service." What Williams dismissed as "electioneering and intrigues" by his opponents, the Oneidas saw as an attempt to rid their community of an ineffective and inattentive spiritual leader who "had failed in all his promises for long years, and how it was owing to his want of good faith, his fraud and deceit, that they were in the wilderness, utterly abandoned, without schools, churches, or religious privileges of any kind."[86]

Charges of this sort had arisen before, but in 1832 and 1833 Williams confronted them without his greatest supporter. John Henry Hobart had died in September 1830. His successor as bishop of New York, Benjamin Onderdonk, knew Williams but was also more willing than Hobart to listen to Williams's critics. Onderdonk learned that Williams, according to Episcopal missionary Jackson Kemper, did not officiate, was held by his neighbors "in no estimation," was "greatly in debt," and "has had two executions of him lately when some of his cattle were seized and sold." In response to the reports he had received from the Oneidas, from Davis, from Cadle and Kemper, Onderdonk decided to recall Williams.[87]

Williams told Hanson he might have fought these charges. He suggested that "there were loud whispers heard here and there," and that many in the community thought Onderdonk had done him an injustice, and that an audience still hungered for his performance. Instead of fighting back, he decided in September 1833 to deliver a farewell sermon. He gave a copy of the text to Hanson, who included an excerpt in his book. "If you have discerned anything of the Savior in me," Williams told his audience, "imitate it." If they saw anything in Williams "contrary to the Spirit of the Gospel," they should reject it. Williams told them that he had acted on the "purest motives." He cared for them and would continue to care for them.[88]

With his clerical career in ruins, Williams wrote a long letter to the "Trustees" of the Ogden Land Company. A month earlier, he had learned that Ogden and his associates "did not feel themselves authorized to incur any further expenditures until some new advance shall be made towards the removal of our Indians." The company felt that Williams had done about all that he could for them, and they no longer were willing to throw money at the man they had hoped might help them relocate the New York Indians.

Figure 3. Painting of Eleazer Williams by George Catlin, ca. 1833.

Courtesy of the Wisconsin Historical Society, Madison.

Many of the Oneidas had moved west, but the rest, and especially the Senecas, remained committed to their New York homelands. Where Williams led, the Ogden Company's leaders now believed, few Iroquois followed.[89]

Williams was furious. He had worked with the Ogden Company for a decade and a half, always under the promise of "a liberal and handsome compensation." His efforts saved the company thousands of dollars. In the company's service, Williams continued, he "left the pleasant valleys of Oneida for the western wilderness and have suffered much in health and reputation and have expended all the little property I had to promote their interest." He had

Oct. 26, 1927
View of Fox River, taken from Eleazer Williams's home.

Figure 4. Fox River, as viewed from the home of Eleazer Williams in 1927.

Courtesy of the Wisconsin Historical Society, Madison.

done important work, and he told the Ogden trustees that he would assist them no further:

> unless I immediately receive twelve hundred dollars and be secured
> with a certain sum which will be stated to you hereafter. I have
> already suffered so much in relying upon the promises of the Com-
> pany and their reluctance, hitherto, to advance me the little sums
> I have demanded, of them all which have impelled me to take the
> course I have now stated. The grounds I have taken, I shall maintain
> it fearlessly. I know too well the task they have now in hand for me to
> have hand in it and run the risk any longer for compensation merely
> upon fair promises.[90]

None of the investors answered. The Ogden trustees knew that Williams's influence had declined, and they could see that too many Indians remained in New York for their liking. Williams's threat carried no weight because they no longer needed his assistance.

So he left. He retired to his farm on the Fox River. He went in peace and in solitude, he told Hanson, in hopes that he might recover, at long last, his broken health, "worn down by fatigue, anxiety and sorrow." He had few resources and numerous small debts. He spent Christmas 1833 at the farm, and he remained in Wisconsin until autumn 1834. He may have leased some of his land to tenants, but he felt the need to find something more secure. He was neither a farmer nor a landlord by temperament or experience. He left Wisconsin, and his wife and his child, on 31 October 1834. He headed back to New York. He would return to Wisconsin only for the shortest of visits, and had little more to do with his small family.[91]

The Life of a Misanthrope

Eleazer Williams "languished for want of support" during the years he served as a missionary, and now found himself "indigent." He sent a bill to Daniel Bread for his services to the Oneidas. It was an act of pique, and a reflection of his powerlessness to undo the changes that had come to his life. Though the Oneidas of the First Christian Party remained "exceedingly anxious that our children should be educated as white children are," they told their federal agent George Boyd that they could not "bear the expense of paying a teacher" and that they would not consider Williams for that job any longer even if they could. Williams found himself in a difficult spot. How could it have been otherwise? His talent lay in ministering to native peoples. He worked well with white policy-makers and possessed the necessary skills—facility in English and familiarity with the language of law, treaty, and land that ruled intercultural diplomacy—that enabled him to serve as a broker between Indians and those who sought their land and their souls. Williams was a professional Indian, a role that required that he keep both native people and white patrons happy. A man-in-between, in this sense, he appealed to audiences that expected different things, and whose interests inevitably clashed. Williams tried to keep his hand in the game. He continued to do the only job he knew. Williams watched the Oneidas, and he watched their neighbors. He watched the conduct of Indian affairs in Wisconsin, New York, and Washington. For the space of almost half a decade, few sought out his assistance or advice. They simply did not see him as worthy of their trust or their continued investment. The native people with whom he worked distrusted him. As for white leaders in church and state, despite Williams's efforts to conform to their expectations of what an Indian was and what one might become, they cast him aside when he lost the certain cachet that came with being useful to those in power. It's an old story, that of the use and abuse of Indians in American history.[1]

Williams left Wisconsin in the fall of 1834. He made his way slowly eastward toward Albany, and from there he planned to head toward St. Regis. He took his time. He spent three days "in an obscure Dutch tavern" a bit east of Schenectady, one observer recalled, where he did nothing but "smoke his pipe and eat hard-boiled eggs."[2] In Albany, late in November, he "was suddenly attacked with dizziness and pain in the head, which compelled me to put an end to my journey for the present." He rested, but soon carried on. He arrived at St. Regis at the end of the first week in December.[3]

This began a span of years during which Williams lived the "life of a misanthrope," A. G. Ellis wrote, "spending but little of his time at Green Bay, but mostly traveling up and down the lakes, and between Buffalo and the Atlantic states and cities." He did so on small stipends, on borrowed money, and on the hope of future gains. He lived a life of disarticulation, now divorced from any community, an acquaintance of many but a friend of few. He left his wife and adolescent son behind, after making poor decisions about the leasing of their lands that caused the family hardship. His autobiographical writings ceased. These may have been years for Williams when, it seemed, nothing of significance happened.[4]

*   *   *

New York State's agent to the Mohawks at St. Regis listed Williams as a resident and member of the community as early as 1832. That year, for the first and last time, Williams received a share of the St. Regis annuity.[5] The roots he sank there remained shallow, and he found himself on the margins of a community that must have seemed even more remote than what he knew in the vicinity of bustling Green Bay. Just over three hundred Mohawks lived on the American side of the St. Regis Reservation. On occasion, the leaders of this small community placed their confidence in Williams, as they had in his father, to represent them on various matters before the state government in Albany. He must have been able to talk himself into a job, and convince the Akwesasnes that whatever they had heard, his experience in dealing with state policy-makers offered certain advantages. It is difficult beyond this to reconstruct his activities in any detail. What is clear is that Williams hoped to remain near the heart of American Indian policy.[6]

The continuing efforts of the Ogden Land Company and their allies in the national government provided him with the opportunity. These well-connected company men believed that pressure on the Wisconsin lands of the immigrant Indians would increase, just as it earlier had done in New York. This was the problem with the removal policy. Aside from its moral shortcomings (and these were considerable), it could never provide a complete solution to the challenge of frontier pressure on Indian lands. Enough Iroquois expressed publically an interest in removal to convince easily persuaded federal authorities that widespread support for the policy existed. "A considerable revolution," the commissioner of Indian affairs learned in 1835, was taking place "in the minds of the leading chiefs" of the Senecas. Thompson Harris, a Seneca, saw removal as a "mode of remedy of the evil which has hitherto counteracted the progress of civilization among the Indians."[7] Williams asked Cass, now Andrew Jackson's secretary of war, whether the New York Indians would be compelled "to surrender the governance of the Green Bay lands after having labored for a series of years and had expended thousands and thousands of dollars to obtain the same?" Cass had already told Vice President Martin Van Buren that "the time will soon come, when circumstances will require them to remove, and it appears to me that it will be much better to purchase out their title now, if they are disposed to sell, and transfer them to the country west of the Mississippi." The Akwesasnes, Williams told Cass, with some reluctance are "disposed to negotiate with the Government for the surrender of their lands at Green Bay," probably because so few had actually gone there. Citing Iroquois statements in favor of removal, and their own assumptions about their fate if native peoples remained in their homelands, spokesmen for the Ogden Company called upon the United States to offer the Iroquois lands in the Indian Territory in exchange for their lands in New York and Wisconsin. Andrew Jackson, always entirely supportive of plans to advance removal, appointed the Dutch Reformed minister John Schermerhorn to negotiate the deal.[8]

Schermerhorn had proved himself a capable negotiator of Indian treaties, at least from the perspective of those who wanted the Indians gone. In 1835, he negotiated the treaty that three years later would send the Cherokees westward along their "Trail of Tears." In preparing for his council with the New York Indians, Schermerhorn consulted with Ogden Company officials and with New York's governor William Marcy. Schermerhorn first intended to visit the Oneidas at Duck Creek. Secretary of War Cass authorized Schermerhorn to make two proposals to the Wisconsin Iroquois, which differed little in their effect. The Indians could sell their Wisconsin lands to the United States, and use the proceeds from that sale to pay for their own removal and sub-sistence expenses, or they could exchange their Green Bay lands for an equal quantity of lands west of the Mississippi, with the United States covering the expense of their removal and providing them with one year's subsistence.[9]

Williams returned to Wisconsin for the council Schermerhorn convened at Duck Creek. Determined to reinsert himself into the conduct of American Indian policy, Williams carried with him a document signed by "the chiefs, Trustees, and principal men of the St. Regis Indians in the State of New York," nominating and appointing "Eleazer Williams, alias Onewanengiyake our Attorney." Williams managed to convince Schermerhorn, who was new to Indian affairs in the north, that he still possessed considerable influence. If he opposed the treaty, Williams told the commissioner, then no treaty could be made. But Schermerhorn was in luck. Williams told him that he would provide assistance, and "show his disinterestedness even at the risk of his interest; and endeavor to effect the objects of the Government because he believed it was for the best interest of the Indians to remove to the Indian Territory." This assistance, Williams made clear, came with a price. He men-tioned to Schermerhorn the deed he and his wife had obtained to their lands in Wisconsin. Williams told Schermerhorn that "he wished the same secured to him in the treaty." Title recognized by the United States stood superior to any title one might obtain from Indians, and with that title, Williams could sell the land, raise some money, and clear his debts. Schermerhorn would do what he could. He told Williams that he and his superiors understood well all that he had done for the Indians in "obtaining and settling this country, which but for him never would have been settled by them."[10]

The council opened on 12 September 1836. Schermerhorn told the Indians that the pressure upon their lands would continue. White settlers, he said, would not rest. All of history taught "that the Indians always had been obliged to retire under such circumstances before the tide of civiliza-tion pressing upon them." The Indians need not worry, and they had nothing to fear. Schermerhorn, like so many officials involved in the formation and conduct of American Indian Policy before and during the Jacksonian era, saw dispossession as justice. He could help them. The Indians could sell their lands on "very advantageous terms," or they could wait "until, by the force of circumstances, which neither they nor the government could control, they were compelled to change their situation."[11]

Daniel Bread spoke for the Oneidas, and served as the principal negotia-tor for the Indians. They could not have missed Schermerhorn's threat. Leave now or be overrun by aggressive settlers the government would not restrain.

This was not news to the Iroquois. They had heard this, and seen this, before. Still, Bread recited for Schermerhorn the history of the Oneidas' westward movement. He explained to him the labors they had undertaken in making a new home for themselves at Green Bay. Iroquois pioneers, they had done all that federal officials had asked of them, assisting them in winning American Independence, transforming elements of their culture, and leaving their homelands in New York. They did not want to sell their lands in Wisconsin and they did not want to relocate again. But Bread, reflecting the exasperation and frustration of a leader with few good options, "saw how it was, all the Indians must go west, west, Mississippi, Mississippi—he hated the word Mississippi—he was sick of it." He felt that there was little that he could do. Bread knew that "the U. States wished their lands [and] they must go for they were in the power of the Government—they were weak and could not risk their power and policy." Bread exposed the lies at the center of the government program of voluntary removal.[12]

Bread explained the New York Indians' objection to an exchange of lands, but he signed the treaty Schermerhorn presented him on 16 September. So did several other Oneidas and Iroquois from other communities gathered at Duck Creek. Solomon Davis and A. G. Ellis signed as witnesses. Like Bread, Williams signed the treaty, and he appears to have done so without reservation.[13] Still, Schermerhorn included nothing in the document about Williams's deed because, he explained, he had not been authorized by the Department of War to do so. But he did advocate for Williams, recommend that the commissioner of Indian Affairs allow Williams's claim and confirm his deed. Schermerhorn pointed out that Williams "rendered very essential aid in my whole negotiations." Schermerhorn claimed he could not have done it without Williams. Indeed, Schermerhorn told C. A. Harris later that "let us say & think of Williams what we please, had it not been for him the New York Indians would never have had the Green Bay Country nor settled there & he is justly entitled to a very liberal consideration for the services he has rendered the Indians & the government of the United States." Williams performed admirably.[14]

After extracting a most reluctant agreement from the New York Indians in Wisconsin, Schermerhorn moved on to Buffalo Creek to obtain the approval of Iroquois remaining in New York. Once again, Schermerhorn proposed to them "a permanent home south west of the Missouri River." Williams attended the council at Buffalo Creek, but played no role in the negotiations. The Senecas and the other members of the Six Nations gathered there made clear that they had no interest in removal. Schermerhorn blamed the opposition on Quaker missionaries who, he believed, stood firmly against any policy that threatened their work among the tribe. The Senecas refused to sign the Duck Creek treaty.[15]

Defeated in New York, Schermerhorn moved on to Washington, where he arrived in December 1836. He tried to persuade the Senate's Indian Affairs Committee to approve the agreement despite the Senecas' refusal to sign, but president-elect Martin Van Buren's Whig opponents postponed any consideration of the treaty. Williams now recognized that Schermerhorn simply lacked the power to promote his interests, so he joined those who opposed the Duck Creek agreement. Schermerhorn understood why. Williams did so, Schermerhorn pointed out to the Commissioner of Indian Affairs, specifically "because no reservation was made in the treaty for the lands conveyed to him by the Indians at Green Bay some years since." The new Van Buren administration, like its predecessor, firmly supported removal. The Democrats in New York were weakest in the western part of the state, a region swept by religious revivals and a variety of moral reform movements that Democrats traditionally had opposed. By appealing to western New Yorkers who favored Indian Removal and the opening of native lands to white settlement, Democrats hoped to make inroads into what many considered a Whig stronghold.[16] The failure in 1836 seems to have produced few hard feelings. The new president reappointed Schermerhorn to try again in 1837, and Schermerhorn still believed that removal might be more easily effected with Williams's cooperation than without.[17]

Yet any objective observer could see that the Indians opposed removal. As early as November 1832, more than thirty Seneca chiefs, along with several Oneidas, assembled "at the council house at Buffalo Creek." Facing enormous pressure from the Ogden Company to leave the state, the chiefs publicly proclaimed that they would never sell their lands "so long as we continue to be Chiefs of this nation," and that "so long as our nation continues to exist we will remain on these Reservations in the State of New York." One year later, a council at Buffalo Creek declared that it was "the decided Resolution of the Senecas, Oneidas, and Onondagas, viz., 'to part with no more of our Territory.' We hope," they continued, that "our White Brothers will not feel dissatisfied with us for this determination and looking back upon the vast patrimony which was once our fathers."[18] The Onondagas living at Buffalo Creek, in 1837, appealed to President Van Buren, asking him not to remove them. "Our Great Father," they said, "many years ago requested us to embrace civilized life, cultivate our lands, and become industrious, build houses to live in and barns to put our grain in." They had done so, and "if we leave our home here and go

west we must in some measure lose our industrious habits and become lazy—
and lose all we hold dear on earth." They asked the president to honor the
terms negotiated years before at Canandaigua, and to leave them alone in the
free use and enjoyment of their lands. One week later, a group of Oneidas told
Van Buren that they had listened to Schermerhorn's proposals but "decided in
council to remain on our Lands in the State of New York."[19]

This was part of how removal worked. Some Indians reluctantly signed
relocation treaties. The leaders of other tribes refused, so federal officials
looked for cracks in the armor, and found other Indians, who might sign the
treaty. The policy was voluntary only in the limited sense that government
officials usually found someone who could be bribed or coerced or otherwise persuaded to sign. It happened like this among the Southeastern tribes,
whose stories dominate popular understandings of the removal policy. But it
also occurred in New York state. The Ogden Company and its allies focused
upon the Senecas when it renewed its efforts to secure Iroquois removal.
Company officials quietly signed agreements with Heman B. Potter, Orlando
Allen, Henry P. Wilcox, and the federal sub-agent James Stryker, "to use
their best endeavors and exertions to dispose and induce the said Indians to
adopt and pursue the advice and recommendations of the Government." The
company no longer relied on influential Indians like Williams. Stryker and
Potter each could count on receiving the enormous sum of $10,000 if they
succeeded in causing 40,000 acres of Seneca land to change hands. The "contractors," as the Company called them, all of whom had close ties to the state
Democratic machine, were authorized as well to draw on Ogden Company
resources to bribe Indian leaders.[20]

In the meantime, Schermerhorn had become a problem. New York
Indians denounced him, as did the Cherokees, who continued to campaign
against what they viewed as a corrupt and fraudulent treaty. Senators and
congressmen in the northeast heard these complaints, and began asking
questions about Schermerhorn's conduct. Best to cut him loose. In the fall
of 1837, Van Buren and Commissioner of Indian Affairs Corey A. Harris
revoked Schermerhorn's commission and replaced him with Ransom H. Gillet, a former New York congressman and a law partner of New York Democratic senator (and Van Buren ally) Silas Wright. Schermerhorn decided to
stick around anyway and assist Gillet.[21]

Despite his disappointment with the outcome of the Duck Creek proceedings, Williams once again offered his assistance. On federal dollars, he
traveled to Green Bay, in Schermerhorn's words, "to do what he could to prepare the minds of the Indians of the Six Nations there to send a delegation" to

the planned council at Buffalo Creek. Williams assured Schermerhorn that he would attend the council as a delegate from the St. Regis. When he returned to Buffalo in the fall of 1837, he assured Stryker that most of the Indians with whom he spoke favored emigration, and that those who stood opposed, like Daniel Bread, "are in the minority whatever they may affirm." Williams knew this was not true. He denigrated and discredited those who disagreed with him, and emphasized his own ability to broker an important deal with Indian tribes. But he could only make a living in this line of work now by being dishonest, by portraying himself as a man who spoke with authority when in reality he spoke only for himself. Everyone who dealt with Williams, in Wisconsin, New York, or elsewhere, had to ask themselves if they could believe the things he said and the tales that he told. He promised much: that he understood better than his detractors what was in the Indians' best interest; that despite the protests of a few vocal malcontents and their Quaker allies, most of the Indians remaining in New York and Wisconsin wanted to exchange their lands. Like the "government chiefs" of an earlier generation, Williams played the role of a broker, mediating relations between the state and the federal government and its allies and a number of native communities. But in 1838 Williams represented only himself, and the notion that he represented anyone else was a deliberately constructed falsehood. The speculators and the land barons and the government men who wanted to claim that they had rid their states of its Indian inhabitants at least in part believed Williams. They relied upon him for information, for a glimmer of good news to counter the numerous petitions, protests, and pleas that flooded state and federal offices from Iroquois people and their allies opposed to removal. These protests had little effect on Williams, who offered his assistance to the United States and its Ogden Company partners in negotiating one of the most demonstrably corrupt Indian treaties in United States history.[22]

If the Senecas removed, both federal officials and Ogden Company investors hoped, the rest of the New York Indians soon would follow. For it was the Senecas, Stryker reported, who "are the owners of all the valuable lands in the state held by the New York Indians with the exception of tracts at Oneida, St. Regis, and Tuscarora," and "they comprise in number more than half the New York Indians, and their removal will dispose of the question as to all the others." The company and its allies brooked no opposition. Schermerhorn, for instance, threatened to prosecute white missionaries like Asher Wright who, in his view, violated the Trade and Intercourse Act of 1834, which made it a crime for any person to "send any talk, speech, message, or letter to any Indian nation, tribe, chief, or individual, with an intent to produce a contravention or infraction of any treaty or other law of the United States, or to disturb the peace or tranquility of the United States." Congress intended through this provision to prohibit white interlopers from stirring up hostility among the Indians. Schermerhorn knew better, but for him Indian removal was an end that justified nearly any means. The missionary Wright had hoped to protect the Indians' interests and in so doing, he ran afoul of Schermerhorn, who contorted the language of a law designed to protect Indians and directed it toward their dispossession and relocation.[23]

Schermerhorn and the contractors intimidated the white opponents of Indian removal. But how to obtain the assent of the Senecas to a removal treaty when they and their longhouse kin had expressed clearly their disinterest in relocation? Though Gillet denied any wrongdoing, as did Schermerhorn, their deeds are well documented in an enormous stack of depositions and other documents collected by Quakers who saw themselves as guardians of the Senecas' interests. Gillet, according to these documents, bribed Indians to persuade their brethren to accept relocation in the west.[24] He and his associates met with Senecas in a tavern, the better to "facilitate" the negotiations with gifts of alcohol. They used threats of violence, too. Schermerhorn told the Seneca chiefs, they claimed, that "if we do not consent to emigrate to the West, that measures will be taken by the General and State Governments by which we shall be made to remove." When Gillet met with Seneca chief John Tate, "a company of armed soldiers from the City of Buffalo came up and surrounded the Council House," and reportedly "carried off" a number of opponents of removal.[25] Simple fraud, though, was much easier. The Senate, aware of questions about the integrity of the treaty process, urged Gillet to obtain evidence that the Indians actually understood and approved of the treaty. Soon thereafter, a number of Seneca chiefs who had opposed any removal found that they had signed statements indicating that they understood and approved of the Buffalo Creek Treaty. According to the Seneca chiefs in question, the "agents of the Ogden Land Company," they said, "have taken private Indians to the Commissioners pretending to him that they were chiefs and have hired them to misname themselves by adopting the names of chiefs in the opposition and have so obtained many [of the] names now affixed" to the treaty. In other words, they found imposters. Gillet, the chiefs added, was "as ready to deceive as any agents of the Company."[26]

Through these means, the commissioner and the contractors obtained enough signatures to produce the Buffalo Creek treaty. Under its terms, the New York Indians ceded to the United States all their claims to land in Wisconsin and New York. The Ogden Company obtained the prize it had sought for so long, all of the Senecas' remaining lands. In exchange for this cession, the United States set aside a large tract of land in the Indian Territory as a "future home" for the "Senecas, Onondagas, Cayugas, Tuscaroras, Oneidas, St. Regis, Stockbridges, Munsees, and Brothertowns residing in the state of New York," as well as those who earlier had relocated to Wisconsin. If they did not leave their homes for these lands within "five years, or such other time as the President may, from time to time, appoint, they shall forfeit all interest in the lands so set apart."[27]

If any of this interested Eleazer Williams, he did not say so. His writings suggest that he wanted one thing, and he obtained it in the ninth article of the Buffalo Creek Treaty. The federal commissioners agreed that title to the Wisconsin lands would be made out to Williams and his wife, which "he is to hold in fee simple, by patent from the President, with full power and authority to sell the same." As Williams made clear to John Holloway Hanson, this tract of 4,800 acres had belonged to his wife, and her family before her, for generations. It was not a bribe to obtain his support. In addition to agreeing to confirm Williams's rights to his lands, the United States agreed to pay to the St. Regis at the time of their removal, or at some other point in time chosen by the president, "the sum of five thousand dollars, as remuneration for monies laid out by the said tribe, and for services rendered by their chiefs and agents in securing title to the Green Bay lands and in removing to the same." Williams felt entitled to the lion's share of these funds as well. When Gillet traveled to St. Regis to explain the Buffalo Creek treaty to the chiefs on the American side, they agreed to accept "one thousand dollars, part of the sum of five thousand dollars mentioned in the provisions for the St. Regis Indians," leaving the rest, presumably, for Williams. They must have done so reluctantly. They must have felt that the treaty, in a sense, presented them with a fait accompli, for they do not seem to have appointed Williams in this instance to represent them. Yet as "chief and agent" of the St. Regis Mohawks, he had no problem putting pen to paper to sign a fraudulent treaty. He did so because it offered him a way to solve his own considerable financial problems. He hoped to benefit once the Senate ratified and the president proclaimed the treaty. That proved more difficult than anyone had anticipated.[28]

* * *

If the federal government intended the Buffalo Creek treaty to secure the removal of the Indians from New York and Wisconsin, its commissioners and negotiators must have been disappointed. Word of the tactics employed by the Ogden Company and the U.S. commissioner arrived quickly in Washington, owing to the work of determined Seneca opponents of removal and reformers interested in the Seneca missions. As a result, President Van Buren moved cautiously with regard to the treaty. He wanted his party to gain votes in heavily Whig western New York, and he believed removal could help, but not if voters perceived the treaty as corrupt and fraudulent. Many Whigs had been critical of Andrew Jackson's aggressive push for Indian removal. A massive campaign by the Senecas and their Quaker allies ensured that political leaders in Washington received detailed information on the practices employed by Ransom Gillet and his gang.[29]

Eleazer Williams nonetheless did what little he could to speed the process along. He wrote to Van Buren in March 1838, and reminded him of the grant of lands included in the ninth article of the treaty. Williams told the president that if he and the Senate did not confirm his "reservation," he was to "receive in lieu thereof ten thousand dollars and have the pre-emption right to purchase the said lands at government price." Both Williams and Van Buren knew that the Buffalo Creek treaty said no such thing, and Williams quickly shifted the tone of his argument. Best to avoid telling tales that could easily be proven false. Rather than relying solely on a bald-faced lie told to the president of the United States, Williams appealed to Van Buren's sense of obligation, and here he stood on stronger ground. "I have a strong claim upon the government," he wrote, "for remuneration for services rendered." He explained to Van Buren that "it can be clearly shown that the General Government have, by my exertions, received more than two millions of acres from the Winnebagos, Menominees, and New York Indians."[30]

A few months later, Williams sent a "memorial" to the president. He presented himself now as "Chief and Agent of the St. Regis Tribe of Indians." He raised the issue of the five thousand dollars allocated to the Akwesasne leadership for the part they played in the relocation to Wisconsin. Williams stated that he and the commissioners long had understood that the "$1000 should be paid to the St. Regis Indians, and the remaining $4000 to your memorialist for services & monies expended by him."[31] Though the treaty said no such thing, both Gillet, grudgingly, and Schermerhorn, willingly, shared in this interpretation. Williams continually called for the ratification and proclamation of the treaty, and continually pestered those who he thought might influence the process. Never did he state that the treaty would benefit the Indians involved, though this he may have believed, or that removal was in their best interest. Treaty in hand, he wanted land and money. He asked Gillet, the commissioner, to see what he could do in Washington and "to have the good-ness to procure, in behalf of my wife (Mary Hobart Williams) and myself the patent of land reserved in the treaty."[32]

Williams kept on the move. He still entertained thoughts of returning to Wisconsin, for he entered into a contract to have a two-story house built there in November 1839. A look at the sparse diary kept by his wife, however, sug-gests he seldom visited home. On 9 September 1836, for instance, she noted that "Mr. Williams arrived from New York, after being absent two years, from home." Twelve days later he left again. The diary of Mary Hobart Williams is full of family business. She described how her son helped her work their land, sowing and harvesting oats. Her own family visited her often. Her father and mother visited. This she described in the diary. Williams returned in May 1837, she wrote, but in October he departed once again for New York. He would not return for another nine months.[33]

The community of immigrant New York Indians, which Eleazer Williams unquestionably helped found, developed without him. In 1838, the same year in which he signed the Buffalo Creek treaty, the Wisconsin Oneida popula-tion stood at 654. Two years later, the Methodist missionary Henry Coleman believed the population had reached a thousand. "Of these," Coleman wrote, "the larger portion attended the Episcopal mission."[34]

But not for long. The Methodist mission grew in membership. Coleman described the Sunday morning congregation. "The men," he wrote, "who had doffed their blankets and were clad in the garb of American citizens," sat on one side, with the women, "still in petticoats and blankets, to the other side." The mission complex consisted of a church and a schoolhouse, where "both boys and girls were taught the elements of education."[35] Had federal officials not looked so fervently toward their removal, they might have noticed that the Oneidas, whether Methodist or Episcopalian, had done much to adopt a settled life in the western Great Lakes. George Boyd called them "good farm-ers," and noted that under the direction of Solomon Davis, Williams's great rival, "their moral condition is improving rapidly." Boyd believed that they "in due time will become valuable citizens." A. G. Ellis, who had little good to say about anyone or anything, described the Oneidas as "an agricultural people, spending but a small share of their time in the chase." Like Boyd, he believed that if "they could be persuaded to become *temperate* and to learn the *English language*, they would soon be prepared to enter on the privileges and duties of citizenship."[36]

As the Wisconsin Oneidas built farms and fences, raised grains and live-stock, and sang Christian hymns in their churches, they redefined Iroquois identity in the West. Removal did not destroy Indian cultures, but it did force changes. Their language survived, as Ellis indicated. As anthropologist Jack Campisi asserted in his study of the Oneidas, they "brought with them to Wisconsin the complex of beliefs associated with individual health, societal well-being, and balance and equilibrium in the universe, and these continued to exert influences throughout the nineteenth century." In addition, Campisi continued, "Oneida herbalists administered to the sick. Dreamers were called upon to diagnose the specific cause of ailments and recommend an appropriate curing agent. Medicines were prepared to ward off witches, guarantee success in love, and assure victory in games such as lacrosse."[37]

Campisi, however, saw signs of declension as well. The Wisconsin Oneidas, he wrote, no longer recited the two great founding stories of the Haudenosaunee, those of the creation of this world on Turtle's back and of the founding of the Iroquois League, that clan matrons no longer condoled chiefs, and that clan relations became less important in the lives of individual Oneidas than the connections forged by religious affiliation.

But the Oneidas in Wisconsin unquestionably saw themselves as authentically Iroquois, the assertions of anthropologists who focused on cultural continuity notwithstanding. An 1838 treaty at Washington established for them a reduced reservation on the basis of one hundred acres for each member of the community. They had transformed this new land—the land they struggled to obtain a legal recognition of their right to settle upon—into a homeland by the middle decades of the nineteenth century. They defended their community. They demanded from the government the appointment of agents of quality and character to protect them from "cunning and evil disposed white men." When the officials in the Indian department considered appointing A. G. Ellis as their agent, for instance, the Oneida chiefs announced that they could have no confidence in a man they believed to be so dishonest, and that should he be appointed, "it will require a great deal of *rubbing* and *scouring* to keep the chain of friendship bright between you and us." The language of Iroquois diplomacy, quite obviously, survived. They complained when they believed that government officials had failed to pay their annuities on time. They complained of the huge numbers of white people encroaching on their lands. "Collisions and difficulties are frequently arising and are in fact of almost daily occurrence between the Oneidas and the whites."[38]

Eleazer Williams said nothing about these changes. He did not write to federal officials to boast of the Oneidas' progress, or to describe their devotion to Christianity, or to lodge protests or to protect their rights. The work of dreamers and herbalists and healers would have meant little to him, for he was not part of that world. He remained entirely absorbed in his drive to obtain what he believed had been promised him at Buffalo Creek. Ill health, in fits and starts, continued to afflict him.[39]

Despite his apparent weakness, Williams continued to clamor for four of the five thousand dollars pledged to the Akwesasne Mohawks and the title to his land. When he learned that Van Buren had submitted the treaty to the Senate early in 1840, despite the obvious evidence of fraud, he reminded those men he thought able to influence the process once again of his contributions and all the hardships he had suffered in the service of government policy. He reminded New York state senator Erastus Root that "I have expended large sums of money (and much of it borrowed) to assist the New York Indians in procuring the G. Bay lands." Without the proper recognition of his title, he wrote, he could not sell the lands and extricate himself from his financial difficulties. Without a good title, "it will be my ruin." The Senate voted in favor of the treaty in the spring of 1840, but it did not do so with the two-thirds necessary to obtain ratification. Nonetheless, Williams asked the president "to order that the Patent be issued for the land which I supposed to be reserved for me and my wife." Williams was "greatly embarrassed & actually in distress in my temporal concerns," and only the title to the lands and the right to sell them could save him.[40]

The president issued Williams the patent for his wife's lands, 4,800 acres in all in Wisconsin, in July 1840. But the money did not arrive. The Buffalo Creek treaty remained the subject of intense criticism by the Senecas, especially, and their Quaker allies. In 1842, these Quakers met with officials of the Ogden Land Company and a small number of Senecas. They negotiated the Supplemental, or Compromise, Treaty at Buffalo Creek. The Senecas, of course, had been deeply dissatisfied with the loss of all four of their reservations under the terms of the 1838 agreement. They might have parted with a portion of the lands on each of these reservations if their return could be effected, but they would not have chosen to relinquish any of them in their entirety. Under the 1842 Supplemental Treaty, however, that is precisely what happened. The Cattaraugus and Allegany reservations, where the Quakers had concentrated their efforts, would remain in the Senecas' possession. Tonawanda and Buffalo Creek belonged now to the Ogden Land Company. Most of the Indians at Buffalo Creek moved to Cattaraugus.[41]

Meanwhile, Oneidas who remained in New York State continued to sell their lands. In June 1840, 578 Oneidas remained in New York. Some of them, members of the First Christian Party, "disposed to migrate to Upper Canada or elsewhere beyond the limits of the said State," sold about 1,500 acres of their remaining lands in Madison and Oneida counties. On 8 March 1841, the Oneidas negotiated another treaty with the state. Only thirty-six Oneidas expressed a willingness to migrate, and they sold to the state their portion of the remaining lands, a piecemeal dispossession. Five days later, members of the Methodist Orchard Party negotiated a similar contract. Of the ninety-eight members of the Orchard Party, forty-four decided they no longer could remain on their lands and live the life they were accustomed to living. Sensing that things might be better in the "Delaware London District Upper Canada or elsewhere," they sold their proportional share of the Orchard Party lands, about 217 acres.[42]

In May 1842, sixteen more members of the Orchard Party left for Canada. The members of this "Emigration Party" sold 76 acres, leaving the "Home Party of the Orchard Indians" with 191 acres. The same day, Oneidas from the First and Second Christian Parties signed a similar agreement. This emigrating group intended to move to Green Bay. They totaled fifty in number. But 102 of their friends and family members chose to remain behind.[43] A state census of the Oneida lands in 1845 indicated that 157 Oneidas in all still resided in "the Oneida Creek Valley." Twenty-one Oneidas lived among the Onondagas to their west, and two with the Tuscaroras. Thirty Oneidas lived on the Seneca reservations in the western part of the state and, New York's census-takers guessed, 722 lived in Wisconsin. The state officials guessed that only twenty Oneidas had moved to Canada. Their data testify to the magnitude of the Oneida diaspora.[44]

The Oneidas found themselves scattered in a small number of pockets across Canada, New York, and Wisconsin, but few Senecas felt compelled to leave the state. In the summer of 1845, the U.S. War Department authorized Abraham Hogeboom to oversee the relocation of a party of New York Indians to new homes in the Indian Territory, today's Oklahoma and Kansas, provided he could gather together a party of at least 250 emigrants. Any number less than that, the commissioner of Indian Affairs felt, would not justify the expenses involved in transporting an emigrant party across the continent. Once Hogeboom had assembled his party, his instructions read, he should notify the commissioner, and await further directions. To the commissioner's dismay, and the misfortune of the emigrants, Hogeboom ignored this portion of his orders. By the summer of 1846, he had rounded up between 183 and 215 prospective emigrants, and departed without word for the Indian Territory. Because, according to Commissioner William Medill, "no intelligence of these unauthorized proceedings was received until the party was a considerable distance on the route," the department was unable to make "those preliminary arrangements that were requisite for their reception and comfortable accommodation in their new country." Predictably grim results followed. Because of lack of adequate preparation, and on account "of the season being unusually warm and unhealthy," eighty-two of the emigrants died over the course of 1846 and 1847. Ninety-four of the original emigrants returned home in 1847. Only a handful chose to remain in the Indian Territory. According to the federal agent stationed in western New York, these survivors of the policy of Indian removal, "with scarcely an exception," returned home "in a destitute condition, and many of them are yet suffering from disease."[45]

Historians of removal often focus on the grand tragedies, like the Cherokee Trail of Tears. But removal operated at different levels, sometimes resulting in the relocation of only small numbers of Indians at a time. The cumulative effect may have been equally effective in bringing about nearly complete dispossession, but the process affected native communities in different ways. These stories of dispossession and removal played themselves out apart from Eleazer Williams. He wrote frequently to federal officials, but no longer to float schemes for Indian removal or to advocate this or that policy. He did not call upon the men involved in Indian affairs to support the Christianization of the Indians. He wanted what he felt was his, and the evidence suggests that despite having finally obtained a sound title to his Wisconsin lands, he struggled to get by. In 1842, he told one correspondent that "we are in a miserable situation in regard to money concerns." His creditors continued to pursue him, placing liens on his property in Wisconsin.[46]

He did what he could. He leased parcels of his wife's land to a number of individuals like Joseph Allor, who obtained the right "to make hay on the premises or prairie belonging to the aforesaid Eleazer Williams," provided that he paid to Williams's agent a third of the hay he cut. He tried, with little success, to persuade the Mohawks at Akwesasne to pay him a share of their annuity. He appealed to the Ogden Company, as well. Thomas Ludlow Ogden wrote to tell Williams that he was "sorry to hear of your indisposition," but that he could not accept his "draft" on the company's accounts.[47]

He appealed for assistance, taking advantage of an emerging national media that an earlier generation of native leaders would not have had at their disposal. The same canal and steamboats that carried goods throughout the country and facilitated the early republic's "Market Revolution" could carry traveling lecturers, itinerant ministers, and confidence men, transmitting their message to like-minded audiences over an increasingly broad swath of territory. As a professional Indian, Williams used this new media. He wrote a letter, signed with the pen name "an Episcopalian," to church leaders in spring 1843, "to make known to you that Mr. W. is in needy circumstances." Williams had rendered himself unpopular, "an Episcopalian" pointed out, because his practices did not accord well with those of the "High Church Party." Should "some of your congregations be disposed to extend the hand of charity towards him," he wrote, "no doubt it will be gratefully received."[48]

That Williams employed a pseudonym in appealing for funds suggests that he understood that many in the Episcopalian establishment no longer believed him, and that his performance no longer moved them. He donned a new guise in this instance in order to generate financial support. It seems not to have worked. Still, Williams ached to remain a part of the broader Christian community. He wrote to Hobart's successor, Bishop Benjamin T. Onderdonk, reminding him of the "false and frivolous charges" conjured by his enemies "to prevent my long continuance as a Missionary among the Oneidas at New York and at Green Bay." Williams knew that he had always been something of a theological sampler, but argued that "it was immaterial with me whether I was ranked among the *high* or *low* church men, provided I served the Lord Jesus Christ faithfully as one of his servants in the Church." He fought the charges against him as best he could, but by now, he told Onderdonk, he had seen enough. Sick and broke, and believing he could "be no longer serviceable to the Church with a constitution broken down like mine, my voice and lungs in a feeble state, subject to fits, and above all my temporal interests having become so embarrassed," he asked the Diocese of New York to dismiss him "from the Ministry of the Protestant Episcopal Church." The Church had celebrated and boasted of his successes, but it did nothing to support him. He claimed that he could take no more.[49]

But that was not exactly true. In August 1841, just three months after he wrote to Onderdonk, Williams traveled to Oneida Castle in New York to commemorate "their eighth triennial anniversary" since he had converted the Pagan Party to Christianity. He felt grateful for the opportunity, he said. "Nothing less than the love and respect I have for the Oneida Nation, and a disposition to do what is within my power to aid in commemorating an event in which I was deeply interested," he wrote, "would have induced me to hazard a feeble voice in addressing you—a voice long unused to speak in public."[50]

He remembered fondly the day he first preached to the Pagan Party nearly a quarter of a century before, and "the glorious event, when six hundred of the Oneida Nation ... embraced the Christian faith under the ministry of him who now addresses you." It was a big moment, "the most interesting and solemn hour you have ever known," and one "big with consequences which will extend through all eternity." He felt immense pride for what he had accomplished during his few short years at Oneida, and "with heart felt gratitude," Williams rejoiced "that the attachment which was then formed, has been preserved with most of you, without abatement."[51]

Williams offered a message of hope to his small audience. He described God's mercy "toward fallen, self-ruined, and justly condemned man." He spoke of the greatness of God's grace, "and the abundance of that love which has been manifested towards us." God sent his son not just to save his chosen people, after all, and he cared as much about "the salvation of the poor benighted Heathens, the Pagans of Africa and Hindostan, as . . . those in the Holy Land."[52] Williams did not see native peoples as cursed, and he severely criticized those who felt their sins were so great that no hope for salvation remained. God knew all, but God loved all, Williams said. "Dare you for a moment entertain the blasphemous idea," he told his audience, "that God sent his Son into the world, to execute a work which after all he was not able to perform, and of course, that his purpose of love will fail of accomplishment." Williams told the Oneidas, who listened to him as they sat in a homeland that shrank ever more each year, to read their Bibles. "Yes," Williams said, "read the thousand great and precious promises of God, to the distressed, the broken-hearted, self-abused sinner, and say you are prepared to think that God is not sincere and will not fulfill his promise?" Have faith, he told them. For "if the blood of Christ can save a world, surely it must be sufficient for all your guilt."[53]

This was Williams at his best. He was perhaps at his most honest and his most heartfelt, giving a powerful performance that conveyed the Word of God to native peoples who might have hungered for something to inspire hope for the future. Williams had done important work, and he reminded the Oneidas of what they had accomplished together. But he could carry this tune only so far, and the anger and frustration he felt from the defeats and setbacks he had suffered soon manifested itself. He told a self-serving story of victimization, a story he very much might have believed. He complained of those who had conspired to end his missionary career among the Oneidas. He spoke of how his enemies worked not only against the humble missionary, but against the will of God.

Satan followed Williams to the Oneida country, he said, determined "to put an end to the glorious work he had initiated among them." He came in the form of men, cloaked as Christians, who scattered the flock and introduced divisions. Williams saw himself as the first of their victims, but he was not the only one. "Extreme is the guilt of those who scatter poison-ous errors, or sow discord among the Brethren and cause divisions and offenses in the Churches—who seduce the People from their Pastor, and weaken the salutary instructions." These, Williams said, "are the open ene-mies of Christ."[54]

Williams's work had been undone by Solomon Davis and others, but he still hoped to resume his ministerial career, despite what he had written to Onderdonk. He wrote to Jackson Kemper, whose jurisdiction as Episcopal bishop for the Northwest included Wisconsin. He attempted to defend him-self against the charges he faced. But Kemper, in the fall of 1842, said Wil-liams stood accused of preaching in Davis's parish without permission, and as a result Kemper forbade Williams from officiating in Wisconsin.[55]

Williams told an audience of Oneidas in Wisconsin that he had been treated unfairly by the bishop, and that Kemper's capricious decision was extraordinary, illegal, and "contrary to the apostolic injunction." He had tried to be a team player. After his recall in 1833, he told the Oneidas, he had avoided them. Only the final illness of two friends brought him back. Williams told the Oneidas that even then he hesitated, "but duty, humanity, sighs, and tears of a dying fellow creature, finally overcame my scruples and I hastened to prepare the exit of my dying friend by affording him all the con-solations which the church offers on such solemn occasions."[56]

Solomon Davis opposed this act of benevolence, Williams recalled. Davis objected as well to a number of addresses Williams gave before Oneida Meth-odists in Wisconsin in 1833. Williams had not known that Davis claimed jurisdiction over Methodists, and thought the claim utterly unwarranted. "God forbid any Bishop or minister of the Protestant Episcopal Church should ever assume such an attitude over others and that particularly over the Indians, who would ever be free as the air they breathe." Williams read to his audience the charges Davis laid out against him: Williams was "in the habit of constantly neglecting the worship of the church," and so had "lost entirely the confidence and respect of the Oneidas;" Williams, Davis con-tended, was a "hindrance to the interests of religion and the church among them," and Williams had "been in some way ministerially connected with other denominations."[57]

Williams tried to respond, though he must have realized that he stood little chance of success. He must have missed Hobart greatly. Williams had not neglected his duties, he said. His home in Wisconsin stood ten miles from the nearest church. That distance, his own poor health, and his poverty and lack of support made travel difficult. And if Williams had lost the respect and trust of the Oneidas, he argued, this was largely the result of Davis's constant backbiting. If speaking to Methodists or consoling a dying friend hindered "the interest of religion among the Oneidas," as Davis charged, Williams did not stand much of a chance. "It is painful in the extreme," Williams said, that Davis, "a man professing to be a Christian, . . . would manifest such uncharitable spirit, as to build his complaints or charges upon such weak and slender foundations, on order to scandalize the object of his fear, and upon whose ruin he would build himself up, and maintain his position where he gets his bread." And as for the charge that Williams had worked too closely as a minister with other congregations, Williams rejected that claim out of hand. None of the arguments he made mattered. Kemper, whom Williams compared most unfavorably to Hobart, remained unmoved. Kemper simply did not believe him.[58]

Williams felt himself deeply wronged, and there can be no doubt that Davis's relentless criticism took its toll. He continued to move about, but some Oneidas, it seemed, retained some fondness for Williams, or respected him and all that he had done. On the Fourth of July 1844, Oneidas in Wisconsin apparently defied Davis and encouraged Williams to begin to raise the funds necessary "to have translated and printed in their own language, some small treatises on religion for adults, and catechisms and hymns for the benefit of their children."[59] A year later, at least some of the Oneida chiefs at Duck Creek invited Williams "once more to resume your Station among us, as our religious instructor." They accused "wicked white men" like Davis of generating opposition. They no longer trusted Solomon Davis, for one thing, but also their morals were a mess. "The immorality of our People has been growing," they told Williams, "and it may now be justly said to an alarming degree."[60] Some Indians clearly wanted Williams back, and the Society for the Propagation of the Gospel believed, in 1846, that Williams was worth once again some small investment.[61]

*   *   *

The drift continued, as did the constant laments that Williams lacked the resources to make ends meet. Whatever small stipend he received from the Society for the Propagation of the Gospel, or whatever small fee he collected on those very rare occasions when he preached, it never seemed enough to support the style of life that Williams expected to live. He moved frequently. He lived in hotels in New York and seldom returned to his wife and his home in Wisconsin. Certainly this misanthropic life, as Ellis described it, was not working out, if we believe that Williams was as straitened as he claimed.

It is clear that his financial problems—the costs of his travel, especially, led him to enter into arrangements that hurt other people. Williams told John Holloway Hanson of the considerable hardships he faced and how he mortgaged the Wisconsin lands he had fought so long to secure to pay a number of judgments against him. Williams's creditors gave him two years to redeem the note, and in July 1844 he asked them for more time. They gave Williams an extension—from April until September 1844, but still he fell short.[62]

All this was a surprise, it seems, to Mary Hobart Williams. In August 1844, just before the deadline, she wrote to Amos A. Lawrence of Boston, their creditor. She told him that she did not understand that by signing the mortgage "I was conveying away all my right & title to my portion of the land." Except the letter was not written by Mary. Once again, it appears in Eleazer's hand. Lawrence met Williams in Boston, and paid his debt on the 4,800 acres. Lawrence believed that he had through this transaction purchased half of the tract, and that he would hold a mortgage for Williams on the rest. Williams never paid off the debt, and Lawrence ended up with thousands of acres of Wisconsin land that his descendants claimed he never wanted. Some of it he sold, some he donated, including a sizable piece that became the site of Lawrence University. Mary Hobart Williams continued to live on a small piece of this land, but she no longer held the title. Williams acted as if the land belonged to him only until his debts jeopardized his ownership of the massive tract. Then, he willingly played the Indian victim of white duplicity and fraud. Williams must have gone into this with his eyes wide open, and surely he knew what was at stake, but he hinted to Hanson that the widely respected Lawrence had deceived him, a claim that not even Hanson believed.[63]

The news did not get better. In the fall of 1845, Williams wrote to Eunice Storrs, a member of the extended Williams family in the Connecticut River Valley. He had just learned that his brother John, who had accompanied him to Longmeadow nearly half a century before, had drowned along with five others on the St. Lawrence. His youngest brother, meanwhile, suffered from tuberculosis and, Williams wrote, "was not likely to continue much longer." At some point during these years he wrote a sermon blasting Roman Catholics in terms the most nativist Know-Nothing would have loved. But the sentiment could not ring true, and the sermon was itself a work of plagiarism, stolen from a collection of essays first published in Scotland several decades before. Even his anti-Catholicism seemed labored and insincere. He continued to play roles, to try out new characters. He claimed to see much about him that filled him with dread. Perhaps he did. He played an Iroquois Free Soiler. The annexation of Texas and its seizure "by lawless adventurers and speculators, their shameless prostration of the inalienable rights of man to life, liberty and the pursuit of happiness in a land where, by the Mexican constitution, human liberty has been permanently established," left him worried for the future. Or so he said.[64]

"At no time in my life, my brethren," Williams wrote in the text of a speech that we do not know if he ever delivered, "have I been more perplexed, dismayed, & disheartened than at present." Alluding to a long history of crimes committed against native peoples, Williams addressed himself to the citizens of the United States. "Our fathers were in possession of this country when you first set your foot upon it," and "they received you as friends." Indians showed the newcomers boundless generosity. It brought them nothing. No good came from befriending white people. "Instead of [a] blessing," he wrote, "it has been a curse to them, instead of joy, weeping and mourning has followed them, yea, instead of health and life, and here my heart bleed at the thought, a general malady, and death in its terrible form have visited them."[65]

And the situation was getting worse. "Americans," Williams wrote, "you boast that liberty is the standard of your Government & do you confirm this, by enslaving several hundred thousand of your fellow men, merely because their color is a little darker shade than your own[?]" Americans were hypocrites, Williams claimed, for enslaving Africans "under the tree of liberty" and for cheating and slaughtering native peoples. In the fragment of yet another speech, Williams wrote that Americans have asked Indians to respect "the Government which have caused to have our lands taken from us by force; but arbitrary power can command no respect." Americans asked Indians for their lands, and now they had them, "but do not ask for our confidence and love—hatred is all that can follow." It was, quite obviously, an angry statement and one that sounds almost uncharacteristic. Perhaps the professional Indian, no longer able to earn a living in his chosen line of work, had become thoroughly disillusioned. Perhaps after getting these sentiments off his chest, he thought through the consequences that might follow from proclaiming them. There is no way of knowing for sure. But that is not much of a problem. Whether he delivered these words or not,

Williams wrote them down. The choppy grammar suggests that he wrote
these words quickly, and the anger he expressed was that of an Indian man
reflecting upon the injustices heaped upon people more like him than not in
an American empire of liberty.[66]

*   *   *

And so the man who lost whatever faith he held in the justice of the American republic began to pursue with more energy the money he felt he was
owed and that he felt had been guaranteed to him at Buffalo Creek. He asked
the commissioner of Indian affairs for permission to travel to Washington to
look into the matter. Commissioner William Medill said Williams did not
need his permission, but he told Williams to "bear in mind that the Department cannot bear any part of your expenses." Knock yourself out, Medill
seemed to suggest.[67]

Writing once again from Wisconsin in June 1846, Williams made his
pitch to M. L. Martin, the Wisconsin Territory's congressional delegate. The
St. Regis, Williams wrote, wanted the $1000 dollars they believed belonged
to them as a result of the treaty. But, Williams wrote, they did not deserve it.
The St. Regis spent only $500 in trying to obtain lands in Wisconsin, while
he "expended large sums of money to effect the same in behalf of the tribe for
which I have received no remuneration." Revising the history of his relationship with Akwesasne, Williams claimed that he had reached an understanding with the Mohawks that of the remaining one thousand dollars, he would
receive half.[68]

Williams retained an attorney in Washington, Philip R. Fendall, to pursue
his claim. The federal agent in New York, meanwhile, presented Williams's
appeal to the council at St. Regis in September 1846. The chiefs at Akwesasne disagreed with Williams's reconstruction of the events. "The claim of
Eleazer Williams upon said tribe, for services rendered and monies advanced
by him," was, according to the American officials present, "unanimously
rejected."[69]

What to do? Williams told Hanson many stories, and Hanson certainly
sympathized. But Williams did not tell Hanson everything, and out of these
silences important truths about Williams emerge. Williams said little to Hanson about his family life, for instance, beyond what it shed on his identity as
the Dauphin. His marriage suffered, a casualty of distance and the death of
the baby Margaret Anne, whom they buried in 1830. Mary Hobart Williams

still grieved deeply almost eight years later. He wrote to her about it in May 1838. He danced around the issue and avoided the pain that tore at his wife. He wrote of small matters—of how the water and the ice on Duck Creek and the Fox River had done great damage, he had heard, and how he feared that the crops had been ruined. He criticized Mary for refusing his advice to plant the potatoes on higher ground. He was looking for the right words.[70]

Williams urged her to reflect on matters religious. He asked her to think beyond the next harvest and to consider her salvation. "You are sensible that we have corrupt hearts & need cleansing by the blood of Jesus Christ," he wrote. "We live in a world," he told Mary, "full of deceit." Certainly he knew this to be true. "We are constantly surrounded with many temptations, both from men & the devil." These were shallow things, and they could not be trusted. He begged Mary to consider this. Please, "my dear Mary," Williams wrote, "nothing in this life would make me more happy than to find that you are serving God, and living in humility, as one who is devoted to Christ & preparing for heaven." They must concentrate on the things that mattered. "Let no longer the world & its vanities be upon the upper most in your mind or thoughts—forsake them—& give yourself to God and Jesus Christ who had redeemed you by his most precious blood."

Perhaps she lost her faith after the death of her child. Perhaps Williams wrote words that he, in this moment of clarity, might live by as well. Williams had never lacked for words. But in this letter, his desperation is palpable. He and Mary had to "set a good example before the only child we have & for his sake let us live as the friends of God—so that when he grows up, he may see that we have lived in the ways of virtue & piety." They lived in a "wicked and deceitful world"—he kept returning to this—and "we are troubled in various ways—sometimes by slander—wicked tongues are always at work." They must "live and so conduct ourselves as to give a lie to all their wicked insinuations."

He would pray for Mary, but he urged her to pray for herself, as well. "How happy it would be, should we as a family, finally by the mercy of God, to meet all, with our departed beloved *Anne*, in heaven, where, we shall all be happy without end & sing praises to God to all eternity." He finally said the child's name. They were not happy like that now. Williams begged his wife "to seek that religion which will make you happy here—happy in the hour of death, & a glorious immortality beyond the grave." He wrote these words to her, he said in closing, "because I love you," and he asked her "to accept them as coming from my heart, yes, as coming from an affectionate husband—'*til death do us part*.'"[71]

What else might he have said? Lots of things, perhaps. In trying to heal his wife's broken heart he relied upon the Christian faith that rested at the center of his own identity, and the center of his soul. These words, it seems, could not assuage the grief of a mother forced by cruel circumstance to bury her child. And this may not have been their only loss. Williams wrote in his diary for 1841 that Mary again became pregnant, and again the child died in infancy. There is no record of the child's burial, and she died before baptism, he wrote. It is possible that Williams made this story up, a small plot point in his dauphin performance.[72] We cannot be certain. What is clear, however, is that Eleazer Williams and Mary Hobart Williams parted long before death. Distance separated them because Eleazer Williams chose to leave Wisconsin. He returned only rarely, and only for short stays. If Williams did tell Hanson this story, Hanson did not feel the need to include it, one more loss suffered by a man who he felt had suffered so much already.[73]

*　*　*

Williams likewise must not have said much to Hanson about his discovery during the first half of the 1840s that his life story interested people, of his growing awareness of his connections to an exciting episode in New England's past. He could not do so, of course, and at the same time convince Hanson that he descended directly from Louis XVI and Marie Antoinette. The Deerfield Raid, the capture of the Reverend John, his family, and the story of the unredeemed captive, Williams understood, captured the public's imagination. He might market his own story. He had always told stories: as a missionary to the Indians, or as a victim of plots and intrigues, or as a guardian and shepherd forsaken by those he aided so greatly. Now he dug deeper into his own past. A great deal of time had passed since he had played the descendant of an unredeemed captive. He began to contribute his expertise to those seeking to reconstruct Deerfield's history. Charles de Saileville, for instance, an amateur historian, sent to Williams his manuscript about Eunice Williams. Williams corresponded with the famous historian Francis Parkman about the Williams family history.[74] In September 1846, he delivered an address at Deerfield to commemorate the anniversary of the Rev. John Williams's death, 117 years before. Williams hoped, through his retelling of the events of that day, "to commemorate the excellencies and true characteristics of his grandsire."[75] And two years later, Williams left with friends a manuscript entitled "The Life or Memoir of Eunice Williams the Captive, or my Great Grand Mother." Williams wanted the manuscript published and he believed that it would "sell well."[76] His story—that of the Indian missionary who descended from Puritans and Indian captives, still possessed relevance and the power to move audiences. Williams valued the story and took pride in this element of his past. But not for long. He jettisoned the story of his actual past—his lived experience and that of his ancestors—for a new story, fabricated entirely out of whole cloth. He was no longer a professional Indian. He was, perhaps, a king.

CHAPTER SIX

The Confidence Man

Eleazer Williams once had been well known as a missionary. He never seems to have wavered in his belief in the importance of bringing Christianity to native peoples, even if his own efforts in that endeavor lacked consistency. Federal officials involved in American Indian policy, and the land speculators in league with them who coveted Iroquois land, valued the assistance he gave them in dispossessing the New York Indians and leading some of them to Wisconsin. For a time it seems that he shared their goals, if not all their motives, because he saw removal as a way to insulate his followers from the lawlessness of aggressive white settlers and the wreckage that might come from living on a frontier. They accorded him a great deal of respect. He knew personally and corresponded with several secretaries of war, commissioners of Indian affairs, and presidents of the United States. But much of that now lay in the past. By the 1840s, Williams had fallen on hard times. The Oneidas who relocated to Green Bay, at least in part at his urging, had cast him out of their community. They felt he paid less attention to their spiritual concerns than to his own interests, and they believed he remained too close to those who clamored for their lands. The Oneidas who remained in New York State for the most part felt little affection for the missionary who had spent only a few short years with them. In addition to falling out of favor in the native communities where he had ministered, Williams remained in debt, hounded by those who sought to attach what little property he still had. And his marriage had grown cold. Williams visited his home in Wisconsin only occasionally and only for short periods of time. He spent much of his time shuttling back and forth between the nation's capital where he continued to pursue various schemes on behalf of Indians he claimed still to represent and for himself, and the Mohawk reservation at St. Regis, where he hoped to revitalize his flagging clerical career by establishing a mission school and an Episcopal church.

Williams always had relied on access to powerful white Americans to make his living, to put food on his table and a roof over his head. He believed in what he was doing, helping them as he helped himself and the Indians. Removal, the preaching of Christianity—it all made sense to Williams. Land sales he saw as fundamental to both of these processes. But when his patrons no longer needed his assistance, Williams had little choice but to embark on another course. He never set out to become a confidence man. Who does? Like all people, Williams made choices about his identity, about how he presented himself to others. Like all people, as well, he confronted forces that in a variety of ways limited the choices open to him. For much of his career, he exploited his Indian identity, his expertise, as a missionary, broker, diplomat, and leader. But he rejected that identity as well. Now he most urgently attempted to persuade government officials that he deserved a pension for his services during the War of 1812. No mere soldier, he served the United States as superintendent-general of the Northern Indian Department and commander of the Corps of Observation, Williams claimed. No mere messenger or translator, he told those who he thought mattered that he served as the leader of an impetuous and daring force of horse soldiers that tenaciously harassed the enemy, risked their lives to gather valuable intelligence, and, by war's end in the far north, helped save the American republic. During these years, as well, Williams met the Reverend John Holloway Hanson on that Northern Line train and convinced him, and others, that he was no Indian but rather the dauphin, the child of Louis XVI and Marie Antoinette, and an heir to the throne of France. No mere missionary to the Indians, he was a "Lost Prince" from whom everything had been taken in the French Revolution but who, in all his humility, would labor still among the Indians in the American wilderness.

These two elaborate stories possessed much in common. One might draw from them the easy conclusion that Williams craved the admiration of white Americans and status within their society—a point that a number of historians have made as they depicted Williams as a tragic figure trapped between Indian and white worlds—but this, of course, does not answer all of our questions. Both of these stories after all, required performance. If well-cast and well-received, they might provide Williams with a livelihood, and a way to make ends meet. Admiration and status he saw, then, not as ends in themselves but as ways to make a living in a world where he found few other options appealing. Williams found himself unable to make an honest living.

The American people, in the middle of the nineteenth century and at other times since, have respected men of martial valor and accomplishment. Andrew Jackson, William Henry Harrison, and Zachary Taylor—the careers of all three men make this abundantly clear. A liar might have claimed that he participated in this or that battle, fought alongside this or that American hero, or performed some heroic deed. Williams did more than this. He fabricated a history, a personal account complete with documentation in the form of a wartime journal that he wrote long after the fact. He played a role, with full knowledge that a compelling portrayal could bring financial rewards. The citizens of the new nation retained a fascination with aristocracy and monarchy as well, despite their republican roots. Nathaniel Hawthorne learned this during the years he spent in diplomatic service, working at the United States consulate in Liverpool.[1] Williams understood this well. He read about the French Revolution, about the tragic history of the child of Louis XVI and Marie Antoinette. He took bits and pieces that he read and heard and learned and cobbled it into a character that captured the imagination of a surprisingly large number of people. These were more than lies and tales that he told, and during the last decade or so of his life, Eleazer Williams became a confidence man, a schemer, telling stories, creating characters and backstory and imagery, and inhabiting this world in order to convince others that they should give him their money. He inhabited these personae, and played these roles, for much of the rest of his life. Identity could be a fluid thing in the American republic, offering the schemers and the dreamers, and the men on the make and the desperate, a range of opportunities to advance their interests and invent themselves anew. But Williams learned as well that there were limits to the confidence white Americans might place in dark-skinned strangers.

*   *   *

And so we return to that train on the Northern Line, where John Holloway Hanson and Eleazer Williams met for the first time in autumn 1851. In this and in their subsequent meetings, Williams explained to Hanson how he confirmed the suspicions he had long held—that he was different, that he was a man out of place with too much of his past unclear to him. The most important part of the story Williams told Hanson involved another steamboat journey, one that took place in fall 1841, a decade before the two men met in northern New York. It was then, Williams told Hanson, that he crossed paths with François-Ferdinand-Philippe-Louis-Marie d'Orléans, the French prince de Joinville. The third son of Louis Philippe, then king of France, Joinville left Buffalo on 13 October 1841 aboard the steamboat *Columbus* bound for Green Bay. Newspapers reported on Joinville's progress, and anyone capable of reading them could have known of the comings and goings of this representative of the French royal family. On 18 October, the boat reached Mackinac Island, and there Williams and his son boarded.[2]

Quite a coincidence. Williams may have sought out Joinville, a man of obvious wealth and influence. He could tell him a story, or tell him a lie. Perhaps he could perform for him some service or favor that produced a gift, a present or a kind word. This may have been the way it happened. Or Williams might have transformed a chance encounter with French royalty during one of his many journeys through the Great Lakes into a vital plot point in his dauphin drama. Both of these possibilities seem more likely than the scene Williams described for Hanson.

Williams said that Joinville had asked about him several times as he traveled from Buffalo through the Great Lakes. Joinville, in Williams's telling, wanted to meet the great missionary to the Indians at Green Bay. Because the ship's captain John Shook "knew of no other gentleman in that capacity excepting myself," he asked Williams if he might arrange a formal introduction between his two passengers. Shook later gave Hanson an affidavit, swearing that this story was true.[3] Joinville, Williams suggested, may have sought out Williams because he had heard that the missionary was "skilled in Indianology and acquainted with the Northwest," or because he thought Williams might serve as an interesting tour guide during his travels on the western Great Lakes. These, he admitted, might seem like possibilities. But Williams dismissed them. Joinville, Williams told Hanson, sought him out because of his secret ties to the French throne. This Williams learned on that remarkable day. When he and Joinville finally met, Williams was sitting on a barrel. "The Prince," he said, "not only started with evident and involuntary surprise when he saw me, but there was great agitation in his face and manner—a slight paleness and a quivering of the lip—which I could not help remarking at the time, but which struck me more forcibly afterwards in connection with the whole train of circumstances, and by contrast with his usual self-possessed manner." Quickly shaking off his initial surprise, observers recalled, Joinville "received Williams with an embrace and went with him to his cabin where the two sat in close conversation until a late hour, about two in the morning."[4]

Joinville approached Williams with unstinting courtesy. He asked Williams if he would "not be intruding too much upon your feelings and patience were I to ask some questions in relation to your past and present life among the Indians." During the journey from Mackinac to Green Bay, he and Joinville spoke of the history of the French in America. They spoke about missions to the Indians, of their improvability, and of Christianity. They spoke of the assistance France had provided the American rebels during the Revolution. Louis XVI, Joinville said, had felt a true regard for America, something too few of its citizens recognized. On the Fourth of July, "when throughout the U.S. the nation was celebrating its independence," Joinville wished that there would be "an especial salute fired to the memory of the King who had contributed so much to the result."[5]

The courtesies continued. Joinville offered to take Williams's son to France for an education. When Joinville learned that Williams and his wife had an infant daughter, and that the child had not yet received baptism, Joinville offered to serve as the baby's godfather. When Williams received upon arrival in Green Bay "the melancholy intelligence that the lovely babe was in her grave, buried the preceding Sunday" Joinville extended his sympathy. He took Williams by the hand. "Descendant of the suffered race," he said to Williams, "may you be supported in this affliction."[6]

Joinville was polite and interested. So Williams tells us. Throughout their time together, Williams wrote, Joinville's "eyes were intensely fixed upon me, eyeing my person from the crown of the head to the sole of my feet." He had something on his mind, something that Williams needed to hear. They arrived at Green Bay. Williams wished to know what Joinville wanted to tell him. But first, some errands. He visited briefly in the afternoon with some members of his wife's family in Green Bay—tellingly, he did not go see his grieving wife—before retiring for the evening to the Astor House Hotel, where Joinville and his retinue were staying. They met in Joinville's quarters. "The gentlemen of his party were in an adjoining room, laughing and carousing," Williams recalled. Joinville had something to tell Williams, but he asked from Williams for "some pledge of secrecy, some promise that I would not reveal to any one what he was going to say." Williams agreed, "provided there was nothing in it prejudicial to any one." Williams signed an agreement to that effect, though he did not keep a copy of the document.[7]

Joinville told Williams that he had not been born in North America. Williams had suspected this, but not what followed. "You are of foreign descent; you were born in Europe, sir, and however incredible it may at first seem to you, I have to tell you that you are the son of a king." Williams was "overcome," he told Hanson, "and thrown into a state of mind you can easily imagine." All that he knew as true was false, and many of the suspicions he felt were now confirmed. Stunned and shaken, he asked Joinville to tell him more.[8] Williams had suffered much, Joinville said. Joinville was willing to tell Williams the secret of his birth, but in doing so, he said, "it was necessary that a certain process should be gone through in order to guard the interests of all parties concerned." Williams wondered what Joinville meant. The prince rose from his chair, and took from his trunk a document that he laid before Williams. There was also on the table pen and ink and wax and an old seal. It was heavy, Williams told Hanson, and he could not be sure whether it was made from gold or silver or an alloy, but it looked to him like the seals used by the old French monarchy.

The document Joinville placed in front of Williams was printed in parallel columns of French and English. Williams mulled over the document. He "continued intently reading and considering it for a space of four or five hours." During this time, the prince came and went, but mostly he stayed with Williams in the room, quietly watching him. They spoke little. The document, Williams told Hanson, "was a solemn abdication of the crown of France . . . with all accompanying names and titles of honor according to the custom of the old French monarchy, together with a minute specification in legal phraseology of the conditions, and consideration, and provisos, upon which the abdication was made." After searching so long for the dauphin, Joinville now wanted Williams to disappear.[9]

Williams told Hanson that he did not know what to do. He should have kept a copy of this document too but, he told Hanson, "it is very easy for you, sitting quietly there, to prescribe the course which prudence and self-interest would dictate." At last, Williams made his decision. He refused to sign the abdication. He told Joinville that "I felt that I could not be the instrument of bartering away with my own hand the rights pertaining to me by my birth, and sacrificing the interests of my family." He was poor but he would not sacrifice his honor.[10]

With this, Joinville's patience finally ran out. He had sat, waiting, a long time. It was not that long a document. He had traveled far to find Williams. He "assumed a loud tone," and "accused me of ingratitude in trampling on the overtures of the King, his father." Williams was not going to be yelled at by a man he now believed to be his inferior. He replied angrily to Joinville. Williams told Joinville that "by his disclosure, he had put me in the position of a superior." Williams had a stronger claim to the throne than did Joinville, he said, and he demanded to be shown some respect. When Williams spoke in these terms, he said, "the Prince immediately assumed a respectful attitude, and remained silent for several minutes."[11]

After Williams refused to sign the abdication, he and Joinville parted ways. Williams claimed that this startling news left him devastated, that "it filled my inward soul with poignant grief and sorrow." Joinville's revelation, he confided in his diary, "was not only new but awful in its nature, to learn for the first time that I am connected by consanguinity with those whose history I had read with so much interest, and for whose sufferings in prison and the manner of their deaths, had moistened my cheeks with sympathetic tear." Williams wondered how this could be so. "Is it true, that I am among the number who are thus destined to such degradation—from a mighty power to a helpless prisoner of the state? From a palace to a prison and dungeon—to be exiled from one of the finest Empires in Europe to be a wanderer in the wilds of America—from the society of the most polite and accomplished countries to be associated with the ignorant and degraded Indians?"[12] Williams wrote in his journal for the last day of October 1841, that "my refusal" to sign Joinville's abdication document could produce "no earthly good to me, but I save my honor, and it may be for the benefit of generations yet unborne." He was, at times, "an unhappy man, and in my sorrow and mournful state, I would with a sigh cry out, like David, O my Father, O my Mother." But at other times, Williams seemed to accept his fate. Joinville left him feeling enormously confused, torn about what he should do next. "It is the will of heaven," he wrote. "I am in a state of obscurity, so shall I remain." All he could do was "endeavor, with all humility, to serve the King of Heaven, to advance his holy cause among the ignorant and benighted people which has been my delight."[13]

Though Joinville later claimed that this conversation never took place, other observers at Green Bay, perhaps eager to claim some connection to big events, lent support to elements of Williams's story. According to a very elderly Wisconsinan named Mary Allen, her grandmother met with Joinville on Mackinac Island. The prince, Allen said, asked for her grandmother's opinion of Eleazer Williams. She said that she believed Williams "had no Indian blood in his veins." Then, according to Allen, she proceeded to tell a story that "staggered" the prince. Allen's grandfather collected engravings, she said. One evening, Williams leafed through the collection and stopped at a face that seemed to him disturbingly familiar. Williams seemed stunned, agitated, as if he had seen a ghost. He "arose to his feet, trembling from limb to limb; the cold perspiration was pouring down his face; he caught hold of my chair as a support." It was a compelling act Williams repeated on a number of occasions. Allen's grandmother seems to have bought it entirely. Williams, shaken, bade his hosts good night, with tears in his eyes. After he departed, Allen's grandmother hurried across the room to look at the engraving that had so struck Williams and found it was "Simon the Jailer," the sadistic torturer of the child dauphin.[14]

Yet if Joinville's message troubled Williams, and if images of the dauphin's tormentors haunted him, he did little about it at the time. He confided in the pages of the journal that he gave to Hanson that "my soul is troubled within me," and that he could find no peace. "Hours have I spent in the solitary wilderness mourning over my fate and the fate of my family," he wrote in an entry for late in November.[15] But he said nothing publicly. As we have seen, he did little as well to patch the holes in his home life, and he failed in his efforts to rejoin polite society in Wisconsin. He struggled with debt. He could not pay his attorney. He did what he could to get by, almost always on the move, an Indian man-on-the-make in Jacksonian America.[16]

Only in 1848, after he received word of the "melancholy death of my reputed father," did the dauphin story emerge publicly. In February that year, Williams told Hanson, he received a report from Baton Rouge "that a respectable French gentleman, by name of Belanger, had lately died in or near New Orleans." Belanger, on his deathbed, revealed "a secret which had been locked up in his bosom since 1795," that "the Rev. Gentleman who bears the name of Eleazer Williams . . . was really and truly the son of Louis XVI, King of France." Belanger claimed that he had rescued the dauphin from the Temple in June 1795 and carried the child who became Eleazer Williams to America. The mysterious Belanger placed him, for safekeeping, among the Iroquois in Canada.[17]

In reality, there was no Belanger. H. E. Eastman, an acquaintance of Williams and a man who "had some business relations" with him, told the Wisconsin antiquarian John Y. Smith he had written a story in the 1840s in which he cast Williams as the dauphin. Belanger was Eastman's creation. Eastman intended his story, he wrote, as nothing "more than a romance, which he might, sometime, publish." Williams, Eastman recalled, "was amused and flattered by the idea," and asked to borrow the manuscript. Eastman thought that this occurred sometime late in 1847. From these and other ingredients, Williams conjured his character and molded his performance. Joinville? That encounter was a fiction. The dead baby Joinville would have baptized—that, too, was probably an invention.[18]

Williams nonetheless began to correspond with those who he hoped might spread his story. He told Mary of his encounter with Joinville. Though she may not have cared that "the long talk" of his "foreign descent is true," and that this caused him "a great grief and sorrow," others found Williams's

tale fascinating. He claimed that he had "already become in a measure subject of history in both hemispheres," but he said only enough to allow his
audience, or his correspondents, to draw their own conclusions. He told one
woman, for instance, that he could not "affirm at this moment, to the extent
you would have me," that he and the dauphin were one. Nonetheless, the
encounter with Joinville, and the story of the mysterious Belanger, certainly
led him "into the belief of my foreign birth." In a letter to Mrs. R. V. Hotchkiss, he suggested that there "are some circumstances corroborating with this
idea which have come to my knowledge, and which I must confess, do carry
strong indications" that he was the dauphin. But none of it could matter, he
suggested. Though he was broke, and "although royalty and a family title may
be connected with your correspondent, and these may sound high with men
of the world," he wrote to Hotchkiss, "yet your correspondent would view
his station to be sufficiently honorable when it is said to be an Indian missionary." He could set aside his claims to the throne of France and return
contentedly to his mission, which he could do more easily and with more
effectiveness if Hotchkiss contributed to the funds he hoped to collect "for
the building of the church" at St. Regis.[19]

Williams encouraged those interested in doing so to broadcast his story.
Writing to newspaperman Joshua Leavitt, the editor of the New York *Independent*, Williams included a capsule history of the dauphin story. Williams
wanted the piece published anonymously. That was in March of 1848. He
wrote that "an heir to the throne of Louis XVI is still living," and that the child
Belanger hid "among the Indians of the North was truly and really the son
of Louis XVI." Williams met with the occasional reporter passing through
Green Bay, when he was there, convincing one that his "appearance, manner, conversation, and mode of expression are not those of an Indian, but of
a Frenchman," and another that he was "a chief of the St. Regis Indians," and
that his features "were not only unlike those of an Indian, but were," somehow,
"directly in opposition to them." He told friends along the Connecticut River
that he "did not know what to believe in regard to his origin," and that he could
not tell "whether he is the Dauphin or not." He did nothing to dissuade them
when they "compared his features with the engraved heads of Louis XVI and
Louis XVIII" they found lying around "and found a striking resemblance."[20]

Over the course of the following year, a number of newspaper stories
appeared making the claim that Eleazer Williams and the dauphin were
one. A story appeared in the *Buffalo Commercial Advertiser* emphasizing
Williams's European features. In March of 1849, Leavitt published a piece
under the title "The Lost Dauphin," likely the piece Williams submitted to

him, claiming that Williams was "a man incapable of lending himself to any scheme of deception in this business, even if the facts did not conclusively show, as they do, that he could have had no possible motive for becoming an imposter." Leavitt did not know Williams very well. A story in the *United States Democratic Review* in the summer of 1849, based on interviews conducted with Williams, emphasized his physical traits. Williams possessed dark hair and skin, but not so much darker than that of other Europeans. More importantly, "his mouth is well-formed, and indicative of mingled firmness and benignity of character." And even more revealing was his possession of "the full protruberant Maximilian lip, the distinctive feature of the Austrian family." That feature was not found in Indians, and seldom among Americans. Elements of these stories were widely reprinted and commented upon, and any of them could have been the article Hanson saw that so awakened his interest in Eleazer Williams.[21]

But it remained a small story, spreading no further than the narrow scope of wherever Williams happened to be. Williams continued to cobble together plans to make ends meet. He attempted to sell to the secretary of state in New York, for instance, "Marquette's original journal and map, which with other papers he had found in a box in the wall of a church at Sault St. Louis . . . at a time when it was abandoned and in ruins." The missionary and advocate for Indians played at fraud. He might have got away with it, had not the secretary of state asked the historian John Gilmary Shea for advice. Shea said that in fact the documents already had been discovered, that the church Williams referred to had never stood in ruins, and that Williams was either attempting to defraud the state of New York or "had fallen into a delusion."[22]

But it was not all petty crime. Williams needed to make a living, and with all the old paths closed, he did what he could to get by. He even asked L. U. Sigourney, a Connecticut acquaintance, to present an appeal to Jenny Lind, the Swedish opera singer, whose tour of the United States P. T. Barnum sponsored. Lind gave generously to charities, and perhaps she might lend some support to Williams. Sigourney failed to catch Lind, who stayed in Hartford for only a few hours, and was too busy with the "necessary preparations for her concert" to receive guests. Sigourney did send Williams five dollars, a consolation prize of sorts as support "for your charitable & Christian designs" for "our poor red brethren." He continued to petition congressmen and senators and the governor of New York to obtain what he felt entitled to for his service during the War of 1812.[23]

The frequent turnover in the White House during the two decades before the Civil War meant regular turnover in the administration of Indian Affairs as well, and opportunities for Williams to ingratiate himself with those in charge and convince them of his usefulness. In August 1850, for example, Williams offered his advice to Commissioner of Indian Affairs Luke Lea. A dozen years after the Buffalo Creek Treaty, everyone seemed to recognize that the Iroquois in New York and Wisconsin had no interest in removing to the Indian Territory. What to do, then, with the 1.824 million acres provided for them in the West in the treaty? Williams thought that the New York Indians might relinquish these claims "provided the arrangement be liberal on the part of the United States." The states of New York and Wisconsin, he told Lea, had changed their conduct toward their Indian residents, so he was "not surprised that the Indians . . . preferred to remain as they are." They knew that removal produced only suffering and, as a result, Williams thought, "it is the general opinion among the most prudent, sensible, and judicious part of the Six Nations, that 'the time has come for them to take their chance with the rest of their fellow men, and get their livelihood by cultivating the earth.'" Any removal, Williams thought, "would greatly retard, if not finally, put an end to the progress they are now making to become as their Brethren, the Americans." But "in order to ascertain more generally the views and wishes of the Six Nations, it will be necessary, for me to visit their several cantons, which extends more than one thousand miles from Green Bay." He would need funding from the commissioner's office to undertake this mission.[24]

Williams continued to pursue the Buffalo Creek funds. In the summer of 1850 a group of St. Regis chiefs wrote to President Zachary Taylor, indicating that in their view Williams deserved the entire four thousand dollars remaining from the treaty. "He is the only person," they wrote, "who has rendered any service in procuring the Green Bay lands." So Williams told Hanson, who observed that "if ever there was a clear case of right and justice, it was this."[25] But Ransom Gillet, who negotiated the original treaty, felt the money should go to the tribe as a whole and not to "Priest Williams," who "is said to have a power of some sort, but informal and insufficient." Gillet thought that "without prompt and decisive movements," Williams would try to keep money that would otherwise greatly aid the St. Regis Mohawks. Gillet encouraged the St. Regis leaders to resist with petitions of their own.[26]

Congress finally voted to appropriate the funds in 1851, and early in 1853 appointed a commissioner to determine how best to distribute them. The commissioner, Stephen Osborn of Buffalo, felt that much of the money ought to go to Williams, but he would not defy the chiefs, who believed that "the entire amount should be paid to the American party of the Indians" at St. Regis. The commissioner called on Gillet for advice, and he argued once again that with the grant of lands to him in the treaty, Eleazer Williams had received enough.[27]

The story infuriated Hanson, when Williams told him about it. The land, after all, had belonged to Williams's wife, and the government did nothing more than recognize her title to it. "The private property of Mrs. Williams, previous to her marriage, and which, according to the treaty of 1838, Mr. Williams claimed *in his own right and in that of his wife,* is represented by Mr. Gillet as an extravagant remuneration for his services." Osborn was replaced, and a new commissioner appointed. By the middle of 1853, the four thousand dollars, Hanson noted with disgust, had been "paid over by government to the very Indians, who, previous to the influence of Mr. Gillet, had renounced all right and title to it."[28]

*   *   *

Williams spent many years pursuing this money, but he also hoped to reestablish himself as a missionary. At first Williams hoped to return to Wisconsin to minister, with the church's blessings, to the Oneidas. "If they are satisfied with the purity of my intentions," he informed Jackson Kemper, "and the prospect of usefulness among them, there will be sufficient inducement for me to serve them." Williams reminded Kemper of all he had done, and why this mattered. "I would wish to labor as a humble Missionary of the Cross among a people where my former exertions were abundantly blessed by God by the conversion of six hundred Pagans to the Christian faith—and for whose benefit I have spent ten thousand dollars of my own money and property to sustain the mission of the Episcopal Church as well as assisting them in their temporal interests, and who are still indebted to me about $8000, in procuring the tract of land which gives them now a home and a living." He rested on his laurels, reprising a successful role, but he was broke, and he needed a job. "How true is that saying by the late venerable Bishop Hobart," that nothing could be "more calamitous to the interests of a clergyman than a condition of debt."[29]

But the Oneidas did not want Williams back. "We have made diligent inquiry throughout the nation," wrote a group of important First Christian Party leaders, "and have not found one in the nation among those who are attached to the Church & who are at all interested in religious matters, who have wished or now wish that Mr. Williams become their minister." Williams was not welcome. "We are persuaded that while among us, his aim was not to benefit us but to destroy us as a nation." Williams, they wrote, "watched over us more like a wolf ready to seize upon and devour us than as a shepherd whose care would be to protect and shield us from danger." Williams, they said, was a liar who would say anything to benefit himself. He openly disrespected the church and laughed at it "as a cold and lifeless body incapable of imparting more than the form of godliness to its members." They did not consider Williams "worthy to serve as a minister of the Church in any place." It was as if he had never accomplished a thing, and his past efforts no longer mattered. Williams tried to convince church officials of all he had done. He tried to convince them that he might do more in the future. And he tried to convince them to believe him rather than his critics.[30]

Williams asserted that the charges he faced stemmed from the hard feelings of his clerical rivals and factionalism among the Oneidas. The enigmatic H. G. Woutman, who identified himself as "secretary to my master (the very honorable Eleazer Williams)," reminded the Episcopal Diocese of New York that Williams's "zeal in the cause of missions, and his success among the Pagans of the Oneida tribe, is known in the historical page" of both Europe and the United States. An alcoholic whose body authorities would later fish from the Fox River, and who it seems began following Williams after he claimed he was the dauphin in the late 1840s, Woutman argued "that at this moment there is a great interest taken in the welfare of your humble Missionary, among some of the most respectable characters in America, England, France and Austria." Best to reinstate Williams, Woutman argued, for the world was watching.[31]

Williams made his arguments as to why the Episcopal diocese of New York ought to consent to his return to Wisconsin. Each step of the way, Jackson Kemper countered Williams's claims. Kemper, who viewed Williams as an incompetent and self-aggrandizing missionary who had mismanaged church resources, learned from Solomon Davis that Williams consistently neglected his duties. Davis told Kemper that Williams had not "expended one dollar for the benefit of the Oneidas but, to the contrary, *has taken thousands from them.*" Kemper did not mince words. He told Williams that he could not consent to his return to Wisconsin. "I have often deeply mourned that a clergy man of your talents and attainments should have utterly wasted the best years of your life." Find something else to do, Kemper wrote, or a mission field where you are welcome.[32]

And that is what Williams did. He told the Standing Committee of the New York diocese that if they would not facilitate his return to Green Bay, then perhaps they might support his efforts to open a school and mission enterprise at St. Regis. Before the diocese could lend Williams its support, however, its leaders wanted to sort out as much as possible what had happened in his relationship with the Oneidas and whether Williams was worth backing financially. Protestant missions struggled at St. Regis, something Williams remembered from his own experience. Many in the community— "the most venal and heartless set of beings in human shape, ever debauched by a low-bred priest"—maintained their ties to the Catholic Church.[33] Still, Williams tried to gain the support of the church. By 1851 he had, he said, "established a school in the eastern part of their reservation, where the Indian Children to the number of twenty-two are taught in the rudimental books of the English education." With church support, he believed that he could firmly establish the Protestant Episcopal Church as an alternative to Catholicism among the Mohawks. But, as always, he needed money. "Yes, Rev'd Sir," he wrote to one member of the board, "I have actually spent about ten thousand dollars of my own money in sustaining, for a series of years, one of her missionary stations among these people." He had nothing left to give but his labor and his commitment. He was willing to travel to raise money. He would go to Connecticut and Massachusetts, where interest in missions was great. He had received invitations to preach in Vermont. He would go and seek funds "wherever I may be permitted to deliver an address in behalf of my establishment and take up collections."[34]

Williams wished that the church would find its way to aid him. "It is revolting to my feelings, at times, to be thus acting as a supplicant in behalf of those who were once Lords of the soil," he wrote, "but it is the work of my ascended and exalted Redeemer, I will and must perform his work as one of his Disciples." He could do something with the church's approval, but so much more with their financial support.[35] He promised much and made his case to men who knew him by reputation, and had learned much about this "wily Indian" from his detractors. So he worked to refute his critics' charges. He elicited letters from supporters. He played for sympathy. He suggested that he suffered unjustly from the hostility of jealous and bitter rivals. The men who sat on the New York Diocese Standing Committee read Williams's letters and those written by his opponents. They remained skeptical about Williams's claims. But in the end, his critics seem to have relented, so long as he did his work in northern New York and not in Wisconsin. Even Jackson Kemper suggested that the New York diocese "try him again, for he has talents." Kemper had heard Williams's claim that he was the dauphin. He knew well that these beliefs were, as he politely noted, "unfounded," and he did not know why Williams was making these claims, but Kemper thought that these odd "notions relative to France" will "neither injure him nor impair his usefulness."[36]

Williams thus won from the Episcopal diocese at last its limited blessings to carry on his work among the Mohawks. Had the diocesan officials consulted with the Indians at St. Regis, however, they might have reconsidered. The Mohawks were unhappy about a number of things. They did not like how the agent appointed by the state of New York distributed their annuity. He gave too much to people with no legitimate claim to the money. Among those claimants, the St. Regis chiefs pointed out, was Williams, who claimed "that he is entitled to some $400 for his share of the annuity of this tribe, which he has neglected to draw." They pointed out that Williams was not a member of the St. Regis community, and that he never had been. They hoped that Williams didn't fool state officials into thinking otherwise.[37]

The St. Regis Mohawks also did not like the state-supported teacher on the reservation. He lived far from them in a hotel run by a proprietor who had rendered himself unpopular by his refusal to serve Indians at the hotel bar. The state's agent, J. J. Seaver, thought that much of this difficulty originated with the Catholic priest, who was "violently opposed to anything Protestant" and willingly took "advantage of their ignorance & superstition to work his purposes in their minds."[38]

Seaver thought highly of the state's teacher. A bigger problem, he thought, was "an old Indian," Eleazer Williams, who was "anxious to supplant the present teacher, and uses all his cunning to bring him in disrepute among the Indians." Seaver warned state officials that Williams was on his way to Albany to level his charges against the current teacher. Seaver wanted government officials in the state capital to "be on their guard respecting the confidence they may place in his statements." He could see that Williams was not to be trusted.[39]

Williams ran a small school on the margins of Fort Covington, just off the reservation, at least for a time. Franklin Hough, who visited him there in June of 1852, a bit more than half a year after Williams met Hanson, found him "very intelligent." Hough seldom met, he wrote, "with a white man who has a more ready flow of language or who is more interesting in conversation." Williams showed Hough the same dress he had shown to Hanson, made of "a most splendid quality of silk . . . whatever may have been its history." But upon reflection Hough thought that Williams "possessed an ingenious faculty for collating the plausible coincidences which make up the warp and woof" of the dauphin tale.[40]

When Williams met Hanson, then, in the fall of 1851, he had regained the right to minister to the Indians, to open a school in a community where he had few connections, few friends, few resources, and little respect. By the time he met Hanson in the fall of 1851, Williams now knew, rightly or wrongly, that he would not obtain the money that he felt had been a part of the Buffalo Creek Treaty. As yet he had received nothing from his efforts to obtain a pension for his service or his father's losses during the war. Whatever stipend he received from the diocese was small, and was probably not adequate to defray the costs of his frequent travel. Williams often mentioned his hardships, but it did not interest Hanson much. Hanson might have spent more time on this part of Williams's story, the patriot and missionary spurned and rejected by the country he saved and the people to whom he ministered. He might have described Williams's dogged efforts to win the necessary approval to resuscitate his clerical career. But Williams led Hanson down another path. Albert Gallatin Ellis, Williams's protégé, chronicler, and critic, pointed out that his one-time patron conjured the dauphin tale "to give him notoriety, to repair his damaged fortunes, and enable him to re-enter those high circles in which, he has for so many years failed to appear."[41]

* * *

In December 1852 Williams traveled to New York City to meet with Hanson and discuss the fruits of his research, a manuscript Hanson intended to submit in the very near future to *Putnam's Magazine.* Hanson's friend and patron, Francis L. Hawks, also attended the meeting. He had known, he said, both Hanson and Williams for years. Williams struck Hawks, despite his reputation, as "a worthy and truthful man." He said that Williams was often slower than Hanson and he in seeing the connections between the bits of evidence that established his identity as the dauphin. If Williams did not always know where Hanson and Hawks were leading him, he played it well. When they showed him how the pieces of the puzzle fit together, Hawks said, Williams's "countenance would light up with a smile, and he would say, 'I see it now but I never saw it before.'"[42]

Hanson and Williams checked their notes. It is likely that they ironed out a few details. Three weeks later, Hanson placed his essay in the hands of George Putnam. And six weeks after that, it appeared in *Putnam's* with the title, "Have We a Bourbon Among Us?" Hanson produced a list of more than two dozen "facts" that he felt helped make his case. Hanson told the stories of Joinville and Belanger, and how a number of French émigrés believed that the dauphin had been secreted out of France and carried to America. Le Ray de Chaumont, for instance, who Hanson believed had been involved in the project to hide the dauphin, "had much dealing with the Indians in the neighborhood where Mr. Williams was brought up," and once in conversation "made a remote allusion to the Dauphin." Then there was Colonel De Ferrier, who lived among the Oneidas, and the Abbé de Colonne who lived near Kahnawake, "both of whom believed the Dauphin to be alive, and in America."[43]

Williams's name did not appear in the baptismal register at Kahnawake, suggesting that his actual birthplace was someplace else. The Catholic priests at that place, Hanson asserted, seemed remarkably keen on luring Williams back to Roman Catholicism. Williams convinced Hanson of the authenticity of the dead Marie Antoinette's gown in his possession and that "the varied marks on his body"—scrofulous scars on his knees, and scars on his face—"correspond exactly with those known to have been on the body of the Dauphin."[44]

Hanson asserted as well that Williams's "reputed mother" did not acknowledge him to be her child," that Williams closely resembled Louis XVIII, and "that he has none of the characteristics of an Indian." Hanson repeated a story similar to that told by others: "a gentleman of distinction," he wrote, showed to Williams some engravings and lithographs he had acquired during a recent stay in Europe. At the sight of one, "and without seeing the name, Williams was greatly excited and cried out, 'Good God! I know that face. It has haunted me through life,' or words to that effect." It was, of course, an engraving of Simon the Jailer.[45]

Hanson attempted to make his case. He believed that the evidence he presented showed "1st. That Louis XVII did not die in 1795." Second, that a cabal of French royalists secretly carried the dauphin to America and to a spot near where Eleazer Williams grew up. Hanson believed that the evidence showed clearly that Williams was not an Indian and, therefore, "that Mr. Williams is Louis XVII." Hanson asserted that his evidence was "irresistible," and that he stood willing to stake "his reputation as a man of common sense and common discernment on the issue."[46]

A number of critics took that bet. *Putnam's*, one pointed out, frequently published sensational stories, though few of them seemed as absurd as Hanson's. Williams, another pointed out, was several years too young to be the dauphin and, besides, his mother, who certainly ought to have known, in fact gave a deposition in which she stated that Eleazer Williams was her fourth child and "that her son Eleazer very strongly resembled his father Thomas Williams, and that no person whatever, either clergyman or others, ever advised her or influenced her, in any manner, to say that he was her son" (which of course Williams and Hanson asserted was evidence that Catholic priests and others had done just that).[47]

Williams's mother disputed Hanson's findings, but so did the prince de Joinville. His representative described Hanson's piece as an "absurd invention." Though Joinville did meet with Williams briefly in 1841, and did send him some books as a token of his friendship, "all the rest, all which treats of the revelation which the Prince made to Mr. Williams, of the mystery of his birth, all which concerns the pretended personage of Louis XVII, is from one end to the other a work of imagination, a fable woven wholesale, a speculation upon the public credulity."[48] One New York paper suggested that the evidence presented by Hanson in behalf of "this half-breed minister" was so deficient that if "ten times multiplied and the products multiplied by ten millions," it would not be "sufficient to implicate, much less convict, a thrice convicted five point or Ann Street rowdy of petty larceny."[49] A critic in the *Christian Enquirer* pointed out how "Mr. Williams has been very unfortunate in losing all the documents on which his story is grounded." This critic thought it implausible that the dauphin might recover from the horrendous suffering he faced to become "a remarkably healthy man, carrying even into his age uncommon freshness and activity." This was, it seemed, surely "a wondrous instance of the benefit of a sea voyage and an out-door life." A critic in the *Literary Messenger* thought Williams's act when he saw the engraving of Simon part of his con, and suggested that Williams was "probably on the look-out for a sensation."[50] Others thought Williams's grip on reality weak. "The limits between fact and dream" for Williams "have become quite hazy," thought the *Christian Enquirer*, and the kindness shown him long before by Joinville "gave an exhaltation to his fancy which was not favorable to his observing nor to his reasoning powers." The *Southern Quarterly Review*, unconvinced by Hanson, thought Williams either a white man or a half-breed overtaken by an "unhappy monomania."[51]

Some skeptics were willing to grant Hanson that Eleazer Williams was not an Indian but a representative of "the best of humankind," but they still thought him an imposter, a play-actor. Those who believed that Williams was an Indian felt sorry for him on occasion. "The true pity," wrote one observer of the controversy "is that Mr. Williams has permitted his confidence to be diverted from his truly honorable ancestry, and from the high office to which he has been ordained, to dream of descent from vulgar kings." The passive voice was important: as an Indian, Williams could not possess the requisite sophistication and cunning to compose so complicated a tale. Williams should take pride in his descent from Eunice Williams, and leave things at that.[52]

Hanson responded to his critics. He gathered additional evidence, took affidavits from those who could provide additional support for his claims, and found witnesses to the encounter between Williams and Joinville. He challenged the veracity of the deposition given by Mary Ann Williams, Eleazer's mother, and challenged his critics' claims and exposed their biases. "To those who have charitably attributed to me the origination of a moon hoax to sell a magazine, or the credulity of adopting the baseless tale of a monomaniac," Hanson wrote, "I reply with all good nature, that I am content to leave the case to speak for itself, quite satisfied with the approbation of those, neither few, nor stupid, nor credulous, who entertain with me, the strongest conviction of the high probability that beneath the romance of the incident there is here the rocky substratum of indestructible fact."[53]

Hanson did not stop there. Like his critics, he came to believe increasingly that the science of racial difference, as it existed in the middle of the nineteenth century, offered important evidence that could support or refute Williams's claim. Hanson took Williams for examination by a panel of medical experts in New York City. Hanson's doctors found that Williams was neither crazy nor an Indian. One physician concluded that Williams had "a lofty aspect, strongly marked outline of figure, obviously European complexion," and consistent with the illnesses of the imprisoned dauphin, "a slight tinge of scrofulous diathesis." Another found that

the physical development of Mr. Eleazer Williams is that of a robust European, accustomed to exercise, exposure to open air, and indicative of the benefit of a generous diet, and a healthy state of the digestive organs. He might readily be pronounced of French blood. His general appearance and bearing are of a superior order; his countenance in repose is calm and benignant; his eyes hazel, expressive and brilliant, and his whole contour, when animated, indicates a sensitive and improvable organization. . . . There are no traces of the aboriginal or Indian in him. Ethnology gives no countenance to such a conclusion. The fact is verified by anatomical expression, and no unsoundness of mind or monomania has been manifested by any circumstance evinced in communication with him.[54]

Hanson included this and other medical testimony in his lengthy biography of Williams, *The Lost Prince*, published by Putnam's in January 1854. Indeed, Hanson had Williams examined by Dr. H. N. Walker of Hogansburg. Walker informed Hanson in a letter published in *The Lost Prince* that Williams had "no ethnological connection with the St. Regis Indians, nor with any other Indians I have ever known." If Williams was an Indian, "it is in the absence of all those ethnological signs discernable in form, features, texture of the skin, hair, and other similar tokens well-known to the profession, which, as far as my observations and information extend, are considered decisive."[55]

*   *   *

Eleazer Williams did not sit idly by as this debate played itself out in the papers. He spoke frequently, and found more pulpits open to him, and larger audiences willing to listen to him than ever before. He toured to raise money to support himself and his missionary enterprise. Skeptics, intent on exposing "the ridiculous humbug lately published by Putnam," attended his talks. But the faithful and the curious came out to see the dauphin on tour as well. They responded with enthusiasm, according to most accounts, to Williams's call for donations. Indeed, Williams reported to his old antagonist Jackson Kemper that "my appeal to the churches in your Atlantic cities has been responded well to my satisfaction."[56]

We do not have a complete record of what Williams told these audiences, but by piecing together a number of accounts, along with fragments found in Williams's papers, it is possible to arrive at some sense of how he constructed his appeal. Certainly he spent some time describing the state of his mission. "I have from 18 to 25 scholars," he told one audience, "who have made a good progress in the first rudiments of an English education." Philanthropists had provided a small amount of funding but he could do so much more with additional support. He had yet to build the church, he said, and the brutal northern New York winter made clear the inadequacy of his schoolhouse. With students eager, and their families supportive, all that was required was the assistance of Christians to bring this mission to fruition.[57]

In Troy, New York, Williams preached to his audience about the hope of eternal life, God's precious gift to mankind. And then, according to the Troy *Daily Traveler*, Williams "proceeded to address his hearers in behalf of the American Indians." Employing the well-worn image of the vanishing American, Williams appealed to the consciences of his audience. The Indian, he said, was once "the sole possessor, the undisputed Lord" of a "vast domain" which included "the broad lands which you now enjoy." The Indians' losses were the white man's gain. When "the broad Atlantic bore upon its bosom . . . the ships of another nation, freighted with the subjects of a foreign prince," the Indians met them "upon the beach," where the newcomers stood help-lessly, with "the ocean behind, and the vast wilderness before them."[58]

The newcomers came with the "avowed object" of bringing "the savage from heathenism to Christianity—to bring him from the darkness of bar-barous life, to the light of Christian truth." It had not worked out very well. "Mark the history of the succeeding years," he said, "to see the Indian fading away before the aggressive march of the white man," the "moral and physical degradation to which he was led." It was the white man who bore responsibil-ity, Williams continued, he "who pressed the accursed bowl to his lips." The white man "added the vices of civilized life to those of savage existence," and "proclaimed the gracious design of bringing the savage people to the light of glorious gospel" while robbing them "of the possessions, and for the products of his toil gave him in return the worthless beads and tinsel trappings, which swelled the coffers of the white man's cupidity and avarice." All Native Ameri-can history, Williams told his audience, was "a history of wrong."[59]

He spoke at Grace Church in Brooklyn in February of 1853, shortly after the publication of Hanson's essay. A month later, when he arrived in Wash-ington upon "business with the Chief of the Indian Bureau," a large number of onlookers "assembled in the lobbies to take observation of the Rev. Eleazer Williams." He spent time in Philadelphia before returning to Green Bay for a brief visit in July.[60]

By the fall he was in Hoboken, where Hanson lived. He preached at St. Paul's and "his theme was Judgment, and the Judgment Day." He may have returned to St. Regis for the winter, but by the spring of 1854 Williams increased the frequency with which he preached, and with which he spun his tale. In March he appeared at churches in Baltimore, sometimes twice in a day. On 26 March he gave three Sunday sermons, morning, afternoon, and evening, at Ascension, Grace, and Advent Churches. At each of these perfor-mances, large audiences gathered to hear him speak "of his mission among the Indians, and the words he uttered fell from his lips with increased effect from the convictions many had that the representative of a long line of French kings spoke to them." He made short trips that spring to New York City, and to Camden, New Jersey, but he spent most of his time in Philadel-phia, where, according to one newspaper, "he has preached in the Church of the Ascension, in St. Peter's, St. James's, St. Mark's, in Christ Church, and we believe in pretty much all the Episcopal Churches in the city." At each stop, he spoke about the condition of the Indians, "and the duty which the American people owe to the Aboriginals of the land." He uttered the well-worn lines used by many before him who had advocated for the Indians.

Williams raised "a handsome amount towards the object of ameliorating the condition of the red men of the forest," while creating "a profound sensation in the minds of those who have investigated the facts in relation to his own most remarkable history."[61]

It is worth noting that Williams, as the dauphin, continued to do what he long had done. He preached, perhaps his greatest talent. He called on white audiences to support his missionary enterprise. And this appeal pulled in substantial crowds. Yet many of those who attended his presentations and dropped their coins in the collection plate were drawn in more by Williams's claim to be the dauphin than by a desire to support missionary activity among the Mohawks at Akwesasne. Certainly those who promoted Williams's appearances employed the story "of the Lost Prince" and "a son of the late Louis XVI" who was now "an humble missionary among the Indians, our red brethren of the forest," to generate interest in their churches. Reverend Williams, the Middletown, Connecticut, *Sentinel and Witness* reported early in 1855, was "believed to be the son of the unfortunate Louis XVI and his equally unfortunate Queen, Marie Antoinette." That a humble missionary like Williams, "descended from the race of kings, of more than three score in number, should, in the providence of God, in a foreign country be an ambassador of the King of Kings, to the feeble and scattered remnants of those who were once themselves, the lords and kings of an immense domain, is certainly a consideration fraught with material for reflection and interest."[62] Indeed. But Williams himself appears to have said little about his parentage, and this frustrated some of those who came to hear him preach. They wanted him to address specifically where he stood on the question of his asserted royal identity. As the Washington, D.C., *Daily National Era* pointed out in the spring of 1854, "Mr. Williams either does or does not profess to believe that he is the son of Louis XVI." He should take a stand and do so publicly. "If he does, he should say so; if he does not, he should not permit any one, whether to give him or his mission éclat, or for whatever purpose, to place him in an equivocal position before the world." Williams clearly had used the notoriety to generate interest in his missionary activity.[63]

Some in those audiences found the notion that Williams was the dauphin entirely unbelievable. But they did not base their skepticism on the obvious problems with the story: Williams was too young by a few years, for instance, and he had no documentary evidence to support his most spectacular claims. Instead, they focused on a variety of "racial" characteristics that to them seemed to demonstrate that Williams was an Indian or, at best, a "half-breed," both of which of course disqualified any claim that he might be the dauphin.

Williams engaged in his performance at the tail end of a period where science had come to define native peoples of the "American Race" as inferior to "Caucasians." Indeed, he spent more time in Philadelphia than in any other city, and Philadelphia long had been the center of American racial science. Though the environmentalism of early eras did not disappear entirely during the Antebellum era, it certainly had come under attack. Charles Caldwell, for instance, one of the most important of these scientists of race, after examining the heads of members of an Indian delegation visiting Washington, D.C., asserted that the "native bent" of white people led them toward civilization, while with Indians, the reverse was true. "Savagism, a roaming life, and a home in the forest, are as natural to them, and as essential to their existence, as to the buffalo or the bear. Civilization is destined to exterminate them in common with the wild animals among which they have lived, and on which they have subsisted." The only hope for their survival, Caldwell thought, was cross-breeding with white people. "By the requisite means, half and quarter-breeds and those having still less Indian in them, may be educated, and rendered useful members of civil society."[64]

These pseudo-scientific inquiries led rather mechanically to lists of characteristics that defined the different races. Often these were little more than stereotypes, and they could not account with much ease for those native people who had managed to "improve," but those interested in this science acted on its assumptions. Samuel George Morton, so enthusiastic a collector of human skulls that his friends jokingly called his Philadelphia study an "American Golgotha," believed that in their measurement lay the key to understanding racial difference. He cleaned the skulls, coated them with varnish, measured their angles, and determined their volume by filling the cranium with pepper seed or buckshot or liquid mercury.[65]

From his studies, Morton deduced the intellectual and physical inferiority of American Indians relative to Caucasians. If Caucasians, for instance, possessed "naturally fair skin," hair that was "fine, long and curling and of various colors," with a skull "large and oval" and a face "small in proportion to the head, of an oval form, with well-proportioned features," by contrast, a "brown complexion, long, black, lank hair, and deficient beard" marked "the American race." In Indians, Morton wrote, "the cheek bones are large and prominent, and incline rapidly toward the lower jaw, giving the face an angular conformation." The Indians' "upper jaw is often elongated and much inclined outwards, but the teeth are for the most part vertical. The lower jaw is broad and ponderous, and truncated in front." The teeth are also "very large, and seldom decayed," Morton continued, "for among the many that remain in the skulls in my possession, very few present any marks of disease, although they are often much worn down by attrition in the mastication of hard substances." Their hair was always straight and black, and among the Indians, "no trace of the frizzled locks of the Polynesian, or the wooly texture of the negro, has ever been observed."[66]

Morton could read the skulls and deduce more than mere physical characteristics. "The bold physical development of the American savage," he wrote, "is accompanied by a corresponding acuteness in the organs of sense." Indians were "vigilant," a product of "the constant state of suspicion and alarm in which the Indian lives." They spoke "in a slow and studied manner, and to avoid committing himself he often resorts to metaphorical phrases which have no precise meaning." They employed subterfuge against their enemies, whom they pursued relentlessly. The Iroquois especially, Morton said, "possessed all the other Indian characteristics in strong relief." They "paid little respect to old age; they were not much affected by the passion of love, and singularly regardless of the connubial obligations; and they unhesitatingly resorted to suicide as a remedy for domestic or other evils." The Iroquois, he said, "were proud, audacious, and vindictive, untiring in the pursuit of the enemy, and remorseless in the gratification of their revenge."[67]

Morton died in 1851, but the ideas he and his cohort of fellow race scientists advanced provided a vocabulary and a widely disseminated and understood set of conceptual categories. Few doubted "the intellectual and moral superiority over all other races of men" of white Americans, and they knew that differences in physical traits could determine racial difference.[68] A persuasive performance as the dauphin might have offered Williams an escape from these increasingly rigid measures, a means to avoid the easy categorization of those who may have viewed him as a degraded savage, whatever his achievements. Perhaps this offered an additional motive for Williams to assume this role. But these standards for defining red and white and the differences between them could entrap as well. Williams confronted these conceptual categories when he presented himself to audiences as the dauphin.

Williams's critics thus dismissed his claims not primarily on the basis of their implausibility, or because they thought that Williams was deluded (though some did), but because in racial terms he did not seem to evidence any of the characteristics they associated with noble European birth. They did not denounce him as a confidence man. They said simply, whatever his claims to the contrary, that according to the canons of race "science" he was Indian and not white. The author of a piece that appeared in the *New York Herald*, for instance, who wrote under the pseudonym St. Clair and who claimed to have met Williams several years before, argued that "no man acquainted with our aboriginal race, and who has seen Mr. Williams, can for a moment doubt his descent from that stock." Of Williams, he wrote, "his color, his features, and the conformation of his face, testify to his origin." He looked like a "half-blood Indian," and not at all like a Bourbon.[69] A. G. Ellis, for his part, said Williams was "unquestionably a half-breed Mohawk Indian, having all the distinctive features of the race: the black straight hair, the black eyes, the copper color and high cheek bone; and all who knew him when young remarked this." Years later, Ellis described Williams as "dark enough for 3/4 Indian," and he clearly believed color did not lie. C. C. Trowbridge, who knew Williams in Wisconsin and respected him for a time, laughed at the dauphin story. Williams "had all the peculiarities of a half-breed Indian, as undoubtedly he was. . . . If he had been otherwise, mentally or morally, his hair and complexion would have stamped him as of mixed savage and civilized blood."[70]

Science came readily to the assistance of those who doubted Williams's clams to be the dauphin. Peter A. Browne, for instance, a race expert in Philadelphia who could "ascertain the race of an individual by the hair upon his head, with as inevitable certainty as a phrenologist can determine character by bumps," concluded from his examination of Williams that "there is a difference in the diameter of the hairs of Mr. Williams," and that "some are oval, some cylindrical," and that "therefore he is a cross of Indian and white" and "consequently he is not the Dauphin." There was little that Williams could say in a debate like this. He could tell no tale, it seemed, powerful enough to circumvent what Americans considered established science.[71]

Indeed, Williams's journey as the dauphin carried him back through Longmeadow, Massachusetts, where he spent his adolescence receiving an education in Calvinism from the descendants of his Puritan forbears, and nearby Springfield. Now, four decades later, he returned not as the descendant of a Puritan child carried into the wilderness but as the son of a French king and his queen. He sat for a daguerreotype in Springfield. He might have faced the camera. That was, after all, the purpose of the daguerreotype, to represent that subject's true likeness. But the man who captured Williams's image evidently had something else in mind. He took a profile, a side view, with the light coming from above. The image highlighted Williams's "Indian" features, his high cheekbones, for instance. Poses such as this were relatively rare. The image constituted a racialist text, a commentary on Williams's chosen identity as the dauphin. He could not possibly be the dauphin, his critics pointed out, because he possessed the

Figure 5. Eleazer Williams, daguerreotype, ca. 1854.

Courtesy of the Longmeadow Historical Society, Longmeadow, Massachusetts.

racial features they associated with American Indians. Williams's ability to define who he was thus ran into assumptions strengthened by the emerging American science of racial difference. And against that standard, Williams struggled to measure up.

But Williams still had his advocates, and they too framed their views in terms of Williams's racial traits. Hanson asserted that "there are certain characteristics of the Indian race which are all but indelible, and appear after the lapse of centuries, even on the cheek of beauty." Hanson looked at Williams closely and knew him well. "When the fact of origin has died into a tradition," he wrote, "you can mark the red blood coursing with a duskier hue beneath the mantling blush brought from other climes, and imparting fixity and palor to its softness. Skin, hair, craniological formation in the closer degrees of affinity, present ready and infallible tests."[72]

And so it went. A correspondent from a New York paper, the *Courier de Etats Unis*, found that Williams did not look like an Indian and that to him, "the forehead and the lower part of the face show a great analogy to certain physiognomies of" the Bourbons. Williams reminded the writer "entirely of Louis XVIII, whose countenance has remained perfectly fixed in our memory."[73] Another New Yorker reported that although Williams's complexion was "rather dark," having "become somewhat bronzed by exposure," his features were "heavily moulded, with the full Austrian lip, eyes dark hazle, and hair, dark, fine, and curling, somewhat sprinkled with gray." Williams was of medium height, full-chested, broad across the shoulders, "and inclined to emboument, which is a well-known characteristic of the Bourbons." A correspondent from a Troy, New York, newspaper concluded that some thought Williams was of mixed racial descent, but he could find no evidence of that himself. In Williams's features "we could trace no works of the Indian. They are decidedly European."[74]

Artists familiar with the Bourbons thought Williams looked about right to be a part of the family. Hanson spoke with M. B. H. Muller, a pupil of David and Gros. According to Hanson, Muller "was at once struck with the remarkable likeness to the royal family of France, and identified the color of Mr. Williams's eyes, bright hazel, with those of the Dauphin, having frequently seen authentic portraits of him in France." Chevalier Giuseppe Fagnani involved himself as well, asserting that Williams looked like a Bourbon to him.[75] Known in America as "the portraitist of crowned heads and statesmen," Fagnani had lived in Europe "in intimate acquaintance with the families of the Sicilian and Spanish Bourbons." When Williams sat for a portrait in Fagnani's New York studio, the "general Bourbonic outline" of Williams's face impressed him. The "upper part of his face," Fagnani wrote, "is decidedly of a Bourbon cast, while the mouth and lower part resembled the House of Hapsburg." Fagnani depicted a man with light skin, hazel eyes, and light colored hair that had turned gray. Williams, he believed, could well be the dauphin because he demonstrated so many physical markers of "the Bourbon race."[76]

While in Philadelphia in the spring of 1854, Williams subjected himself to medical examination once again. The doctors—this time from the Pennsylvania College of Physicians, the Jefferson Medical College, and the U.S. navy—found that Williams possessed scars consistent with those received by the dauphin, as Hanson had claimed. Further, they found that

Figure 6. Eleazer Williams, painting by Giuseppe Fagnani.
Courtesy of the National Portrait Gallery, Washington, D.C.

his skin, where it has not been exposed to the weather, is that of a pure white man. His hair is of a silken fineness and curls freely. His hands and feet, his wrists and ankles are very small, indicating an ancestry unaccustomed to any hard use of their bodily organs. His countenance and reception are peculiarly benign and gracious—totally free from the reserve and austerity of the Indians.[77]

This was another point that some of Williams's audiences raised. Not only did he look like a European and unlike an Indian, but he did not *act* in ways Indians were believed to act. In Williams's "mental likeness," one newspaper reported, "there is something closely allied to the best Bourbon traits," though the paper gave its readers no sense of how those traits might be measured. He did not speak like an Indian, though these observers said nothing about how they thought Indians spoke. But he was talkative and articulate and bright, traits all that his company did not associate with their Indian ideal. In Camden, New Jersey, Williams impressed the group who had gathered to meet with him after one of his dauphin performances. "Much to our surprise," one observer wrote, "we found him easy in manners, free and agreeable in conversation, with the polished bearing of a gentleman accustomed to refined and cultivated society." In no way, they wrote, did Williams "resemble the Indian, but in zeal for their spiritual interests and temporal welfare; and we venture to say, that of a hundred intelligent and observant men, familiar with the Indian character, visiting him without any previous intimation of his being of Indian extraction, not one would have even the most remote thought of his being of any other than European origin."[78]

*   *   *

John Holloway Hanson died in New York City in October 1854. "Many tears must flow from the death of one so amiable and pious, as well as so able and earnest minded, as Mr. Hanson," read his obituary in the *New York Times*, "but none, we are sure, will mingle more freely or more warmly, than those of his venerable and simple, yet, he verily believed, *royal* friend, who has been fated to bear the humble name of ELEAZER WILLIAMS."[79] That might have been so, but whatever grief Williams felt, he did not join the distinguished list of city clergy who attended Hanson's funeral, even though he was in the area. He stayed away, and he continued to tell his story, and pass the collection plate, for his humble mission to the St. Regis Mohawks.

In November he preached in Bridgeport and Hartford, Connecticut. He appealed for funding to build his church at St. Regis, as always, and according to reports "raised considerable money for that purpose." Shortly after New Year's in 1855 he preached at Trinity Church in New Haven to an overflow audience, and a couple of days after that at Christ Church in Middletown. He raised close to sixty dollars that night, and convinced the editor of the local paper of the sincerity of his desire to preach to the Indians. Williams "may have been deprived of a rich earthly crown," but "he will receive a far more brilliant crown in heaven."[80] Within a week, he had returned to New York City, before preaching in Albany in March and Troy in the summer. As late as September an observer in Troy noted that "his appearance is said to excite much interest wherever he goes."[81]

So it seemed. In each city where he preached, he still drew a crowd, and still managed to collect funds. That much is clear. But he spoke less frequently, and he began to devote his energies increasingly to older causes he had pursued over many years. Williams always had come to the cities in search of his fortune: New York, after the War of 1812, to become a missionary to the Indians, to Albany and to Washington, D.C., to influence the conduct of American Indian policy. A professional Indian, Williams was well known and for a time widely respected by those who wanted to ameliorate the Indians' condition or save their souls or seize their lands or all three. From these men, Eleazer Williams derived his income, and to keep their favor, he told them what he thought they needed to hear.

But the performances began to seem hollow, and when these men decided that Williams could no longer provide them with what they wanted, they cast him off. Williams became a confidence man, following a new path, the dauphin "humbug" as one newspaper described it. He created an elaborate backstory and he came to the cities to tell it. He told a story that drew on feelings and sentiments and images and questions that resonated with white urban Americans in the antebellum republic.

Williams began his career as an Indian who emerged from a humble upbringing to become an important missionary. Now he cast himself as a man born at the top, forced by circumstances out of his control to the very bottom. In the first half of the nineteenth century, with large numbers of Americans leaving the countryside for America's growing cities, many hoped to rise through the social ranks while others hoped to preserve their status. Whether Eleazer Williams was the dauphin or not raised questions about truth, the fluidity of identity in an allegedly open society, and the confidence one might place in strangers.[82] Like Barnum's Joice Heth exhibition, which preceded William's dauphin career by a decade and a half, Williams's tour presented to his audiences questions of authenticity and race, in a society where both of these categories were contested. He played upon that uncertainty. He invented himself. He told his tales. But he also found that powerful forces limited the choices he made.[83]

So as the curious assembled to hear him speak, they asked themselves the same question: Was he or wasn't he? Was Eleazer Williams the son of the king of France or an Indian from the northern wilds? Was he white or red, civilized or savage, or something in between? As those in the audience contemplated those questions, they looked closely at Williams. They watched his behavior, studied his comportment. They measured his color, his features, his hair, against what they believed to be the identifiers of "white" and "red." Members of the audience began with the exciting premise that the Lost Dauphin may have surfaced in America. They ended up talking about race. In this sense, we might view Williams's audiences as a series of concentric rings with him at the center. There was Hanson, of course, and a small number of others, who stood in his inner circle. The physicians who examined him, for Williams, comprised a most intimate audience. Then came those who saw Williams in person, who listened to him preach, and watched his performance. And beyond these came a larger audience still, who followed the resulting debate in the popular press. They all assessed the evidence they found before them, up close or from afar. Together, from wherever they watched, they considered and calculated the fraction of Indian blood that flowed through his veins. And some of them placed money in the collection basket when it passed them by, whatever they felt about his northern mission.

Williams moved on. He continued to pursue his efforts to publish his linguistic work. He developed a surprisingly complex syllabary for the Mohawk language given his language skills, an unnecessarily cumbersome thing with more than 180 characters, many of which closely resembled each other. He wrote histories—the biography of his father that I have cited many times in this book, and biographies of Louis Cook and William Gray. He sent them to Franklin Hough, giving "full permission to make such use of them as might be deemed proper, but expressing a wish that if published, the language should be slightly amended, and grammatical errors corrected, as the papers had been hastily prepared and time had not been found to give them the necessary revision for the public eye."[84]

He continued to advocate for native peoples, even if his efforts won him little support and few friends. He involved himself, for instance, in a long-standing Mohawk claim to lands in the state of Vermont. The land in question comprised "nearly one-half of the state, and covers its most valuable agricultural portions," wrote a journalist from Ogdensburg, New York. The state wanted to settle this claim, and it met with a Mohawk delegation in the summer of 1855, for which Williams served as an interpreter, and as "our true and lawful attorney" with the power "to receive from the State of Vermont any pay or compensation for lands within the limits of said State and to discharge all liabilities, claims or dues on such lands from the State of Vermont, and in all things fully release all such claims, and further bind the St. Regis Indians and several members of said tribes respectively."[85]

Williams and the Vermonters confronted the legacy of the 1796 Seven Nations Treaty that his father had negotiated. The Mohawks assumed that they had not included the Vermont lands in the cession. The state, through its representative J. H. Hotchkiss, was not buying. Though willing to consider the Mohawks' claim and settle it upon what he considered reasonable terms, Hotchkiss pointed out that "your title to the land in Vermont is not only doubtful, but it is utterly denied, and it has never been admitted that you have any legal claim, and you ask compensation for the lands your ancestors once occupied as their hunting ground." And these lands, Hotchkiss argued, the Mohawks had abandoned long before settlers moved into the region. "The people of Vermont have already paid very dear for their lands." Tell us what you want to quit this claim, Hotchkiss said, but do not ask for too much. "The smaller the sum you claim the greater will be the probability that the Legislature will allow it."[86]

When they met with Hotchkiss again in October 1855, the Mohawks asked for $89,600, or four cents an acre for their "Ancient hunting grounds in Vermont." Williams did not attend the council. Perhaps he recognized that Hotchkiss would never agree to that amount, and that the prospect of a reasonable settlement was doomed. (In fact, Hotchkiss thought the request was "entirely out of the question" when he received it.) Perhaps opposition to Williams's presence had emerged at St. Regis. It is not possible to tell, for Williams said nothing about the matter. But he did preach while in Vermont, striking one observer with the "mild, benevolent, Christian expression, that forbids the thought that any Indian blood is in his veins." When the plate was passed, "a handsome sum of money was collected to aid the St. Regis Indians in building a church."[87]

Williams lived off of this money. He had no other significant source of income. He committed a fraud, using funds collected from audiences curious about the dauphin and willing to chip in for an Indian mission to provide him with a meager livelihood. He exploited the nostalgia and sympathy white audiences in the northern states felt for native peoples with whom they no longer had to contend for control of the land and its resources. At the same time, Williams continued to pursue a pension for his military service during the War of 1812 and his share of the money set aside in the ninth article of the Buffalo Creek Treaty. He petitioned both federal and state authorities for a pension.[88] He wrote in his own behalf, and in behalf of his "reputed mother." He asked the commissioner of Indian affairs to forward to him copies of documents that he felt would help him justify his claim to the Buffalo Creek money.[89] And as he did this, Williams continued to cast himself as a representative of the St. Regis Mohawks. He wrote to the commissioner of Indian Affairs, and to others in the commissioner's office, about the St. Regis share in the so-called Kansas Lands, those set aside for the New York Indians in the Indian Territory at Buffalo Creek in 1838. All this he did without significant support at St. Regis. Early in 1858, the chiefs on the American side at St. Regis wrote to officials in New York to make sure that they understood that Williams did not represent them. Williams told state officials that the St. Regis wanted to become citizens, and that they favored the division of their lands into individual parcels, a policy that later would come to be known as allotment. The chiefs informed the state that those who supported Williams were "men not to be relied upon as representing the wishes of his tribe." Whatever Williams said, "we do not wish any division of our lands, nor nothing of the kind."[90]

His efforts with Congress did make some headway. In May of 1858, Congressman Schuyler Colfax of Indiana introduced a bill passed by the Senate the month before that allowed Williams "the sum of four thousand dollars, in full for his claim arising under the ninth article of the treaty with the Six Nations of Indians." The second section of the act gave to Williams a pension of $219 for his military service. But the legislation went no farther than that.[91]

The Last of Eleazer Williams

Early in 1858 Eleazer Williams met with Asher Wright, the long-serving Presbyterian missionary to the Senecas with whom he had been acquainted for more than a quarter century. They met at the Merchants' Hotel in Albany. Williams, Wright wrote later, had told him much over the years about "what he knew of his own history." Williams had explained to Wright how "he became early aware that he was watched and cared for by distinguished strangers, who kept themselves constantly informed of everything which concerned him." Wright recalled that when he recited the well-rehearsed story of his encounter with Joinville, Williams's "eyes flashed with indignation that the Prince should imagine him mean enough to sell his birthright and throw away the inheritance of his children for any amount of filthy lucre."[1]

Asher Wright was nobody's fool. He knew all about dishonesty. He witnessed the Ogden Company, its hirelings and its friends in high places at work. He understood the lengths those who coveted Indian land would travel to achieve their ends. Their lies menaced the people to whom he ministered. They pretended to act in the Indians' best interest, but all they wanted was their land. They would say or do anything to achieve their goals. The story Williams told was different, his storytelling of another order. It was performance. Something in it tugged at Wright. He could not say if Williams was the Dauphin. Of course he had his doubts. Still, Wright possessed not "the slightest doubt of the sincerity" of Williams's "own belief in them."[2]

To what extent can we become the stories we tell? To Wright, Williams genuinely believed that he was the Dauphin. Wright found some part of the performance compelling, a testament to Williams's skills. From his account, we can detect something of the forcefulness with which Williams spun his tales. Eleazer Williams needed to tell stories, whether about his service in

war, or as he held court in the Skenandoah house at Oneida Castle, or as
he searched for wisdom in Holy Scripture. He told stories to instruct those
who listened to him about the incredible power of God's grace. These are
the stories that clerics long have told their congregations, as they provided
consolation to those in pain, comfort and hope to seekers, and validation to
the confident and righteous. Williams was indeed a talented preacher. But
not all his audiences were Indian Christians. Not all of them sought solace or
salvation. Some of them wanted Oneida lands. They looked forward to transforming a dwindling Iroquoia into an emergent Empire State. William told
these men stories too, and some of them got him in trouble: that the Indians
to whom he ministered in New York favored removal, whatever a few unrep-
resentative malcontents might claim; that most Indians would be happier in
the West than in their people's ancestral homeland; that in fact they wanted
Williams to continue as their minister, that they trusted him still, and that
they relied upon him. Oneidas told whoever they thought might listen that
the stories Williams told were untrue, that he was a liar, and that he stood in
favor of policies and programs that they opposed. Williams's stories led the
Oneidas in Wisconsin and New York to cast him out of their community.
They saw through his act. The stories he told, and the roles he played, to
them, caused more harm than good.

So he began to tell new stories. He became a war hero, and he became the

For much of his career, then, Eleazer Williams played Indian. Or, more
accurately, he was an Indian playing to the expectations and assumptions
white elites held about what an Indian could be. Exhibiting gentility and
refinement, literacy, Christianity, and patriotism, Williams offered proof positive, it seemed, that native people might find some place for themselves in an
Anglo-American, Christian republic. This was a demanding performance, for
as he conducted his Indian work, Williams witnessed the injustice the citizens
of the republic heaped upon his countrymen: rustled livestock, cut timber,
stolen lands, and relentless encroachment. Whatever his misgivings, he aided
the nation's political and business leaders in their efforts to dispossess the Iroquois and drive them to new homes in the West. He expected this assistance
to buy him a livelihood, but by the middle of the 1830s, he found many of the
paths he had followed closed to him. He had to do something else to get by.[3]

So he began to tell new stories. He became a war hero, and he became the
dauphin. Whether he stood at the pulpit, calling on his audience to accept
his message, or spoke of his service during the War of 1812, Eleazer Williams performed. When he met with the Ogden Company men, offering his
services as missionary and agent in the cause of Indian removal, and when
he attempted to persuade audiences that he was a worthy recipient of their

charity, he attempted to gain their confidence. For him, this playacting was terribly serious business. In each of the guises he wore, he looked to make a living: a salary, a stipend, a pension, or contributions for a mission that existed mostly in his mind.

In an era known for its men-on-the-make and hustlers, its confidence men, counterfeiters, and painted women, Williams was not alone in his role-playing. Americans in the antebellum republic moved frequently, aided by a far-reaching "transportation revolution." Cities grew. Some of the uprooted and the rootless learned to take advantage of the confusion and the anonymity these changes permitted. Motion came easy, and the committed performer stood a reasonable chance of inventing him- or herself anew. Forgers, swindlers, and frauds might prosper, if only for a time.[4]

The possibility that the person to whom one spoke was not who or what they claimed to be loomed large in the literature of the era. P. T. Barnum, of course, exploited this uncertainty. Herman Melville placed this concern at the center of his difficult exploration of the antebellum American psyche.[5] Many expressed concerns that the traditional social and economic norms that governed face-to-face interactions might no longer apply. If all looked toward the main chance, to get ahead, and so many of those who one encountered were strangers here today and gone tomorrow, how could one determine in whom they might safely place their confidence?[6]

Play actors and performers: they seemed to be everywhere. Blackface minstrelsy, for instance, where white male actors played a number of stock African American characters, entertained huge audiences in the northern cities. The audience, largely Democratic and largely proletarian, gathered together and relished the small amount of security that came from knowing that an inferior racial caste lay beneath them. The audiences knew that the actors were white, a fact made clear in the promotional materials that announced each performance. Minstrel actors put on a costume, not a disguise.[7] But if minstrels served the needs of an anxious white audience, some antebellum role-players acted their parts in ways that threatened the social order. The itinerant faith healer Henry Tufts traveled about New England, for instance, preaching in the animated manner of a New Light minister. It was all an act. "I found it in no way difficult to cajole my ignorant followers," Tufts wrote, "into believing whatever idle tale I was pleased to fabricate." He gloated. "How easy to deceive is the unreflecting multitude!" He played upon the faith of his audience, collected what he could, and moved on.[8]

Tufts aimed at the pocketbooks of those who crossed his path. Runaway slaves who managed to pass as white, or as freed people of color, meanwhile, looked to blur the stark line between black slavery and white freedom that defined the Southern racial order. These runaways played difficult roles, parts that forced them to adopt the speech patterns, the manners, and the costume of those above them in the hierarchies of a slave society. Individuals like Okah Tubbee, born a slave, made a living for himself as an Indian. He traveled widely. He appeared in P. T. Barnum's museum in the 1840s. He played Indian to earn a living, but also to escape that dividing line between black and white. With this playacting came very high stakes. A successful performance allowed the actor to forge an identity as someone other than a slave, to find employment, perhaps, to practice a trade, and to establish and enjoy ties of kinship and family. Hundreds of runaways did so during the antebellum period, but the risk of failure, the dangers that came with offering an unconvincing performance, remained considerable.[9]

Performers were everywhere. Williams was not the only native person to play roles, to craft an identity, to carve out a space for himself in the white man's republic. George Copway, like Williams, served as a missionary. Like Williams, he spent much of his career earning a living as a professional Indian. He wrote about the history and the culture of the Ojibwe. He called for the creation of a Native American homeland west of the Great Lakes. He told white people stories, some of them untrue, intended to cast himself in a most positive light. He claimed expertise he did not have, influence he no longer possessed. Like Williams, Copway's white patrons soon grew weary of him. He spoke poorly and preached ineffectively, one critic suggested, and with his "discursive imagination," Francis Parkman wrote in 1849, "facts grow under his hands into preposterous shape and dimensions." He begged supporters for financial assistance. He looked for income wherever he could. He may have traveled to Central America, to join the filibustering expedition of William Walker, and he certainly attempted to recruit Canadian Indians to fight for the Union cause in the American Civil War. Like Williams, Copway found it difficult to get by, once his audiences no longer found his performances interesting or of use.[10]

Copway confronted the same forces against which Williams contended. Both struggled to make ends meet, despite a life spent perfecting the roles they played. Williams learned how to dress, how to convince his audiences of his civility and his refinement. By doing so he persuaded a series of patrons that he might aid them in war, help them Christianize the Indians and relocate them to new homes in the West where they might be civilized. He persuaded some that he was the lost child of a French king and queen. He understood what his audiences wanted to see in a preacher, a leader, and a king. He had to watch the reactions of his audiences, to read the crowd. He had to adjust his performance accordingly. Some parts of the act worked well—witness the repeated accounts of Williams feigning shock and confusion upon viewing an engraving of Simon the Jailer. He needed to convince these audiences. He sought not the applause and acclaim that went to the accomplished performer, however, but whatever income might result from a compelling performance. Some of the tales he told clearly with the intent to deceive. Some of his tales involved exaggeration, or evasion, or puffery. We can see, if we look, evidence that Williams used gestures and silence to convince those with whom he interacted that what was false actually was true. It is difficult to overstate the challenges of this endeavor, for if Williams wrote his own story and constructed his own characters, in the end he relied upon an audience to validate and reward his efforts.[11]

If many of the American confidence men threatened, as historian Karen Haltunnen put it, to undermine "social confidence among men and women, to reduce the American republic to social chaos," Williams may have stood apart in one more way.[12] Those who found Williams's performances unconvincing at the end did not denounce him as a crook, a thief, or a liar. His con hardly threatened the social order at all. He asked his audiences to donate money to support a mission. He had been a missionary in the past, and wanted to be one again. In Williams's confidence game, he did not turn his back on this part of his past. He added a twist, an extraordinary tale designed to generate interest. In this respect, he bore similarities to showmen and promoters such as Barnum and others like him during this era of cheap amusements and broadsides.

Barnum appealed to race, to patriotism, to the unusual and unbelievable, to draw an audience. Williams went with nostalgia, an appeal that resonated with Americans' interest in monarchy. And he appealed as well to the notion of the "Vanishing American," that condescending and romantic depiction of the Native American past that tugged at so many of his contemporaries. But on this cold winter day in Albany, Williams told Asher Wright a new story, one that he had not told him before over the many years they had known one another. Williams said that his long struggle to regain his rights was coming to a close. He may have spoken of his claims to the French throne, but what he said could have applied just as well to his long-standing attempts to acquire a pension for service during the War of 1812, or justice, as he saw it, based on the terms of the 1838 Buffalo Creek treaty. As he and Wright visited, Williams "spoke of his failing health: said he was fast wearing out." He told Wright that he worried about his son John, who worked as a fireman aboard a Great Lakes steamboat, a child and now a man for whom he had done little. Williams knew that the end was near.[13]

*   *   *

Williams last saw his son in July 1857, half a year before he met with Wright. He had returned to Green Bay to find some papers he needed to advance his claims before Congress. Either his wife or his son, presumably, could have looked through his papers for the documents he needed. It was a long journey indeed for an elderly man to undertake merely to search for a handful of documents he probably knew did not exist. Perhaps Williams wanted to see his family one last time. It is hard to find another reason why he would undertake so long and tiring a journey. But he stayed with his family for only two nights, one with his son in Green Bay and the other with Mary at Duck Creek. If there was something he wanted to complete, or something that he wanted to say, he did it quickly. He could not find the documents he sought, or apparently anything else, during this final journey to Wisconsin. He was most at home away from home.[14]

By the spring of 1858, he had returned to Washington. He wanted to keep an eye on the legislation that might at long last bring him a pension or the St. Regis moneys. Williams stayed at a boardinghouse on Pennsylvania Avenue. One night he stayed up late. He called out loudly enough for the other tenants to hear, "Assassin! Assassin! Save me from the Assassin!' Then he sat himself upon the floor, and placed a weapon, the "assassin's dagger," beside him. He waited.

The other boarders rushed to Williams's assistance. They found him lying on the floor, "totally exhausted." As they helped him to his feet, he told them he had been sitting at his desk, "arranging papers" while "engaged in literary labors." The assassin quietly entered Williams's room, and advanced on him with an uplifted dagger. "I've got you at last, have I?" This, he said, the assassin "exclaimed through his teeth." But his attacker did not count on the old man's strength. Williams fought with his attacker, and drove him off. According to the account that appeared in the *New York Times*, "the contest was desperate but short," and "the villain finding that he could not accomplish his hellish purpose," fled from the house into the night.[15]

Williams staged this event to garner attention, to keep people talking about him, his claims, and his royal descent. Newspapers that covered the assassination attempt identified Williams not as an Indian but as a claimant to the throne of France. To convince the credulous that he remained a significant enough figure that someone, for some reason, would send a midnight assassin to kill him was, in the end, part of the con, a way to keep the dauphin story alive. It was an appeal for sympathy as well, a plea that appears just a little bit pathetic.

Williams told a number of people that he feared assassins. He wrote a letter to his friend Edward Henry a year and a half before the episode in Washington. He asked for $150 to help finance his trip to the capital. He could not make the trip without financial assistance, for his health, he wrote, "for nearly two years past" has been "somewhat in a precarious state, in consequence of the poison (as stated by my attending physicians) having been administered to me while at Philadelphia." Two weeks after the mysterious assassination attempt, Williams again asked Henry for money—another $150 on a short-term loan—that he would repay in ninety days. "I hope you will make a great effort in my behalf in this matter," he pleaded, for "I have every reason to believe that a large sum is now within my reach." He expected to receive his pension at long last.[16] There is no telling how much money letters like these netted Williams. Nor is there any evidence that anybody bothered to poison Williams or that, in Washington, any sort of manhunt followed the assassination attempt he described. Williams's story grew cold. When he passed through Albany in May 1858, the local paper reported that "the Lost Bourbon" spent two or three days in town. "For a 'Lost' personage," the *Albany Evening Journal* indicated, Williams "turns up very often." Still, the paper noted, the old man "caused a sensation wherever he appears." He was a sick man by this point, on his way back to St. Regis, but Williams still could draw a crowd.[17]

He returned to Hogansburg. His mission never got much off the ground, and the very small number of Protestants at St. Regis provided him with "few opportunities . . . for the exercise of a clergyman among the people with whom he had been associated the greatest part of his life." Earlier visitors to his home thought it "presented an aspect of cheerless desolation, without a mitigating ray of comfort, or a genial spirit of homelight." He owned little furniture, Franklin B. Hough noted, "save a scanty supply of broken chairs and invalid tables," with "his pantry and sleeping room disordered and filthy." By the end he had moved into "an attractive house in the style of a French chateau," a structure that stood apart, architecturally and physically, from the other homes on the reservation.[18]

Williams died here on 28 August 1858. He died in poverty and there was "no doubt," one of his obituaries noted, "that he suffered at last from want of attention and other necessaries."[19] That claim, in turn, drew a response from Hiram Walker, one of the physicians who attended Williams during his final illness. The treasurer of the "Fund for Aged and Infirm Clergymen" provided money to pay for Williams's medical care, which allowed for a housekeeper, two nurses, and a doctor, "who visited once daily for twenty days and twice daily for forty-six days and sometimes three or four times a day." Williams suffered from a terrible final illness, Walker wrote, but not from a want of care.[20]

He died in the morning. He was seventy. He died from a combination of things: "first, angina pectoris; second, acute bronchitis; third, erysipelas and rubrum eczema, and lastly a species of anasarca (subsidiary) and gangrene as a finality." His last words, by all accounts, were "Lord Jesus Christ, have mercy on me, and receive my spirit." On that point, nobody protested.[21]

*   *   *

William Ward Wight noted that when Eleazer Williams "was wrapt in his shroud, not an Indian brave attended his funeral" on the St. Regis Reservation. The charlatan and con man died alone, Wight believed, unloved and unmourned. Wight found something fitting in that end. Lyman Draper, that great compiler of Wisconsin history, was more explicit in his denunciation. Williams, he wrote, "aped greatness, but accomplished nothing." Had Williams possessed "integrity of character, and discarded his impractical fancies, he might have proved a blessing to the Indian race." If only Williams had rested content as a missionary. If only he had not aspired to something above his station, Draper suggested, the story might have turned out better. But Williams, in Draper's view, could not do this. For every writer like A. de Grasse Stevens who saw Williams's life as one of constant injustice in which "his fortune fell from him, his adopted country but scantily rewarded his services on its behalf, his Indian flock time and again repudiated his care, he was persecuted by those whom he had aided, and every sorrow that human nature is prone to devolved upon him but did not crush him," there were more like Draper who considered his life "a comparative failure," at least if judged "by the limited fruits of his splendid opportunities."[22]

In the years after Williams died, newspapers continued to report new developments in his story: Francis Vinton's reminiscence of his time with Williams in Newport in the 1840s when Williams, once again, acted dazed and confused after viewing an engraving of Simon the Jailer in a collection of French Revolutionary annals, or the efforts of his son John to acquire his father's pension for military service. The authors of these stories as time passed described Williams as a romantic oddity, one of a number of pretenders to the French throne who surfaced during the nineteenth century. Mark Twain, writing in the *Buffalo Express* in September 1869, described the many forms native peoples had taken, the many roles they had played over time. "I poked around your northern forests," Twain's "Wildman" told the reporter, "among your vagabond Indians, a solemn French Idiot, personating the ghost of a dead Dauphin, that the gaping world might wonder if we had 'a Bourbon among us.'"[23]

Those who study Native American history and the history of the Iroquois in particular, have been less willing to dismiss Williams as a harmless buffoon. If, as John Schermerhorn asserted, the removal of the New York Indians owed significantly to Williams's efforts, those on the receiving end of these policies viewed Williams as complicit in a grave crime against native peoples. They have described him as the author or abettor of many of the bad things that have happened to the New York Indians. Williams willingly participated in the dispossession of the Iroquois. There can be no denying this. But the process began decades before Williams arrived in central New York and continued for a quarter century after he left. Williams worked hard to make removal a reality, took pride in his efforts, and constantly reminded his patrons of the importance of his labors. But other native leaders in New York advocated removal as well. Like Williams, they hoped that their people might outrun their problems in the West. Indeed, it is difficult to believe that dispossession and removal would not have occurred had Williams not come along, given the relentless pressure New Yorkers placed upon the Indians to give up their lands. Williams climbed aboard a swiftly moving train. He did so willingly, looking to his own advantage. At times he took the controls, but he did not set its course.

And if Williams actively involved himself in the Christianization and in the dispossession of New York's Indians, he remained apart from many important events and developments occurring across a broader Iroquoia: the determined efforts of many Iroquois people to hang on to their remaining lands in New York State; the development of the *Gaiwiio*, the Code of Handsome Lake, a nativist religious response to the problems confronting reservation Iroquois in the first decade of the nineteenth century; the emergence, out of crisis, of a representative form of government among the Seneca Nation of Indians, still functioning today, under a constitution older than those of more than half the American states; and the campaign of political resistance waged by New York's Indians and their allies against the state's efforts to tax them, to allot their lands, curtail their movement, and subject them to state jurisdiction. These are important parts of the Iroquois story. Eleazer Williams knew of all these things, but said almost nothing about them. We learn little from his writings about the Oneidas who lived in Wisconsin and New York, or about the Mohawks. He tells us little about the lived experience of Iroquois peoples. He says little about their struggles and their successes. Within and without. His homes, at Little Kakalin and at Akwesasne, stood apart from his neighbors.

Eleazer Williams understood perfectly well the difference between truth and lies, between reality and fantasy. He told stories and performed roles. He took advantage of a world that made inventions of this sort easy. He moved about freely. He found ready audiences filled with individuals who shared his interests. He learned much about what these audiences wanted to hear, and he gave it to them. He needed the approval of whites because he needed to make a living. He played the role of a catechist, a missionary, a leader, and an advocate for native peoples. He saw himself as a man wronged by many who had not appreciated all that he had attempted to do for them. He played that role, too, the victim. His critics—and there were many—would have accepted these labels for him at times, but they would have added to this list a dishonest man, a faithless guardian, a charlatan, and a bad debt.

As Williams moved through the many worlds of the Iroquois in the first half of the nineteenth century, he always performed and played roles. Kahnawake; the river towns and the clerical community in the Connecticut River Valley; the extended Williams family in New England; the American military during the War of 1812; and the missionary arms of the Episcopal Church. He spent time in the divided Oneida community in central New York; worked with missionaries, Ogden Land Company investors, and the U.S. Department of War. He ministered to the Oneida and immigrant Indian community established in Wisconsin, helping out in some capacity as New York Indians became pioneers. He negotiated with Menominees and Winnebagos, for the New York Indians and for himself, and interacted with the *habitant* communities and military officers at Green Bay—all before he reached thirty.

In all these, he attempted to play the roles he saw before him: a Williams redeemed, a soldier, a missionary, an actor in Indian affairs; and he made his living through the relationships he established with powerful and well-connected white men on his American odyssey. But eventually these paths were closed to him. Williams made choices during his life that left him with the sense that he could not earn an honest living. He did not put this belief down in writing but, like Samson Occom, he did complain of the ill treatment and the injustice he faced; he had done so much for the white men who saw in him a valuable ally that he lost credibility among his native supporters.[24] Native peoples at times could earn livelihoods with some autonomy in early America, even if doing so often proved to be extremely difficult.[25] But Williams became, in this sense, a man with no country. He could not live on the margins of white settlements, fishing and farming and trading with his neighbors. He was on his own, divorced from any larger community. That was a product of his background, his lived experience, and, no doubt, his own personality. And his were skills that required connection to others. In the 1830s, with nearly all those connections severed, he described his life as "a catalogue of poverty, affliction, disappointment, and abuse from my fellow men."[26] He traveled constantly, borrowing money and accepting the gifts of those who craved for whatever reason to claim that they knew royalty. Williams spent his few remaining years at Hogansburg, just off the reservation. He lived, it seems, off of the small sum he had raised during his speaking tour, but he remained poor. If he taught school—and the evidence that he did is less than clear—he did so seldom and occasionally. A small church may have stood nearby, but he had no congregation. Catholicism retained its influence over Mohawk Christians at St. Regis, and Williams never succeeded in building the Episcopal establishment he asked his audiences to support. In the end, king and patriot, Dauphin and wartime Superintendent of Indian affairs, were characters Williams played, with limited success, in a decades-long struggle to make ends meet.

ABBREVIATIONS

AEDNY   Archives, Episcopal Diocese of New York

APS   American Philosophical Society, Philadelphia

ASPIA   *American State Papers. Documents, Legislative and Executive, of the Congress of the United States*, 38 vols.; Class 2: *Indian Affairs*, 2 vols. (Washington, D.C.: Gales and Seaton, 1832)

EWP   Eleazer Williams Papers, State Historical Society of Wisconsin, Area Research Center, Cofrin Library, University of Wisconsin-Green Bay

EWP-Newberry   Eleazer Williams Papers, Newberry Library, Chicago

HSP   Historical Society of Pennsylvania, Philadelphia

IIM   *Iroquois Indians: A Documentary History of the Diplomacy of the Six Nations and Their League*, Microfilm, 50 reels. (Woodbridge, Conn.: Research Publications, 1984)

LR-OIA-6N   Correspondence of the Office of Indian Affairs, Letters Received, 1824–1881, M234, RG75. Six Nations Agency, 1824–1834, Microfilm Reel 832

LR-OIA-Emigration   Correspondence of the Office of Indian Affairs, Letters Received, 1824–1881, M234, RG75. Emigration, 1829–1851, Microfilm Reel 597

LR-OIA-GB   Correspondence of the Office of Indian Affairs, Letters Received, 1824–1881, M234, RG75. Green Bay Agency, 1824–1880, Microfilm Reels 315–19

LR-OIA-NY	Correspondence of the Office of Indian Affairs, Letters Received, 1824–1881, M234, RG75. New York Agency, 1829–1880, Microfilm Reels 583–96
NA	National Archives, Washington, D.C.
NYPL	New York Public Library, New York
NYSA	New York State Archives, Albany
NYSL	New York State Library, Albany
PJCC	*The Papers of John C. Calhoun*, ed. W. Edwin Hemphill (Columbia: University of South Carolina Press, 1969)
SHSW	State Historical Society of Wisconsin, Madison
TPUS	*The Territorial Papers of the United States*, ed. Clarence E. Carter and John Porter Bloom. 28 vols. (Washington, D.C.: GPO, 1934–1956)
Whipple Report	New York State Legislature. Assembly, Doc. 51, *Report of the Special Committee to Investigate the Indian Problem of the State of New York*, Appointed by the Assembly of 1888. 2 vols. (Albany, N.Y.: Troy Press, 1889)
WHSC	*Collections of the State Historical Society of Wisconsin*

NOTES

Preface

1. General Albert G. Ellis, "Recollections of Rev. Eleazer Williams," *WHSC* 8 (1879): 346–47.

Prologue. On the Northern Line

1. John Holloway Hanson, *Poems of the Rev. John Holloway Hanson* (New York: Pott and Amery, 1869), 19–22; Francis Hawks to William Berrien, 4 September 1852, AEDNY. Information on Hanson's career was found in his obituary, which appeared in the *Church Journal*, (New York) 19 October 1854.

2. Hanson, *Poems*, 20; Samuel W. Durant, *History of St. Lawrence Co., New York, With Illustrations and Biographical Sketches* (Philadelphia: L. H. Everts, 1872), 293; *Journal of the Proceedings of the Bishops, Clergy, and Laity of the Protestant Episcopal Church in the United States of America* (New York: Daniel Dana, 1847), 247.

3. Francis Hawks to William Berrien, 4 September 1852, AEDNY; *Church Journal*, 19 October 1854.

4. Hanson, *Poems*, 15–17.

5. Ibid.; Stephen Elliott, Bishop of the Diocese of Georgia, to the Clerical Members of the Standing Committee of the Diocese of New York, 10 November 1845, AEDNY.

6. J. H. Hanson, *The Lost Prince: Facts Tending to Prove the Identity of Louis the Seventeenth of France, and the Rev. Eleazer Williams, Missionary Among the Indians of North America* (New York: G. P. Putnam, 1854), 336–37. Hanson most likely saw a story that appeared under the title "History of the Dauphin," *United States Democratic Review* 133 (July 1849): 11–16.

7. Information on the Ogdensburg Railroad has been recovered from a Northern New York railroad advertisement in the *Burlington Sentinel*, 30 November 1854, and *The Railroad Jubilee: An Account of the Celebration Commemorative of the Opening of Railroad Communication Between Boston and Canada* (Boston: J. H. Eastburn, 1852), 248; Wellington Williams, *Appleton's Railroad and Steamboat Companion* (New York: D. Appleton, 1849), 228.

8. Hanson, *Lost Prince*, 337–38.

9. Ibid., 338.

10. Ibid.

11. Biographical works that have informed my thinking include Thomas P. Slaughter, *The Beautiful Soul of John Woolman: Apostle of Abolition* (New York: Hill and Wang, 2008) and *The Natures of John and William Bartram* (Philadelphia: University of Pennsylvania Press, 2005); Paul E. Johnson, *Sam Patch: The Famous Jumper* (New York: Hill and Wang, 2003); Paul E. Johnson and Sean Wilentz, *The Kingdom of Matthias: A Story of Sex and Salvation in Nineteenth-Century America* (New York: Oxford University Press, 1994); Martha Hodes, *The Sea Captain's Wife: A True Story of Love, Race, and War in the Nineteenth Century* (New York: Norton, 2006); Patricia Cline Cohen, *The Murder of Helen Jewett* (New York: Knopf, 1998); Elaine Forman Crane, *Killed Strangely: The Death of Rebecca Cornell* (Ithaca, N.Y.: Cornell University Press, 2002); and John Ruston Pagan, *Anne Orthwood's Bastard: Sex and Law in Early Virginia* (New York: Oxford University Press, 2002). Biographies and life histories treating native figures are less common, but worth reading are John Demos, *The Unredeemed Captive: A Family Story from Early America* (New York: Knopf, 1994); and Allan Greer, *Mohawk Saint: Catherine Tekakwitha and the Jesuits* (New York: Oxford University Press, 2005).

12. Hanson, *Lost Prince*, 338–39.

13. Hanson, *Lost Prince*, 39–40, 42; Maurice Vitrac, *The King Who Never Reigned* (New York: John McBride, 1909), 17.

14. Hanson, *Lost Prince*, 64–66; Vitrac, *King*, 99. Even in Hanson's time, there was a large literature on the fate of the Dauphin and his treatment during the Revolution. See John S. C. Abbott, *History of Marie Antoinette* (New York: Harper, 1849); A. de Beauchesne, *The Bourbon Prince* (New York: Harper, 1853); and Hugh de Normand, *Two Eras of France, Or, True Stories from History* (Auburn, N.Y.: Alden, Beardsley, 1854).

15. Hanson, *Lost Prince*, 70–82.

16. "The Dauphin," *New York Evangelist*, 17 February 1853. On the death of the dauphin and persistent questions that somehow the child had survived his imprisonment, see Deborah Cadbury, *The Lost King of France: Revolution, Revenge, and the Search for Louis XVII* (London: Fourth Estate, 2002), vi–viii.

17. Cadbury, *Lost King of France*, viii; Hanson, *Lost Prince*, 339.

18. Hanson, *Lost Prince*, 175; E. J. Devine, *Historic Caughnawaga* (Montreal: Messenger Press, 1922), 316.

19. Devine, *Historic Caughnawaga*, 316; Mrs. R. S Martin, "The Uncrowned Hapsburg," *Ladies' Repository* (February 1874).

20. Hanson, *Lost Prince*, 187; A. de Grasse Stevens, *The Lost Dauphin, Louis XVII, or Onwarenhiiaki, the Indian Chief* (Sunnyside, Kent: George Allen, 1887), 61.

21. Elizabeth E. Evans, *The Story of Louis XVII of France* (London: Swan Sonnenschein, 1893), v; and Nicholas Hondrocostas, "Eleazer Williams: Missionary and Pretender, 1789–1858" (M.S. Thesis, University of Wisconsin, 1959), 126, for early assessments of Hanson's abilities.

22. Hanson, *Lost Prince*, 340–42. On anti-Catholicism in antebellum New York, see David Brion Davis, "Some Themes of Counter-Subversion: An Analysis of Anti-Masonic,

Anti-Catholic, and Anti-Mormon Literature," *Mississippi Valley Historical Review* 47 (September 1960): 205–24; Jenny Franchot, *Roads to Rome: The Antebellum Protestant Encounter with Roman Catholicism* (Berkeley: University of California Press, 1994).

23. Ogden Ross, *The Steamboats of Lake Champlain, 1809–1930* (1930; repr. Burlington: Vermont Heritage Press, 1997), 67, 69.

24. J. H. Hanson, "Have We a Bourbon Among Us?" *Putnam's Magazine*, February 1853, 198.

25. Ibid.

26. Ibid., 199.

27. Ibid. Williams, in fact, had many books at his Hogansburg home. See the inventory of his estate in the Franklin County Surrogate's Court Records, Franklin County Courthouse, Malone, N.Y.

28. Hanson, *Lost Prince*, 344; "History of the Dauphin," *United States Democratic Review* 133 (July 1849): 15.

29. Hanson, *Lost Prince*, 347; "Louis XVII," *Littell's Living Age*, 7 August 1869.

30. Hanson, *Lost Prince*, 348–49.

31. See Hanson, *Poems*.

32. Hanson, *Lost Prince*, 351.

33. Franklin B. Hough, *A History of St. Lawrence and Franklin Counties, New York, from the Earliest Period to the Present Times* (Albany, N.Y.: Little and Co., 1853), 111; Hanson, *Lost Prince*, 353.

34. William A. Starna, "When Two Are One: The Mohawk Community at St. Regis (Akwesasne)," *European Review of Native American Studies* 14, 2 (2000): 39–40; Frederick W. Seaver, *Historical Sketches of Franklin County* (Albany, N.Y.: J.B. Lyon, 1852), 575. For population on the St. Regis/Akwesasne Reservation see the census dated 13 March 1824, LR-OIA-6N; Jasper Parrish to Thomas McKenney, 15 January 1827, LR-OIA-6N; Indian census of the State of New York, 1 October 1830, LR-OIA-6N; Hough, *St. Lawrence and Franklin*, 177.

35. Seaver, *Franklin County*, 577, 583–89; Hough, *St. Lawrence and Franklin*, 67.

36. Hanson, *Lost Prince*, 353; Hough, *St. Lawrence and Franklin*, 175. Williams, at the time Hanson and Hough visited him, rented his lodgings in Fort Covington.

37. Hanson, *Lost Prince*, 352. According to the 1850 U.S. Census, Ransom Harrington, a twenty-eight-year-old innkeeper, and his father Amariah B. Harrington lived with their families in Moira. One of them was the man Hanson interviewed.

38. Hanson, *Lost Prince*, v.

Chapter 1. Pilgrim and Patriot

1. Eleazer Williams, Autobiographical Writings, EWP Reel 3; *The Redeemed Captive: A Narrative of the Captivity, Sufferings and Return of the Rev. John Williams . . . for Sabbath Schools* (New York: S.W. Benedict, 1833), 5–6.

2. Richard I. Melvoin, *New England Outpost: War and Society in Colonial Deerfield* (New York: Norton, 1987), 149–56; Evan Haefeli and Kevin Sweeney, *Captors and*

Captives: The 1704 French and Indian Raid on Deerfield (Amherst: University of Massachusetts Press, 2003), 26–27.

3. On the Williams family captivity, see John Demos, *The Unredeemed Captive: A Family Story from Early America* (New York: Knopf, 1994), 120–52.

4. Evan Haefeli and Kevin Sweeney, "Revisiting *The Redeemed Captive:* New Perspectives on the 1704 French and Indian Raid on Deerfield," *William and Mary Quarterly* 3rd ser. 52 (January 1995): 31–37. On Iroquois warfare in the long seventeenth century, see Daniel K. Richter, *The Ordeal of the Longhouse: The Iroquois in the Era of European Colonization* (Chapel Hill: University of North Carolina Press, 1992); Jon Parmenter, *The Edge of the Woods* (Lansing: Michigan State University Press, 2011).

5. Melvoin, *Outpost*, 281; Robert L. Hall, "Eleazer Williams: Mohawk Between Two Worlds," *Voyageur* 19, 1 (2002): 11; Geoffrey Buerger, "Eleazer Williams: Elitism and Multiple Identity on Two Frontiers," in *Being and Becoming Indian: Biographical Studies of North American Frontiers*, ed. James A. Clifton (Chicago: Dorsey Press, 1989), 116–17; William Ward Wight, *Eleazer Williams: Not the Dauphin of France* (Chicago: Fergus Printing, 1903), 8. On Europeans who chose to remain with their captors, see James Axtell, "The White Indians of Colonial America," in *The European and the Indian: Essays in the Ethnohistory of Colonial North America* (New York: Oxford University Press, 1981), 168–206.

6. On alcohol in Indian communities in early America, see Peter Mancall, *Deadly Medicine: Indians and Alcohol in Early America* (Ithaca, N.Y.: Cornell University Press, 1995); and Maia Conrad, "Disorderly Drinking: Reconsidering Seventeenth-Century Iroquois Alcohol Abuse," *American Indian Quarterly* 23 (1999): 1–12; Richter, *Ordeal*, 85–86, 94, 263–68. On the founding of Kahnawake, see David Preston, *The Texture of Contact: European and Indian Settler Communities on the Frontiers of Iroquoia, 1667–1763* (Lincoln: University of Nebraska Press, 2009), 28–30; Allan Greer, *Mohawk Saint: Catherine Tekakwitha and the Jesuits* (New York: Oxford University Press, 2005), 89–110.

7. Gerald F. Reid, *Kahnawa:ke: Factionalism, Traditionalism, and Nationalism in a Mohawk Community* (Lincoln: University of Nebraska Press, 2004), 6–7; Preston, *Texture of Contact*, 39.

8. Parmenter, *Edge of the Woods*, 131–52; David Blanchard, "The Seven Nations of Canada: An Alliance and a Treaty," *American Indian Culture and Research Journal* 7, 2 (1983): 6. For the St. Lawrence Valley as a focus of Iroquois activity, see Jose Antonio Brandao, *"Your Fyre Shall Burn No More": Iroquois Policy Toward New France and Its Native Allies to 1701* (Lincoln: University of Nebraska Press, 1997).

9. Parmenter, *Edge of the Woods*, 154–55; Greer, *Mohawk Saint*, 98.

10. Reid, *Kahnawa:ke*, 12; Blanchard, "Seven Nations," 6.

11. See Jon Parmenter, "After the Mourning Wars: The Iroquois as Allies in Colonial North American Campaigns, 1676–1760," *William and Mary Quarterly*, 3rd ser., 64 (January 2007): 39–82.

12. Barbara Graymont, *The Iroquois and the American Revolution* (Syracuse, N.Y.: Syracuse University Press, 1971), 60, 67.

13. Eleazer Williams, *Life of Te-ho-ra-gwa-ne-gen, Alias Thomas Williams, A Chief of the Caughnawaga Tribes of Indians in Canada* (Albany, N.Y.: J. Munsell, 1859), 21.

14. On the Iroquois diaspora following the American Revolution, see Colin G. Calloway, *The American Revolution in Indian Country: Crisis and Diversity in Native American Communities* (New York: Cambridge University Press, 1995), 128–57; Alan Taylor, *The Divided Ground: Indians, Settlers, and the Northern Borderland of the American Revolution* (New York: Knopf, 2006), 133–36; and Karim M. Tiro, *The People of the Standing Stone: The Oneida Nation from the Revolution Through the Era of Removal* (Amherst: University of Massachusetts Press, 2011), 157–86.

15. Reid, *Kahnawa:ke*, 12–13; Blanchard, "Seven Nations," 17; Jack Aaron Frisch, "Revitalization, Nativism, and Tribalism Among the St. Regis Mohawks," Ph.D. dissertation, Indiana University, 1970, 71–72; Duane Hamilton Hurd, *History of Clinton and Franklin Counties, New York* (Philadelphia: J.W. Lewis, 1880), 22.

16. Franklin B. Hough, *A History of St. Lawrence and Franklin Counties, New York, From the Earliest Period to the Present Times* (Albany, N.Y.: Little and Co., 1853), 147; Blanchard, "Seven Nations," 17–18; Taylor, *Divided Ground*, 345.

17. Hough, *St. Lawrence and Franklin*, 126; Petition of William Gray to New York State Legislature, 19 February 1800, Legislative Assembly Papers, Series A1818, 30: 337–40, NYSA; Williams, *Life of Thomas Williams*, 43–45; Frederick W. Seaver, *Historical Sketches of Franklin County* (Albany, N.Y: J. B. Lyon, 1852), 582.

18. Speech of New York Agents to Indians of St. Regis, March 1795, Legislative Assembly Papers, Series A1818, 40: 287–90, NYSA; Proceedings of Treaty Between Seven Nations of Canada and New York State, 23–31 May, 1796, Legislative Assembly Papers, Series A1818, 40: 299, NYSA; Taylor, *Divided Ground*, 345–46. The 1793 version of the Indian Trade and Intercourse Act reads "that no purchase or grant of land . . . from any Indians or nation or tribe of Indians . . . shall be of any validity, unless the same be made by a treaty or convention entered into pursuant to the constitution."

19. Proceedings of a Treaty between the Seven Nations of Canada and New York State, 23–31 March, 1796, Legislative Assembly Papers, Series A1818, 40: 299–314, NYSA.

20. *Indian Affairs: Laws and Treaties*, Charles J. Kappler, comp. (Washington, D.C.: GPO, 1904), 2: 45; Blanchard, "Seven Nations," 19; William A. Starna, "When Two Are One: The Mohawk Community at St. Regis (Akwesasne)," *European Review of Native American Studies* 14, 2 (2000): 40.

21. Hough, *Franklin and St. Lawrence*, 151, 154; Williams, *Life of Thomas Williams*, 47–52.

22. Milo Milton Quaife, ed., *John Long's Voyages and Travels in the Years 1768–1788* (Chicago: Lakeside Press, 1922), 9–10; E. J. Divine, *Historic Caughnawaga* (Montreal: Messenger Press, 1922), 380.

23. Eleazer Williams, Autobiographical Writings, EWP, Reel 3; Demos, *Unredeemed Captive*, 242–43; Buerger, "Eleazer Williams," 117.

24. Note, Nathaniel Ely Papers, Longmeadow Historical Society, Longmeadow, Massachusetts; Nathaniel Ely Diary, Eleazer Williams Collection, Missouri Historical

Society (Microfilm Copy at Pocumtuck Valley Memorial Association Library, Deerfield, Mass.); John H. Hanson, *The Lost Prince: Facts Tending to Prove the Identity of Louis the Seventeenth of France, and the Rev. Eleazer Williams, Missionary Among the Indians of North America* (New York: G. P. Putnam, 1854), 188–89; Michael Batinski, *Pastkeepers in a Small Place: Five Centuries in Deerfield, Massachusetts* (Amherst: University of Massachusetts Press, 2004), 43; *Proceedings at the Centennial Celebration of the Incorporation of the Town of Longmeadow, October 17th, 1883, with Numerous Historical Appendices and a Town Genealogy* (Longmeadow, Mass.: Centennial Committee, 1884), 230–31.

25. Thomas Williams to Nathaniel Ely, 1806, Nathaniel Ely Papers, Longmeadow Historical Society, Longmeadow, Mass.; Hall, "Eleazer Williams," 12.

26. Williams, Autobiographical Writings, EWP, Reel 3; Hanson, *Lost Prince*, 188–89. On Iroquois children in New England, see the discussion running through Linford Fisher, *The Indian Great Awakening: Religion and the Shaping of Native Cultures in Early America* (New York: Oxford University Press, 2012). For the experience of another Indian child raised with non-Indians in southern New England, see William Apess, *A Son of the Forest and Other Writings*, ed. Barry O'Connell (Amherst: University of Massachusetts Press, 1992), 4–21.

27. Note, Ely Papers; *Proceedings at Centennial Celebration*, 231; Linda M. Rodgers and Mary S. Rogeness, eds., *Reflections of Longmeadow* (Kennebunk, Me.: Phoenix Press, 1983), 34.

28. Hanson, *Lost Prince*, 203.

29. Ibid.

30. Ibid., 191–92, 194, 469; J. K. Bloomfield, *The Oneidas* (New York: Alden Bros., 1907), 155.

31. J. H. Hanson, "Have We a Bourbon Among Us?" *Putnam's Magazine* (February 1853), 202.

32. Hanson, *Lost Prince*, 190.

33. Ibid., 188.

34. Ibid., 197; Nathaniel Ely Diary, 28 October 1800.

35. Eleazer Williams, Journal Fragments, EWP, Reel 3.

36. Nathaniel Ely Diary, 28 February 1804; Williams, *Life of Thomas Williams*, 57–58.

37. Williams, *Life of Thomas Williams*, 58.

38. Hanson, *Lost Prince*, 207–8; Nathaniel Ely Diary, 28 May 1804.

39. Nathaniel Ely Diary, 11 October 1804; Eleazer Williams, Journal Fragments, EWP, Reel 4; Eleazer Williams to William Sprague, 15 February 1855, in *Annals of the American Pulpit, or Commemorative Notices of Distinguished American Clergymen of Various Denominations*, ed. William B. Sprague (New York: Robert Carter and Brothers, 1859), 238.

40. Eleazer Williams, Autobiographical Writings, EWP; A. G. Ellis, "Advent of the New York Indians into Wisconsin," *WHSC* 2 (1856): 418; Thomas Williams to Nathaniel Ely (1806), Ely Papers, Longmeadow Historical Society; Nathaniel Ely Diary, 5 February 1806. See Ely's entry for 1 May 1806 as well.

41. This depiction of Eleazer Williams's time in southern New England differs from that offered by Buerger, in "Eleazer Williams," 117, and Hall, "Eleazer Williams," 12. For Williams's departure from Brockway's household, see Nathaniel Ely Diary, 20 July 1803, and Williams, Autobiographical Writings, EWP, Reel 3.

42. Nathaniel Ely Diary, 4 May 1803, 21 May 1804, and 30 November 1804; William Patten to Nathaniel Ely, 11 February 1803, Nathaniel Ely Papers, Longmeadow Historical Society, Longmeadow, Massachusetts; George Sheldon, "Was There a Bourbon Among Us?" *Springfield Republican* (1903) in Sheldon Clippings File, Pocumtuck Valley Memorial Association Library, Deerfield, Massachusetts; "To the Honorable Senate and Honorable House of Representatives of the Commonwealth of Massachusetts in General Court Assembled, in Boston, in May of 1806," in Correspondence about Eleazer Williams and the "Lost Dauphin," also Notes and an Article Written by George Sheldon, Pocumtuck Valley Memorial Association Library.

43. Arthur Burt to EW, 12 June 1803, EWP, Reel 4.

44. Eleazer Williams, Journal Fragment, EWP, Reel 3.

45. "Ode for Independence, 1793, Composed and Set to Music by Dr. Willard," in Nathan Williams, *A Sermon Delivered in Stafford on the Anniversary of American Independence, July 4th, A. D. 1793* (Hartford, Conn.: Hudson and Goodwin, 1793) copied into EWP, Reel 6.

46. George Caleb Bingham, *An Astronomical and Geographical Catechism*, 9th ed. (Boston: Carlisle, 1806), 18–19.

47. Eleazer Williams, Autobiographical Fragments, EWP. On the vanishing Indian as a motif in American culture, see Brian W. Dippie, *The Vanishing American: White Attitudes and U. S. Indian Policy* (Middletown, Conn.: Wesleyan University Press, 1982). For Indians in southern New England in the decades after the American Revolution, see Daniel R. Mandell, *Behind the Frontier: Indians in Eighteenth Century Eastern Massachusetts* (Lincoln: University of Nebraska Press, 1996); idem., *Tribe, Race, History: Native Americans in Southern New England, 1780–1880* (Baltimore: Johns Hopkins University Press, 2008).

48. Eleazer Williams, Autobiographical Writings, EWP, Reel 3; E. Brooks Holifield, "Let the Children Come: The Religion of the Protestant Child in Early America," *Church History* 76 (December 2007): 754, 760, 763, 776.

49. Holifield, "Children," 767–68; Isaac Watts, *The Child's Catechism: To Which Are Added a Serious Address to Children, and Some Important Verses on Various Subjects* (Montreal: Nahum Mower, 1809), 2, 9–10.

50. Holifield, "Children," 753; David E. Stannard, *The Puritan Way of Death: A Study in Religion, Culture, and Social Change* (New York: Oxford University Press, 1977); Joseph F. Kett, "Growing Up in Rural New England, 1800–1840," in *Anonymous Americans: Explorations in Nineteenth Century Social History*, ed. Tamara K. Hareven (Englewood Cliffs, N.J.: Prentice-Hall, 1975), 5–6.

51. Thomas Williams to EW, 10 February 1803, EWP, Reel 2; Eleazer Williams, Journal Fragments, EWP, Reel 4; Nathaniel Ely Diary, 2 April 1803; Hanson, *Lost Prince*, 206.

52. Eleazer Williams, Autobiographical Writings, EWP, Reel 3.

53. Ibid.; Jonathan Pritchard to Eleazer Williams, 27 September 1802, EWP, Reel 2.

54. Eleazer Williams, Journal Fragments, 18 February 1802, EWP, Reel 2; Hanson, *Lost Prince*, 201; Nathaniel Ely Diary.

55. Eleazer Williams, Autobiographical Writings, EWP, Reel 3.

56. Ibid.

57. Ibid.

58. Ibid.

59. Ibid.; Buerger, "Eleazer Williams," 118.

60. James Axtell, "Dr. Wheelock's Little Red School," in Axtell, *Natives and Newcomers: The Cultural Origins of North America* (New York: Oxford University Press, 2001), 183; Tammy Schneider, "'This Once Savage Heart of Mine': Joseph Johnson, Wheelock's Indians, and the Construction of Christian/Indian Identity, 1764–1776," in *Reinterpreting New England Indians and the Colonial Experience*, ed. Colin G. Calloway and Neal Salisbury (Boston: Colonial Society of Massachusetts, 2003), 258; Fisher, *Indian Great Awakening*, 145–47, 158; Eleazer Williams to "Respected Sir," n.d., EWP, Reel 2; Nathaniel Ely to Rev. Morse, 27 August 1807, EWP, Reel 2; Buerger, "Eleazer Williams," 118; Hall, "Eleazer Williams," 12.

61. Eleazer Williams, Autobiographical Writings, EWP, Reel 3.

62. Eleazer Williams to Mrs. Elizabeth Ely, 25 July 1808, EWP Reel 2; Nathaniel Ely Diary, 18 March 1808. Williams kept the Bible Ely gave him his entire life. It is housed in the EWP, Box 9, Folder 1.

63. Eleazer Williams to Mrs. Elizabeth Ely, 25 July 1808, EWP, Reel 2.

64. Eleazer Williams to "Respected Sir," 2 May 1810, EWP, Reel 2.

65. Enoch Hale, writing in *Christian's Magazine*, 1 June 1811.

66. Pastor Storrs to Rev. Dr. Romeyn, 6 April 1811, *Longmeadow Centennial*, 231–32; Demos, *Unredeemed Captive*, 244; *Christian's Magazine*, 1 June 1811.

67. Thomas C. Reeves, "The Anti-Catholic Movement in Wisconsin," *Wisconsin Magazine of History* 68 (Spring 1985): 188–90; Edwin Ryan, "The Oxford Movement in the United States," *Catholic Historical Review* 19 (Spring 1933), 24–25, 34–35.

68. Samuel Worcester, writing in *The Panoplist, and Missionary Magazine*, September 1811; "Religious Intelligence," ibid., June 1813; "Pecuniary Accounts of the Board," *Connecticut Evangelical Magazine and Religious Intelligencer*, December 1812. Williams quoted Romans 9:3 and Ephesians 3:8, writing in *Christian's Magazine*, 1 June 1811. Useful on Native American engagement with the larger economy is Daniel H. Usner, Jr., *Indian Work: Language and Livelihood in Native American History* (Cambridge, Mass.: Harvard University Press, 2010).

69. Eleazer Williams, Autobiographical Writings, EWP, Reel 3.

70. "Extracts from the Letters of Eleazer Williams, of the Iroquois Nation, Who Is Now in a Course of Education Under the Direction of the American Board of Commissioners for Foreign Missions," *Panoplist and Missionary Magazine*, June 1, 1813, 21–22.

71. Eleazer Williams, Autobiographical Writings, EWP, Reel 3. Certainly such sentiments existed at St. Regis. In a biographical sketch of Louis Cook he wrote late in life for

the New York antiquarian Franklin B. Hough, Williams charged that the descendants of Gray and Thomas Williams continued to suffer on account of their Protestantism and the role they played in the sale of Mohawk land. See the Sketch of Colonel Louis, in "Essays of Eleazer Williams, re. Indian Affairs," Franklin B. Hough Papers, Box 91, Folder 9, NYSL.

72. For the best discussion of these years, see Roger H. Brown, *The Republic in Peril: 1812* (New York: Norton, 1971); Reginald Horsman, *The Causes of the War of 1812* (Philadelphia: University of Pennsylvania Press, 1962); Donald R. Hickey, *The War of 1812: A Forgotten Conflict* (Urbana: University of Illinois Press, 1989); John K. Mahon, *The War of 1812* (New York: De Capo, 1991); and the works cited below.

73. Carl Benn, *The Iroquois in the War of 1812* (Toronto: University of Toronto Press, 1998), 3; Alan Taylor, *The Civil War of 1812: American Citizens, British Subjects, Irish Rebels, and Indian Allies* (New York: Knopf, 2010), 3, 140–41.

74. Taylor, *Civil War*, 276–77, 290–91; Alan S. Everest, *The War of 1812 in the Champlain Valley* (Syracuse, N.Y.: Syracuse University Press, 1981), 45.

75. Governor Daniel D. Tompkins to Thomas Grosvenor, 12 February 1812, in *The Public Papers of Daniel D. Tompkins, Governor of New York, 1807–1817*, ed. Hugh Hastings (Albany, N.Y.: J. B. Lyon, 1902), 2: 480–84; Benn, *Iroquois*, 196, for Iroquois warrior population at Akwesasne, Kanesatake, and Kahnawake. Federal agents interested in effecting a purchase of Seneca lands in the West at nearly the same time abandoned the idea of a cession, given the impending threat of a British invasion across the Niagara River. See Jasper Parrish to S. M. Hopkins, Esq., 15 September 1812, Subject Files, Indians, Box 2, NYPL.

76. Tompkins to Grosvenor, 12 February 1812, in *Public Papers of Tompkins*, 2: 480–84; Jack Frisch, "Revitalization, Nativism, and Tribalism," 79–81; Benn, *Iroquois*, 30–31; Everest, *War of 1812*, 50, 63–68; David Blanchard, *Kahnawake: A Historical Sketch* (Kahnawake: Kanien'kehaka Raotitiohkwa Press, 1980), 11.

77. Williams, *Life of Thomas Williams*, 71–72; Benn, *Iroquois*, 4, 61–65; Carl Benn, "Iroquois External Affairs, 1807–1815: The Crisis of the New Order," in *The Sixty Years' War for the Great Lakes, 1754–1814*, ed. David Curtis Skaggs and Larry L. Nelson (East Lansing: Michigan State University Press 2001), 292; Eleazer Williams, Autobiographical Writings, EWP, Reel 3; Frederick J. Seaver, *Historical Sketches of Franklin County* (Albany, N.Y.: J.B. Lyon, 1918), 581.

78. Hanson, *Lost Prince*, 221; *Plattsburgh Republican*, 11 December 1886.

79. Taylor, *Civil War*, 180, 182; Everest, *War of 1812*, 47; *Plattsburgh Republican*, 11 December 1886; Eleazer Williams, Autobiographical Writings, EWP, Reel 3.

80. *Plattsburgh Republican*, 11 December 1886; Eleazer Williams, Autobiographical Writings, EWP, Reel 3; Ellis, "Advent," 418; and letters of Henry Dearborn to George Graham, 18 February 1816; Henry Dearborn to Eleazer Williams (Copy) 5 August 1812; Henry Dearborn to Benjamin Mooers, 6 August 1812, all in Bailey-Moore Collection, Feinberg Library Special Collections, SUNY-Plattsburgh, Plattsburgh, New York.

81. Franklin B. Hough, *A History of St. Lawrence and Franklin Counties, New York, from the Earliest Period to the Present Times* (Albany, N.Y.: Little and Co., 1853), 202–3; Williams, *Life of Thomas Williams*, 71–72.

82. Benjamin P. Mooers to Wade Hampton, 28 August 1813, Bailey-Moore Collection.

83. Hanson, *Lost Prince*, 224; Bloomfield, *Oneidas*, 158.

84. Williams, *Life of Thomas Williams*, 66–70.

85. Hanson, *Lost Prince*, 236; *Plattsburgh Republican*, 11 December 1886; Letters of Mooers to Dearborn, 3 August 1813; D. Erwin to Benjamin Mooers, 11 May 1813; Lewis Cook to Benjamin P. Mooers, 18 January 1813, all in Bailey-Moore Collection. See also the *Plattsburgh Republican*, 6 June 1814. For an account that takes seriously Williams's accounts of the war in the north and the Battle of Plattsburgh, see Keith A. Herkalo, *The Battles at Plattsburgh, September 11, 1814* (Charleston, S.C.: History Press, 2012).

86. Mooers to Colonel Pinckney, 31 May 1814, Bailey-Moore Collection; Benson J. Lossing, *The Pictorial Field Book of the War of 1812* (New York: Harper and Brothers, 1868), 236, 373–76; Hanson, *Lost Prince*, 249–50.

87. Hanson, *Lost Prince*, 247, 252; James Ripley Jacobs, *Tarnished Warrior: Major-General James Wilkinson* (New York: Macmillan, 1938), 299.

88. Taylor, *Civil War*, 269, 329–30.

89. Izard quoted in Taylor, *Civil War*, 290, 306; *Plattsburgh Republican*, 3 June 1887; Lossing, *Field Book*, 584–85; David Curtis Skaggs, "The Sixty Years' War for the Great Lakes, 1754–1814: An Overview," in Skaggs and Nelson, *The Sixty Years' War*, 16.

90. *Plattsburgh Republican*, 5 March 1887; Taylor, *Civil War*, 382–83; Thomas Ridout, *Ten Years of Upper Canada in Peace and War, 1805–1815: Being the Ridout Letters* (Toronto: William Briggs, 1890), 319–20.

91. Hickey, *War of 1812*, 190; Herkalo, *Battles at Plattsburgh*, 49–62; George F. G. Stanley, *The War of 1812: Land Operations* (Ottawa: Macmillan, 1983), 345; Skaggs, "Overview," 16–17; Taylor, *Civil War*, 402–3.

92. *Plattsburgh Republican*, 5, 19 March 1887.

93. *Plattsburgh Republican*, 26 March 1887; Ridout, *Ten Years*, 320; Jon Latimer, *1812: War with America* (Cambridge, Mass.: Harvard University Press, 2007), 352.

94. *Plattsburgh Republican*, 26 March 1887.

95. Hanson, *Lost Prince*, 266.

96. Williams, *Life of Thomas Williams*, 78–80; Herkalo, *Battles at Plattsburgh*, 101–35; Stanley, *Land Operations*, 248; Ridout, *Ten Years*, 317–24; Hickey, *War of 1812*, 193.

97. Williams, *Life of Thomas Williams*, 76–88.

98. *Plattsburgh Republican*, 2 April 1887; Eleazer Williams, Autobiographical Writings, EWP, Reel 1; Hanson, *Lost Prince*, 269.

99. 1 Timothy 1:15 (KJV). Williams left off the last clause of the passage, "of which I am chief."

100. Eleazer Williams, Autobiographical Writings, EWP, Reel 3; Benn, "External Affairs," 299–300.

101. Abstracts of War of 1812 Payrolls, Series B0810, NYSA; War of 1812 Military Service Records, NA.

102. Henry Dearborn to Benjamin Mooers, 18 February 1816; George Graham to Mooers, 29 February 1816; Mooers to Col Pinckney, 31 May 1814; EW to Mooers, 22

November 1816, all in Bailey-Moore Collection. See also the report, "Eleazer Williams, Heir of Thomas Williams," House Report 303, 35th Cong., 1st Sess., 17 April 1858.

103. Eleazer Williams to David Ogden, 12 December 1817; David A. Ogden to John C. Calhoun, 9 March 1818, both in Indian Papers, Related to Proposed Removal to the West, Indians, Box 1, File 31, NYPL; Eleazer Williams to David A. Ogden, 31 January 1818, Onondaga, Oneida, Miscellaneous, Indians, Box 1, File 35, NYPL.

104. Lewis Cass to the Chiefs of the New York Indians at Green Bay, 4 May 1828, LR-OIA-6N; Lewis Cass to John Eaton, 5 December 1830, M574, Reel 8; Office of Indian Affairs, Special Files, File 73, NA.

105. *Journal of the United States House of Representatives*, 2 February 1829, 229; 12 February 1829, 275.

106. "History of the Dauphin," *United States Democratic Review* 133 (July 1849): 13. Kenny Franks, in his essay on Eleazer Williams in *American National Biography* suggests that Williams wrote the essay. This is unlikely, given that the story told in this essay about Williams's actions during the war differs from his standard account. Sean Harvey, "'Translated from the Dominions of Darkness': Native Missionaries, Language, and Scientific Authority in the Nineteenth Century," paper presented at American Historical Association Convention, 9 January 2011.

107. "Memorial of Eleazer Williams, Praying a Pension for Services Rendered During the Last War with Great Britain," Records of the Committee on Pensions, 31st Cong., 1st Sess., NA. Williams was not the only Iroquois ally of the United States to complain about lack of payment for military service rendered. See Benn, *Iroquois*, 147.

108. "Memorial of Eleazer Williams."

109. Ibid.; Senate Report 311, 31st Cong., 2nd sess., 20 February 1851.

Chapter 2. Soldier of Christ

1. John Holloway Hanson, *Poems of the Rev. John Holloway Hanson* (New York: Pott and Amery, 1869), 21–22.

2. Eleazer Williams, Autobiographical Writings, EWP, Reel 2; J. K. Bloomfield, *The Oneidas* (New York: Alden Brothers, 1907), 167.

3. J. H. Hanson, "Have We a Bourbon Among Us?" *Putnam's Magazine*, February 1853, 203.

4. Eleazer Williams to "Respected Sir," n.d., EWP, Reel 2; Williams, Autobiographical Writings, EWP, Reel 3.

5. Copy of Remarks Made to Bishop Hobart by T. L. Ogden, 14 December 1814, David Ogden Papers, Clements Library, University of Michigan; *IIM*. On the Ogden Land Company, see Barbara H. Conable, "A Steady Enemy: The Ogden Land Company and the Seneca Indians," Ph.D. dissertation, University of Rochester, 1995.

6. Eleazer Williams, Autobiographical Writings, EWP, Reel 3; Bloomfield, *Oneidas*, 169–70.

7. J. H. Hobart, "Conversion of Indian Tribes," *Churchman's Magazine*, May/June 1815, 101–2. See also a later appeal, using nearly identical language, in "Bishop Hobart's

Address," *Christian Visitant,* 23 December 1815, 232; James Montgomery to Jackson Kemper, 8 June 1815, EWP, Reel 2; Eleazer Williams, Autobiographical Writings, EWP, Reel 3.

8. Eleazer Williams to Bishop Benjamin Onderdonk, 3 August 1815, EWP, Reel 2; Essays, Rev. Eleazer Williams re. Indian Affairs, Franklin B. Hough Papers, Box 91, Folder 9, NYSL.

9. Eleazer Williams to Onderdonk, 3 August 1815, EWP, Reel 2; and Eleazer Williams to Onderdonk, 3 March 1816, EWP, Reel 2; Eleazer Williams, Autobiographical Writings, EWP, Reel 3.

10. John Anthony and Moses Sconnoto to Eleazer Williams, 9 December 1814, EWP Reel 2; John H. Hanson, *The Lost Prince: Facts Tending to Prove the Identity of Louis the Seventeenth of France, and the Rev. Eleazer Williams, Missionary Among the Indians of North America* (New York: G. P. Putnam, 1854), 274; Eleazer Williams, Autobiographical Writings, EWP, Reel 3.

11. Eleazer Williams, Autobiographical Writings, EWP, Reel 3.

12. Karim Tiro, *The People of the Standing Stone: The Oneida Nation from the Revolution Through the Era of Removal* (Amherst: University of Massachusetts Press, 2011), 138; Eleazer Williams, Autobiographical Writings, EWP, Reel 3.

13. Eleazer Williams, Autobiographical Writings, EWP, Reel 3; Historical Notes, EWP, Reel 4.

14. On these nativist movements, see Gregory Evans Dowd, *A Spirited Resistance: The North American Indian Struggle for Unity, 1745–1815* (Baltimore: Johns Hopkins University Press, 1992); and Anthony F. C. Wallace, *Death and Rebirth of the Senecas* (New York: Knopf, 1970). On relations between Indians and whites during the late colonial period in the Oneida country, see David Preston, *The Texture of Contact: European and Indian Settler Communities on the Frontiers of Iroquoia, 1667–1783* (Lincoln: University of Nebraska Press, 2009) and David J. Silverman, "The Curse of God: An Idea and Its Origins Among the Indians of New York's Revolutionary Frontier," *William and Mary Quarterly* 66 (July 2009): 514–20. On Onoquaga, see Colin Calloway, *The Revolution in Indian Country: Crisis and Diversity in Native American Communities* (Cambridge: Cambridge University Press, 1995), 108–28, and Daniel R. Mandell, "'Turned their Minds to Religion': Oquaga and the First Iroquois Church, 1748–1776," *Early American Studies* 11 (Spring 2013): 211–42.

15. Laurence M. Hauptman, *Conspiracy of Interests: Iroquois Dispossession and the Rise of New York State* (Syracuse, N.Y.: Syracuse University Press, 1999), 38; David J. Silverman, *Red Brethren: The Brothertown and Stockbridge Indians and the Problem of Race in Early America* (Ithaca, N.Y.: Cornell University Press, 2010), 157; Silverman, "Curse," 526; Tiro, *People of the Standing Stone,* 12–16.

16. On the Oneidas and Kirkland, see Barbara J. Graymont, *The Iroquois and the American Revolution* (Syracuse, N.Y.: Syracuse University Press, 1972), 34–47; Alan Taylor, *The Divided Ground: Indians, Settlers, and the Northern Borderland of the American Revolution* (New York: Knopf, 2006), 54–58; Tiro, *People of the Standing Stone,* 12–19, 39–64; Laurence M. Hauptman and L. Gordon McLester, III, *Chief Daniel Bread and the*

Oneida Nation of Indians of Wisconsin (Norman: University of Oklahoma Press, 2002), 19. For Warren Johnson's observations, see *In Mohawk Country: Early Narratives About a Native People*, ed. Dean R. Snow, Charles T. Gehring, and William A. Starna (Syracuse, N.Y.: Syracuse University Press, 1996), 262.

17. Anthony Wonderley, "An Oneida Community in 1780: Study of an Inventory of Iroquois Property Losses During the Revolutionary War," *Northeast Anthropology* 56 (1988): 23–25, 30.

18. On alcohol, see Silverman, *Red Brethren*, 142–44; Joseph Glathaar and James Kirby Martin, *Forgotten Allies: The Oneida Indians and the American Revolution* (New York: Hill and Wang, 2006), 302.

19. Hauptman, *Conspiracy of Interests*, 28–29; Taylor, *Divided Ground*, 142–202.

20. William N. Fenton, *The Great Law and the Longhouse: A Political History of the Iroquois Confederacy* (Norman: University of Oklahoma Press, 1998), 609.

21. *Indian Affairs: Laws and Treaties*, comp. Charles J. Kappler (Washington, D.C.: GPO, 1904), 5–6; *Proceedings of the Commissioners of Indian Affairs Appointed by Law for the Extinguishment of Indian Titles in the State of New York*, ed. Franklin B. Hough (Albany, N.Y.: J.J. Munsell, 1861), 86–107; J. David Lehman, "The End of the Iroquois Mystique: The Oneida Land Cession Treaties of the 1780s," *William and Mary Quarterly* 47 (October 1990), 536–38, 544; Anthony Wonderley, "Good Peter's 'Narrative of Several Transactions Respecting Indian Lands': An Oneida View of Dispossession, 1785–1788," *New York History* 84 (2003): 237–73. The state negotiated a similarly fraudulent treaty with the Onondagas. See Michael Leroy Oberg, "Good Neighbors: The Onondagas and the Fort Schuyler Treaty of September 1788," *New York History* 88 (Fall 2007): 391–418. The problems that occurred in New York were not unique. North Carolina, Georgia, and the short-lived "State of Franklin" also embarked on aggressive Indian policies in defiance of federal Indian commissioners. See the relevant documents in *ASPIA*, vol. 1.

22. Francis Paul Prucha, *The Great Father: The American Indian and the United States* (Lincoln: University of Nebraska Press, 1984), 89; William A. Starna, "'The United States Will Protect You': The Iroquois, New York State, and the 1790 Nonintercourse Act," *New York History* 83 (Winter 2002): 4–33; Karim M. Tiro and Cesare Marino, eds., *Along the Hudson and the Mohawk: The 1790 Journal of Count Paolo Andreani* (Philadelphia: University of Pennsylvania Press, 2006), 59; Jeremy Belknap, *Journal of a Tour from Boston to Oneida, June 1796* (Cambridge, Mass.: John Wilson and Son, 1882), 21, 23; Tiro, *People of the Standing Stone*, 65, 103.

23. Notes on Council with Oneida Indians, Timothy Pickering Papers, Massachusetts Historical Society, Boston, 60: 217–41; Silverman, *Red Brethren*, 127. On Indian dispossession generally during these years, see Stuart Banner, *How the Indians Lost Their Land: Law and Power on the Frontier* (Cambridge, Mass.: Harvard University Press, 2005), 112–91.

24. Notes on Council with Oneida Indians, Pickering Papers, 60: 217–41.

25. Kappler, *Laws and Treaties*, 2: 35. On the Treaty of Canandaigua, see Jack Campisi and William A. Starna, "On the Road to Canandaigua: The Treaty of 1794," *American*

Indian Quarterly 19 (1995): 467–90; Fenton, *Great Law and the Longhouse*, 622–706. The total number of non-uniformed employees of the national government in 1801, the first year for which good figures exist, was less than 3,000, and the vast majority worked in customs and other revenue-related functions, or for the postal service. Only 214 federal employees resided in New York State, nearly all in the vicinity of New York City, and almost all employed in customs. Never more than two federal Indian agents served in the state, assisted by an occasional interpreter who worked when called upon. See James Stirling Young, *The Washington Community, 1800–1828* (New York: Columbia University Press, 1966), 29; Leonard D. White, *The Federalists: A Study in Administrative History, 1789–1801* (New York: Macmillan, 1948), 256.

26. On the 1798 accord, see John Adams to the Members of the United States Senate, 3 May 1798, in *ASPIA*, 1: 636. On 1802, see Henry Dearborn to Thomas Jefferson, 5 March 1802, and Thomas Jefferson to Members of the United States Senate, 27 December 1802, *ASPIA*, 1: 663–64. On 1805, see Jack Campisi, "Ethnic Identity and Boundary Maintenance in Three Oneida Communities," Ph.D. dissertation, State University of New York at Albany, 1974, 104; Whipple Report, 259–80.

27. Erastus Granger to Henry Dearborn, 21 December 1808, quoted in Tiro, *People of the Standing Stone*, 123.

28. Sterling Leonard, "Biographical account of Sewell Newhouse," Typescript, ca. 1948, MM 1/23, Feinberg Library Special Collections, SUNY-Plattsburgh.

29. Historical Notes, EWP, Reel 4; James Taylor, Jonathan Thomas, and others to the Pennsylvania Yearly Meeting Indian Committee, 26 November 1798, Letters to the Pennsylvania Yearly Meeting, Indian Committee, Haverford College Library Special Collections, Haverford, Pa.; Jacob Taylor and Others to Brethren of the Oneida Nation, 6 January 1800, Letters to Pennsylvania Yearly Meeting Indian Committee; Petition of Oneida Indians to New York State Legislature, 27 February 1798, Legislative Assembly Papers, Correspondence and Reports Relating to Indians, 1783–1831, A1823, NYSA. On Occom's career, see Silverman, *Red Brethren*, 55–67; W. Deloss Love, *Samson Occom and the Christian Indians of New England*, reprint (Syracuse, N.Y.: Syracuse University Press, 2000).

30. Hauptman, *Conspiracy of Interests*, 52–53; General A. G. Ellis, "Advent of the New York Indians into Wisconsin," *WHSC* 2 (1856): 419. On Jenkins's subsequent career after he left Oneida, see the annual report of the Board of Directors of the Northern Missionary Society in *Christian Herald*, 29 November 1817. On Kirkland's limitations as a speaker of the Oneida language, see the commentary in Tiro and Marino, eds., *Along the Hudson and Mohawk*, 70n69.

31. Bloomfield, *Oneidas*, 150; Vivian C. Hopkins, "De Witt Clinton and the Iroquois," *Ethnohistory* 8 (Spring 1961): 114–16; Franklin B. Hough, *A History of St. Lawrence and Franklin Counties, New York, from the Earliest Period to the Present Times* (Albany, N.Y.: Little and Co., 1853), 174; Tiro, *People of the Standing Stone*, 121–22.

32. Skenandoah quoted in Hauptman, *Conspiracy of Interests*, 43–44, 47.

33. Karim Tiro points out that the massive eruption of Mt. Tambora in Indonesia produced an ash cloud that caused darkened skies and that ruined harvests in central

New York. Snow fell in June 1816, a year without a summer. See Tiro, *People of the Standing Stone*, 138–39.

34. Geoffrey E. Buerger, "Eleazer Williams: Elitism and Multiple Identity on Two Frontiers," in *Being and Becoming Indian: Biographical Studies of North American Frontiers*, ed. James H. Clifton (Chicago: Dorsey Press, 1989), 122; Eleazer Williams to Dr. Stewart, 14 November 1817, EWP, Reel 2; Reginald Horsman, "The Origins of Oneida Removal to Wisconsin, 1815–1822," in *Oneida Indian Journey: From New York to Wisconsin, 1784–1860*, ed. Laurence M. Hauptman and L. Gordon McLester, III (Madison: University of Wisconsin Press, 1999), 57; Ellis, "Advent of the New York Indians," 419; Tiro, *People of the Standing Stone*, 138–39.

35. Extract of Minutes, Northern Missionary Society Meeting, 2 May 1816; James Mairs and Christian Miller, Committee Report to Northern Missionary Society, June 1816; Minutes of the Board, 4 September 1816, all in Papers of the Northern Missionary Society of New York, Rutgers University Library Special Collections, New Brunswick, N.J. Eleazer Williams's translation work appeared as Samuel Blatchford, *An Address Delivered to the Oneida Indians, September 24, 1810, Translated at the Request of the Board of Directors of the Northern Missionary Society by Eleazer Williams* (Albany, N.Y.: Churchhill and Abbey, 1815).

36. Eleazer Williams, Autobiographical Writings, EWP, Reel 3.

37. Ibid.

38. Eleazer Williams, "A Method of Daily Prayer," EWP, Reel 6; idem., "Occasional Prayers," EWP, Reel 5.

39. Catechism assembled by Eleazer Williams, EWP, Reel 5.

40. Eleazer Williams, Autobiographical Writings, EWP, Reel 3.

41. "Go out into the highways and hedges, and compel them to come in, that my house may be filled," Luke 14: 23 (KJV); Eleazer Williams, Autobiographical Writings, EWP, Reel 3.

42. Eleazer Williams, Autobiographical Writings, EWP, Reel 3; Bible passages highlighted by Williams, EWP, Reel 2; Sermon on Psalm 107: 4–7, EWP Reel 5. Terence J. O'Grady, "The Singing Societies of Oneida," *American Music* 9 (Spring 1991): 67–91.

43. Ellis, "Advent of the New York Indians," 420; Eleazer Williams, Autobiographical Writings, EWP, Reel 3; Sermon on John 8:34, EWP Reel 5; Tiro, *People of the Standing Stone*, 139.

44. Eleazer Williams, Autobiographical Writings, EWP Reel 3.

45. Ibid.

46. Ibid.

47. Ibid.

48. Ibid.

49. Ibid.

50. Ibid.

51. Ibid; *Christian Herald,* 1 March 1817, 361.

52. *Christian Herald*, 1 March 1817, 361; Ellis, "Advent of the New York Indians," 420; Hauptman, *Conspiracy of Interests*, 56; Bloomfield, *Oneidas*, 146; Luna M. Hammond Whitney, *History of Madison County, State of New York* (Syracuse, N.Y.: Truair, Smith, 1872), 112.

53. Eleazer Williams to Bishop Hobart, n.d., EWP, Reel 2; Eleazer Williams, Autobiographical Writings, EWP, Reel 3; Ellis, "Advent of the New York Indians," 420; Frank W. Merrill, *The Church's Mission to the Oneidas* (Fond du Lac, Wis.: P.B. Harper, 1902), 12.

54. Merrill, *Mission*, 12; Eleazer Williams, Autobiographical Writings, EWP, Reel 3; Appendix to Eleazer Williams, *Prayers for Families and for Particular Persons, Selected from the Book of Common Prayer* (Albany, N.Y.: G.J. Loomis, 1816), 20.

55. Clipping from the *Onondaga Gazette*, 30 July 1817, EWP Reel 3; Hobart's survey printed in *Christian Journal and Literary Register*, 19 March 1817.

56. "Mission of the Protestant Episcopal Church in the State of New York to the Oneida Indians," *Christian Journal and Literary Register*, 1 September 1818; "Religion, from the Utica *Patriot*," *National Register: A Weekly Paper*, 10 October 1818; "Address by Bishop Hobart to the Convention of the Protestant Episcopal Church," *Christian Journal and Literary Register*, 1 December 1818; Bloomfield, *Oneidas*, 151; Charles Wells Hayes, *The Diocese of Western New York: History and Recollections*, 2nd ed. (Rochester, N.Y.: Scranton, Wetmore, 1905), 49–51.

57. "Oneida Indians," *Religious Intelligencer*, 26 December 1818.

58. Eleazer Williams, Autobiographical Writings, EWP, Reel 3.

59. Ibid.; "Report of the Committee of the Board of the Hamilton Baptist Missionary Society," *Western New York Baptist Magazine*, 1 February 1820.

60. Hanson, *Lost Prince*, 278; Bloomfield, *Oneidas*, 169; "Third Annual Report of the New York Protestant Episcopal Missionary Society," *Christian Journal and Literary Register*, 1 December 1819.

61. Ellis, "Advent of the New York Indians"; idem, "Fifty-Four Years' Recollections of Men and Events in Wisconsin," *WHSC* 7 (1876): 207–68; idem, "Recollections of Rev. Eleazer Williams," *WHSC* (1879): 322–52.

62. Ellis, "Recollections of Eleazer Williams," 347; idem, "Advent of the New York Indians," 448–49.

63. A. G. Ellis to Eleazer Williams, n.d., EWP, Reel 2. The famous Wisconsin historian and chronicler Lyman Draper, in his introduction to Ellis's "Fifty-Four Years," 207, stated that Ellis first met Williams in November 1819. Ellis, in his "Recollections of Eleazer Williams," 322, says he met Williams for the first time in November 1820.

64. Hauptman and McLester argue that Ellis "helped foster the 'greatness' of the missionary's reputation" and that in his writings Williams's "less desirable qualities are minimized while his magnetic leadership is stressed." See Hauptman and McLester, *Daniel Bread*, 10. Hauptman and McLester have, in this instance, badly misread Ellis's scathing critique of Williams.

65. Ellis, "Recollections of Eleazer Williams," 323.

66. Ibid., 324.

67. Ibid., 329–30. On singing, see Tiro, *People of the Standing Stone*, 14–15, 87–88, 139.

68. Williams actually used twelve characters. Ellis, "Recollections of Eleazer Williams," 331, 322–23; Eleazer Williams, *Gaiatonsear Ionteweienstagwa Ongwe Onwe Gawennontakon: A Spelling Book in the Language of the Seven Iroquois Nations* (Utica, N.Y.: William Williams, 1820); Williams, *Prayers for Families*. I am indebted to Roy Wright for helping me to understand the significance of Williams's writings in Mohawk. See also Sean Harvey, "'Translated from the Dominions of Darkness': Native Missionaries, Language, and Scientific Authority in the Nineteenth Century," paper presented at the American Historical Association Annual Meeting, Boston, January 2011). For additional evidence of Williams's talents as a linguist see the two-volume manuscript Iroquois grammar he completed, at the Buffalo and Erie County Historical Society in Buffalo, New York (Eleazer Williams, Iroquois Grammar, 2 vols., Mss. W-68).

69. Ellis, "Recollections of Eleazer Williams," 325, 335.

70. On the harsh treatment meted out to Indians by the frontier population, see Jabez Hyde to David A. Ogden, 31 March 1819, Ogden Family Papers, NYPL.

71. Ibid., 331–33; Ellis, "Advent of the New York Indians," 421.

72. For studies that repeat Ellis's claim, see Judy Cornelius, "Tribal Discord and the Road to Green Bay," in Hauptman and McLester, *Oneida Indian Journey*, 128; Howard Greene, *The Reverend Richard Fish Cadle: A Missionary of the Protestant Episcopal Church in the Territories of Michigan and Wisconsin in the Early Nineteenth Century* (Waukesha, Wis.: privately printed, 1936), 150; Herbert S. Lewis, ed., *Oneida Lives: Long-Lost Voices of the Wisconsin Oneidas* (Lincoln: University of Nebraska Press, 2005), xx–xxi. Both Geoffrey Buerger and Laurence M. Hauptman have expressed some skepticism toward Ellis's claim. See Buerger, "Elitism," 123, and Laurence M. Hauptman, "The Gardener: Chief Daniel Bread and the Planting of the Oneida Nation in Wisconsin," in *Seven Generations of Iroquois Leadership: The Six Nations Since 1800* (Syracuse, N.Y.: Syracuse University Press, 2008), 90–91.

73. Hanson, *Lost Prince*, 297. The Rev. George Copway, also known by his Ojibwe name of Kahgegagahbowh, promoted the idea of establishing a territory for the Ojibwe and other Great Lakes Algonquian peoples in the 1840s within the boundaries of today's South Dakota. Copway may have drawn his inspiration from James Duane Doty, who governed the Wisconsin Territory in the early part of that decade. The U.S. Senate, in August 1842, rejected Doty's proposal that such a territory be established where native peoples might begin farms, develop their own form of territorial government, and, perhaps, join the Union as an Indian state. See Cecilia Morgan, "Kahgegagahbowh's (George Copway's) Transatlantic Performance: Running Sketches, 1850," *Cultural and Social History* 9, 4 (2012): 529; and Donald B. Smith, "The Life of George Copway, or Kah-ge-ga-gah-bowh (1818–1869) and a Review of His Writings," *Journal of Canadian Studies* 23 (October 1988): 19–22.

74. George A. Schultz, *An Indian Canaan: Isaac McCoy and the Vision of an Indian State* (Norman: University of Oklahoma Press, 1972), 67–68, 80–81, 95–96; Isaac McCoy,

Remarks on the Practicability of Indian Reform, Embracing Their Colonization (Boston: Lincoln and Edmands, 1827), 36.

75. Eleazer Williams to Jedidiah Morse, 22 July 1822, EWP-Newberry; Schultz, *Canaan*, 61; William Buell Sprague, *The Life of Jedidiah Morse, D.D.* (New York: Anson D. F. Randolph, 1874), 167–68, 171–72. See also George Seldon to Rev. John Chester, 8 November 1819, Jedidiah Morse Collection, Olin Library Special Collections, Cornell University, Ithaca, N.Y.

76. Morse quoted in Sprague, *Morse*, 171–72; Jedidiah Morse to John C. Calhoun, 4 February 1820, *PJCC*, 4: 634–35; Joseph W. Phillips, *Jedidiah Morse and New England Congregationalism* (New Brunswick, N.J.: Rutgers University Press, 1983), 209–11.

77. Calhoun to Morse, 7 February 1820, *PJCC*, 4: 648–51; Calhoun to Superintendents and Agents for Indian Affairs, and Officers of the Army of the United States, 7 February 1820, *PJCC*, 4: 651; Morse to Calhoun, 15 August 1820, *PJCC*, 5: 332; Eleazer Williams, Autobiographical Fragments, EWP, Reel 3.

78. On Williams's influence, see Rev. John Henry Hobart to John C. Calhoun, 25 January 1820, *PJCC*, 4: 604. See also Buerger, "Elitism," 116–23; Hauptman and McLester, *Daniel Bread*, 33.

79. Hanson, *Lost Prince*, 276.

80. Ibid., 287.

81. Ibid., 292; Tiro, *People of the Standing Stone*, 143.

Chapter 3. The Prospect of Great and Good Things

1. Whipple Report, 369; Historical Documents Regarding the Claims of the St. Regis Indians Against the State of New York, RG 10, Indian Affairs, Library and Archives of Canada, 14–18; Receipts Dated 18 and 19 March, 1816, Entry Documentation Submitted by the Indian Commissioner for Annuities Paid to Indians, 1796–1825, Series A0832, NYSA Box 7, Folder 4; Franklin B. Hough, *A History of St. Lawrence and Franklin Counties, New York, from the Earliest Period to the Present Times* (Albany, N.Y.: Little and Co., 1853), 159; Karim Tiro, *The People of the Standing Stone: The Oneida Nation from the Revolution Through the Era of Removal* (Amherst: University of Massachusetts Press, 2011).

2. Treaty with the Second Christian Party of Oneidas, 27 March 1817, Whipple Report, 284–87; General A. G. Ellis, "Advent of the New York Indians into Wisconsin," *WHSC* 2 (1856): 420; Mrs. L. M. Hammond, *History of Madison County, State of New York* (Syracuse, N.Y.: Truair, Smith, and Co., 1872), 112; Madison County Deed Book, Book O, 444–45, 448–49; Book T, 31–32, Madison County Clerk's Office, Wampsville, N.Y.; Receipts, NYSA A0832, Box 7, Folder 4; James H. Smith, *History of Chenango and Madison Counties, New York* (Syracuse, N.Y.: D. Mason., 1880), 735.

3. Historical Documents Regarding the Claims of the St. Regis Indians Against the State of New York, RG 10, 17–19, Library and Archives of Canada; Receipts, NYSA A0832, Box 7, Folder 4; John Tayler to Eleazer Williams, 2 September 1817, John Tayler Papers, Box 1, Folder 4, NYSL; Hough, *St. Lawrence*, 160.

4. J. H. Hanson, *The Lost Prince: Facts Tending to Prove the Identity of Louis the Seventeenth of France, and the Rev. Eleazer Williams, Missionary Among the Indians of North America* (New York: G.P. Putnam, 1854), 294–95.

5. See the discussion in Stuart Banner, *How the Indians Lost Their Land: Law and Power on the Frontier* (Cambridge, Mass.: Harvard University Press, 2007), 191–214.

6. Jasper Parrish to John C. Calhoun, 3 November 1819, *PJCC*, 4: 395.

7. Jasper Parrish struggled to protect Seneca livestock from white rustlers. See his complaints in LR-OIA-6N.

8. For attempts to protect the Indians, see Governor Daniel D. Tompkins, Report to the Assembly Committee on Indian Affairs, 12 February 1812, in *The Public Papers of Daniel D. Tompkins, Governor of New York, 1807–1817*, ed. Hugh Hastings (Albany, N.Y.: J.B. Lyon, 1902), 2: 482–83; New York Session Laws, Chapter 34, 40th Session, 2 February 1817; "Oneida Indians," *Religious Intelligencer*, 26 December 1818; Vivian Hopkins, "DeWitt Clinton and the Iroquois," *Ethnohistory* 8 (Spring 1961): 135; David J. Silverman, *Red Brethren: The Brothertown and Stockbridge Indians and the Problem of Race in Early America* (Ithaca, N.Y.: Cornell University Press, 2010), 150–53.

9. On the first Cherokee Removal crisis, see Gregory Evans Dowd, *A Spirited Resistance: The North American Indian Struggle for Unity, 1745–1815* (Baltimore: Johns Hopkins University Press, 1992), 161–66; and William G. McLoughlin, "Thomas Jefferson and the Origins of Cherokee Nationalism, 1806–1809," *William and Mary Quarterly* 3rd ser. 32 (1975): 547–80.

10. Alexander Dallas to Daniel D. Tompkins, 5 August 1815, quoted in Annie Heloise Abel, "The History of Events Resulting in Indian Consolidation West of the Mississippi," *Annual Report of the American Historical Association for the Year 1906* (Washington, D.C.: GPO, 1908), 305–6n; Barbara M. Conable, "A Steady Enemy: The Ogden Land Company and the Seneca Indians," Ph.D. dissertation, University of Rochester, 1995, 56.

11. Dowd, *Spirited Resistance*, 167–73, 185–90.

12. Brian W. Dippie, *The Vanishing American: White Attitudes and U.S. Indian Policy*, (Middletown, Conn., 1982), 45–78; Bernard W. Sheehan, *Seeds of Extinction: Jeffersonian Philanthropy and the American Indian* (Chapel Hill: University of North Carolina Press, 1973); Dowd, *Spirited Resistance*, 117.

13. On the Ogden Company, the best study remains Conable, "Steady Enemy," but see also Laurence M. Hauptman, *Conspiracy of Interests: Iroquois Dispossession and the Rise of New York State* (Syracuse, N.Y.: Syracuse University Press, 1999), chaps. 9–12. For a discussion of the right of preemption and what it entails, see N. Bruce Duthu, *American Indians and the Law* (New York: Penguin, 2008), 69–74, and, generally, Blake A. Watson, *Buying America from the Indians: Johnson v. McIntosh and the History of Native Land Rights* (Norman: University of Oklahoma Press, 2012).

14. Robert Troup to Jasper Parrish, 24 August 1810, Huntington Library, HM 8900, *IIM*; David Ogden to Jasper Parrish, 10 March 1818, and David Ogden to Jasper Parrish, 5 September 1818 in Ogden Family Papers, NYPL; Jasper Parrish to John C. Calhoun, 3 December 1818, Closed Docketed Case Files, Docket 301, Records of the Indian Claims

Commission, Box 2674, NA; Hauptman, *Conspiracy of Interests*, 121–24; Reginald Hors-man, "The Origins of Oneida Removal to Wisconsin, 1815–1822," in *The Oneida Indian Journey: From New York to Wisconsin, 1784–1860*, ed. Laurence M. Hauptman and L. Gordon McLester III (Madison: University of Wisconsin Press, 1999), 55–58; Conable, "Steady Enemy," 58; Lewis Cass to Headmen of the Six Nations, 30 May 1817, Indian Affairs, Field Office Papers, Michigan Superintendency, Letters Sent, vol. 2, NA.

15. David A. Ogden, Memorial to the President of the United States, 1817, David Ogden Papers, William L. Clements Library, University of Michigan, *IIM*.

16. Ibid.

17. Report of the Committee of the New York State Legislature, Legislative Assembly Papers 41: 143–48, NYSA, *IIM*; Resolution of the New York State Senate, New York State Legislative Assembly Papers, 41: 149, NYSL. On these attitudes in general, see Reginald Horsman, *Race and Manifest Destiny: The Origins of American Racial Anglo-Saxonism* (Cambridge, Mass.: Harvard University Press, 1981).

18. On these developments, see David A. Nichols, "Land, Republicanism and Indians: Power and Policy in Early National Georgia," *Georgia Historical Quarterly* 85 (Summer 2001): 199–226; Cynthia Cunfer, "Local Origins of National Indian Policy: Cherokee and Tennessean Ideas About Sovereignty and Nationhood, 1790–1811," *Journal of the Early Republic* 23 (Spring 2003): 21–46; Tim Alan Garrison, "Beyond *Worcester*: The Alabama Supreme Court and the Sovereignty of the Creek Nation," *Journal of the Early Republic* 19 (1999): 423–50.

19. David A. Ogden to John C. Calhoun, 16 March 1819, Ogden Papers, William L. Clements Library, University of Michigan, *IIM*.

20. John C. Calhoun to David A. Ogden, 19 August 1818, *PJCC*, 3: 56–57.

21. Hauptman, *Conspiracy of Interests*, 19–20.

22. Ibid. See also John C. Calhoun to Jasper Parrish, 14 May 1818, *PJCC*, 2: 294.

23. William Troup to Jasper Parrish, 24 August 1818, RG 279, Docket 301, Records of the Indian Claims Commission, Box 2674, NA.

24. Eleazer Williams to David Ogden, 12 December 1817; David A. Ogden to John C. Calhoun, 9 March 1818, both in Indian Papers, Related to Proposed Removal to the West, Indians, Box 1, File 31, NYPL; Eleazer Williams to David A. Ogden, 31 January 1818, Onondaga, Oneida, Miscellaneous, Indians, Box 1, File 35, NYPL.

25. Eleazer Williams, Autobiographical Writings, EWP, Reel 3; Ellis, "Advent of the New York Indians," 421; Silverman, *Red Brethren*, 161–62.

26. "Narrative of Jabez B. Hyde," in *Narratives of Early Mission Work on the Niagara Frontier and Buffalo Creek*, ed. Frank Severance, *Collections of the Buffalo and Erie County Historical Society*, vol. 6 (Buffalo, N.Y.: Buffalo and Erie County Historical Society, 1903), 248.

27. Oneida Petition to the President, 11 November 1818, Letters Received by the Secretary of War, Registered Series, 1801–1860, M221, Reel 182, NA.

28. Eleazer Williams, Autobiographical Writings, EWP, Reel 3; William Buell Sprague, *The Life of Jedidiah Morse, D.D.* (New York: Anson D. F. Randolph, 1874), 171–75; David Ogden to Lewis Cass, 2 June 1820, Ogden Family Papers, NYPL.

29. Rev. J. H. Hobart to John C. Calhoun, 25 January 1820, *PJCC*, 4: 604; Thomas Ludlow Ogden to Peter Buell Porter, 25 January 1820, RG 279, Docket 301, Records of the Indian Claims Commission, Box 2674, NA; Horsman, "Origins," 60; Ellis, "Advent of the New York Indians," 417; Hauptman, *Conspiracy of Interests*, 121–27.

30. Eleazer Williams to Morris Miller, 24 May 1820, Gratz Collection, Historical Society of Pennsylvania, Philadelphia; Eleazer Williams to John C. Calhoun, 4 February 1820, Letters Received by the Secretary of War, Main Series, M221, Reel 87, NA; Jedidiah Morse to John C. Calhoun, *PJCC*, 4: 634–35; likely Jedidiah Morse, *The American Geography* (Boston: Thomas and Andrews, 1812).

31. John C. Calhoun to Eleazer Williams, 9 February 1820, *PJCC*, 4: 658.

32. John C. Calhoun to Lewis Cass, 9 February 1820, *PJCC*, 4: 656; John C. Calhoun to George Gibson, 9 February 1820, *PJCC*, 4: 657; John C. Calhoun to Decius Wadsworth, 9 February 1820, *PJCC*, 4: 657–658; John C. Calhoun to Jasper Parrish, 9 February 1820, *PJCC*, 4: 657.

33. Hauptman, *Conspiracy of Interests*, 148.

34. Eleazer Williams, Autobiographical Writings, EWP, Reel 3: Eleazer Williams to John Henry Hobart, 16 May 1820, EWP, Reel 2; Thomas Ogden to David Ogden, 12 February 1820, Ogden Family Papers, NYPL .

35. Eleazer Williams to John Henry Hobart, 16 May 1820, EWP, Reel 2.

36. Ibid.; Laurence M. Hauptman and L. Gordon McLester, III, *Chief Daniel Bread and the Oneida Nation of Indians of Wisconsin* (Norman: University of Oklahoma Press, 2002), 34.

37. Hanson, *Lost Prince*, 290.

38. Jeanne Kay, "The Land of La Baye: The Ecological Impact of the Green Bay Fur Trade, 1634–1836," Ph.D. dissertation, University of Wisconsin, 1977, 11; Alice E. Smith, *The History of Wisconsin*, vol. 1, *From Exploration to Statehood* (Madison: State Historical Society of Wisconsin Press, 1973), 104; Kerry A. Trask, "Settlement in a Half-Savage Land: Life and Loss in the Metis Community at La Baye," *Michigan Historical Review* 15 (Spring 1989): 4–5, 14–16.

39. Trask, "Settlement," 7–8; Kay, "La Baye," 207; James W. Biddle, "Recollections of Green Bay in 1816–1817," *WHSC* 1 (1855): 61.

40. Trask, "Settlement," 1–2; John Haeger, "A Time of Change: Green Bay, 1815–1834," *Wisconsin Magazine of History* 54 (Summer 1971): 286; Suzanne Elizabeth Moranian, "Ethnocide in the Schoolhouse: Missionary Efforts to Educate Indian Youth in Pre-Reservation Wisconsin," *Wisconsin Magazine of History* 64 (Summer 1981): 247.

41. Smith, *Wisconsin*, 98; Patrick J. Jung, "Forge, Destroy, and Preserve the Bonds of Empire: Euro-Americans, Native Americans, and Metis on the Wisconsin Frontier, 1634–1856," Ph.D. dissertation, Marquette University, 1997, 184–86; idem., "Soldiering at Fort Howard, 1816–1841: A Social History of a Frontier Fort at Green Bay, Part II" *Voyageur* 12 (Summer/Fall 1995): 27–29; Biddle, "Green Bay," 52.

42. Lewis Cass to John C. Calhoun, 27 May 1819, *TPUS*, 10: 831; Cass to Calhoun, 17 April 1818, *TPUS*, 10: 745–46; James W. Oberly, "Decision on Duck Creek: Two Green

Bay Reservations and Their Boundaries, 1816–1996," *American Indian Culture and Research Journal* 24, 3 (2000): 44–46; Jung, "Forge," 189–90.

43. Francis Paul Prucha, *Lewis Cass and American Indian Policy* (Detroit: Wayne State University Press, 1967), 5; Kay, "La Baye," 211; Patrick J. Jung, "To Extend Fair and Impartial Justice to the Indian: Native Americans and the Additional Court of Michigan Territory, 1823–1836," *Michigan Historical Review* 23 (Fall 1997): 31.

44. *Indian Affairs: Laws and Treaties*, comp. Charles J. Kappler (Washington, D.C.: Government Printing Office, 1904), 2: 138; Trask, "Settlement," 24; Colin G. Calloway, "The End of an Era: British-Indian Relations in the Great Lakes Region after the War of 1812," *Michigan Historical Review* 12 (Fall 1986): 8–9; David R. M. Beck, *Siege and Survival: History of the Menominee Indians, 1634–1856* (Lincoln: University of Nebraska Press, 2002), 87.

45. Hauptman and McLester, *Daniel Bread*, 46; Smith, *Wisconsin*, 112–13; Kay, "La Baye," 1v, 212; John Haeger, *Men and Money: The Urban Frontier at Green Bay, 1815–1840* (Mt. Pleasant: Clarke Historical Society, Central Michigan University, 1971), 6.

46. Porlier and Lawe quoted in Trask, "Settlement," 26; Jeanne Kay, "John Lawe: Green Bay Trader," *Wisconsin Magazine of History* 64 (Winter 1980): 13.

47. Beck, *Siege and Survival*, 86.

48. *Detroit Gazette*, 28 July 1820, quoted in Ellis, "Advent of the New York Indians," 422; Jedidiah Morse to John C. Calhoun, 15 August 1820, *PJCC*, 5: 331–32.

49. Jedidiah Morse to John C. Calhoun, 15 August 1820, *PJCC*, 5: 331–32; Oneida Delegates to Lewis Cass, 12 August 1820, C. C. Trowbridge Manuscripts, Burton Historical Collection, Detroit Public Library, *IIM*; Horsman, "Origins," 61.

50. Jedidiah Morse to John C. Calhoun, 15 August 1820, *PJCC*, 5: 332; Morse to Calhoun, 3 October 1820, *PJCC*, 5: 371.

51. Lewis Cass to David A. Ogden, 11 December 1820, C. C. Trowbridge Manuscripts., Burton Historical Collection, Detroit Public Library, *IIM*; Sprague, *Morse*, 183–84; Lewis Cass to John C. Calhoun, 11 November 1820, *TPUS*, 11: 69–70; Cass to Deputies of the Oneidas, 11 December 1820, C. C. Trowbridge Manuscripts, Burton Historical Collection, Detroit Public Library, *IIM*; Beck, *Siege and Survival*, 91.

52. David A. Ogden to John C. Calhoun, 14 February 1821, *PJCC*, 5: 631; Eleazer Williams, Autobiographical Writings, EWP, Reel 3; Petition of the Oneidas Indians to the President of the United States, 10 April 1821, RG 279, Docket 301, Records of the Indian Claims Commission, Box 2674, NA.

53. Green Bay and Prairie du Chien Papers, 1774–1895, Indian Affairs, Volume 74, SHSW; Albert Gallatin Ellis, "Recollections of Eleazer Williams," *WHSC* 8 (1879): 335; Robert Troup to Peter Porter, 7 July 1821, RG 279, Docket 301, Records of the Indian Claims Commission, Box 2674, NA; John C. Calhoun to Eleazer Williams, 4 June 1821, *PJCC*, 6: 169; Horsman,"Origins," 61.

54. Geoffrey E. Buerger, "Eleazer Williams: Elitism and Multiple Identity on Two Frontiers" in *Being and Becoming Indian: Biographical Studies of North American Frontiers*, ed. James H. Clifton (Chicago: Dorsey Press, 1989), 127.

55. Eleazer Williams, Autobiographical Writings, EWP, Reel 3; Albert Gallatin Ellis, "Fifty-Four Years' Recollections of Men and Events in Wisconsin," *WHSC* 7 (1876): 325–26.

56. Tiro, *People of the Standing Stone*, 143–46; Ellis, "Recollections of Eleazer Williams," 327–28.

57. For examples of his storytelling, see Eleazer Williams to John Tayler, 28 March 1822, EWP-Newberry.

58. Oneida and Onondaga Chiefs to the President of the United States, 8 August 1821, RG 279, Docket 301, Records of the Indian Claims Commission, Box 2675, NA; Ellis, "Advent of the New York Indians," 426.

59. Eleazer Williams, Autobiographical Writings, EWP, Reel 3; Ellis, "Recollections of Eleazer Williams," 327–28.

60. Robert Troup to Peter Porter, 7 July 1821, RG 279, Docket 301, Records of the Indian Claims Commission, Box 2679,NA; Ellis, "Fifty-Four Years," 210–11.

61. Ellis, "Fifty-Four Years," 211–13; Journal of C. C. Trowbridge's Trip to Green Bay in Company with the Oneida Indians of New York, July-September 1821, C. C. Trowbridge Manuscripts, Burton Historical Collection, Detroit Public Library, *IIM*; James W. Oberly, *A Nation of Statesmen: The Political Culture of the Stockbridge-Munsee Mohicans, 1815–1972* (Norman: University of Oklahoma Press, 2005), 33; Beck, *Siege and Survival*, 91–92. Jacob Konkapot's interest in land sales and removal appears to have predated that of Williams. See John Tayler to Nathan Williams, 25 May 1814, John Tayler Papers, Box 1, Folder 4, NYSL.

62. Jacob Brown to John C. Calhoun, 27 September 1819, *PJCC*, 4: 345–46.

63. Trowbridge Journal, *IIM*.

64. Ibid.

65. Ibid.; Eleazer Williams, Autobiographical Writings, EWP, Reel 3; C. C. Trowbridge to Lewis Cass, 7 September 1821, Documents Relating to the Negotiation of Ratified and Unratified Treaties with Various Indian Tribes, 1801–1869, T494, Reel 8: 14–15, NA.

66. Eleazer Williams to John C. Calhoun, 29 November 1821, *PJCC*, 6: 543.

67. Eleazer Williams, Autobiographical Writings, EWP, Reel 3; Trowbridge to Cass, 7 September 1821, T494, Reel 8:17.

68. Cornelius Beard to John C. Calhoun, 25 January 1822, *PJCC*, 6: 633; Beck, *Siege and Survival*, 93; Eleazer Williams to John C. Calhoun, 29 November 1821, RG 75, M221, Letters Received by the Secretary of War, Registered Series, 1801–1860, NA.

69. Eleazer Williams, Autobiographical Writings, EWP, Reel 3.

70. Nicolas Garmigontaya, Hendrick Schuyler, Peter Yaramynem, Moses Schuyler, Christopher Schuyler, Martin Quinney, and Abraham Schuyler to William Lacey, 25 February, 1823, in Abel, "History of Events," 317n.

71. Eleazer Williams, Autobiographical Writings, EWP, Reel 3; "Journals of the Rev. Thompson S. Harris," in *Narratives of Early Mission Work*, ed. Severance, 291–92; Peter Summer and Other Oneida Indians to John C. Calhoun, 22 January 1822, *PJCC*, 7: 178; Ellis, "Recollections of Eleazer Williams," 336.

72. Hanson, *Lost Prince*, 292.

73. Nicolas Garmigontaya, Hendrick Schuyler, Peter Yaramynem, Moses Schuyler, Christopher Schuyler, Martin Quinney, and Abraham Schuyler to William Lacey, 25 February 1823, in Abel, "History of Events," 317n; William B. Lacey to Bishop J. H. Hobart, 25 February 1822, in Abel, "History of Events," 318n; Hanson, *Lost Prince*, 293.

74. Declaration of Oneida Chiefs in General Council Assembled, 29 February 1822, EWP, Reel 1.

75. John C. Calhoun to Lewis Cass, 8 May 1822, and John C. Calhoun, Circular Letter to Indian Agents and Officers of Government in Michigan Territory, 8 May 1822, LR-OIA-NY, Reel 583; John C. Calhoun to Assistant Commissaries of Subsistence in Michigan Territory, 8 May 1822, *PJCC*, 7: 100.

76. Journal of A. G. Ellis, Fragment, EWP, Reel 7; Ellis, "Fifty-Four Years," 223.

77. Journal of A. G. Ellis, Fragment, EWP, Reel 7; Eleazer Williams, Autobiographical Writings, EWP, Reel 3.

78. Journal of A. G. Ellis, Fragment, EWP, Reel 7.

79. Beck, *Siege and Survival*, 95, Oberly, *Nation of Statesmen*, 34–35; Karim M. Tiro, *The People of the Standing Stone: The Oneida Nation from the Revolution to the Era of Removal* (Amherst: University of Massachusetts Press, 2011), 142–43; Ellis, "Advent of the New York Indians," 428; idem, "Fifty-Four Years," 225.

80. Eleazer Williams, Autobiographical Writings, EWP, Reel 3. See also Thomas L. McKenney to John C. Calhoun, 5 July 1821, *PJCC*, 6: 244–45.

81. Jung, "To Extend Fair and Impartial Justice," 27–29; idem, "Soldiering at Fort Howard, Part II," 28.

82. Eleazer Williams, Autobiographical Writings, EWP, Reel 1, Reel 3; John Lawe to Jacques Porlier, 2 November 1823, "The Fur Trade in Wisconsin, 1821–1825," *WHSC* 20 (1911): 320.

83. Rachel Swamp, WPA Interview, quoted in Hauptman, *Oneida Indian Journey*, 126; Tiro, *People of the Standing Stone*, 78; Laurence M. Hauptman, "The Gardener: Chief Daniel Bread and the Planting of the Oneida Nation in Wisconsin," in *Seven Generations of Iroquois Leadership: The Six Nations Since 1800* (Syracuse, N.Y.: Syracuse University Press, 2008), 85.

84. Eleazer Williams, Autobiographical Writings, EWP, Reel 1; Oberly, *Nation of Statesmen*, 38–39; Silverman, *Red Brethren*, 172–74; Jasper Parrish to Thomas L. McKenney, 26 February 1827, LR-OIA-6N; Receipt/Bill, EWP, Reel 2.

85. Hanson, *Lost Prince*, 299.

86. Eleazer Williams to John Henry Hobart, 15 May 1823, Francis L. Hawks and General Collection of Early Episcopal Church Manuscripts, RG 117, Archives of the Episcopal Church, Austin, Texas; A. Parker Curtiss, *History of the Diocese of Fond du Lac and Its Several Congregations* (Fond du Lac, Wis.: P. B. Haber, 1925).

87. "Letter from Eleazer Williams, the Indian Catechist," *Churchman's Magazine*, March 1823, 92–94; Eleazer Williams to John C. Calhoun, 27 December 1822, *PJCC*, 7: 395; Eleazer Williams, Autobiographical Writings, EWP, Reel 3. Eleazer Holmes

Ellis was born on 26 August 1825. See Christ Episcopal Church Records, SHSW, Area Research Center, Cofrin Library, University of Wisconsin, Green Bay, Reel 2.

88. Ellis, "Fifty-Four Years," 226; William Clarke Whitford, "Early History of Education in Wisconsin," *WHSC* 5 (1869), 331–351.

89. Eleazer Williams to John Henry Hobart, 15 May 1823, Hawks Collection.

90. Ellis, "Fifty-Four Years," 226–228; J. K. Bloomfield, *The Oneidas* (New York: Alden Brothers, 1907), 181; Robert L. Hall, "Eleazer Williams: Mohawk Between Two Worlds," *Voyageur* 19, 1 (2002): 15; Trask, "Settlement," 15; Eleazer Williams, Autobiographical Writings, EWP, Reel 3.

91. Ellis, "Fifty-Four Years," 228.

92. Ibid., 242–43.

93. Ibid., 231; Eleazer Williams, Autobiographical Writings, EWP Reel 3.

94. Eleazer Williams to John C. Calhoun, 27 December 1822, *PJCC*, 7: 395. On the shortage of funds experienced chronically by Indian missionaries, see the explanation offered by Solomon Davis in his letter to Mr. M. Van Wagenen, treasurer of the Committee for the Propagation of the Gospel in the State of New York, 10 November 1823, in the Hawks Collection. Davis intended to open his school at Oneida after Williams's departure from New York. He expected that a school where "the instruction of the boys should, in addition to reading, writing, and arithmetic, embrace a practical knowledge of the mode of agriculture, and that the girls also be instructed in spinning, weaving, sewing and other domestic branches," would cost $344 a year to operate, a sum far greater than what he, or Williams in Wisconsin, received from the Episcopal Church. See also Davis to Rev. John McVicker, 5 July 1824, Hawks Collection.

95. John C. Calhoun to Albert Gallatin Ellis, 12 August 1823, EWP, Reel 2; *Philadelphia Recorder*, 9 April 1825; Bloomfield, *Oneidas*, 176; Trask, "Settlement," 26.

96. Ellis, "Fifty-Four Years," 233; Howard Greene, *The Reverend Richard Fish Cadle: A Missionary of the Protestant Episcopal Church in the Territories of Michigan and Wisconsin in the Early Nineteenth Century* (Waukesha, Wis.: privately printed, 1936), 46.

97. Eleazer Williams, Sermon, 4 July 1823, EWP, Reel 1.

98. Ibid.

99. Margaret Scannadoa, Nelly Scannadoa, Rachel Schermerhorn, Martin Denny, Daniel Bread, Peter Webster, and Peter John to George Boyd, 5 April 1824, EWP, Reel 2; "For the Reformer: Missionaries Among the Indians," *Reformer*, 136–37.

Chapter 4. A Failed Performance

1. General Albert Gallatin Ellis, "Recollections of Eleazer Williams," *WHSC* 8 (1879): 334; Eleazer Williams to John C. Calhoun, Williams Collection, Missouri Historical Society, *IIM*; Laurence M. Hauptman and L. Gordon McLester, III, *Chief Daniel Bread and the Oneida Nation of Indians of Wisconsin* (Norman: University of Oklahoma Press, 2002), 52; Karim M. Tiro, *The People of the Standing Stone: The Oneida Nation from the Revolution Through the Era of Removal* (Amherst: University of Massachusetts Press, 2011), 146–48.

2. "Propagation of the Gospel," ca. 1820s, EWP, Reel 6; Eleazer Williams to "Right Reverend Sir," n.d., EWP, Reel 2.

3. Undated scrap, EWP, Reel 2; Eleazer Williams to "Right Reverend Sir," n.d., EWP, Reel 2.

4. John Lawe to Jacques Porlier, 2 November 1823, in "The Fur Trade in Wisconsin, 1812–1825," *WHSC* 20 (1911): 320.

5. Eleazer Williams, Autobiographical Writings, EWP, Reel 3. On Denny, see Hauptman and McLester, *Daniel Bread*, 30, 38.

6. Eleazer Williams to Rev. George Boyd, 29 June 1824, EWP, Reel 2; Williams, Plan for Education, EWP, Reel 6.

7. Williams, Plan for Education, EWP, Reel 6; "To All Who Love the Prosperity of Zion and Are Disposed to Aid in the Propagating the Gospel Among, and the Civilization of the Heathen," 4 July 1844, broadside, in EWP, Reel 2.

8. On this point I have found useful the discussion on stages of civilization in Drew McCoy, *The Elusive Republic: Political Economy in Jeffersonian America* (Chapel Hill: University of North Carolina Press, 1980); and Ronald L. Meek, *Social Science and the Ignoble Savage* (New York: Cambridge University Press, 1976).

9. Eleazer Williams, Plan for Education, EWP, Reel 6; Eleazer Williams to Timothy Clowes, 28 October 1824, EWP, Reel 2. Important works on Indian education include Brenda Child, *Boarding School Seasons: American Indian Families, 1900–1940* (Lincoln: University of Nebraska Press, 1998); Amanda J. Cobb, *Listening to Our Grandmothers' Stories: The Bloomfield Academy for Chickasaw Females, 1852–1949* (Lincoln: University of Nebraska Press, 2007); and Devon Mihesuah, *Cultivating the Rosebuds: The Education of Women at the Cherokee Female Seminary, 1851–1909* (Urbana: University of Illinois Press, 1993).

10. George Boyd to Jackson Kemper, 31 August 1824, EWP, Reel 2; "Indians Within the United States," *Christian Herald and Seaman's Magazine*, 3 January 1824; *Zion's Herald*, 15 May 1823; Eleazer Williams to Timothy Clowes, n.d., EWP, Reel 2.

11. See Entry Documentation Submitted by the Indian Commissioners and Indian Agents for Annuities Paid to Indians and for Other Expenditures, NYSA A0832, Box 7, Folder 5.

12. Abundant evidence for this exists for the Senecas. Less evidence appears for the St. Regis, for whom records generally are less numerous. For a Seneca example, see the speech of Red Jacket to Erastus Granger, 27 November 1815, in *The Collected Speeches of Segoyewatha, or Red Jacket*, ed. Granville Ganter (Syracuse, N.Y.: Syracuse University Press, 2006), 183–84.

13. Whipple *Report*, 372–75.

14. Treaty of 26 August 1824 in Whipple Report, 287–89. The following November, the state legislature enacted a law authorizing the commissioners of the state land office to issue letters patent for Eleazer Williams "or his assignee, Erastus Willard, in the manner stipulated in the said treaty with the Oneida Indians." *New York Session Laws*, 47th Session, Chapter CCCV, 24 November 1824, 359. Williams received letters

patent to the tract from the commissioners of the State Land Office in the spring of 1825.

15. Eleazer Williams to Timothy Clowes, n.d., EWP, Reel 2; Eleazer Williams, Autobiographical Writings, EWP, Reel 3; J. H. Hanson, *The Lost Prince: Facts Tending to Prove the Identity of Louis the Seventeenth of France, and the Rev. Eleazer Williams, Missionary Among the Indians of North America* (New York: G. P. Putnam, 1854), 302

16. General Albert G. Ellis, "Fifty-Four Years' Recollections of Men and Events in Wisconsin," *WHSC* 7 (1876): 234–36; "Documents Relating to the Episcopal Church and Mission in Green Bay, 1825–1841," *WHSC* 14 (1898): 450n–451n. The territorial legislature formally incorporated the Christ Church charter in the fall of 1829. See *Acts Passed at the Second Session of the Third Legislative Council of the Territory of Michigan* (Detroit: Sheldon McKnight, 1829), 14; Christ Episcopal Church Records, SHSW Area Research Center, Cofrin Library, University of Wisconsin, Green Bay.

17. Eleazer Williams, Autobiographical Writings, EWP Reel 1; EWP Reel 3.

18. Ibid., Reel 3.

19. Magdalene W. to George Boyd, 4 February 1826, EWP, Reel 2.

20. There might be more to the name, for the Reverend John Williams of Deerfield, Eunice's father, named one of his children Eleazer. This Eleazer Williams married a Mary Hobart, the "third daughter of Rev. Nehemiah Hobart." The couple settled in Mansfield, Connecticut. The name "Mary Hobart," then, in addition to deriving from Williams's mother and most important patron, was an old Williams family name, and perhaps a signifier of Eleazer Williams's identification at this point in his career with his English forbears. See *The Commemorative Services of the First Church in Newton, Massachusetts, on the Occasion of the Two Hundred and Twenty-Fifth Anniversary of its Foundation* (Boston: The Society, 1889), 88–89.

21. Eleazer Williams, Autobiographical Writings, EWP, Reel 1; Mary Hobart Williams to Mrs. Hobart (1826), EWP, Reel 2.

22. J. K. Bloomfield, *The Oneidas* (New York: Alden Brothers, 1907), 169.

23. Eleazer Williams, Autobiographical Writings, EWP, Reel 1; Bloomfield, *Oneidas*, 186.

24. Solomon Davis to Mr. M. Van Wagenen, 10 November 1823, and Solomon Davis to Rev. John McVicker, 5 July 1824, in Francis L. Hawks and General Collection of Early Episcopal Church Manuscripts, RG 117, Archives of the Episcopal Church, Austin, Texas.

25. Bloomfield, *Oneidas*, 186; *Zion's Herald*, 6 September 1826; "Bishop Hobart's Address to the Oneida Indians," *Gospel Messenger and Southern Episcopal Register*, October 1826, 311.

26. "Bishop Hobart's Address," 311.

27. Eleazer Williams to John Henry Hobart, 2 August 1826, Hawks Collection.

28. Ibid.; Duane Hamilton Hurd, *History of Clinton and Franklin Counties, New York* (Philadelphia: J.W. Lewis, 1880), 227. On the Peru Iron Company, see John Denis Haeger, *The Investment Frontier: New York Businessmen and the Economic Development*

of the Old Northwest (Albany: State University of New York Press, 1981), 14–15; and Gordon C. Pollard and Haagen D. Klaus, "A Large Business: The Clintonville Site, Resources, and Scale at Adirondack Bloomery Forges," *Industrial Archaeology* 30, 1 (2004): 19.

29. *Zion's Herald*, 6 September 1826; *Boston Recorder and Religious Telegraph*, 1 September 1826; Bloomfield, *Oneidas*, 187–88; Eleazer Williams, Autobiographical Writings, EWP, Reel 1.

30. Jacob Jamieson to James Barbour, 26 September 1827, LR-OIA-6N; Brad Devin Edward Jarvis, "Preserving the Brothertown Nation of Indians: Exploring Relationships Amongst Land, Sovereignty, and Identity, 1740–1840," Ph.D. dissertation, University of Minnesota, 2006, 252; Hauptman and McLester, *Daniel Bread*, 37.

31. Taylor Spence, "The Endless Commons: Indigenous and Immigrants in the British-American Borderland, 1835–1848," Ph.D. dissertation, Yale University, 2012, 46–52.

32. Brothertown Chiefs to President John Quincy Adams, 17 January 1827, LR-OIA-6N; Albert Gallatin Ellis, "Advent of the New York Indians into Wisconsin," *WHSC* 2 (1856): 430.

33. David R. M. Beck, *Siege and Survival: History of the Menominee Indians, 1634–1856* (Lincoln: University of Nebraska Press, 2002), 98–99; Jarvis, "Brothertown," 233–34; James W. Oberly, *A Nation of Statesmen: The Political Culture of the Stockbridge-Munsee Mohicans, 1815–1972* (Norman: University of Oklahoma Press, 2005), 42.

34. Thomas L. McKenney to Henry B. Breevoort, 8 March 1825, *TPUS*, 11: 657–58. On the formation of the Office of Indian Affairs and McKenney's role in it, see Francis Paul Prucha, *The Great Father* (Lincoln: University of Nebraska Press, 1984), 163–65.

35. Eleazer Williams, Autobiographical Writings, EWP, Reel 1.

36. Lewis Cass to Thomas L. McKenney, 3 September 1825, M21, Letters Sent, Office of Indian Affairs, 1824–1881, Reel 419, NA; Beck, *Siege and Survival*, 98; Jarvis, "Brothertown," 257–58; David J. Silverman, *Red Brethren: The Brothertown and Stockbridge Indians and the Problem of Race in Early America* (Ithaca, N.C.: Cornell University Press, 2010), 174–75.

37. Jarvis, "Brothertown," 366; Robert W. Venables, "Victim versus Victim: The Irony of the New York Indians' Removal to Wisconsin," *American Indian Environments: Ecological Issues in Native American History*, ed. Christopher Vecsey and Robert W. Venables (Syracuse, N.Y.: Syracuse University Press, 1980), 142–43.

38. John Metoxen to Eleazer Williams, 23 July 1827, EWP, Reel 2. The notes are in EWP, Box 6.

39. Thomas L. McKenney, *Memoirs, Official and Personal* (Lincoln: University of Nebraska Press, 1973), 81, 83; Silverman, *Red Brethren*, 174–75; Francis Paul Prucha, *American Indian Treaties: The History of a Political Anomaly* (Berkeley: University of California Press, 1994), 141–42.

40. Jarvis, "Brothertown," 159–160; Beck, *Siege and Survival*, 99–100; Silverman, *Red Brethren*, 175.

41. *Indian Affairs: Laws and Treaties*, comp. Charles J. Kappler (Washington, D.C: GPO, 1904), 2: 281–82; Beck, *Siege and Survival*, 101; Oberly, *Nation of Statesmen*, 42–43.

42. Jarvis, "Brothertown," 263–64; William Troup, Thomas L. Ogden, and B. W. Rogers to James Barbour, 16 October 1827, LR-OIA-6N; William Troup, Thomas L. Ogden, and B. W. Rogers to Thomas L. McKenney, 20 December 1827, LR-OIA-6N.

43. Eleazer Williams, Autobiographical Writings, EWP, Reel 1; Hanson, *Lost Prince*, 307, 309.

44. Hanson, *Lost Prince*, 309–10; Eleazer Williams, Autobiographical Writings, EWP, Reel 1.

45. Hanson, *Lost Prince*, 309; Thomas Ludlow Ogden to Thomas L. McKenney, 21 January 1829, LR-OIA-GB, Reel 315.

46. Memorial of the New York Indians to Congress, 26 January 1829, *IIM*.

47. Kappler, *Laws and Treaties*, 2: 283.

48. Jasper Parrish to Thomas L. McKenney, 15 January 1827, LR-OIA-6N; Parrish to McKenney, 12 April 1829, LR-OIA-6N; Nathan Sargent to Thomas L. McKenney, 6 April 1829, LR-OIA-6N.

49. Tiro, *People of the Standing Stone*, 151; Whipple Report, 291–93.

50. Thomas L. McKenney to T. L. Ogden, 26 January 1829, *TPUS*, 12: 14; Jasper Parrish to Thomas L. McKenney, 13 April 1829, LR-OIA-6N; Petition of the First Christian Party, New York State Assembly, Legislative Assembly Papers, 41: 423–32, NYSA.

51. Reginald Horsman, "The Origins of Oneida Removal to Wisconsin, 1815–1822," in *The Oneida Indian Journey: From New York to Wisconsin, 1784–1860*, ed. Laurence M. Hauptman and L. Gordon McLester III (Madison: University of Wisconsin Press, 1999), 65–67; Jack Campisi, "The Wisconsin Oneidas Between Disasters," ibid., 71; Justus Ingersoll, "Census of the Indians in New York State," 1 October 1830, LR-OIA-6N; "Estimated Census, 13 March 1834, LR-OIA-6N.

52. Davis quoted in Tiro, *People of the Standing Stone*, 143–44. On Bread's acting according to traditional norms of leadership, see Hauptman and McLester, *Daniel Bread*, xiii, 27–28. Between March 1817 and April 1830, Oneidas signed seven deeds granting lands to the State of New York: three by the First Christian Party (26 August 1824, 13 February, 8 October 1829); two by the Orchard Party (2 February 1827, 3 April 1830); and two by the Second Christian Party (17 March 1817, 1 February 1826). Fifty-two individuals signed these deeds, but only five (Daniel Bread, Henry Powless, John Cornelius, Jacob Cornelius, and William Cornelius) signed three of the agreements. None signed more than three, and nine individuals signed two agreements. Eleazer Williams signed only the treaty negotiated with the Second Christian Party on 17 March 1817, and he did so as a witness. Williams signed no other Oneida land cession treaties. The relevant documents are included in the Whipple Report, 284–305.

53. Laurence M. Hauptman, "The Gardener: Chief Daniel Bread and the Planting of the Oneida Nation in Wisconsin," in *Seven Generations of Iroquois Leadership: The Six Nations Since 1800* (Syracuse, N.Y.: Syracuse University Press, 2008), 88–89.

54. On this era in Iroquois history generally, see Tiro, *People of the Standing Stone*, 129–56; Silverman, *Red Brethren*, 149–83; Matthew Dennis, *Seneca Possessed: Indians, Witchcraft, and Power in the Early American Republic* (Philadelphia: University of

Pennsylvania Press, 2010); and Laurence M. Hauptman, *Conspiracy of Interests: Iroquois Dispossession and the Rise of New York State* (Syracuse, N.Y.: Syracuse University Press, 1999).

55. See the discussion in Stuart L. Banner, *How the Indians Lost Their Land: Law and Power on the Frontier* (Cambridge, Mass.: Harvard University Press, 2007), 191–227.

56. Samuel C. Stambaugh, "Report on the Quality and Conditions of the Wisconsin Territory, 1831," *WHSC* 15 (1900): 405–7; "Marsh's Report to the Scottish Society, 1831," in "Documents Relating to the Stockbridge Mission, 1825–1848," *WHSC* 15 (1900): 58–59; On post-removal Indian communities, see John Bowles, *Exiles and Pioneers: Eastern Indians in the Trans-Mississippi West* (Cambridge: Cambridge University Press, 2007); Stephen Warren, *The Shawnees and Their Neighbors, 1795–1870* (Urbana: University of Illinois Press, 2005); and Andrew Denson, *Demanding the Cherokee Nation: Indian Autonomy and American Culture, 1830–1900* (Lincoln: University of Nebraska Press, 2004).

57. "St. Paul's Church, Detroit," *Episcopal Watchman*, 2 September 1828; Eleazer Williams, Autobiographical Writings, EWP, Reel 1; Eleazer Williams to Unknown, 1 October 1828, EWP, Reel 2; William Clarke Whitford, "Early History of Education in Wisconsin," *WHSC* 5 (1869), 327–328; "Narrative of Morgan L. Martin," *WHSC* 11 (1888): 390; Stambaugh, "Report on the Wisconsin Territory," 406–7.

58. Histories of Jacksonian Indian policy are numerous, with many scholars focusing upon the Southeastern tribes. Among the best examples are William G. McLoughlin, *Cherokee Renascence in the New Republic* (New Haven, Conn.: Yale University Press, 1986); Ronald N. Satz, *American Indian Policy in the Jacksonian Era* (Lincoln: University of Nebraska Press, 1975); Brian Dippie, *The Vanishing American: White Attitudes and American Indian Policy* (Middletown, Conn.: Wesleyan University Press, 1982); and Reginald Horsman, *Race and Manifest Destiny: The Origins of American Racial Anglo-Saxonism* (Cambridge, Mass.: Harvard University Press, 1981).

59. On what I have called here "frontier federalism," see Cynthia Cunfer, "Local Origins of National Indian Policy: Cherokee and Tennessean Ideas About Sovereignty and Nationhood, 1790–1811," *Journal of the Early Republic* 23 (Spring 2003): 21–46; and David A. Nichols, "Land, Republicanism and Indians: Power and Policy in Early National Georgia, 1780–1825," *Georgia Historical Quarterly* 85 (Summer 2001): 199–226.

60. On the debate, see Francis Paul Prucha, *American Indian Policy in the Formative Years: The Indian Trade and Intercourse Acts, 1790–1834* (Cambridge, Mass.: Harvard University Press, 1962), 224–25; and Francis Paul Prucha, ed., *Cherokee Removal: The "William Penn" Essays and Other Writings by Jeremiah Evarts* (Knoxville: University of Tennessee Press, 1981); Dippie, *Vanishing American*, 64–65.

61. T. L. Ogden to Thomas McKenney, 23 December 1829, LR-OIA-Emigration. On McKenney's break with the Jackson Administration, see McKenney, *Memoirs*, 256–84.

62. Cornelius Baird and Jacob Jamieson to John Quincy Adams, 7 January 1828, LR-OIA-6N; Lewis Cass to the Chiefs of the New York Indians at Green Bay, 4 May 1828, LR-OIA-6N.

63. Lewis Cass to John Eaton, 5 December 1830, M574, Reel 8; Office of Indian Affairs, Special Files, File 73, NA.

64. On the New Yorkers' distrust, see the Petition of the New York Indians, 3 May 1830, LR-OIA-GB, Reel 315; For Eaton's instructions to the commissioners, see John Eaton to Erastus Root, Jarvis McCall, and John Mason, 9 June 1839, LR-OIA-GB, Reel 315.

65. Ellis's report, 1830, LR-OIA-GB, Reel 315; "Journal of the Proceedings of the Board of Commissioners Appointed by the President, 7 June 1830," LR-OIA-GB, Reel 315.

66. Commissioners' Report, LR-OIA-GB, Reel 315; Hauptman and McLester, *Daniel Bread*, 55.

67. Commissioners' Report, LR-OIA-GB, Reel 315; Beck, *Siege and Survival*, 107.

68. Eleazer Williams, Autobiographical Writings, EWP, Reel 1; Hauptman and McLester, *Daniel Bread*, 65. For Stambaugh's sympathy for the Menominees, see John W. Hall, *Uncommon Defense: Indian Allies in the Black Hawk War* (Cambridge, Mass.: Harvard University Press, 2009), 183. On Williams's daughter, see Holy Apostles Episcopal Church Records, SHSW Area Research Center, Cofrin Library, University of Wisconsin, Green Bay.

69. *Western Recorder*, 21 December 1830; Calvin Colton, *Tour of the American Lakes, and Among the Indians of the North-West Territory in 1830: Disclosing the Character and Prospects of the Indian Race*, 2 vols. (London: Frederick Westley and A. H. Davis, 1833), 2: 164–65.

70. Lyman C. Draper, "Additional Notes on Eleazer Williams," *WHSC* 8 (1879): 364–65; John Y. Smith, "Eleazer Williams and the Lost Prince," *WHSC* 6 (1870): 335.

71. Samuel Stambaugh to John H. Eaton, 8 March 1831, LR-OIA-GB, Reel 315; Eleazer Williams, letter dated 27 July 1831, EWP, Reel 2.

72. A Brief Exposition of the Claims of the New York Indians to Certain Lands at Green Bay, in the Michigan Territory, 20 January 1831, M668, Reel 6, NA. See also Brothertown Petition to Andrew Jackson, 27 December 1830, LR-OIA-6N; Memorial of John W. Quinney, Eleazer Williams, and Others, 15 February, 1831, M668, Reel 6, NA; Samuel Stambaugh to George Porter, 2 November 1831, M234, LR-OIA-GB, Reel 315.

73. Kappler, *Laws and Treaties*, 2: 319–20, 324.

74. "A Brief Exposition of the Claims"; Memorial of John W. Quinney, Eleazer Williams, and Others, 15 February 1831, M668, Reel 6, NA.

75. Ellis, "Advent of the New York Indians," 437.

76. T. L. Ogden and William Troup to Lewis Cass, 18 October 1831, LR-OIA-6N; Ellis, "Advent of the New York Indians," 439.

77. Eleazer Williams, Autobiographical Writings, EWP Reel 1; Eleazer Williams to Mary Williams, November 1831, EWP Reel 2; George Porter to Lewis Cass, 3 February 1832, LR-OIA-GB, Reel 315; Jarvis, "Brothertown," 282–83; Hauptman and McLester, *Daniel Bread*, 70.

78. George Porter to Lewis Cass, 24 January, 1833, Joshua Porter Papers, SHSW.

79. Speech of Grizzly Bear, October 1832, Documents Relating to the Negotiation of Ratified and Unratified Treaties with Various Indian Tribes, 1801–1869, T494, Reel 2, NA.

80. Kappler, *Laws and Treaties*, 2: 378–80; Hauptman, "The Gardener," 91; Governor George Porter to Lewis Cass, 3 February 1832, LR-OIA-GB, Reel 315; Form for Fundraising, 10 May 1832, EWP, Reel 2; C. A. Baker to Jonas Earll, 1 February 1831, LR-OIA-6N.

81. Eleazer Williams, Autobiographical Writings, EWP, Reel 3.

82. Ibid.

83. For the deed to Williams, LR-OIA-6N; Hanson, *Lost Prince*, 320. On *Johnson v. McIntosh* (1823) see Banner, *How the Indians Lost Their Land*, 178–90.

84. "Meeting of Oneida at Green Bay," *Episcopal Register*, 21 April 1832; Blank Contribution Sheet, 10 May 1832, EWP, Reel 2; William Ward Wight, *Eleazer Williams: Not the Dauphin of France* (Chicago: Chicago Historical Society, 1903), 27–28. On Davis's enterprise, see "Stage Passengers—Look Out!" *Evangelical Magazine and Gospel Advocate* 1 (1830).

85. Ellis, "Recollections of Eleazer Williams," 344.

86. Eleazer Williams, Autobiographical Writings, EWP, Reel 3; Hauptman and McLester, *Daniel Bread*, 89–90.

87. Eleazer Williams, Autobiographical Writings, EWP, Reel 3; Jackson Kemper, "Journal of an Episcopalian Missionary's Tour to Green Bay, 1834," *WHSC* 14 (1898): 423–24; Hauptman and McLester, *Daniel Bread*, 90.

88. Hanson, *Lost Prince*, 319.

89. Eleazer Williams to the Trustees of the Ogden Land Company, September 1833, EWP, Reel 2.

90. Ibid.

91. Hanson, *Lost Prince*, 320; Eleazer Williams, Autobiographical Writings, EWP, Reel 3. For information on Williams's debts, see the Certificate of Notice, 30 March 1833, EWP, Reel 2; Eleazer Williams to John Lawe, 10 June 1833, Grignon, Lawe, and Porlier Papers, SHSW Area Research Center.

Chapter 5. The Life of a Misanthrope

1. Eleazer Williams, Autobiographical Writings, EWP, Reel 3; Eleazer Williams to Henry Baird, 10 January 1837, Henry S. Baird Papers, Clippings, ca. 1899–1907, Wisconsin Manuscript V, Box I, Folder 4, SHSW; Chiefs of the First Christian Party to Agent George Boyd, 16 June 1834, LR-OIA-GB, Reel 316.

2. A. G. Ellis to Lyman C. Draper, Joseph Brant Papers, 1710–1789, Draper Manuscript Collection, Series F, Volume 19, SHSW.

3. John Holloway Hanson, *The Lost Prince: Facts Tending to Prove the Identity of Louis the Seventeenth of France, and the Rev. Eleazer Williams, Missionary Among the Indians of North America* (New York: G.P. Putnam, 1854) 320; A. G. Ellis, "Recollections of Rev. Eleazer Williams," *WHSC* 8 (1879): 343–44; Eleazer Williams, Autobiographical Writings, EWP, Reel 3.

4. Ellis, "Recollections of Eleazer Williams," 343–44; Diary of Mrs. Eleazer Williams, 1 June 1835, EWP, Reel 7. For information on Williams's debts, see the Certificate of Notice, 30 March 1833, EWP, Reel 2.

5. State of New York, in Account with James B. Spencer, Agent for Paying Annuities, Entry Documentation Submitted by the Indian Commissioners and Indian Agents for Annuities Paid to Indians for Other Expenditures, NYSA A0832, Box 7, Folder 6; James B. Spencer to A. C. Flagg, 14 July 1834, NYSA A0832, Box 7, Folder 6.

6. Stephen Parrish to Jasper Parrish, 25 January 1828, LR-OIA-6N; John Schermerhorn to Carey A. Harris, 10 June 1837, LR-OIA-NY, Reel 583; Franklin B. Hough, *A History of St. Lawrence and Franklin Counties, New York* (Albany, N.Y.: Little and Co., 1853), 167; St. Regis Chiefs to Eleazer Williams, 24 March 1835, NYSA A0832, Box 7, Folder 6.

7. James Stryker to Elbert Herring, 28 June 1835, LR-OIA-NY, Reel 583; Thompson Harris to Lewis Cass, 20 March 1835, LR-OIA-NY, Reel 583; See also the statement of the "Seneca chiefs in favor of Removal," September 1837, LR-OIA-NY, Reel 583; and Barbara Conable, "'A Steady Enemy': The Ogden Land Company and the Seneca Indians," Ph.D. dissertation, University of Rochester, 1995, 118.

8. Eleazer Williams to Lewis Cass, 4 June 1836, LR-OIA-NY, Reel 583; Eleazer Williams to Lewis Cass, 30 June 1836, LR-OIA-NY, Reel 583; Lewis Cass to Eleazer Williams, 22 June 1836, Letters Sent by the Office of Indian Affairs, 1824–1881, M21, 9, NA.

9. Conable, "Steady Enemy," 118; Laurence M. Hauptman and L. Gordon McLester III, *Chief Daniel Bread and the Oneida Nation of Indians of Wisconsin* (Norman: University of Oklahoma Press, 2002), 92; James W. Van Hoeven, "Salvation and Indian Removal: The Career Biography of Rev. John Freeman Schermerhorn, Indian Commissioner," Ph.D. dissertation, Vanderbilt University, 1972, 229–30, 233–35.

10. Williams's Mohawk name first appears in the written record in 1815. It was spelled differently in different documents, but all of them possessed a similarity to the name that the Mohawks had granted to Sir William Johnson seventy-five years before: Warraghiyagey. Williams may well have adopted the name to link himself to the Crown's superintendent of Indian Affairs in the Northern Department. In making sense of Williams's Mohawk name, I am indebted to Roy Wright and Darren Bonaparte. On Williams's power of attorney, see the document from the St. Regis leaders to Eleazer Williams, 5 August 1836, LR-OIA-NY, Reel 583; Anthony Dickens to C. A. Harris, 8 December 1837, LR-OIA-NY, Reel 583; and Schermerhorn to [illegible], 28 December 1836, LR-OIA-NY, Reel 583.

11. John Schermerhorn, Speech to New York Indians at Green Bay, in Duck Creek Proceedings, RG46, Records of the United States Senate, Treaty of 16 September 1836, NA.

12. LR-OIA-NY, Reel 583; Stuart L. Banner, *How the Indians Lost Their Land: Law and Power on the Frontier* (Cambridge, Mass.: Harvard University Press, 2005), 191–227.

13. The Duck Creek Treaty is reprinted in "Some Wisconsin Indian Conveyances, 1793–1836," *WHSC* 15 (1900): 20–24.

14. Schermerhorn, Report on the Duck Creek Council, December 1836, LR-OIA-NY, Reel 583; Schermerhorn to C. A. Harris, 24 November 1837, LR-OIA-NY, Reel 583.

15. Schermerhorn to Andrew Jackson, 20 August 1836, LR-OIA-NY, Reel 583; Schermerhorn to United States Senate, 28 December 1836, RG 46, Records of the United States Senate, Treaty of 16 September 1836; Van Hoeven, "Schermerhorn," 240; Hauptman and McLester, *Daniel Bread*, 92–94.

16. For New York politics in this period, see Whitney R. Cross, *The Burned-Over District: The Social and Intellectual History of Enthusiastic Religion in Western New York, 1800–1850* (Ithaca, N.Y.: Cornell University Press, 1950); Paul Johnson, *A Shopkeeper's Millennium: Society and Revivals in Rochester, New York, 1815–1837* (New York: Hill and Wang, 1978); Paul E. Johnson and Sean Wilentz, *The Kingdom of Matthias: A Story of Sex and Salvation in Nineteenth-Century America* (New York: Oxford University Press, 1994); Stephen J. Valone, "William Seward, Whig Politics, and the Compromised Indian Removal Policy in New York State, 1838–1843," *New York History* 82 (2001): 107–34; and Henry S. Manley, "Buying Buffalo from the Indians," *New York History* 28 (July 1947): 315.

17. Schermerhorn to Commissioner of Indian Affairs, 30 October 1837, LR-OIA-NY, Reel 583; Van Hoeven, "Schermerhorn," 243–44, 249.

18. Proclamation of Seneca Chiefs, 3 November 1832, Indian Treaties Collection, Buffalo and Erie County Historical Society, in IIM; Gathering of Six Nations at Onondaga, 15 October 1833, LR-OIA-6N; Records of Seneca Council, 15 October 1837, LR-OIA-NY, Reel 583.

19. Onondaga Chiefs, Petition to the President of the United States, 11 August 1837, LR-OIA-NY, Reel 583; Oneida Petition to the President, 17 August 1837, LR-OIA-NY, Reel 583. For additional information on the Oneidas' fears, see Ransom H. Gillet to Corey A. Harris, 27 December 1837, LR-OIA-NY, Reel 583.

20. Conable, "A Steady Enemy," 129–30; Manley, "Buying Buffalo," 314–16.

21. Laurence M. Hauptman, *Conspiracy of Interests: Iroquois Dispossession and the Rise of New York State* (Syracuse, N.Y.: Syracuse University Press, 1999), 185; Van Hoeven, "Schermerhorn," 255–56; Chief John Ross to William S. Coodey, December 1837, in *The Papers of Chief John Ross*, ed. Gary Moulton (Norman: University of Oklahoma Press, 1985), 1: 574.

22. Schermerhorn to C. A. Harris, 21 July 1837, LR-OIA-Emigration; United States Statutes-at-Large, 24th Cong., Sess. 2, Chap. 31; James Stryker to C. A. Harris, 6 November 1837, LR-OIA-NY, Reel 583; Schermerhorn to C. A. Harris, 22 November 1837, LR-OIA-NY, Reel 583.

23. Trade and Intercourse Act of 1834, in *Documents of United States Indian Policy*, 3rd ed., ed. Francis Paul Prucha (Lincoln: University of Nebraska Press, 2000), 65; Conable, "Steady Enemy," 124. See also Ransom H. Gillet to C. A Harris, 27 December 1837, LR-OIA-NY, Reel 583.

24. Agreements between John and Joseph Snow, and R. H. Gillet, 9 July 1837, Indian Committee Reports, Philadelphia Yearly Meeting, Society of Friends, Box 4, 1831–1839,

Haverford College Library, Haverford, Pennsylvania, in IIM. The Society of Friends published many of the documents related to the council at Buffalo Creek. See *The Case of the Seneca Indians in the State of New York, Illustrated by Facts* (Philadelphia: Merrihew and Thompson, 1840), a damning indictment.

25. Seneca Chiefs, Speech to President Martin Van Buren, ca. 1838, Quaker Collection, Philadelphia Yearly Meeting, Indian Records, Box 33, Haverford College Library, in IIM; Affidavit of John Tate, Indian Committee Records, Philadelphia Yearly Meetings, Box 4, 1831–1839, Haverford College Library, in IIM.

26. Seneca Chiefs' Depositions, 8 February 1839, Indian Committee Records, Philadelphia Yearly Meeting, Society of Friends, Box 4, 1831–1839, Haverford College Library, IIM.

27. *Indian Affairs: Laws and Treaties*, comp. Charles J. Kappler (Washington, D.C.: GPO, 1904), 2: 504.

28. Ibid., 505; Supplemental Article to the Treaty of January 15, 1838, Documents Relating to the Negotiation of Ratified and Unratified Treaties with Various Indian Tribes, 1801–1869, T494, Reel 4, NA; Ransom Gillet to C. A. Harris, 11 October 1838, LR-OIA-NY, Reel 583. A month after the federal commissioners negotiated the 1838 treaty at Buffalo Creek, Commissioner of Indian Affairs Corey A. Harris met with representatives from the Oneidas of Wisconsin in Washington. The Oneidas ceded the lands they obtained in the 1831 and 1832 Menominee treaties and in return received a reservation out of those ceded lands of approximately 65,000 acres. See Kappler, *Laws and Treaties*, 2: 517–18.

29. Hauptman, *Conspiracy of Interests*, 188–90; Valone, "William Seward," 113–14. On opposition to Jacksonian Indian policy in general, see Christine Bolt, "The Anti-Slavery Origins of Concern for the American Indians," in *Anti-Slavery, Religion and Reform: Essays in Memory of Roger Antsey*, ed. Christine Bolt and Seymour Drescher (Folkestone: Dawson, 1980), 233–53; Jeremiah Evarts, *Cherokee Removal: The William Penn Essays and Other Writings*, ed. Francis Paul Prucha (Knoxville: University of Tennessee Press, 1982); Mary Hershberger, "Mobilizing Women, Anticipating Abolition: The Struggle Against Indian Removal in the 1830s," *Journal of American History* 86 (June 1999): 15–40; Natalie Joy, "Cherokee Slaveholders and Radical Abolitionists: An Unlikely Alliance in Antebellum America," *Common-Place* 10 (July 2010); Linda Kerber, "The Abolitionist Perception of the Indian," *Journal of American History* 62 (September 1975): 271–95; William G. McLoughlin, *Cherokee Renascence in the New Republic* (New Haven, Conn.: Yale University Press, 1986); Michael Leroy Oberg, "William Wirt and the Trials of Republicanism," *Virginia Magazine of History and Biography* 99 (August 1991): 305–26; Alisse Portnoy, *Their Right to Speak: Women's Activism in the Indian and Slave Debates* (Cambridge: Cambridge University Press, 2005); and Ronald N. Satz, *American Indian Policy in the Jacksonian Era* (Lincoln: University of Nebraska Press, 1975).

30. Eleazer Williams to Martin Van Buren, 2 March 1838, LR-OIA-NY, Reel 583.

31. Eleazer Williams to Martin Van Buren, 10 July 1838, LR-OIA-GB, Reel 317.

32. Eleazer Williams to Ransom H. Gillet, 18 September 1838, LR-OIA-NY, Reel 583; Williams to Secretary of War Joel Poinsett, 29 June 1838, LR-OIA-NY, Reel 583; Williams to T. Hartley Crawford, 30 November 1838, LR-OIA-NY, Reel 583.

33. Articles of Agreement Between Eleazer Williams and Horace Hood, 29 November 1839, EWP, Reel 2; Diary of Mrs. E. Williams, EWP, Reel 7.

34. Jack Campisi, "The Wisconsin Oneidas Between Disasters," in *The Oneida Indian Journey: From New York to Wisconsin, 1784–1860*, ed. Laurence M. Hauptman and L. Gordon McLester, III (Madison: University of Wisconsin Press, 1999), 71; Henry Coleman, "Recollections of the Oneida Indians, 1840–1845," *Proceedings of the State Historical Society of Wisconsin at its Fifty-Ninth Annual Meeting*, (Madison: SHSW, 1912), 152–53.

35. Coleman, "Recollections," 156–58.

36. Statement on the Number of Each Tribe of Indians Within the Green Bay Sub-Agency, 30 November 1841, LR-OIA-GB, Reel 318; A. G. Ellis to Henry Dodge, 24 September 1845, LR-OIA-GB, Reel 319; Campisi, "Between Disasters," 71.

37. Campisi, "Between Disasters," 72–77.

38. Oneida Petition to Territorial Governor Henry Dodge, 15 March 1839, John Lawe and George W. Lawe Papers, SHSW; Oneida Chiefs to Commissioner T. Hartley Crawford, 14 July 1845, *TPUS*, 28: 861; Governor Dodge to Commissioner Crawford, 1 December 1840, *TPUS*, 28: 253; Oneidas from Duck Creek, Petition to William L. Marcy, 10 July 1845, LR-OIA-NY, Reel 586; Oneida Council Minutes, 20 November 1845, LR-OIA-GB, Reel 319.

39. O. E. Strong to Eleazer Williams, 10 November 1839, EWP, Reel 2; Eleazer Williams to Dr. Armstrong, November 1841, EWP, Reel 2.

40. Eleazer Williams to Erastus Root, 10 February 1840, EWP, Reel 2; Eleazer Williams to Martin Van Buren, 19 June 1840, LR-OIA-NY, Reel 584.

41. On Williams's deed, see Deborah B. Martin, *History of Brown County, Wisconsin, Past and Present* (Chicago: S. J. Clarke, 1913), 112. See also Conable, "Steady Enemy," 242–60; Hauptman, *Conspiracy of Interests*, 188–212. After a long legal battle the Tonawanda Senecas won in 1857 the right to purchase back a portion of their reservation, even after they had opposed with a tremendous level of unanimity all attempts to acquire their lands. That story is told by Laurence M. Hauptman in *The Tonawanda Senecas' Heroic Battle Against Removal: Conservative Activist Indians* (Albany: State University of New York Press, 2011).

42. Whipple Report, 310–12, 329–55.

43. Ibid., 361–62.

44. Population Census of Indian Reservations, 1845, A1832-78, NYSA.

45. *Annual Report of the Commissioner of Indian Affairs*, 1846, 215–216, 231–35; Conable, "A Steady Enemy," 326–33; Report of Sub-Agent W. P. Angel, in *Annual Report of the Commissioner of Indian Affairs*, 1847, 891.

46. Eleazer Williams, unaddressed letter, March 1842, EWP, Reel 2; Lien, dated 1843, EWP, Reel 2.

47. Articles of Agreement with Joseph Allor of Wisconsin, 26 July 1841, EWP, Reel 2; Articles of Agreement with Augustus Lavine, 21 August 1841, EWP, Reel 2; Eleazer Williams to the Chiefs of the American Party at St. Regis, n.d., EWP, Reel 2; T. L. Ogden to Eleazer Williams, 12 July 1841, EWP, Reel 2.

48. "An Episcopalian" to Rev. Dr. Milner, 7 March 1843, EWP, Reel 2; Eleazer Williams to "Respected Sir," March 1848, EWP, Reel 2.

49. Eleazer Williams to Bishop Benjamin T. Onderdonk, 12 June 1841, EWP, Reel 2.

50. Eleazer Williams, *The Salvation of Sinners Through the Riches of Divine Grace: Two Homilies Pronounced at the Oneida Castle in the Audience of the Oneida Indians at Their Eighth Triennial Anniversary Since the Conversion of Six Hundred Pagans of That Tribe to the Christian Faith* (Green Bay, Wis.: Republican, 1842), 3.

51. Ibid., 8–9.

52. Ibid., 4–5, 13.

53. Ibid., 17.

54. Ibid., 9–10.

55. Jackson Kemper to Eleazer Williams, 21 September 1842, Eleazer Williams Collection, Missouri Historical Society (microfilm copy at Pocumtuck Valley Memorial Association Library, Deerfield, Mass.); Robert D. Slocum, *The Path of Duty: Jackson Kemper and the Missionary Episcopate* (n.p., 1985), 1.

56. Eleazer Williams, Speech on Treatment by Bishop Kemper, EWP, Reel 7.

57. Ibid.

58. Ibid.

59. Broadside, "To All Who Love the Prosperity of Zion and Are Disposed to Aid in the Propagating the Gospel Among, and the Civilization of the Heathen," 4 July 1844, EWP, Reel 2.

60. "To The Reverend Eleazer Williams, Beloved Brother," 1845, EWP, Reel 2.

61. "Society for Propagating the Gospel," *Christian Register*, 27 November 1847; Judy Cornelius, "Tribal Discord and the Road to Green Bay," in Hauptman and McLester, *Oneida Indian Journey*, 149

62. Eleazer Williams to William J. Eustis, 3 September 1844, EWP, Reel 2; Hanson, *Lost Prince*, 330–31. A copy of one of Williams's expense sheets appears in EWP, Box 11, Folder 1. It indicates the significant amount of money he spent on travel and lodging.

63. Mary Hobart Williams to Amos Lawrence, 18 August 1844, EWP, Reel 2; Hanson, *Lost Prince*, 331; William Lawrence, *Life of Amos A. Lawrence* (New York: Houghton, Mifflin, 1899), 69.

64. Eleazer Williams to Eunice Storrs, 30 September 1845, EWP, Reel 2; Eleazer Williams, "Essay on Roman Catholicism," EWP-Newberry. Williams replaced references to Scotland in the original with references to the United States. See William McGavin, *The Protestant: Essays on the Principal Points of Controversy Between the Church of Rome and the Reformed* (Middletown, Conn.: Edwin Hunt, 1835), 1: 45–47; Blank Petition Opposing Texas Annexation, EWP, Reel 6.

65. Notes to a Speech, EWP, Reel 7.

66. Ibid.; Speech Fragment, EWP, Reel 2.

67. William Medill to Eleazer Williams, 24 December 1845, *TPUS*, 28: 902–3.

68. Eleazer Williams to M. L. Martin, 6 June 1846, LR-OIA-NY, Reel 586.

69. Certified Copy of Minutes of Council at St. Regis, 21 September 1846, LR-OIA-NY, Reel 586; William P. Angel to William Medill, 1 October 1846, LR-OIA-NY, Reel 586. Williams's correspondence with Fendall is voluminous. See EWP, Box 11, Folder 1. See also P. R. Fendall to Samuel J. Potts, 9 March 1837, LR-OIA-NY, Reel 583.

70. Eleazer Williams to Mary Hobart Williams, May 1838, EWP, Reel 1.

71. Ibid. On child death in the nineteenth century, see Nancy Schrom Dye and Daniel Blake Smith, "Mother Love and Infant Death, 1750–1920," *Journal of American History* 73 (September 1986): 329.

72. Eleazer Williams, Journal for 1841, EWP, Reel 4.

73. On the Williams children, see Publius V. Lawson, *Prince or Creole: The Mystery of Louis XVII* (Menasha, Wis.: Geo. Banta, 1905), 276. I consulted the baptismal and burial records for both Holy Apostles and Christ Church.

74. Evan Haefeli and Kevin Sweeney, *Captive Histories: English, French, and Native Narratives of the 1704 Deerfield Raid* (Amherst: University of Massachusetts Press, 2006), 2, 222.

75. Charles de Saileville to Eleazer Williams, 12 June 1842, Eleazer Williams Collection, Missouri Historical Society (microfilm copy at Pocumtuck Valley Memorial Association Library); *Biographical and Historical Discourse, (In Two Parts with Notes) Delivered at Deerfield, Mass, September 7th and 8th, 1846, on Commemoration of the Death of the Rev. John Williams, the First Pastor of that Place*, EWP-Newberry. Williams also learned that a market of some sort still existed for his language skills. The American Philosophical Society in 1840 considered publishing "a grammar of the Mohawk dialect of the Iroquois language or of the five ancient Confederated Nations—containing rules and exercises; intended to exemplify the Indian syntax, according to the best authorities, Preceded by succinct rules relative to the pronunciation . . . by Eleazer Williams." See Eleazer Williams to P. S. Du Ponceau, 24 June 1838, Gratz Collection, HSP, and Minutes of the Historical and Literary Committee, American Philosophical Society, 8 January and 10 July 1840, APS.

76. A Discourse Delivered at Deerfield, 12 June 1846, EWP, Reel 3; Eleazer Williams to Joshua Leavitt, 17 March 1848, EWP, Reel 2.

Chapter 6. The Confidence Man

1. Nathaniel Hawthorne, *Our Old Home and English Note-Books* (Boston: Houghton Mifflin, 1863), 1: 33; Stanley Weintraub, *Victorian Yankees at Queen Victoria's Court: American Encounters with Victoria and Albert* (Newark: University of Delaware Press, 2011), 67–71.

2. William Ward Wight, *Eleazer Williams: Not the Dauphin of France* (Chicago: Chicago Historical Society, 1903), 1.

3. Eleazer Williams, Journal for 1841, EWP, Reel 4.

4. J. H. Hanson, "Have We a Bourbon Among Us?" *Putnam's Magazine*, February 1853, 204–5; Letter from Henry Caswell, 10 October 1857, reprinted from *Green Bay Historical Bulletin* 1 (Oct.–Dec. 1925) and included in EWP, Reel 1.

5. Hanson, "Have We a Bourbon?" 205; "Visitors on the Frontier," Henry S. Baird Papers, W. S. Mss., V, Box 4, Folder 8, SHSW; Wight, *Williams*, 1; Eleazer Williams, Journal Fragments, EWP, Reel 4.

6. Eleazer Williams, Journal for 1841, EWP, Reel 4. This would be the second child Williams and his wife lost, if the story is true. No burial record exists for any Williams child other than Margaret Anne Williams.

7. Hanson, "Have We a Bourbon?" 205–6.

8. Ibid., 206.

9. Ibid.

10. Ibid.

11. Ibid.

12. Eleazer Williams, Journal for 1841, EWP, Reel 4.

13. Ibid.; "Is Louis XVII in New York?" *Literary Messenger*, 5 February 1853.

14. Mary H. Allen, "The Lost Prince: A Reminiscence of 1830," *The Critic* (April 1900).

15. Eleazer Williams, Journal for 1841, EWP, Reel 4.

16. For the characterization of the Jacksonian period as one dominated by men-on-the-make, see Bray Hammond, *Banks and Politics in America from the Revolution to the Civil War* (Princeton, N.J.: Princeton University Press, 1957); Eleazer Williams to Henry Baird, 29 December 1847, Henry and Elizabeth Baird Papers, 1798–1837, Box 2, Folder 1, SHSW; Eleazer Williams to Philip R. Fendall, EWP, Box 11, Folder 1.

17. Eleazer Williams to "My Correspondent in Europe," August 1849, EWP, Reel 2; Eleazer Williams to Mr. Ostrander, October 1848, EWP, Reel 2; Hanson, "Have We a Bourbon?" 197; Robert L. Hall, "Eleazer Williams: Mohawk Between Two Worlds," *Voyageur* 19, 1 (2001): 11; Geoffrey Buerger, "Eleazer Wiliams: Elitism and Multiple Identity on Two Frontiers," in *Being and Becoming Indian: Biographical Studies of North American Frontiers*, ed. James H. Clifton (Chicago: Dorsey Press, 1989), 132.

18. H. E. Eastman to John Y. Smith, 27 May, 1872, in John Y. Smith, "Eleazer Williams and the Lost Prince," *WHSC* 6 (1870): 338–39.

19. Eleazer Williams to Mary Hobart Williams, 22 September 1848, EWP, Reel 2; Eleazer Williams to "Rev'd and Dear Sir," 14 June 1848, EWP, Reel 2; Letter, dated August 1848 from Green Bay, with the heading "The Following Extract of a Letter from Rev. E. Williams (or the Dauphin) to His Correspondent in Europe," EWP, Reel 2; Eleazer Williams to Madam R. V. Hotchkiss, 25 February 1850, EWP, Reel 2.

20. Eleazer Williams to J. Leavitt, 18 March 1848, EWP, Reel 2; *Boston Herald*, 24 October 1849; Alfred Cope, "A Mission to the Menominee: Alfred Cope's Green Bay Diary (Part I)," *Wisconsin Magazine of History* 49 (Summer 1966): 318; *Christian Watchman and Reflector*, 6 March 1851.

21. "History of the Dauphin," *United States Democratic Review* 133 (July 1849): 15. For examples of reprints, see *Republican Advocate* (Batavia, N.Y.), 24 July 1849, and *Maine Farmer*, 6 December 1849.

22. Shea's story was recounted by Lyman Draper in an addendum to Smith, "Williams and the Lost Prince," 342.

23. L.U. Sigourney to Eleazer Williams, 11 July 1851, Eleazer Williams Collection, Missouri Historical Society, (Microfilm Copy housed at Pocumtuck Valley Memorial Association Library, Deerfield, MA); Timothy Howe to William L. Marcy, 26 April 1848, LR-OIA-GB, Reel 319; Eleazer Williams to A. S. Loughery, 31 October 1849, LR-OIA-GB, Reel 319.

24. Eleazer Williams to Luke Lea, 14 August 1850, LR-OIA-NY, Reel 587; See also Eleazer Williams to William Medill, 14 May 1849, LR-OIA-GB, Reel 319. On the history of the 1.824 million acres in the Indian Territory, the so-called "Kansas Lands," see Philip Otto Geier III, "A Peculiar Status: A History of Oneida Indian Treaties and Claims: Jurisdictional Conflict Within the American Government, 1775–1920," Ph.D. dissertation, Syracuse University, 1980.

25. See St. Regis Chiefs' petition, 17 June 1850, in J. H. Hanson, *The Lost Prince: Facts Tending to Prove the Identity of Louis the Seventeenth of France, and the Rev. Eleazer Williams, Missionary Among the Indians of North America* (New York: G.P. Putnam, 1854), 325–26.

26. Gillet, quoted in Hanson, *Lost Prince*, 326–28. See also William Seward to Luke Lea, 18 March 1851, LR-OIA-NY, Reel 587.

27. Stephen Osborn to Commissioner of Indian Affairs, 3 April 1853, in Hanson, *Lost Prince*, 328; Gillet to Commissioner of Indian Affairs, in Hanson, *Lost Prince*, 328–29.

28. Ibid., 329.

29. Eleazer Williams to Rev. William Berrian, 28 February 1849, AEDNY; Eleazer Williams to Jackson Kemper, 18 April 1849, AEDNY.

30. Elijah Skenandoah, Cornelius Stevens, Neddy Artisquette, Adam Swamp, Thomas King, Henry Powlis, Daniel Williams, Jacob Cornelius, and Daniel Bread to Bishop Jackson Kemper, 1 June 1849, AEDNY.

31. H. G. Woutman to Benjamin Haight, 29 October 1849, AEDNY; Woutman to Standing Committee, Protestant Episcopal Church, 25 December 1849, AEDNY; Henry Addison (at the order of Eleazer Williams) to Dr. Haight, 5 July 1850, AEDNY; Eleazer Williams to the Standing Committee, 5 December 1851, AEDNY. On Woutman, see the *Plattsburgh Republican*, 30 May 1854. The 1850 federal census listed "Waterman" as a member of Williams's household in Brown County, Wisconsin. The census listed Woutman's place of birth as Holland and his age as fifty-five.

32. Jackson Kemper to Rev. W. Berrian, President of the Standing Committee of the Diocese of New York, 19 June 1849, AEDNY; Jackson Kemper to Eleazer Williams, 5 May 1849, AEDNY; Kemper to Berrian, 5 May 1849, AEDNY.

33. Eleazer Williams to W. Berrian, 29 June 1850, AEDNY; Cincinnati *Weekly Patriot*, 21 May 1853, clipping in EWP, Reel 7; Eleazer Williams to William Berrian,

29 June 1850, AEDNY; Letter to Rev. Dr. Haight from [illegible], 29 November 1851, AEDNY; Eleazer Williams to Haight, 14 April 1851, AEDNY.

34. Eleazer Williams to Rev. John McVicker, 25 November 1851, AEDNY; John G. Newton to the Standing Committee, 16 December 1851, AEDNY.

35. Eleazer Williams to Rev. John McVicker, 25 November 1851, AEDNY.

36. Jackson Kemper to Dr. Haight, 23 August 1851, AEDNY; Letter to Rev. Dr. Haight from [illegible], 29 November 1851, AEDNY.

37. St. Regis Chiefs to Washington Hurt, Comptroller, State of NY, and the Commissioners of the Land Office, 9 August 1850, NYSA A0832, Box 8 , Folder 2.

38. J. J. Seaver to the Hon. P. C. Fuller, 30 October 1851, NYSA A0832, Box 8, Folder 2. On New York's public education system with native peoples, see Ruth Birdseye, *Indian Education in New York State, 1846–1970* (Albany: New York State Education Department, 1970).

39. J. J. Seaver to P. C. Fuller, 30 October 1851, NYSA A0832, Box 8, Folder 2.

40. Franklin B. Hough Diary, 17 June 1852, Franklin B. Hough Papers, NYSL; Lyman Copeland Draper, "Additional Notes on Eleazer Williams," *WHSC* 8 (1879): 360; Williams's own description of his school appears in a letter dated 4 August 1852 in EWP, Reel 7.

41. Ellis quoted in the Syracuse *Daily Star*, 17 March 1853, clipping in EWP, Reel 2.

42. Hanson, "Have We a Bourbon?" 194.

43. Ibid., 211–12.

44. Ibid., 212.

45. Ibid., 212, 196.

46. Ibid., 212–13; "A Bourbon Really Among Us!" *Gleason's Pictorial Drawing Room Companion*, 24 September 1853.

47. "The Iroquois Bourbon," *Southern Quarterly Review* (July 1853); "Rev. Eleazer Williams," *Christian Enquirer*, 12 February 1853; "Summary," *National Era*, 19 May 1853.

48. "Have We a Bourbon Among Us?" *Albany Evening Journal*, 29 March 1853.

49. "New York Correspondence," 12 February 1853, newspaper clipping, EWP, Reel 7.

50. "Reverend Eleazer Williams"; "Is Louis XVII in New York?" *Literary Messenger*, 5 February 1853.

51. "Reverend Eleazer Williams"; "The Iroquois Bourbon."

52. "Reverend Eleazer Williams."

53. J. H. Hanson, "The Bourbon Question," *Putnam's Magazine*, April 1853, 462. Hanson here referred to the New York "Moon Hoax" of 1835. See Mario Castagnaro, "Lunar Fancies and Earthly Truths: The Moon Hoax of 1835 and the Penny Press," *Nineteenth Century Contexts* 34 (July 2012): 253–68.

54. Hanson, *Lost Prince*, 395–97.

55. Ibid.

56. "Editorial Melange," *Gleason's Pictorial Drawing Room Companion*, 10 September 1853; "Eleazer Wiliams Express," newspaper clipping, EWP, Reel 7; Eleazer Williams to Jackson Kemper, 29 September 1853, EWP, Reel 2.

57. Eleazer Williams, letter dated 4 August 1852, in undated and unidentified newspaper clipping, EWP, Reel 7.

58. Troy (N.Y.) *Daily Traveler*, 23 July 1855.

59. Ibid. Williams gave a similar address, at an earlier point in his career, as an Indian, in which he described the efforts of "the man from the East . . . to extirpate *us* from the face of the Earth" (emphasis added). See EWP, Reel 7, Frames 2–3.

60. Albany Newspaper, 9 February 1853, newspaper clipping, EWP, Reel 7.

61. *New York Evening Express*, 19 September 1853; *Philadelphia Enquirer*, 28 March 1854; Philadelphia newspaper clipping, EWP, Reel 7; *Banner of the Cross*, 1 April 1854; *American Courier*, 22 April 1854; *Church Journal*, 13 April 1854.

62. *Sentinel and Witness* (Middletown, Conn.), 9 January 1855, EWP, Reel 7.

63. *Washington Daily National Era*, 2 March 1854, clipping, EWP, Reel 7.

64. Charles Caldwell, *Thoughts on the Original Unity of the Human Race*, 2nd ed. (Cincinnati: J. A. and U. P James, 1852), 80–81; Reginald Horsman, *Race and Manifest Destiny: The Origins of American Racial Anglo-Saxonism* (Cambridge, Mass: Harvard University Press, 1981), 117–18; Bruce Dain, *A Hideous Monster of the Mind: American Race Theory in the Early Republic* (Cambridge, Mass.: Harvard University Press, 2002), vii; Paul Erickson, "The Anthropology of Charles Caldwell, M.D.," *Isis* 72 (June 1981): 253–54.

65. Ann Fabian, *The Skull Collectors: Race, Science, and America's Unburied Dead* (Chicago: University of Chicago Press, 2010), 1, 14–16.

66. Samuel George Morton, *Crania Americana; Or, a Comparative View of the Skulls of Various Aboriginal Nations of North and South America* (Philadelphia: J. Dobson, 1839), 5, 67.

67. Ibid., 74, 191.

68. O. S. Fowler and L. N. Fowler, *Phrenology Proved, Illustrated, and Applied* (New York: Fowler and Wells, 1849).

69. "The Eleazer Williams Humbug," *New York Herald*, undated clipping, EWP, Reel 7.

70. Syracuse *Daily Star*, 17 March 1853; A. G. Ellis to Lyman Draper, 19 January 1880, EWP Reel 7; C. C. Trowbridge to Lyman Draper, 24 September 1872, EWP, Reel 7.

71. "Have We a Bourbon Among Us?" *Daily Dispatch*, 29 August 1854.

72. Hanson, *Lost Prince*, 395.

73. Undated clipping, EWP, Reel 7.

74. "The Bourbon Question," newspaper clipping from 1853, EWP, Reel 7; Troy (N.Y.) *Daily Traveler*, 23 July 1855, EWP, Reel 7.

75. Hanson, *Lost Prince*, 393; J. K. Bloomfield, *The Oneidas* (New York: Alden Brothers, 1907), 210.

76. Hanson, *Lost Prince*, 391–92; New York *Evening Post*, 4 November 1867. Louis XVI was a Bourbon, Marie Antoinette a Habsburg. Fagnani's portrait of Williams was sold with the artist's estate in 1873. See *New York Herald*, 10 June 1873. On two occasions, at least, Fagnani failed in his efforts to sell his portrait of Williams. See *New York Herald*, 19 April, 26 May 1858.

77. Newspaper clipping, EWP, Reel 7.

78. Newspaper Clipping, EWP, Reel 7; Clipping from the *Literary Repository of the Camden Young Ladies' Institute* (Camden, N.J.), 1 May 1854, EWP Reel 7.

79. Coverage of Hanson's death appears in the *New York Times* on 10, 13, and 19 October 1854. His obituary appeared on 13 October 1854.

80. *Waverly Magazine*, 11 November 1854, clipping, EWP, Reel 7; *Sentinel and Witness*, 9 January 1855, clipping, EWP, Reel 7.

81. *Banner of the Cross*, 13 January 1855, clipping, EWP, Reel 7; *Ballou's Pictorial Drawing Room Companion*, 17 March 1855, 29 September 1855; *Daily Traveler*, 23 July 1855, clipping, EWP, Reel 7.

82. John Demos, *The Unredeemed Captive: A Family Story from Early America* (New York: Knopf, 1994), 245–46; Karen Halttunen, *Confidence Men and Painted Women: A Study of Middle-Class Culture in America, 1830–1870* (New Haven, Conn.: Yale University Press, 1982), xv, 1, 30.

83. James W. Cook, *The Arts of Deception: Playing with Fraud in the Age of Barnum* (Cambridge, Mass.: Harvard University Press, 2001); Benjamin Reiss, "P. T. Barnum, Joice Heth, and Antebellum Spectacles of Race," *American Quarterly* 51 (1999): 78–85; Andie Tucher, *Froth and Scum: Truth, Beauty, Goodness, and the Ax Murder in America's First Mass Medium* (Chapel Hill: University of North Carolina Press, 1994), 55–56; Stephen Mihm, *A Nation of Counterfeiters: Capitalists, Con Men, and the Making of the United States* (Cambridge, Mass.: Harvard University Press, 2007), 3.

84. Syllabary, EWP-Newberry; "Essays, Rev. Eleazer Williams—re: Indian Affairs," Franklin B. Hough Papers, Box 91, Folders 8 and 9, NYSL; Journal of Franklin B. Hough, 17 June 1852, NYSL.

85. *St. Lawrence Republican*, 14 November 1854; Minutes of 1855 meeting, Indian Affairs Central Registry File, 1844–1970, RG 10, Vol. 7157, Public Archives of Canada, Ottawa.

86. Minutes of 1855 Meeting.

87. Ibid.; David Blanchard, *Seven Generations: A History of the Kanienkehaka* (Kahnawake: Kahnawake Survival School 1980), 282; *Plattsburgh Republican*, 18 November 1855.

88. *New York Observer and Chronicle*, 3 April 1856.

89. Eleazer Williams to Commissioner of Indian Affairs, 11 February 1856, LR-OIA-NY, Reel 588; Eleazer Williams to J. F. Polk, 23 May 1857, LR-OIA-NY, Reel 588; J. F. Polk to Commissioner of Indian Affairs, 15 January 1858, LR-OIA-NY, Reel 589.

90. Eleazer Williams to Commissioner Charles Mix, 26 May 1858, LR-OIA-NY, Reel 589; Eleazer Williams to James W. Denver, 13 June 1857, LR-OIA-NY, Reel 588; American Chiefs of the St. Regis Indians to Comptroller, State of New York, 16 January 1858, NYSA A0832, Box 8, File 2.

91. H.R. 508, Report No. 303, 35th Cong., 1st sess., 17 April 1858; Report 459, 35th Cong., 1st sess., 29 May 1858, in *Reports of the Committees of the House of Representatives,*

Made During the 1st Session, of the 35th Congress, 6 vols. (Washington, D.C.: James W. Steedman, 1858).

Conclusion. The Last of Eleazer Williams

1. Asher Wright to O. H. Marshall, 28 February 1871, Asher and Laura Wright Letters, Buffalo and Erie County Historical Society.

2. Ibid.

3. The material in this paragraph has been informed by Daniel H. Usner, *Indian Work: Language and Livelihood in Native American History* (Cambridge, Mass.: Harvard University Press, 2009); Philip Deloria, *Playing Indian* (New Haven, Conn.: Yale University Press, 1999); and idem., *Indians in Unexpected Places* (Lawrence: University Press of Kansas, 2006).

4. On this generally, see Karen Haltunnen, *Confidence Men and Painted Women: A Study in Middle-Class Culture in America, 1830–1870* (New Haven, Conn.: Yale University Press, 1982).

5. Herman Melville, *The Confidence Man: His Masquerade* (New York: Dix, Edwards, 1857); Neil Harris, *Humbug: The Art of P. T. Barnum* (Boston: Little, Brown, 1973), 219–23.

6. Haltunnen, *Confidence Men*, 31, 192–93.

7. Robert C. Toll, *Blacking Up: The Minstrel Show in Nineteenth Century America* (New York: Oxford University Press, 1974); William J. Mahar, *Behind the Burnt Cork Mask: Early Blackface Minstrelsy and Antebellum American Popular Culture* (Urbana: University of Illinois Press, 1999); Eric Lott, *Love and Theft: Blackface Minstrelsy and the American Working Class* (New York: Oxford University Press, 1993).

8. On Tufts, see Joshua David Bellin, "Taking the Indian Cure: Thoreau, Indian Medicine, and the Performance of American Culture," *New England Quarterly* 79 (March 2006): 3–36.

9. Amani Marshall, "'They Will Endeavor to Pass for Free': Enslaved Runaway Performances of Freedom in Antebellum South Carolina," *Slavery and Abolition* 31 (June 2010): 166–73; Uri McMillen, "Crimes of Performance," *Souls* 13, 1 (2011): 30–32; Paul Gilmore, "The Indian in the Museum: Henry David Thoreau, Okah Tubbee, and Authentic Manhood," *Arizona Quarterly* 54 (Summer 1998): 38–42. I found useful, as well, Angela Pulley Hudson's forthcoming biography of Oakah Tubbee. I am grateful to Professor Hudson for sharing her work with me.

10. On Copway, see A. Lavonne Brown Ruoff, "Early Native American Writers' Representations of Native Life: George Copway and Charles Eastman," *First Nations of North America: Politics and Representation* 54, 1 (2005): 89–108; Donald B. Smith, "The Life of George Copway, or Kah-ge-ga-gah-bowh (1818–1869)—and a Review of His Writings," *Journal of Canadian Studies* 23 (October 1988): 5–38; Cecilia Morgan, "Kah-gegagahbowh's (George Copway's) Transatlantic Performance: Running Sketches, 1850," *Cultural and Social History* 9, 4 (2012): 527–33. For Indian performance in general, see Joshua David Bellin and Laura Mielke, *Native Acts: Indian Performance, 1603–1836* (Lincoln: University of Nebraska Press, 2011).

11. On this count, I have drawn heavily on Steven C. Bullock, "A Mumper Among the Gentle: Tom Bell, Colonial Confidence Man," *William and Mary Quarterly* 3rd ser. 55 (April 1998): 231–58.

12. Haltunnen, *Confidence Men*, xv.

13. Wright to Marshall, 28 February 1871, Asher and Laura Wright Letters. On Wright's career, see Thomas S. Abler, "Protestant Missionaries and Native Cultures: Parallel Careers of Asher Wright and Silas T. Rand," *American Indian Quarterly* 26 (Winter 1992): 25–37; William N. Fenton, "Toward the Gradual Civilization of the Indian Natives: The Mission and Linguistic Work of Asher Wright," *Proceedings of the American Philosophical Society* 100 (1956): 567–81.

14. Publius V. Lawson, *Prince or Creole: The Mystery of Louis XVII* (Menasha, Wis.: Geo. Banta Publishing, 1905), 262–64.

15. "Reported Attempt to Assassinate the Rev. Eleazer Williams," *New York Times*, 15 April 1858.

16. Eleazer Williams to Edward Henry, 4 December 1856, EWP, Reel 2; Eleazer Williams to Edward Henry, 27 April 1858, EWP-Newberry.

17. *Albany Evening Journal*, 12 May 1858.

18. Hough, writing in the introduction to Eleazer Williams, *Life of Te-ho-ra-gwa-ne-gen, Alias Thomas Williams, a Chief of the Caughnawaga Tribe of Indians in Canada* (Albany, N.Y.: J. Munsell, 1859), 12–14. On Williams's house, the so-called "Lost Dauphin Cottage," that still stands in Hogansburg, N.Y., see Robert Harold MacGowan, *Architecture from the Adirondack Foothills: Folk and Designed Architecture of Franklin County, New York* (Malone, N.Y.: Franklin County History and Museum Society, 1977), 77; and T. Wood Clarke, *Émigrés in the Wilderness* (New York: Macmillan, 1941), 205–6.

19. *Albany Evening Journal*, 3 September 1858; *The Independent*, 9 September 1858.

20. "The Last of Eleazer Williams," *New York Times*, 16 September 1858. On the Fund for Aged and Infirm Clergymen, see *Journal of the Proceedings of the Seventy-Fifth Convention of the Protestant Episcopal Church in the Diocese of New York* (New York: Daniel Dana, 1858), 91, 117. Williams died intestate. An inventory of his estate compiled in December of 1867 revealed he still owned a large number of books at the time of his death, but the furnishings in his home were sparse, at least what remained a decade after he died. The authorities in Franklin County valued the estate at $119.75. The relevant records are housed in the Franklin County Surrogate's Courts Records, Franklin County Courthouse, Malone, N.Y.

21. "The Last of Eleazer Williams."

22. William Ward Wight, *Eleazer Williams: Not the Dauphin of France* (Chicago: Chicago Historical Society, 1903), 17; Lyman C. Draper, "Additional Notes on Eleazer Williams," *WHSC* 8 (1879): 369; A. de Grasse Stevens, *The Lost Dauphin; Louis XVII, or Onwarenhiiaki, the Indian Iroquois Chief* (Sunnyside, Kent: George Allen, 1887), 114.

23. "Had We a Bourbon Among Us?" *New York Evening Post*, 14 August 1868. See also *New York Daily Tribune*, 13 May 1871; "Ridiculous Story," *Albany Argus*, 30 May 1871; "French Pretenders," *New York Tribune*, 9 March 1874.

24. For Occom's lament, see his autobiography in *The Collected Writings of Samson Occom*, ed. Joanna Brooks (New York: Oxford University Press, 2006), 51–58; and David J. Silverman, *Red Brethren: The Brothertown and Stockbridge Indians and the Problem of Race in Early America,* (Ithaca, N.Y.: Cornell University Press, 2010), 80.

25. Valuable discussions of this struggle can be found in Daniel Mandell, *Tribe, Race, History: Native Americans in Southern New England, 1780–1880* (Baltimore: Johns Hopkins University Press, 2010); David J. Silverman, *Faith and Boundaries: Colonists, Christianity, and Community Among the Wampanoag Indians of Martha's Vineyard, 1600–1781* (Cambridge: Cambridge University Press, 2005); Jean M. O'Brien, *Dispossession by Degrees: Indian Land and Identity in Natick, Massachusetts, 1650–1790* (Cambridge: Cambridge University Press, 1997); idem, *Firsting and Lasting: Writing Indians Out of Existence in New England* (Minneapolis: University of Minnesota Press, 2010); and Matthew Dennis, *Seneca Possessed: Indians, Witchcraft, and Power in the Early American Republic* (Philadelphia: University of Pennsylvania Press, 2010), 117–78.

26. Williams, Autobiographical Writings, EWP, Reel 3.

Acts, 57–58; Indian commissioners appointed by, 57 Indian population decline owing to removal, 122; lawlessness of frontier population, 72–73, 75, 79–80; negotiates Seven Nations treaty, 19–21; postwar Indian policy of, 18–21; support for Indian removal, 58, 80, 82–83, 87–88; War of 1812, 38–39; white population growth, 117

New York Times, 202

Northern Missionary Society, 62

Occom, Samson, 50, 60, 206–7

Ogden, David A.: assists Williams, 46; Bowyer sale, 92; Hanson's ties to, 1; Indian removal, 81–82, 83

Ogden, Thomas Ludlow, 86; funds Williams, 87–88, 112, 131; Indian future, 50–51; Indian Removal bill, 125–26; Williams seeks funding from, 153

Ogden Land Company, 46, 51, 197–99, 206; Buffalo Creek treaty, 144–48; Butte des Morts, 120; cuts ties to Williams, 134–36; hires "contractors," 144; and Indian removal, 81–84, 85–88, 97; Menominee treaty, 130–31; and Seneca lands, 69, 144–47; support for Williams, 121; Wisconsin lands, 140

Ogdensburg (New York), 17, 194

Ogdensburg Railroad, 1, 2, 211n7

Onderdonk, Benjamin: continuing distrust of Williams, 154; recalls Williams, 134

Oneida carrying place, 56

Oneida Castle, 66, 198

Oneida Lake, 61

Oneidas, 2, 19; baptism and confirmation of, 67–68; brokers sought by, 53, 97; and Buffalo Creek treaty, 143–44; and Canandaigua treaty, 58–59; Christian missions, 53, 60; culture change, 55–56; factionalism, 53–54, 58–59, 114–15; Green Bay explored by, 91–92, 95–97,

99–100; growing distrust of Williams, 88, 198; invitation to Williams, 52; at Kahnawake, 17; lands lost, 57, 58, 79–80; loss of hope after Revolution, 56; oppose removal, 85–87, 144; population in New York, 152; question Williams's leadership, 68–69; relocation to Wisconsin, 101, 115; subsistence, 61; white settlement and, 54. *See also* Oneidas, Christian party; Oneidas, Orchard Party; Oneidas, Pagan party; Oneidas, Second Christian Party, Oneidas in Wisconsin

Oneidas, Christian Party: American Revolution, 56; in Canada, 151–52; Christianity of described, 62; and Kirkland's mission, 54–55; loss of religious fervor, 60–61; oppose removal, 97; reject Williams, 138; support for removal, 88, 122

Oneidas, Orchard Party: and Canada, 152; land sales by, 122; origins, 122

Oneidas, Pagan Party: becomes Second Christian Party, 64; conversion to Christianity, 62–63; invites Williams to Oneida, 53

Oneida, Second Christian Party: addresses governor, 66; conversion, 62–65; conversion commemorated, 154–55; land sales by, 78; opposition to removal, 94, 97–99; removal to Green Bay, 97

Oneidas in Wisconsin: Bread's importance to, 123–24; culture of, 149–50; Methodism among, 156–57; opposition to Williams, 134, 175–76; population, 149; poverty, 104; reservation established, 150

Onondagas, 2, 17, 19, 58–59, 88, 92; at Buffalo Creek, oppose removal, 123, 143

Onoquaga, 54

Oriskany, Battle of (1777), 55

ACKNOWLEDGMENTS

I first became interested in Eleazer Williams while conducting historical research for the United States Justice Department on issues related to the Oneida land claim. Williams seemed to be everywhere in the record, and for a number of years I thought about trying to tell his story. A number of other projects intervened. I left one job at Geneseo, moved to Houston, and just as quickly returned to upstate New York, an adventure in relocation that I would not recommend to anyone. I kept my eye on Williams and continued to follow his elusive trail. Ten years after I first encountered him, the book is done, though it is a very different project from what I originally envisioned.

Williams was a difficult character to decipher, and I could not have written this book without the advice, encouragement, criticism and questioning offered by a large number of friends and colleagues. Williams left a broad paper trail, and archivists and librarians at a number of institutions helped me track down documents needed to reconstruct the more elusive parts of Williams's story. Jim Folts of the New York State Archives, Wayne Kempton of the Archives of the Episcopal Diocese of New York, and Debra Kimok of the Special Collections Department at SUNY-Plattsburgh's Feinberg Library deserve special mention, but also extremely helpful were Rodney Ross at the National Archives, Helen Long at the Newberry, Christopher Damiani at the Historical Society of Pennsylvania, and Linda Abrams of the Longmeadow Historical Society in Longmeadow, Massachusetts. Archivists at the Cofrin Library at the University of Wisconsin—Green Bay helped me navigate their collections.

Many friends and colleagues, while conducting their own research and teaching their own courses, offered me advice or asked questions or listened to me express the frustrations I felt as I attempted to write the biography of a dishonest man. Alyssa Mt. Pleasant, Todd Romero, James Kirby Martin, Peter Hoffer, Audra Simpson, James Sidbury, Peter Mancall, Karim Tiro, Jon Parmenter, Erik Seeman, Justin Behrend, Andrew Lipman, Julie Fisher, Carl Benn, Rick Hill, Larry Hauptman, Darren Bonaparte, Roy Wright, Sean Harvey,

Andrew Cohen, Evan Haefeli and Ed Countryman all helped in important ways over the years. Dan Richter, Laura Spero, Annette Gordon-Reed, Chris Grasso, Karin Wulf, Buck Woodard, Jim Rice and Alison Parker and the Rochester United States Historians' (RUSH) Group all provided opportunities to present pieces of this project to interested and supportive audiences. Institutional support came from SUNY-Geneseo and, for one year, the University of Houston. Chris Dahl, the recently retired President of SUNY-Geneseo, not only served as a fantastic leader fully committed to the liberal arts, but an administrator who allowed me to return to Geneseo after my year in Texas. I owe him. My family owes him. My colleagues in the Department of History at SUNY-Geneseo have always provided a wonderful environment for working and teaching. And, as always, Stephen Saunders Webb was more than willing to discuss the different aspects of my latest project.

Angela Pulley Hudson, Josh Piker, David Silverman and Tom Slaughter all read the manuscript and offered comments and criticisms that forced me to question my own assumptions, dig deeper in the sources, and tighten my arguments. Angela Workoff, my friend and former student, got me thinking a lot more than I might otherwise have done about how we historians tell the stories we choose to tell. To them all I am very grateful.

At the University of Pennsylvania Press, Alison Anderson, and Kathryn Krug have helped usher this book through the editorial process. Bob Lockhart has asked tough questions and given important encouragement along the way, and made this a stronger book than it otherwise might have been.

Last, I need to thank Leticia Ontiveros and our five children. They view my research trips as "vacations," and my work habits as "eccentricities." Much of the time they were not interested at all in the life of a nineteenth century Indian who claimed to be a king, and I am sure that they are glad that Eleazer Williams has finally left the building. But they do provide the diversions, joys and distractions that ensure that my own life is in no way like Eleazer Williams's.